GEORGE ELIOT IN CONTEXT

Prodigiously learned, alive to the massive social changes of her time, defiant of many Victorian orthodoxies, George Eliot has always challenged her readers. She is at once chronicler and analyst, novelist of nostalgia and monumental thinker. In her great novel *Middlemarch* she writes of 'that tempting range of relevancies called the universe'. This volume identifies a range of 'relevancies' that inform both her fictional and her non-fictional writings. The range and scale of her achievement are brought into focus by cogent essays on the many contexts – historical, intellectual, political, social, cultural – to her work. In addition there are discussions of her critical history and legacy, as well as of the material conditions of production and distribution of her novels and her journalism. The volume enables fuller understanding and appreciation, from a twenty-first-century standpoint, of the life and work of one of the nineteenth century's major writers.

MARGARET HARRIS is Professor of English Literature and Director of Research Development in the Faculty of Arts and Social Sciences, University of Sydney. She has published widely on nineteenth- and twentieth-century English and Australian literature.

GEORGE ELIOT IN CONTEXT

EDITED BY

MARGARET HARRIS

CAMBRIDGE
UNIVERSITY PRESS

University Printing House, Cambridge CB2 8BS, United Kingdom

Cambridge University Press is part of the University of Cambridge.

It furthers the University's mission by disseminating knowledge in the pursuit of education, learning and research at the highest international levels of excellence.

www.cambridge.org
Information on this title: www.cambridge.org/9781107527423

First published 2013
First paperback edition 2015

A catalogue record for this publication is available from the British Library

Library of Congress Cataloguing in Publication data
George Eliot in context / edited by Margaret Harris.
pages cm
Includes bibliographical references and index.
ISBN 978-0-521-76408-7 (hardback)
1. Eliot, George, 1819–1880–Criticism and interpretation. I. Harris, Margaret, 1942– editor of compilation.
PR4688.G396 2013
823′.8–dc23
2012048496

ISBN 978-0-521-76408-7 Hardback
ISBN 978-1-107-52742-3 Paperback

Contents

List of illustrations — *page* viii
Notes on contributors — xii
Preface — xvii
Chronology — xix
Margaret Harris
List of texts and abbreviations — xxxi

PART I LIFE AND AFTERLIFE — 1

1 George Eliot's life — 3
Kathryn Hughes

2 Publishers and publication — 12
Joanne Shattock

3 Editions of George Eliot's work — 23
Joanne Shattock

4 Genre — 34
Nancy Henry

5 The biographical tradition — 41
Margaret Harris

6 Afterlife — 52
Margaret Harris

PART II CRITICAL FORTUNES — 63

7 Critical responses: to 1900 — 65
Juliette Atkinson

8 Critical responses: 1900–1970 74
Juliette Atkinson

9 Critical responses: 1970–present 83
Juliette Atkinson

PART III CULTURAL AND SOCIAL CONTEXTS 93

10 Class 95
Ruth Livesey

11 Dress 104
Clair Hughes

12 Education 113
Elizabeth Gargano

13 Etiquette 122
Judith Flanders

14 Families and kinship 129
Josie Billington

15 Gender and the Woman Question 137
Kyriaki Hadjiafxendi

16 Historiography 145
Joanne Wilkes

17 Industry and technology 153
Richard Menke

18 Interiors 160
Judith Flanders

19 Landscape 168
John Rignall

20 Language 176
Melissa Raines

21 Law 183
Kieran Dolin

22 Metropolitanism 190
John Rignall

23 Money 197
Dermot Coleman

24 Music 206
Delia da Sousa Correa

25 Philosophy 214
Moira Gatens

26 Politics 222
Robert Dingley

27 Race 230
Alicia Carroll

28 Religion 238
Oliver Lovesey

29 Romanticism 248
Joanne Wilkes

30 Rural life 256
Carol A. Martin

31 The science of the mind 264
Pauline Nestor

32 Secularism 271
Michael Rectenwald

33 Theatre 279
Lynn Voskuil

34 Transport 287
Ruth Livesey

35 Travel and tourism 295
Judith Johnston

36 Visual arts 303
Leonée Ormond

Further reading 312
Index 327

Illustrations

1 An 1858 photograph by John Edwin Mayall, of which George Eliot's friend Mme Belloc (Bessie Rayner Parkes) commented that it gave 'the only real indication left to us of the true shape of the head, and of George Eliot's smile and general bearing'. © National Portrait Gallery, London. *page* 7
2 Engraving by Paul Rajon of Frederic Burton's 1864 portrait of George Eliot, commissioned by J. W. Cross as the frontispiece for *George Eliot's Life* (1885). 9
3 The first (anonymous) publication of *Scenes of Clerical Life*, in *Blackwood's Edinburgh Magazine*, January 1857. 16
4 George Eliot's revisions of the opening of chapter 17 of *Adam Bede* for the eighth edition. By permission of Harry Ransom Center, The University of Texas at Austin. 26
5 John Walter Cross (1840–1924), George Eliot's husband and biographer, is seated on the right. © National Portrait Gallery, London. 44
6 Gordon S. Haight (1901–85), Professor of English at Yale from 1933, photographed in 1938. His work on George Eliot, especially his edition of her letters in nine volumes (1954–78), is indispensable. Reproduced by permission of Manuscripts & Archives, Yale University Library. Office of Public Affairs, Yale University. Photographs of Individuals (RU686). 48
7 Still from the set in Florence for *Romola*, directed by Henry King (1924), with (left to right) Dorothy Gish (Tessa), Ronald Colman (Carlo Bucellini), Henry King, unknown, Lillian Gish (Romola). Courtesy of www.doctormacro.com. 57
8 The iconoclastic critic F. R. Leavis (1895–1978; charcoal drawing by Robert Sargent Austin, 1934) included George Eliot in his influential *The Great Tradition* (1948). © National Portrait Gallery, London. 77

9 Barbara Hardy (born 1924; photograph by Bassano, 1974): a key figure in the post-World War II critical rehabilitation of George Eliot. © National Portrait Gallery, London. 80

10 *The Fair Toxophilites* depicts one of the archery contests fashionable in the second half of the nineteenth century, at which young elite women like Gwendolen Harleth were able to display their persons and their dress to best advantage. Dress and headgear could be elaborate as archery was an essentially static affair. *The Fair Toxophilites*, 1872, by William Powell Frith (1819–1909). Royal Albert Memorial Museum, Exeter, Devon, UK/The Bridgeman Art Library. Nationality/copyright status: English/out of copyright. 110

11 As chief architect for the School Board of London, E. R. Robson was responsible for the design of hundreds of schools in London after the Elementary Education Act of 1870. 'Double Class-Room, shewing dual arrangement of desks' is from his *School Architecture; Being Practical Remarks on the Planning, Designing, Building and Furnishing of School-Houses* (1874), which encapsulated the principles he espoused. 114

12 'The Priory – Drawing-Room', engraving from *George Eliot's Life* by J. W. Cross. The room was decorated by the fashionable designer Owen Jones when George Eliot and George Lewes bought the house in 1863. 162

13 Vignette by Myles Birket Foster for the title page of Blackwood's 1874 one-volume edition of *Middlemarch*. 172

14 'Sketches in the Bank of England: Machine for weighing gold' (*Illustrated London News*, 1873). © Trustees of the British Museum. 198

15 George Eliot heard the baritone George Henschel (1850–1934) on a number of occasions, sometimes accompanying himself as in this portrait. Sir Lawrence Alma-Tadema, *Portrait of the singer George Henschel playing Alma-Tadema's piano, Townshend House 1879* (oil on panel). Private collection. Photo © Christie's Images. Reproduced by permission of The Bridgeman Art Library. 209

16 John Tenniel, 'A leap in the dark', *Punch* (3 August 1867). Masquerading as a thoroughbred, Disraeli (who piloted the 1867 Bill through the Commons) gallops at a forbidding hedge labelled

REFORM, while Britannia, terrified, shields her face. John Bright, Gladstone and Lord Derby have pulled up short. 223

17 'The Gipsy Beauty', by W. H. Overend, an illustration from George Smith, *Gipsy Life: Being an Account of our Gipsies and their Children* (1880): characteristic of popular mid- to late-nineteenth-century images of gypsies. 233

18 Soon after the publication of *Scenes of Clerical Life*, 'Shepperton Church' was identified with that at Chilvers Coton, and the town of Milby with Nuneaton. 'Reminiscences of "George Eliot"' (*Graphic*, 8 January 1881) illustrates several of the places depicted in *Scenes*, including a ribbon weaver at a handloom (mentioned in 'Amos Barton': Silas Marner is not George Eliot's only weaver). 242

19 '"You may run away from my words, Sir," continued Mrs Poyser.' Illustration by William Small, engraved by James D. Cooper, for *Adam Bede*, chapter 32, 'Mrs Poyser "has her say out"', in Blackwood's Illustrated Edition (1867). 260

20 George Eliot's grave in Highgate Cemetery, with Jacob Holyoake's nearby (at the left of the image). By permission of Mustapha Ousellam. 277

21 An illustration by D. H. Friston of a scene from W. S. Gilbert's play *The Wicked World* (1873) at the Haymarket Theatre, London. *Illustrated London News*, 8 February 1873, courtesy of John Weedy. 282

22 The opening paragraph of *Felix Holt* evokes the glory of 'the old coach-roads' and 'the rolling swinging swiftness' of coaches like the Birmingham Tally Ho, depicted here by James Pollard (1792–1867). Image after James Pollard, 'The Birmingham Tally Ho Coaches', sourced from Encore Editions. 290

23 Like many travellers, George Eliot initially found Rome overpowering and gained relief by driving into the countryside – an experience shared with Dorothea Casaubon in chapter 20 of *Middlemarch*. Corot's painting of the Campagna *c.* 1830–1 depicts the area as Dorothea might have seen it. Jean Baptiste Camille Corot (French, 1796–1875), *La Cervara, the Roman Campagna* (*c.* 1830–1). Oil on fabric, 97.6 × 135.8 cm. The Cleveland Museum of Art. Leonard C. Hanna, Jr. Fund 1963.91. 301

24 George Eliot shared the opinion common in her day that Raphael was the greatest of all painters. The Sistine Madonna ('this sublimest picture' – *J*, 325) especially moved her during her stay in Dresden in 1858, when she and Lewes frequently visited the Old Masters Gallery. 304

Contributors

JULIETTE ATKINSON is a lecturer in nineteenth-century literature at University College London, currently preparing a monograph on Anglo-French literary relations in the nineteenth century. Her publications include *Victorian Biography Reconsidered: A Study of Nineteenth-Century 'Hidden' Lives* (2010), and an edition of criticism on George Eliot. In 2012, she was awarded a New Scholars Award by the Bibliographical Society of America.

JOSIE BILLINGTON is a Victorian literature specialist in the School of English, and Deputy Director of the Centre for Reading Research, University of Liverpool. Publications include *Faithful Realism* (2002), *Eliot's Middlemarch* (2008) and *Elizabeth Barrett Browning and Shakespeare* (2012).

ALICIA CARROLL, Associate Professor of English at Auburn University, is the author of *Dark Smiles: Race and Desire in George Eliot* (2003). She is currently pursuing a new project entitled 'New Woman Ecologies: From Arts and Crafts to the Great War'.

DERMOT COLEMAN was awarded his doctorate by the University of Exeter in 2011 for a thesis entitled 'Being Good with Money: Economic Bearings in George Eliot's Ethical and Social Thought'. He remains a partner in the investment management firm he co-founded in 1998.

DELIA DA SOUSA CORREA is Senior Lecturer at the Open University. Publications include *George Eliot, Music and Victorian Culture* (2003) and, as editor, *The Nineteenth-Century Novel: Realisms* (2000), *Phrase and Subject: Studies in Literature and Music* (2006) and, with W. R. Owens, *The Handbook to Literary Research* (2010). She is the founding editor of *Katherine Mansfield Studies.*

ROBERT DINGLEY was formerly a senior lecturer in English at the University of New England, New South Wales. He has written extensively on nineteenth-century British and Australian literature and his publications include essays and articles on Jane Austen, Charlotte Brontë, Harriet Martineau, George Eliot and Anna Sewell.

KIERAN DOLIN is Chair of English and Cultural Studies at the University of Western Australia. He is the author of *Fiction and the Law: Legal Discourse in Victorian and Modernist Literature* (Cambridge University Press, 1999) and *A Critical Introduction to Law and Literature* (Cambridge University Press, 2007).

JUDITH FLANDERS is the author of a number of works on the Victorian period, including *Consuming Passions: Leisure and Pleasure in Victorian England* (2006) and *The Victorian City: Everyday Life in Dickens' London* (2012). She is Senior Research Fellow, Humanities Research Institute, University of Buckingham.

ELIZABETH GARGANO is the author of *Reading Victorian Schoolrooms: Childhood and Education in Nineteenth-Century Fiction* (2008). She teaches English at the University of North Carolina at Charlotte.

MOIRA GATENS is Challis Professor of Philosophy at the University of Sydney. Her many publications include *Imaginary Bodies: Ethics, Power and Corporeality* (1996), *Collective Imaginings: Spinoza Past and Present* (with Genevieve Lloyd, 1999) and as editor, *Feminist Interpretations of Benedict Spinoza* (2009). Her current major project is on Spinoza, Feuerbach and George Eliot.

KYRIAKI HADJIAFXENDI is Senior Lecturer at Bath Spa University, currently completing a monograph entitled 'George Eliot, the Literary Market-Place and Sympathy'. Her publications include *Authorship in Context: From the Theoretical to the Material,* edited with Polina Mackay (2007) and, as guest editor, a special issue of *George Eliot–George Henry Lewes Studies,* 'The Cultural Place of George Eliot's Poetry' (2011).

MARGARET HARRIS is Director of Research Development in the Faculty of Arts and Social Sciences at the University of Sydney, where she was previously Challis Professor of English Literature. She edited *The Journals of George Eliot* (with Judith Johnston, Cambridge University Press, 1998).

NANCY HENRY is Professor of English at the University of Tennessee at Knoxville. She is the author of *The Life of George Eliot: A Critical Biography* (2012), *George Eliot and the British Empire* (Cambridge University Press, 2002) and *The Cambridge Introduction to George Eliot* (Cambridge University Press, 2008).

CLAIR HUGHES, formerly Professor of English and American Literature at the International Christian University, Tokyo, is the author of *Dressed in Fiction* (2006) and *Henry James and the Art of Dress* (2001).

KATHRYN HUGHES is Professor of Life Writing at the University of East Anglia. She is the author of *George Eliot: The Last Victorian* (1998) and editor of *George Eliot: A Family History* (2001). Her most recent book is *The Short Life and Long Times of Mrs Beeton* (2005).

JUDITH JOHNSTON formerly taught at the University of Western Australia, and is now an Honorary Associate at the University of Sydney. Her extensive publications on Victorian women's writing include *George Eliot and the Discourses of Medievalism* (2005), *Victorian Women and the Economies of Travel, Translation and Culture, 1830–1870* (2013) and *The Journals of George Eliot* (with Margaret Harris, Cambridge University Press, 1998).

RUTH LIVESEY is Reader in Nineteenth-Century Literature and Thought in the Department of English, Royal Holloway, University of London. She is the author of *Socialism, Sex and the Culture of Aestheticism in Britain, 1880–1914* (2007), co-editor of *The American Experiment and the Idea of Democracy in British Culture, 1776–1914* (2012) and an editor of the *Journal of Victorian Culture.*

OLIVER LOVESEY is Associate Professor of English at the University of British Columbia, Okanagan, author of *The Clerical Character in George Eliot's Fiction* (1990) and editor of Broadview's edition of *The Mill on the Floss* (2007). He recently edited the four-volume set *Victorian Social Activists' Novels* (2011).

CAROL A. MARTIN is Emeritus Professor of English at Boise State University in Boise, Idaho. Her publications include *George Eliot's Serial Fiction* (1994), together with the Clarendon (2001) and Oxford World's Classics (2008) editions of *Adam Bede,* and numerous articles and reviews.

RICHARD MENKE, Associate Professor of English at the University of Georgia, is the author of *Telegraphic Realism: Victorian Fiction and Other Information Systems* (2008).

PAULINE NESTOR is Professor in English at Monash University. Her books include *George Eliot* (2002), *Charlotte Brontë* (1987), *Charlotte Brontë's Jane Eyre* (1992) and *Female Friendships and Communities* (1985).

LEONÉE ORMOND is Professor Emerita of Victorian Studies at King's College London. She has published articles, editions and monographs on many nineteenth- and early twentieth-century artists and writers, including Dickens, George Eliot, George Du Maurier, Frederic Leighton (with Richard Ormond), Tennyson, Thackeray, Barrie, Kipling and Linley Sambourne.

MELISSA RAINES is the author of *George Eliot's Grammar of Being* (2011), a study of George Eliot's manuscripts, syntax and writing process. She has published several articles on George Eliot, and her current work is on the narrative and syntax of Thomas Hardy and Anthony Trollope. She teaches at the University of Liverpool.

MICHAEL RECTENWALD teaches liberal studies at New York University. He is co-author of *Academic Writing, Real World Topics* (with Lisa Carl, 2012) and has also published on science and *Middlemarch*, nineteenth-century secularism, and pre-Darwinian evolutionary thought. He is currently working on a book on secularism in connection with literature, science and religion.

JOHN RIGNALL is Emeritus Reader in English and Comparative Literary Studies at the University of Warwick. He is the author of *George Eliot, European Novelist* (2011), and editor of the *Oxford Reader's Companion to George Eliot* (2000) and *George Eliot and Europe* (1997).

JOANNE SHATTOCK is Emeritus Professor of Victorian Literature at the University of Leicester. Recent publications include an edition of Margaret Oliphant's literary criticism in Joanne Shattock and Elisabeth Jay (eds.), *Selected Works of Margaret Oliphant* (2011) and *The Cambridge Companion to English Literature 1830–1914* (Cambridge University Press, 2010). She edited *The Cambridge Bibliography of English Literature*, vol. 3, 1800–1900 (Cambridge University Press, 1999).

LYNN VOSKUIL teaches Victorian literature and Women's Studies at the University of Houston. She is the author of *Acting Naturally: Victorian Theatricality and Authenticity* (2004) and is currently working on 'Horticulture and Imperialism: The Garden Spaces of the British Empire, 1789–1914', a book project that explores nineteenth-century Britain's fascination with exotic horticulture and plants.

JOANNE WILKES, Professor of English at the University of Auckland, has published *Women Reviewing Women in Nineteenth-Century Britain: The Critical Reception of Jane Austen, Charlotte Brontë and George Eliot* (2010) and the award-winning *Lord Byron and Madame de Staël: Born for Opposition* (1999). She has also edited Gaskell's *Mary Barton* (2005) and periodical criticism by Margaret Oliphant (2011).

Preface

G. A. Sala, in his obituary in the *Illustrated London News*, commented that George Eliot for all her greatness remained 'an abstraction, an impalpability'.[1] Leslie Stephen, in his lengthy and measured tribute in the *Cornhill Magazine*, spoke of the way her work 'set before us a fine sense of its wider relations'.[2] This volume attempts to make 'George Eliot' less abstract by attending to some of the 'wider relations' that establish co-ordinates on her life and work.

George Eliot is notoriously elusive. From its first appearance as the name of the author of the two volumes of *Scenes of Clerical Life* published by William Blackwood and Sons in January 1858, there has been conjecture about the identity of 'George Eliot'. Even before she adopted the pseudonym, the woman baptised Mary Anne Evans had more than once modified the name by which she wanted to be known, becoming Mary Ann and then Marian Evans. When she took up with George Henry Lewes she insisted on being called Marian Lewes. She assumed other names in particular contexts: thus to Lewes she was Polly, Pollian and Madonna, and Mutter to his sons. In correspondence she sometimes chose a whimsical signature ('Medusa', 'Clematis'), and she jokingly assumed another pseudonym, 'Saccharissa', for her essays in the *Pall Mall Gazette* in 1865. Finally, in the last year of her life she became Mrs John Cross.

George Eliot, then, was conscious of herself as a text, managing the ways her names were used. (In this volume, while contributors at times employ various of her names in referring to her, the pseudonym 'George Eliot' is used in full, and not treated as if 'Eliot' is a separable surname.) In these protean manifestations her awareness of the importance of context is demonstrable. Her writing too is insistent on the ways the meaning of a situation or event is conditioned by the circumstances that surround it. Her masterpiece *Middlemarch* provides telling images for the relativity both of individual perception (in the pier glass image in chapter 27) and of knowledge broadly conceived ('that tempting range of relevancies called the universe' – ch. 15). Moreover, as so often in her fiction *Middlemarch* makes play with the double time of the novel, that of the action, and of the time of narration, exhibiting the author's awareness that interpretation and understanding modify with changing historical, economic and social circumstances. More than most writers, George Eliot was conscious of the intellectual and material milieux in which she operated. The essays in this volume discuss both concepts and contexts contemporary with her, and later ones, contemporary with us, to provide as full a range of lenses as possible through which to illuminate her achievement.

The first section of the book offers perspectives on George Eliot's life, particularly her career as an author, and her afterlife. The second section expands an aspect of 'afterlife', and surveys her critical fortunes, providing another set of contexts in which to address her. The third and longest section encompasses 'Cultural and social contexts'. These essays are arranged alphabetically by topic, and do not pretend to be exhaustive. There are also suggestions for further reading: these too are inevitably selective.

I am pleased to acknowledge the support of an Australian Research Council Discovery Grant, 'The Lives of George Eliot' (DP0559432), for work on this volume. Particular assistance at different times has been provided by Rowanne Couch, Jennifer Moore, and Olivia Murphy, and by administrative staff in the School of Letters, Art and Media at the University of Sydney, and I thank them all. Special thanks too to staff of Fisher Library, University of Sydney, especially Michele Parker for her assistance in preparing images. I am grateful to Linda Bree, and latterly Maartje Scheltens, at Cambridge University Press for their encouragement and patient advice during the protracted assembly of the volume. Above all, thanks to the contributors, without whose commitment and enthusiasm *George Eliot in Context* could not have happened at all.

Margaret Harris
University of Sydney

NOTES

1 8 January 1881, 27.
2 *Cornhill Magazine* (February 1881), in David Carroll (ed.), *George Eliot: The Critical Heritage* (London: Routledge and Kegan Paul, 1971), p. 472.

Chronology

Margaret Harris

This chronology refers to 'George Eliot' as 'GE' throughout, without attempting to track the various names by which she was known at different times.

1819	24 May Princess Alexandrina Victoria of Kent, the future Queen Victoria, born.
	22 November Mary Anne Evans (GE) born at South Farm, Arbury, near Nuneaton, Warwickshire, to Christiana, née Pearson, second wife of Robert Evans, estate manager – the youngest of her father's five surviving children, and closest in age to brother Isaac (1813–93) and sister Christiana (1816–59). Scott, *Ivanhoe*; Byron, *Don Juan* (first two cantos).
1820	29 January George III dies, succeeded by George IV.
	March The Evans family moves to Griff House, Arbury. Shelley, *Prometheus Unbound*; Keats, *Hyperion.*
1821	23 February John Keats dies.
1822	8 July Percy Bysshe Shelley dies.
1824–35	GE is educated at a boarding school in Attleborough, then at Miss Wallington's boarding school in Nuneaton, and finally at the Misses Franklin's school in Coventry.
1824	19 April Lord Byron dies.

Goethe, *Wilhelm Meisters Lehrjahre* (1795), translated into English by Thomas Carlyle as *Wilhelm Meister's Apprenticeship.*

1829 Publication of Balzac's *Les Chouans*, the first of the series of seventeen novels entitled *La Comédie Humaine.*

1830 26 June
George IV dies, succeeded by William IV.

26–29 July
The July Revolution in France deposes the Bourbon Charles X in favour of his cousin, Louis Philippe, Duke of Orléans.

15 September
Liverpool and Manchester Railway opens.
Tennyson, *Poems, Chiefly Lyrical*; Stendhal, *Le rouge et le noir.*

1830–3 Charles Lyell, *Principles of Geology.*

1832 22 March
Johann Wolfgang von Goethe dies.

7 June
Royal Assent to the First Reform Bill.

21 September
Sir Walter Scott dies.

December
GE witnesses polling day scuffles in Nuneaton between supporters of Conservative and pro-Reform candidates.
Pandemic cholera outbreak reaches London and Paris.
George Sand, *Indiana.*

1834 25 July
Samuel Coleridge dies.

1836 3 February
Christiana Evans dies.

March
Publication of the first of twenty monthly instalments of Dickens's *Pickwick Papers.*

1837 GE takes over household management for her father following the marriage in May of her sister Chrissey to Edward Clarke, a medical practitioner.

26 June
William IV dies, accession of Victoria.
Carlyle, *The French Revolution.*

1839 GE is learning Italian, Latin and Greek.

1840 January
GE's first published work, a poem, 'As o'er the fields', appears in the *Christian Observer*, signed 'M.A.E.'

10 February
Queen Victoria marries Prince Albert of Saxe-Coburg and Gotha.
GE begins German lessons.

1841 17 March
GE moves to Foleshill, Coventry, with her father in anticipation of brother Isaac's marriage on June 8.

November
GE becomes acquainted with the Coventry manufacturer and author Charles Bray, his wife Cara and her sister Sara Hennell. Her religious belief is challenged, especially when she reads Charles Hennell's *An Inquiry Concerning the Origin of Christianity* (1838).
Carlyle, *On Heroes, Hero-Worship, and the Heroic in History.*

1842 January
GE's refusal to accompany her father to church instigates a 'Holy War' which marks her break with orthodox Christianity. She goes to church again 15 May.

August – September
Chartist riots in support of an extension of the suffrage and parliamentary reform.
Wordsworth, *Poems, Chiefly of Early and Late Years*; Tennyson, *Poems*; Robert Browning, *Dramatic Lyrics.*

1843 Alfred Tennyson becomes Poet Laureate. First volume of Ruskin's *Modern Painters* appears (vol. 5, 1860).

1845 The Great Famine in Ireland consequent on the failure of the potato crop.

1846 15 June
GE's translation of D. F. Strauss, *Das Leben Jesu* (1835–6), as *The Life of Jesus*, begun in 1844, appears anonymously, published in three volumes by John Chapman.

25 June
The House of Lords votes to repeal the Corn Laws, abolishing protective tariffs on the import of grain into Britain.

	4 December GE publishes anonymously the first of five instalments of her 'Poetry and Prose, from the Notebook of an Eccentric' in the *Coventry Herald*, owned by Charles Bray. G. H. Lewes, *Biographical History of Philosophy.*
1847	January Serialisation of Thackeray's *Vanity Fair* begins. 1 July Implementation of a Factory Act which restricts hours worked by women and children. Charlotte Brontë, *Jane Eyre*; Emily Brontë, *Wuthering Heights.*
1848	February Revolution in France and the establishment of the French Second Republic under Louis Napoleon, setting off the 'year of revolution' in Germany, Poland, Italy and the Austrian Empire.
	28 February Publication of Marx and Engels, 'The Communist Manifesto' (in German in London; English translation by Helen Macfarlane 1850). Founding of the Pre-Raphaelite Brotherhood. Elizabeth Gaskell, *Mary Barton.*
1849	GE begins to translate Spinoza, *Tractatus theologico-politicus.*
	31 May GE's father, Robert Evans, dies.
	12 June In company with the Brays, GE travels abroad for the first time. She winters in Geneva, lodging with the D'Albert-Durade family. Cholera epidemic in England.
1850	March GE returns to Coventry, where she lives with the Brays at Rosehill.
	23 April William Wordsworth dies. Alfred Tennyson appointed Poet Laureate.

18 August
Honoré de Balzac dies.
Tennyson, *In Memoriam*; Wordsworth, *The Prelude*; R. W. Emerson, *Representative Men*; Hawthorne, *The Scarlet Letter*; Herbert Spencer, *Social Statics*.

1851 8 January
GE moves to London, where she lodges with publisher John Chapman at 142 Strand, and works with him on the *Westminster Review*. Her review of R. W. Mackay's *The Progress of the Intellect* appears in the January issue.

24 March
GE returns to Rosehill, apparently because of friction in the household at 142 Strand arising from her intimacy with John Chapman.

1 May
Opening of the Great Exhibition held in the Crystal Palace in Hyde Park.

September 29
GE goes to London again, and meets Herbert Spencer and George Henry Lewes (GHL), among others.
First volume of Ruskin's *The Stones of Venice* published (the third and final volume appears in 1853); Melville, *Moby Dick*.

1852 January
First number of the *Westminster Review* for which GE has principal responsibility.
In the course of the year she sees a good deal of *Westminster* contributor and social scientist Herbert Spencer, who makes plain in the summer that he cannot reciprocate her ardent feelings.

1853 17 October
GE moves from Chapman's establishment to 21 Cambridge Street as her relationship with GHL intensifies. She gives up the editorship of the *Westminster*, though still contributing to it and other journals.

October 1853 – February 1856
Crimean War, in which Britain, France, the Ottoman Empire and the Kingdom of Sardinia resisted Russian attempts to expand eastwards into Europe.

	Comte's *Cours de philosophie positive* (1830–42) translated by Harriet Martineau as *Positive Philosophy.*
1854	July Ludwig Feuerbach's *Das Wesen des Christenthums* appears as *The Essence of Christianity*, 'Translated from the Second German Edition. By Marian Evans', published by John Chapman.
	20 July GE leaves London for Germany with GHL, who plans to carry out research on Goethe.
	August – October GE and GHL are based in Weimar. Among other outings they hear Wagner's *Lohengrin* (1850), conducted by Liszt; also *Der fliegende Holländer* (1843) and *Tannhäuser* (1845). GE writes 'Woman in France: Madame de Sablé', published in the October number of the *Westminster Review.*
	3 November They move on to Berlin, where GE begins to translate Spinoza's *Ethics*.
1855	11 March GE and GHL return to England, taking various lodgings before setting up house at 8 Park Shot, Richmond. GE publishes articles in *Westminster Review* and other journals.
	31 March Charlotte Brontë dies.
	October GHL's *Life* of Goethe is published by David Nutt, and reviewed by GE in the *Leader.* Walt Whitman, *Leaves of Grass*; Elizabeth Gaskell, *North and South*; Trollope, *The Warden*, the first of the Barchester chronicles.
1856	April GE's review of the third volume of Ruskin's *Modern Painters* appears in the *Westminster Review*, followed by the major essays 'The Natural History of German Life' in July and 'Silly Novels by Lady Novelists' in October.

6 May
Sigmund Freud born.

8 May
GE and GHL visit Ilfracombe and Tenby from May to August, mainly because of GHL's fascination with marine biology.

August
GHL's 'Sea-Side Studies' begin to appear in *Blackwood's Edinburgh Magazine.*

September
GE starts to write 'The Sad Fortunes of the Reverend Amos Barton', which publisher John Blackwood accepts in November.

1857 1 January
GE's last contributions to the *Westminster* appear in the January issue: the essay, 'Worldliness and Otherworldliness: The Poet Young', together with the 'Belles Lettres' and 'History, Biography, Voyages and Travels' sections.
'The Sad Fortunes of the Reverend Amos Barton', the first of the 'Scenes of Clerical Life', appears anonymously in the January number of *Blackwood's Edinburgh Magazine.* During the year, 'Mr Gilfil's Love-Story' (beginning in March) and 'Janet's Repentance' (beginning in July) are also serialised in *Blackwood's.*

15 March
GE and GHL leave for a visit to the Scilly Isles and Jersey that extends until July, again in the interests of GHL's 'Sea-Side Studies'.
Flaubert, *Madame Bovary*; Baudelaire, *Les fleurs du mal*; Elizabeth Barrett Browning, *Aurora Leigh*; Elizabeth Gaskell, *The Life of Charlotte Brontë*; Trollope, *Barchester Towers.*

1858 5 January
Scenes of Clerical Life, by George Eliot, published in two volumes by William Blackwood and Sons.

April
GE and GHL travel to Munich and Dresden.
Lewes's *Sea-Side Studies* is published in book form by Blackwood.

	The English Woman's Journal is launched by GE's friends Bessie Parkes and Barbara Bodichon.
1859	1 February Blackwood publishes *Adam Bede* in three volumes: it sells 16,000 copies in the first year. GE and GHL move to Holly Lodge, Wandsworth. When Joseph Liggins, the son of a Nuneaton baker, claims to have written *Adam Bede*, GE acknowledges to friends the secret of her authorship.
	July 'The Lifted Veil' is published in *Blackwood's Edinburgh Magazine.* J. S. Mill, *On Liberty*; Tennyson, *Idylls of the King*; Meredith, *The Ordeal of Richard Feverel*; Dickens, *A Tale of Two Cities*; Turgenev, *A Nest of Gentlefolk* (English translation by W. R. S. Ralston in 1869); G. H. Lewes, *The Physiology of Common Life;* Darwin, *On the Origin of Species.*
1860	January First number of the *Cornhill Magazine.*
	24 March GE and GHL visit Italy, returning to England in July. During this sojourn, GHL suggests Savonarola to GE as the subject for a novel, but she sets work on it aside in favour of *Silas Marner.* GHL's eldest son, Charles, leaves Hofwyl School in Switzerland and comes to live with GE and GHL in central London. A consequence is that their attendance at theatre and concerts becomes easier and more frequent.
	4 April *The Mill on the Floss* published in three volumes by William Blackwood and Sons.
1861	2 April Publication of *Silas Marner* in one volume by William Blackwood and Sons. GE and GHL undertake a second journey to Italy, mainly to do research for *Romola*, a novel which caused her immense difficulty. Outbreak of the American Civil War, which continues until May 1865.

29 June
Elizabeth Barrett Browning dies.

14 December
Prince Albert dies.

1862 27 February
Publisher George Smith offers £10,000 for *Romola.* After considerable discussion, GE agrees to accept £7,000 in return for a less punishing schedule for serialisation, and the novel begins publication in the *Cornhill* in July.
Turgenev, *Fathers and Sons* (translated into English by Eugene Schuyler 1867).

1863 6 July
Romola published in three volumes by Smith, Elder.

5 November
GE and GHL move to 'The Priory', Regent's Park, and begin to hold Sunday afternoon receptions.

16 October
GHL's second son, Thornton, goes to seek his fortune in Natal.

24 December
Death of Thackeray.
Mary Elizabeth Braddon, *Lady Audley's Secret.*

1864 4 May
GE and GHL leave for another visit to Italy, returning on June 20, during which GE has the inspiration for *The Spanish Gypsy.*

July
'Brother Jacob' (written 1860) is published in *Cornhill.*
Newman, *Apologia pro vita sua*; Trollope, *Can You Forgive Her?*, the first of the Palliser novels. Tolstoy's *War and Peace* begins publication (completed 1869; first translation into English 1885–6, made by Clara Bell, working from a French translation).

1865 GE writes poetry, together with articles for the newly founded *Pall Mall Gazette* and *Fortnightly Review*, the latter edited by GHL. She begins *Felix Holt.*

10 August
GE and GHL leave for a month's visit to Normandy and Brittany.

	Lewis Carroll, *Alice in Wonderland*; Dickens, *Our Mutual Friend.*
1866	15 June GE returns to Blackwood for the publication of *Felix Holt, the Radical* (3 vols.).
	9 September GHL's third son Herbert sets out to join Thornton in Natal.
1867	August Second Reform Bill. GE and GHL travel in Spain from December to March 1868. Trollope, *The Last Chronicle of Barset* (final novel of the Barsetshire Chronicles); Marx, *Das Kapital*; Zola, *Thérèse Raquin.*
1868	January 'Address to Working Men, by Felix Holt' published in *Blackwood's.*
	25 May *The Spanish Gypsy* published. Robert Browning's *The Ring and the Book* begins publication (completed in four volumes in 1869). L. M. Alcott, *Little Women.*
1869	3 March GE and GHL travel to Italy again, returning in May.
	18 April In Rome GE meets John Walter Cross for the first time. GE is working on poetry, and the beginning of *Middlemarch.*
	8 May Thornton Lewes returns ill from Natal; dies 19 October. Inception of Hitchin College for women, which becomes Girton College in 1873. GE contributes £50, 'From the Author of *Romola*'. J. S. Mill, *The Subjection of Women*; Matthew Arnold, *Culture and Anarchy.*
1870	First Married Women's Property Act; Elementary Education Act.
	9 June Charles Dickens dies. D. G. Rossetti, *Poems.*

	July 19 Outbreak of the Franco-Prussian War: concluded by the Treaty of Frankfurt on 10 May, 1871.
1871	December *Middlemarch* begins part publication. The four-volume edition comes out in December 1872, from Blackwood.
1874	April The first Impressionist exhibition opens in Paris.
	May *The Legend of Jubal and Other Poems* is published by Blackwood. Hardy, *Far from the Madding Crowd.*
1875	June 29 Herbert Lewes dies in Natal. Political instability in the Balkans: the 'Eastern Question' is live through to the Congress of Berlin in 1878 which attempts to balance the competing claims of Britain, Russia and Austro-Hungary in the face of the reduced power of the Ottoman Empire. Henry James, *Roderick Hudson*; Meredith, *Beauchamp's Career*; Trollope, *The Way We Live Now*; GHL, *Problems of Life and Mind* (First Series: *The Foundations of a Creed*, vols. 1 and 2).
1876	February *Daniel Deronda* begins publication in monthly parts; the four-volume edition follows from Blackwood in December.
	May 1 Queen Victoria is proclaimed Empress of India.
	December 6 GE and GHL purchase 'The Heights', Witley, Surrey, as a summer residence. Alexander Graham Bell patents the telephone.
1877	GE concludes an agreement with Blackwood for the Cabinet Edition of her works: the first titles are published in 1878. GHL publishes *Problems of Life and Mind* (Second Series: *The Physical Basis of Mind*). Zola, *L'Assommoir*, one of the series *Les Rougon-Macquart* (1871–93).

1878	November 30 GHL dies. London University becomes the first to offer degrees to women. Hardy, *The Return of the Native*; Gilbert and Sullivan, *HMS Pinafore.*
1879	May Blackwood brings out *Impressions of Theophrastus Such.* GE prepares the final volume of GHL's *Problems of Life and Mind* (Third Series*: Mind as a Function of Organism*) for publication. October 29 John Blackwood dies. Meredith, *The Egoist*; Ibsen, *A Doll's House.*
1880	May 6 GE marries John Cross, and her brother Isaac sends congratulations after years of estrangement. On the wedding journey, for reasons unknown, Cross falls into the Grand Canal in Venice but soon recovers. The married couple moves to Cheyne Walk, Chelsea, on 3 December. May 8 Flaubert dies. December 22 Having caught a chill at a concert, GE dies. Tennyson, *Ballads and Other Poems*; Gissing, *Workers in the Dawn*; Trollope, *The Duke's Children*, the last Palliser novel.
1881	Henry James, *The Portrait of a Lady.*
1882	January 25 Virginia Woolf is born. February 2 James Joyce is born.
1884	Publication of GE's *Essays and Leaves from a Notebook*, prepared by Charles Lewes (Blackwood).
1885	Publication of *George Eliot's Life as related in her letters and journals, arranged and edited by her husband J. W. Cross* in three volumes (Blackwood).
1924	3 November John Cross dies.

Texts and abbreviations

All references to George Eliot's novels and stories, except where specifically indicated otherwise, are to the Oxford World's Classics editions which reproduce the text of Oxford's Clarendon Edition of the fiction if one exists. Chapter references, rather than page references, are provided. Titles are abbreviated as follows:

AB Adam Bede
'BJ' 'Brother Jacob'
DD *Daniel Deronda*
FH *Felix Holt, the Radical*
'LV' 'The Lifted Veil'
M *Middlemarch*
MF *The Mill on the Floss*
R *Romola*
SC *Scenes of Clerical Life* – the individual stories abbreviated as 'Amos', 'Gilfil', 'Janet'
SM *Silas Marner*

The Clarendon Edition published by Oxford University Press is the standard text. To date it comprises:

Thomas A. Noble (ed.), *Scenes of Clerical Life* (1985)
Carol A. Martin (ed.), *Adam Bede* (2001)
Gordon S. Haight (ed.), *The Mill on the Floss* (1980)
Andrew Brown (ed.), *Romola* (1993)
Fred C. Thomson (ed.), *Felix Holt, the Radical* (1980)
David Carroll (ed.), *Middlemarch* (1986)
Graham Handley (ed.), *Daniel Deronda* (1984)
Other writings of George Eliot are from the following sources:

Cross	J. W. Cross (ed.), *George Eliot's life as related in her letters and journals*, 3 vols. (Edinburgh and London. William Blackwood, 1885).
Essays	Thomas Pinney (ed.), *Essays of George Eliot* (London, Routledge and Kegan Paul, 1963). Individual essays are abbreviated as follows: '[The Progress of the Intellect]' as 'Progress'; 'The Natural History of German Life' as 'Natural History'; 'Address to Working Men, By Felix Holt' as 'Address'.
J	Margaret Harris and Judith Johnston (eds.), *The Journals of George Eliot* (Cambridge University Press, 1998).
L	Gordon S. Haight (ed.), *The George Eliot Letters*, 9 vols. (New Haven, CT: Yale University Press, 1954–78).
Poetry	Antonie Gerard van den Broek (ed.), *The Complete Shorter Poetry of George Eliot*, 2 vols. (London: Pickering and Chatto, 2005).
SG	Antonie Gerard van den Broek (ed.), *The Spanish Gypsy by George Eliot* (London: Pickering and Chatto, 2008).
TS	Nancy Henry (ed.), *Impressions of Theophrastus Such* (University of Iowa Press, 1994).

Haight (1968) refers to Gordon S. Haight, *George Eliot: A Biography* (Oxford University Press, 1968).

PART I

Life and afterlife

CHAPTER 1

George Eliot's life

Kathryn Hughes

George Eliot was born Mary Anne Evans on 22 November 1819, although her name changed many times in the course of her sixty-one-year life. Christened 'Mary Anne', she dropped the final 'e' during her pious adolescence, perhaps bothered by its suggestion of a French, that is Catholic, resonance. By the time she was thirty and had left Evangelical Protestantism far behind, 'Mary Ann' had mutated, ironically enough, into the distinctly Gallic 'Marian'. On settling into an unmarried partnership with G. H. Lewes in 1854 Marian insisted on being known as 'Mrs Lewes' or, when signing herself formally, 'Marian Evans Lewes'. Yet by the time of her wedding to John Cross at the end of her life her autograph had changed to 'Mary Ann Cross'. In addition there was the *nom de plume* 'George Eliot' by which she was known professionally throughout her life, and by which she continues to be known today.

George Eliot's ambivalence about her given name may have been to do with the way it placed her precisely in class and regional terms. Mary Ann(e) – customarily shortened to 'Polly' – was a very popular name among the Midland farming community into which she had been born. She was the youngest child of Robert Evans and his second wife Christiana Pearson. Evans had risen from being an enterprising carpenter to become land agent to the Newdigate-Newedegate family, whose holdings stretched from Derbyshire in the North to Kent in the South. Their chief seat, however, was in Midlands Warwickshire, at Arbury Hall near Nuneaton, and it was in a substantial farmhouse, Griff House, just outside the park boundary that Mary Anne lived until she was twenty-one.

Of her two parents, Mary Anne was closer to her middle-aged father whom she often accompanied on his rounds of the estate. Through his expert eyes Mary Anne came to know a landscape that was by no means exclusively pastoral. The Newdigate holdings included a colliery, and in the nearby villages miners lived alongside ribbon-weavers whose livelihood was often strafed by trade depressions. As an adolescent during the struggle for parliamentary reform in the early 1830s Mary Anne had witnessed rioting in the streets of Nuneaton, while as a young woman she ran a clothing club for the local poor. Yet the studious Miss Evans was also given the run of the magnificent library at Arbury Hall by her father's employers. Thus while Mary Anne's childhood adhered to her later prescription of being 'well rooted in some spot of a native land' (*DD*, ch. 3), there was nothing remotely parochial about it. Seven of her eight novels are populated with characters from every stratum of society including weavers, artisans, clergy, aristocrats, lawyers, doctors and farmers, all types which she had first encountered within a few miles of her family home.

Mrs Evans's ill health following the birth and death of twin sons in 1821 may have been the reason why Mary Anne was sent away to school at the age of just five. She spent her most formative years at 'The Elms' in Nuneaton where she forged a strong bond with the assistant mistress, the evangelical Irishwoman Maria Lewis. Mary Anne's piety intensified still further when she transferred to a school in Coventry, run by the daughters of a local Baptist minister. Her ostentatiously 'Quaker' dress, fierce bookishness and proficiency at the piano meant that her awed classmates regarded the formidable adolescent as 'immeasurably superior to themselves' (Cross, I: 26).

In 1836, at the age of seventeen, Mary Ann – now minus the final 'e' – was called home to help nurse her mother, who was dying of breast cancer. Following the marriage of her older sister Christiana in May 1837 she became sole housekeeper to her father and brother Isaac yet also continued the ambitious programme of study begun at school. In her correspondence with Miss Lewis she commented in detail on the historical and religious books she was reading in the slivers of time between domestic duties. She also took language and music lessons from visiting masters.

In 1841 Robert Evans retired, handing over the land agency to Isaac who continued to live at Griff with his new wife. Mary Ann accompanied her father to a handsome house on the outskirts of Coventry, which had been taken to launch the rather plain twenty-one-year-old onto the Midlands marriage market. But these careful plans were disrupted on 2 January 1842 when Mary Ann announced that it would be hypocritical to continue to attend church, since, as she explained a few weeks later, she now believed that Christianity was based on 'mingled truth and fiction' (*L*, I: 128). If Robert Evans was bewildered by Mary Ann's behaviour, her brother was furious. The very close relationship that the siblings had enjoyed as small children had long since cooled, rendering the differences in their temperaments more apparent than ever. According to the highly censorious Isaac, Mary Ann's rebellious attitude was imperilling the good name of the entire Evans clan.

There was no doubt in the Evans family's collective mind as to who was to blame for this reckless reversal in Mary Ann's religious beliefs. Shortly after arriving in Coventry she had been introduced to near-neighbours Charles and Cara Bray. Charles was a ribbon manufacturer and newspaper proprietor who held progressive views on everything from education to marriage while Cara was an intellectually independent woman raised in the Unitarian church. Through the influence of this charismatic pair, amplified by Cara's elder sister Sara Hennell, Mary Ann had started to read some of the new 'Higher Criticism' which threw doubt on the literal truth of the Bible, in particular the supernatural elements in the New Testament's account of the life of Christ. It was this reading, including *An Inquiry Concerning the Origin of Christianity* (1838) by Sara and Cara's brother Charles Christian Hennell, which had loosened Mary Ann's attachment to Anglican observance and nudged her towards the agnosticism that endured for the rest of her life.

After a few painful weeks a truce was called in what Mary Ann dubbed her 'Holy War', and she continued to live with her father as companion and, increasingly, nurse until his death in 1849. In later life she regretted the way in which she had allowed intellectual vanity to cause such pain to the man she called 'The one deep strong love I have ever known' (*L*, 1: 284). However, every minute she could spare from tending the elderly man was spent at Rosehill, the Brays' large house through which passed the radical elite of the day.

It was through the Brays that in 1846 Mary Ann came to publish her first book, *The Life of Jesus, Critically Examined*, a translation from the German of the second edition of D. F. Strauss's *Das Leben Jesu*, which went even further than Hennell in showing that Christianity was based on a series of 'mythi' rather than verifiable historical facts. Despite agreeing with Strauss's intellectual position, Mary Ann found the implications of his outlook bleak. Her next translation – of Ludwig Feuerbach's *Das Wesen des Christenthums* as *The Essence of Christianity* (1854) – was much more compatible. Feuerbach argued that it was in the loving bonds between individuals that one could best reach the divine.

Both these translations were published by the radical publisher John Chapman, a friend of the Brays based at 142 Strand, London, from where he ran a bookshop and publishing business. And it was to this address that Mary Ann moved in 1851. She agreed to work as an uncredited assistant and *de facto* editor on Chapman's flagship publication, the recently acquired *Westminster Review*, while also lodging in the hostel for transient intellectuals run on the premises by his wife. Over the next five years the newly styled 'Marian' not only edited articles from some of the most important thinkers of the day, including J. S. Mill and J. A. Froude, but also reviewed hundreds of books on a range of subjects including history, science and literature. She also pursued love affairs with John Chapman himself and with the bachelor Herbert Spencer, whose rejection caused a serious wound to her already precarious self-esteem.

It was, however, through Chapman and Spencer that, in 1851, Marian met the man who would become her emotional and professional partner for the next twenty-five years. George Henry Lewes was a journalist and author whose complicated private life had long been the subject of London gossip. His wife was conducting an affair with his former best friend and colleague, Thornton Hunt, by whom she would eventually have four children, in addition to three surviving sons by her husband. At the time Lewes became intimate with Marian he had lived apart from his wife for several years but because he had agreed to be named as the legal father of Hunt's children he was unable to seek a divorce.

Marian's decision in July 1854 to 'elope' with Lewes for a nine-month working holiday in Germany caused immense shock. It also set up a pattern of extended travel, both within Britain and abroad, which was to become an important feature of the Leweses' life together. Cara Bray and Sara Hennell were offended that Marian had not revealed the seriousness of her new relationship, let alone taken their advice on such a drastic step. Men of the world who had previously professed admiration for the clever Miss Evans were now incandescent with rage, insisting that no wife or daughter of theirs would be allowed to have anything to do with her. It was for this reason that, on returning from Germany where Lewes had been working on his biography of Goethe, the couple set up home in the anonymous suburbs of south-west London. In this state of near purdah Marian wrote some of her most accomplished essays for the *Westminster Review*, including 'Silly Novels by Lady Novelists' (October 1856), which mounts a searing satire on the conventions of the commercial fiction of the day. Her choice of subject suggests that she might have now been toying with writing a novel of her own.

In November 1856 Lewes sent thirty-seven-year-old Marian's first story to John Blackwood, the Edinburgh publisher whose family firm produced the eponymous monthly magazine to which Lewes regularly contributed scientific articles. Blackwood liked 'The Sad Fortunes of the Reverend Amos Barton', taking on trust Lewes's cover story that it was written by a shy, implicitly male, friend who wished to conceal his identity. When, after a few weeks, Blackwood pressed for a *nom de plume* for his new author, Marian volunteered 'George Eliot' (she later explained that 'the reason she fixed on this name was that George was Mr Lewes's Christian name, and Eliot was a good mouth-filling, easily-pronounced word': Cross, I: 430–1). 'Amos Barton' was followed by 'Mr Gilfil's Love Story' and 'Janet's Repentance', all based on incidents and people that Marian recalled from her youth. Unfortunately, so did many other people: Nuneaton was in an uproar trying to work out the true identity of the mysterious 'George Eliot'. For a time a penniless alcoholic called Joseph Liggins allowed people to think that he was the author, a state of affairs that initially amused Marian and Lewes but eventually forced them into revealing the actual situation.

Figure 1 An 1858 photograph by John Edwin Mayall, of which George Eliot's friend Mme Belloc (Bessie Rayner Parkes) commented that it gave 'the only real indication left to us of the true shape of the head, and of George Eliot's smile and general bearing'.

Marian's first full-length novel, *Adam Bede* (1859), did nothing to disperse the excited chatter. This time it was her late father's Derbyshire relatives who recognised the true story on which the narrative of Hetty Sorrell, the milkmaid who gets pregnant by the young squire and is brought to repentance by a young female Methodist preacher, was based. The novel was a commercial and critical success and resulted in the definitive unmasking of George Eliot as Marian Lewes or, to the watchful eyes of her remaining family in the Midlands, Mary Anne Evans. By this time Marian had revealed her irregular domestic situation to her brother, who responded by breaking off contact and instructing his sister Chrissey to follow suit. It was now too that Lewes travelled to Switzerland to reveal to his three schoolboy sons that he was separated from their mother and living with the rising literary star 'George Eliot'.

It was perhaps the realisation that she might never see her brother and sister again that steered Marian towards the subject matter of her next novel, *The Mill on the Floss* (1860). Set in the Midlands in the early part of the century, it deals with the estrangement of Tom and Maggie Tulliver and features a chorus of maternal aunts who are based on Christiana Evans's fearsome sisters. The book's sales suffered slightly from the fact that its author was now known to be none other than the scandalous Marian Evans. This sense that critical eyes and tongues were judging her leaked into the account of Maggie's exclusion from the town of St Ogg's but also into 'The Lifted Veil' (1859), a short story written around the same time that seethes with a sense of suffocating paranoia.

Gradually Marian's isolation began to lessen and by the autumn of 1860 she had moved with Lewes into the centre of London. This was partly so that Lewes's eldest son Charles could commute easily to his Post Office job. Marian now felt sufficiently confident to attend concerts, theatre and even dinner parties. The longevity of her relationship with Lewes, combined with her new fame and wealth, had softened people's attitudes to her domestic position. Nonetheless, she and Lewes made the decision not to have children of their own in order to avoid further stigma. Significantly, her next novel, the fairy-tale-like *Silas Marner* (1861), concerns a single middle-aged man who adopts a baby that has arrived unexpectedly on his doorstep.

Silas Marner, set in Marian's signature Warwickshire landscape, was a comparatively easy book for her to write. The next would prove the hardest. *Romola* (1863) was an over-researched account of the life of the Dominican friar Savonarola in counter-Reformation Florence. It failed to fulfil Marian's own edict that a novel should not 'lapse anywhere from the

Figure 2 Engraving by Paul Rajon of Frederic Burton's 1864 portrait of George Eliot, commissioned by J. W. Cross as the frontispiece for *George Eliot's Life* (1885).

picture to the diagram' (*L*, 4: 300) and, although well received by intellectual readers of the day, it remains the least popular of all her works. Rather than being published by Blackwood, the book was brought out by George Smith who offered an unprecedented £10,000 for it. Marian had been tempted not so much by the money as by a buried desire to punish Blackwood for not acting more decisively in the Joseph Liggins affair. However, the disappointing result of this collaboration with Smith, Elder pushed Marian into returning to Blackwood's where she remained for the rest of her career.

By 1863 the Leweses were wealthy enough to afford a large house to the north of Regent's Park. Lavishly decorated, 'The Priory' became the setting for their famous Sunday afternoon receptions which attracted the great and the good of the day, including Charles Darwin and a young, star-struck Henry James. Women, too, found themselves drawn to Marian, including Georgie Burne-Jones, wife of the painter, and Princess Louise, daughter of Queen Victoria.

Marian returned to the Midlands of her youth for her next novel. *Felix Holt, the Radical* (1866) is based on her memories of poll-day rioting in Nuneaton in the 1830s. Although the central characters fail to spark, there is no disguising the pleasure with which Marian once again invokes the physical and social landscape of pre-Victorian Warwickshire. The book, however, was not such a popular success as her earlier works. Though the long narrative poem which followed it, *The Spanish Gypsy* (1868), sold well, some sensed that George Eliot's writing career was on the wane.

These were difficult times personally too. In the summer of 1869 Lewes's second son Thornie returned from Africa where he had been farming, just in time to die of spinal tuberculosis. In this moment of greatest devastation, Marian turned again to her earliest memories. The sonnet sequence 'Brother and Sister' (1874) recounts the painful moment when she and Isaac first started to grow apart as children.

With her next novel Marian's reputation and finances spectacularly revived. *Middlemarch*, published mostly in two-monthly instalments throughout 1872, plaits the story of an idealistic doctor arriving in a Midlands market town with that of an equally high-minded young woman who insists on marrying out of misplaced duty and intellectual ambition. The book was an astonishing success and remains today Eliot's most highly regarded book.

Marian's final novel, *Daniel Deronda*, was published in monthly instalments in 1876. Again, it knits together two narratives which seem only tenuously related. The first concerns a young man's discovery of his Jewishness and the second that of a young Englishwoman's marriage into the aristocracy. Although the book sold reasonably well, readers and critics were predictably puzzled by the 'Jewish part' of the book which struck many, then as now, as wordy and lacking in dramatic pace.

The purchase of a country house in Surrey in 1876 should have heralded the beginning of a more tranquil phase for Marian. Instead, her happiness was blighted by Lewes's worsening health. His death in 1878 left her devastated and unable to work, although *Impressions of Theophrastus Such*, which she had been writing during the last months of Lewes's life, duly appeared. One of the few people Marian could bear to see during her early months of bereavement was John Walter Cross, the young banker who had negotiated the purchase of 'The Heights' at Witley and acted as the Leweses' financial advisor.

In 1880 the literary world was rocked by the private life of George Eliot for the first time in twenty-five years. Once again she had slipped away unnoticed to Europe with a man, although this time there had been a bona fide church wedding first. Soon an altogether more damaging story than the mere fact of her marriage to the much younger John Cross was filtering back to London. On arriving in Venice at the climax of the honeymoon, Johnnie had leapt into the Grand Canal apparently in an attempt to commit suicide. Whatever the real reasons behind Cross's sudden and violent depression, there were plenty who liked to attribute it sniggeringly to the oppressive sexual demands of his elderly bride.

In any event, the marriage did not last. A few weeks after the Crosses moved into a new riverside house in Chelsea, Mary Ann caught a chill and died. She had recently celebrated her sixty-first birthday. Despite discreet lobbying, Westminster Abbey refused to bury her, nominally on account of her agnosticism, but quite possibly because of her earlier irregular life with Lewes. Instead, she was interred at Highgate Cemetery next to Lewes. Not until 1980, a full century after her death, was a memorial stone finally dedicated to George Eliot in Poet's Corner.

CHAPTER 2

Publishers and publication

Joanne Shattock

'The simple fact is, she is so great a giant that there is nothing for it but to accept her inspirations and leave criticism alone', the publisher John Blackwood wrote to his colleague Joseph Langford after reading the manuscript of Book Six of *Daniel Deronda* in the spring of 1876.[1] Langford, as George Eliot had anticipated, had expressed doubts about the 'Jewish element' in the novel (*J*, 145). Blackwood reassured him that the latest instalment would remove any concerns he might have. His assessment of George Eliot's stature in 1876 was not exaggerated, and his respect for her work, close to reverence, was the culmination of their twenty-year association.

It was an important relationship to them both. The two were nearly of an age, John Blackwood being born the year before George Eliot, in 1818. The likelihood of a close working relationship let alone friendship between them was not obvious at the outset. Blackwood was gregarious, sporting, intelligent but not an intellectual, and very much at home in male company. He was developing into an astute publisher, with a good judgement of the literary marketplace and of what would appeal to readers of *Blackwood's Edinburgh Magazine*. He also believed in nurturing his authors. He had taken over the editorship of the house magazine from his father in 1845, and assumed the headship of the firm in 1852. The introduction of publisher and author in 1856 came through G. H. Lewes, who was a valued *Blackwood's* contributor.

Lewes sent him the manuscript of 'The Sad Fortunes of the Reverend Amos Barton' on behalf of an unnamed 'friend'. After minor changes the story was published anonymously in two parts in January and February 1857 (see Figure 3). 'Mr. Gilfil's Love Story' followed from March to June, and then 'Janet's Repentance' in five parts between July and November. Blackwood communicated with his new author through Lewes, the adoption of the pseudonym 'George Eliot' serving to mask both her identity and her gender. Midway through the process Lewes cautioned Blackwood against offering too much constructive criticism: 'Entre nous let me hint that unless you have any *serious* objection to make to Eliot's stories, *don't* make any. He is so easily discouraged, so diffident of himself, that not being prompted by necessity to write, he will close the series in the belief that his writing is not relished' (*L*, 2: 363–4). Initially Blackwood abided by Lewes's advice, and kept his comments to a minimum. But as the later parts of 'Janet's Repentance' arrived he could not suppress his concern over the development of the plot, particularly Janet's alcoholism and Dempster's death from delirium tremens. In response George Eliot decided against writing another two stories, and the series was brought to an end. *Scenes of Clerical Life*, by 'George Eliot', was published in two volumes early in 1858.

Blackwood met George Eliot for the first time in February 1858 when he called on Lewes in Richmond. 'She is a most intelligent pleasant woman, with a face like a man, but a good expression', he wrote to his wife; 'I am not to tell Langford the secret even.' Joseph Langford was then running the firm's London office. The letter went on: 'Lewes says he would do ten times the work for me that he would do for any other man, and he does not think any other editor in the world would have been able to induce George Eliot to go on. It was very flattering, as his experience of editors is very great, and he is a monstrous clever fellow' (*L*, 2: 436). The letter is telling in a number of respects. Lewes and Blackwood were to become the two most influential agents in George Eliot's writing career. They did not always act in unison, but as the letter indicates, Blackwood respected Lewes's judgement, and Lewes knew how to get the best from the publisher.

By the time Lewes had forwarded her first story to Blackwood, Marian Evans had been writing and publishing for ten years. She had begun with a number of short articles and reviews for the *Coventry Herald and Observer*, a newspaper owned by her friend Charles Bray. Her first publisher was the London-based John Chapman, who published her translation from the German of D. F. Strauss's *Das Leben Jesu* in 1846. Her name was not on the title page. Through Chapman she was introduced to the radical circle involved with the quarterly *Westminster Review*, which Chapman purchased in the spring of 1851. He also provided her with her first lodgings when she moved to London in January of that year.

Chapman's unorthodox establishment at 142 Strand was the site of an early attachment between them, which soon transformed itself into a professional working relationship from which both benefited. Chapman possessed enormous self-confidence, but acknowledged that he did not have the intellectual credentials to support the editorship of the premier radical periodical of the day. He persuaded Marian Evans to act as his sub-editor, responsible for commissioning and reading articles along with the time-consuming tasks of revising submissions, correcting proofs and making up the review each quarter. Chapman was the public face of the *Westminster*, the proprietor and, to those not in the inner circle, the editor. The quarterly's finances were precarious. Evans was not paid for her editorial duties, but only for her articles.

At 142 Strand she was introduced to a variety of writers and intellectuals, some of them associated with the review, others part of intersecting networks who gathered at Chapman's frequent evening parties. Her visitors included Herbert Spencer, with whom she formed another attachment, Harriet Martineau, George Combe, Bessie Parkes and, most important of all, George Henry Lewes. Number 142 Strand provided the future George Eliot with an invaluable introduction to metropolitan literary life. It also gave her a base from which to lead an independent professional one.

Her editorship of the *Westminster Review* lasted from Chapman's first issue in January 1852 until the January 1854 number. While it provided intellectual stimulus it did not bring in an income, and she needed to supplement the small annuity from her father's estate. During this period she reviewed R. W. Mackay's *The Progress of the Intellect* for the *Westminster* (January 1851) and W. R. Greg's *The Creed of Christendom* for the weekly *Leader* (20 September 1851), which Lewes and Thornton Hunt established in 1850. The two periodicals were to provide a modest income until the end of 1856.

Once she relinquished her editorial responsibilities she began to review regularly for both the *Westminster* and the *Leader*. In March 1854 Chapman asked her to write the 'Belles Lettres' section of the 'Contemporary Literature' feature in each number of the *Westminster*, which paid twelve guineas a quarter (*J*, 58, 64–5). Each 'Belles Lettres' contained short reviews of upwards of thirty works, requiring a phenomenal amount of reading and writing. Gordon S. Haight estimates that the seven 'Belles Lettres' for which she was responsible reviewed 166 different books, and that she probably read many more.[2] Lewes was taken ill in the spring of 1854 and she took over some of his regular reviewing for the *Leader*. Meanwhile, she was preparing a translation of Ludwig Feuerbach's *The Essence of Christianity* which was published in Chapman's Quarterly Series in July. This time her name, Marian Evans, was on the title page, the only occasion it was used on any of her works.

She welcomed Chapman's invitation to review Victor Cousin's book on Madame de Sablé for the *Westminster* when she and Lewes travelled to the continent in the summer of 1854. Two further articles resulted from their stay in Germany, 'Three Months in Weimar' (*Fraser's Magazine*, June 1855) and 'Liszt, Wagner and Weimar' (*Fraser's*, July 1855), the first a reworking of material in her unpublished 'Recollections of Weimar' (*J*, 215–40).

Like many reviewers in the age of anonymity, she learned to maximise her efforts by spreading her material over more than one periodical. She reviewed Charles Kingsley's *Westward Ho!* in the *Leader* (19 May 1855) and included the novel in the 'Belles Lettres' section in the *Westminster* for July 1855. Heinrich Heine, whom she and Lewes had read together while they were in Berlin, featured in a number of her reviews, including the influential essay 'German Wit: Heinrich Heine' for the *Westminster* (January 1856). Anonymity enabled her to write a factual account of Lewes's *Life of Goethe* for the *Leader* (3 November 1855), even though she had provided the translations of many of the German quotations and helped with the preparation of the manuscript. The article avoided an evaluative judgement, but to modern eyes the review still represents a surprising conflict of interest.

Her last year of intensive reviewing, 1856, produced some of her best work: 'The Natural History of German Life', her review-essay on the work of the historical sociologist W. H. von Riehl (*Westminster Review*, July 1856) and the well-known 'Silly Novels by Lady Novelists' (*Westminster Review*, October 1856), both of which set out the principles of her realism, and her last *Westminster* article 'Worldliness and Other-Worldliness: the Poet Young' (January 1857).

Invitations to write for new journals came from several quarters. Probably through Lewes she was drawn to contribute to the pugnacious new weekly *Saturday Review*, writing four articles in 1856. Bessie Parkes urged her to write for the new monthly *English Woman's Journal* which she and Barbara Bodichon, née Leigh Smith, established in 1858. 'I have given up writing "articles," having discovered that my vocation lies in other paths. In fact *entre nous*, I expect to be writing *books* for some time to come' (*L*, 2: 431), she replied. And she stuck to her word. Unlike most of her contemporaries both male and female, who juggled reviewing with the writing of fiction, anxious not to ignore any income stream in a precarious professional life, she had set her mind to writing fiction, and consciously turned her back on journalism. When in 1858 John Blackwood advised against publishing a preface she had prepared for *Adam Bede*, he asked

BLACKWOOD'S EDINBURGH MAGAZINE.

No. CCCCXCV. JANUARY 1857. Vol. LXXXI.

SCENES OF CLERICAL LIFE.—NO. I.

THE SAD FORTUNES OF THE REVEREND AMOS BARTON.

PART I.—CHAPTER I.

Shepperton Church was a very different-looking building five-and-twenty years ago. To be sure, its substantial stone tower looks at you through its intelligent eye, the clock, with the friendly expression of former days; but in everything else what changes! Now, there is a wide span of slated roof flanking the old steeple; the windows are tall and symmetrical; the outer doors are resplendent with oak-graining, the inner doors reverentially noiseless with a garment of red baize; and the walls, you are convinced, no lichen will ever again effect a settlement on—they are smooth and innutrient as the summit of the Rev. Amos Barton's head, after ten years of baldness and supererogatory soap. Pass through the baize doors and you will see the nave filled with well-shaped benches, understood to be free seats; while in certain eligible corners, less directly under the fire of the clergyman's eye, there are pews reserved for the Shepperton gentility. Ample galleries are supported on iron pillars, and in one of them stands the crowning glory, the very clasp or aigrette of Shepperton church-adornment—namely, an organ, not very much out of repair, on which a collector of small rents, differentiated by the force of circumstances into an organist, will accompany the alacrity of your departure after the blessing, by a sacred minuet or an easy "Gloria."

Immense improvement! says the well-regulated mind, which unintermittingly rejoices in the New Police, the Tithe Commutation Act, the penny-post, and all guarantees of human advancement, and has no moments when conservative-reforming intellect takes a nap, while imagination does a little Toryism by the sly, revelling in regret that dear, old, brown, crumbling, picturesque inefficiency is everywhere giving place to spick-and-span new-painted, new-varnished efficiency, which will yield endless diagrams, plans, elevations, and sections, but alas! no picture. Mine, I fear, is not a well-regulated mind: it has an occasional tenderness for old abuses; it lingers with a certain fondness over the days of nasal clerks and topbooted parsons, and has a sigh for the departed shades of vulgar errors. So it is not surprising that I recall with a fond sadness Shepperton church as it was in the old days, with its outer coat of rough stucco, its red-tiled roof, its

Figure 3 The first (anonymous) publication of *Scenes of Clerical Life*, in *Blackwood's Edinburgh Magazine*, January 1857.

whether she would consider reviewing or writing 'miscellaneous papers', adding that the material from her preface would do well in a review. Her response was measured, expressing a willingness to write in service 'to my future self and my fellow novelists', but adding that she read more old books than new, and so was in need of suggestions (*L*, 2: 510, 512–13).

By then the pace of her novel writing had quickened, and there was neither time nor inclination to write articles or reviews. Only in 1865, when Lewes became editor of the *Fortnightly Review* and an advisor to George Smith's newspaper the *Pall Mall Gazette*, did she relent, writing a series of short pieces for the *Gazette* under the pseudonym 'Saccharissa'. She wrote one substantial review for the *Fortnightly*, 'The Influence of Rationalism' (15 May 1865), which was signed 'George Eliot'. Her only non-fictional contribution to *Blackwood's* was 'Address to Working Men, by Felix Holt', written at the publisher's instigation and published in the January 1868 issue.[3]

The decision to bring the *Scenes of Clerical Life* to an end with 'Janet's Repentance' had both positive and negative repercussions. It allowed her to begin *Adam Bede*, the novel that became, in Carol Martin's words, 'the benchmark for all her future novels'.[4] But the fact that the three stories were too short to fill the requisite three volumes demanded by the circulating libraries had an impact on its reception. 'I wish the Series had been long enough to make the statutory 3 vols. as that would have afforded time to fix your reputation more firmly and *familiarly*', Blackwood wrote (*L*, 2: 393). Charles Mudie, the influential proprietor of the largest of the libraries, took 350 copies. But, much to the chagrin of George Eliot and Lewes, he did not advertise the book. 'E. of course takes it as a sign that Mudie doesn't think much of the book. I utterly scout *that* idea', Lewes wrote to Blackwood (*L*, 2: 467). The publisher remained optimistic, conscious that from October 1857 a new novel was in preparation. *Adam Bede* was begun in the expectation that it would be serialised in *Blackwood's*, but this time George Eliot was determined to be further ahead with the writing before publication than she had been with the *Scenes*.[5]

The first thirteen chapters were shown to Blackwood early in March 1858. George Eliot recorded in her journal that after reading the first page he had said, smiling, 'This will do' (*J*, 295). His reactions to subsequent sections remained enthusiastic, although Arthur's seduction of Hetty and possibly the treatment of Methodism led him to hesitate about its suitability for the magazine. In the end the author proposed that it should be published in three volumes and he agreed, offering her £800 for the copyright for four years.

George Eliot and Lewes were eager for a pre-Christmas publication to capitalise on seasonal sales. More urgently, they were anxious that publication should precede any revelation of the identity of George Eliot and the adverse publicity that they feared would almost inevitably ensue. Blackwood did not want *Adam Bede* to compete with Bulwer Lytton's *What will he do with it?*, then completing its serialisation in the magazine. In the end the novel was published on 1 February 1859.

Its reception was totally beyond Blackwood's expectations. Mudie took 500 copies initially, and ordered 200 more. '[W]e may now consider the Bedesman fairly round the corner and coming in a winner at a slapping pace', Blackwood wrote triumphantly on 7 March (*L*, 3: 29). On 12 March Langford reported that Mudie had increased his number of copies to a thousand (*L*, 8: 226). The novel went through seven printings in its first year, and outsold all of George Eliot's other novels in her lifetime.

She had already begun its successor. As early as January 1859 she made some notes on floods in 1770 and 1781, a subject which would feature in the dramatic denouement of her new novel, and on which she would do more research in the following summer. She finished her story 'The Lifted Veil' at the end of April 1859 and in June sent Blackwood 110 pages of what would become *The Mill on the Floss*. He declared himself 'perfectly delighted' with it (*L*, 3: 88). The title was his suggestion. Once again the question of serialisation was raised. In proposing that *Adam Bede* be published in the expensive three-volume format both Lewes and George Eliot knew they were risking the advantages that exposure in a serial would bring, all the more important as sales of *Scenes* had been disappointing.

Now, with the overwhelming success of *Adam Bede* behind them, George Eliot pressed again for the three-volume format, arguing that serialisation in the magazine would 'sweep away perhaps 20,000 – nay, 40,000 – readers' of the more expensive library edition (*L*, 3: 151). A more truthful reason was her dislike of beginning publication before she had completed the writing. '[M]y stories grow in me like plants, and this is only in the leaf-bud', she wrote to Blackwood in August. 'I have faith that the flower will come. Not enough faith, though, to make me like the idea of beginning to print till the flower is fairly out – till I know the end as well as the beginning' (*L*, 3: 133). As John Sutherland points out, most publishers, Blackwood included, regarded magazine serialisation as attracting additional readers rather than putting off those of the library editions which followed it.[6] Magazines such as the *Cornhill* and *Macmillan's* had recently been established by publishers with precisely this aim.

Despite the disagreement, their personal relations remained cordial throughout the summer of 1859. He sent her a puppy, a pug, at the end of

July. In September he offered her £3,000 for the magazine serial and the copyright for four years. He also paid her an additional £400 for *Adam Bede*, based on its continuing healthy sales. Their only serious misunderstanding occurred in the autumn of 1859, when Eliot and Lewes thought Blackwood was not taking the threat to her reputation posed by the lifting of her incognito sufficiently seriously. He in turn was hurt by her cool response to the additional sum he paid her for *Adam Bede*, and irritated by her refusal to part with the copyright of the new novel. The rift was smoothed over, and he eventually offered her £2000 for *The Mill on the Floss*, with publication in three volumes and the copyright retained by her. At the same time he gave up the remaining copyright of *Adam Bede*. The novel was completed in March 1860. Nearly 6,000 copies of the first edition were sold almost immediately following its publication on 4 April 1860. Mudie took 2,000 and in April was 'nibbling at a third thousand', according to Blackwood (*L*, 3: 289).

Her main task over the summer of 1860, after a holiday in Italy, was her story 'Brother Jacob'. In July she mentioned a plan for an 'Italian' novel, for which she had undertaken some preliminary research while abroad. She was occupied from the end of September through to March with *Silas Marner* which, as she told Blackwood 'came *across* my other plans by a sudden inspiration' (*L*, 3: 371). She sent him the first chapters in February, and the rest in March. The story was published in one volume in April 1861.

She resumed her exhausting and exhaustive research on her 'Italian Romance', as Lewes referred to it, on their return to Italy in April 1861. The autumn of 1861 was taken up with preparations for the first collective edition of the novels, the so-called 'Cheap Edition', comprising *Scenes of Clerical Life*, *Adam Bede*, *The Mill on the Floss* and *Silas Marner*, which was to establish the text of the four novels for decades to come.

On New Year's Day 1862, according to her journal, she began to write *Romola*. Later the same month George Smith of the publishing firm Smith, Elder, and proprietor of the monthly *Cornhill Magazine*, out of the blue made her a 'magnificent offer' (*J*, 108). Smith urgently needed a new serial by a big 'name' to revive the *Cornhill*'s circulation following the success of Trollope's *Framley Parsonage* in its first year. Thackeray's *The Adventures of Philip*, the current serial, did not have the attraction of its predecessor, *Lovel the Widower*. As a publisher of fiction, Smith was known for the generous sums offered to his authors, which extended to his payments to contributors to the *Cornhill* – £1,000 a year to Thackeray as editor, and similarly extravagant sums for serialised fiction. His offer to George Eliot was £10,000 for the copyright of an illustrated serial in sixteen monthly parts, to begin in April or May, the largest offer he had yet made to a *Cornhill* contributor.

The offer was breathtaking in financial terms, but less attractive in other respects. She had made her antipathy to monthly serialisation clear to Blackwood and she had not changed her mind. Moreover, she was not sufficiently far on with *Romola* to consider publication in April. A three-part serialisation of 'Brother Jacob' was suggested as a stopgap. She queried the number of instalments Smith wanted, and was unwilling to cede the copyright in perpetuity. Eventually she agreed to produce twelve monthly numbers, with the copyright reverting to her after six years, for the reduced sum of £7,000. The novel in the end ran to fourteen parts.

She did not feel able to discuss Smith's offer with Blackwood until she had accepted it, knowing, she later told him, that it was beyond his usual terms. Blackwood was generous in his reply. Aware of the 'wild sums' being talked about in some quarters, he was not surprised that she had been made such an offer. '[I]t would destroy my pleasure in business if I knew any friend was publishing with me when he thought he could do better for himself by going elsewhere', he told her (*L*, 4: 36). It was a well-judged response.

The writing of *Romola* did not proceed smoothly. She was beset with illness as well as self-doubt throughout its composition. The research was burdensome. As she famously remarked later, 'I began it a young woman, – I finished it an old one' (Cross, 2: 352). One of the few pleasures of the experience was making the acquaintance of Frederic Leighton, who had been chosen as the novel's illustrator. The serial did not revive the *Cornhill*'s fortunes as Smith had hoped, and sales of the magazine continued to drop. *Romola* was duly published in three volumes in 1863.

George Eliot offered Smith her next novel, *Felix Holt, the Radical*, but he refused it, fearing its political subject matter would not appeal to *Cornhill* readers. Blackwood was magnanimous about her return to the firm, offering her £5,000, and publishing *Felix Holt* in three volumes in 1866. The first edition of five thousand sold sufficiently well, but the two-volume edition at twelve shillings moved slowly. 'The next time we take the field together I think we must experiment in a new form', he suggested in September 1866 (*L*, 4: 307).

Blackwood's determination to challenge the stranglehold of the circulating libraries was strengthened by the commercial failure of *Felix Holt*. This played well into Lewes's hands. George Eliot began work on her new novel, which would eventually become *Middlemarch*, in 1868. It promised to be even longer than its predecessors. Four-volume novels were not unknown to Blackwood – he had published Bulwer Lytton's *My Novel* (1853) and *What will he do with it?* (1858) in this format, but had not regarded either as a success. Lewes proposed a compromise, a halfway point between a serial, to which George Eliot was resistant, and a four-volume library edition, for which the libraries could well reduce their subscription and therefore Blackwood's profit. Publication was to be in eight half-volumes or parts, selling for five shillings and published at two-monthly intervals. The outlay of two pounds or forty shillings for the entire novel could be spread over twenty-four months, which would appeal to buyers rather than borrowers. The parts were to have attractive light green wrappers with a vignette on the cover.

Whether the idea was indeed Lewes's, or whether, as John Sutherland suggests, he remembered that Blackwood himself had proposed an experiment of five-shilling parts for one of Bulwer Lytton's novels as early as 1850, the publisher and Joseph Langford agreed to his proposal.[7] The interval between the parts was altered so that the final three 'books' came out at monthly intervals, concluding in December 1872. The eight divisions lent themselves to the structure of the novel. Each of the eight parts or books was given a title which was retained in the volume format. The pressures of serialisation were minimised because the parts did not need to be of exact lengths. Lewes proposed the addition of advertising supplements, thus bulking out each book to more closely resemble a volume of a standard novel. The experiment paid off. In terms of both sales and critical acclaim, *Middlemarch* was a triumph. The format was retained with *Daniel Deronda* in 1876 and used by Chapman and Hall for Trollope's *The Prime Minister* in the same year, but it did not catch on. The tide was turning against the 'three decker' and against the circulating libraries. The future lay in cheap one-volume editions.

George Eliot's relationship with John Blackwood remained strong until the end. Like his famous author, he too was coming to the end of his career. The death in 1861 of his brother William, 'the Major', had led to the latter's son, another William, being taken into the firm, and gradually assuming more responsibility for its running. John Blackwood's death on 29 October 1879 followed less than a year after Lewes's on 30 November 1878 and little more than a year before George Eliot's own in December 1880. She was most certainly the 'giant' he had acknowledged in 1876, but he had played a significant role in establishing her reputation.

NOTES

1 Mrs Gerald Porter, *Annals of a Publishing House: John Blackwood*, 3 vols. (Edinburgh and London: William Blackwood and Sons, 1898), vol. III, p. 392.

2 Haight (1968) discusses her reviews in detail, pp. 176–210.
3 William Baker and John C. Ross, *George Eliot: A Bibliographical History* (New Castle, DE and London: Oak Knoll Press and The British Library, 2002), pp. 422–45, lists her known periodical articles plus misattributions.
4 Carol A. Martin (ed.), *Adam Bede* (Clarendon edn, Oxford University Press, 2001), p. liv.
5 Martin notes that the manuscript of the first four chapters is marked 'End of Part I': Clarendon edn, p. xxvi.
6 J. A. Sutherland, *Victorian Novelists and Publishers* (London: Athlone, 1976), p. 38.
7 Ibid., pp. 200, 203.

CHAPTER 3

Editions of George Eliot's work

Joanne Shattock

In the volatile world of nineteenth-century fiction production, as John Sutherland has rightly observed, 'the publisher's skills were often as instrumental to success as anything the author might contribute'.[1] He points out that George Eliot was fortunate in her choice of publisher, or, to be more precise, her two publishers. Seven publishing houses dominated fiction publishing in the Victorian period, all of them run by comparatively young men, whose talents complemented those of the writers they brought before the public. John Blackwood, of William Blackwood and Sons, and George Smith, of Smith, Elder & Co., were two of the most enterprising, and were responsible for the editions of George Eliot's works that were brought into the public domain during her lifetime.[2]

Of the two, John Blackwood was the longer serving, and the publisher who is credited with successfully marketing 'George Eliot'. The firm of Blackwood kept her name before the public from its first appearance in 1858, with the book publication of *Scenes of Clerical Life*, to *Impressions of Theophrastus Such*, published in 1879, the year before her death – and beyond. George Smith, dubbed 'the prince of publishers', had a reputation for treating his authors generously, as George Eliot discovered when in 1862 he temporarily lured her away from Blackwood for the serialisation of *Romola* in his new house magazine the *Cornhill* and its subsequent publication in three volumes in 1863.

In their publishing strategies both Blackwood and Smith had to meet the demands of the still powerful circulating libraries, which required that novels should be published in expensive three-volume 'library' editions, selling for a guinea and a half, or thirty-one shillings and sixpence, a sum beyond the means of all but the wealthiest of book buyers. Library proprietors, of whom the most influential was Charles Edward Mudie, 'the Leviathan Mudie' as Blackwood called him (*L*, 2: 417), owner of the largest of the libraries, negotiated discounts under the threat of refusing to stock a particular title. Mudie's usual terms were a 10 per cent discount in addition to the standard 25 per cent reduction offered to booksellers. His weekly advertisements were a highly visible announcement that a novel had been 'taken' by his library, an honour which the young Margaret Oliphant described 'a sort of recognition from heaven'.[3]

Victorian fiction publishing operated, as Sutherland observes, by a system which both underpinned the circulating libraries and at the same time sought to circumvent them. John Blackwood in particular grew increasingly exasperated by the stranglehold of the libraries, which included in George Eliot's publishing lifetime a new chain operated by W. H. Smith, and evolved a strategy which challenged the dominance of the 'three decker' on several fronts.

The production of George Eliot's novels coincided with changing technology at the House of Blackwood, which had been slow to adopt the new process of stereotyping. Between 1858, when *Scenes of Clerical Life* came out in volume form, and the early 1860s, after *Adam Bede* and *The Mill on the Floss* were published in three volumes, the firm moved from traditional typesetting, which required the storage of large quantities of standing type, to the more flexible stereotyping or electrotyping, which enabled a speedier production of new editions or reissues of a novel in response to reader demand.

Blackwoods were ahead of their competitors in one respect, in having had since 1817 a house magazine, *Blackwood's Edinburgh Magazine*, which they used to promote the firm's authors. The magazine had always included some fiction, but from the 1850s, with authors such as Bulwer Lytton, Samuel Warren and Margaret Oliphant on their books, serialisation became the first stage of a publication process designed to maximise sales and to keep an author before the public for as long as possible. Monthly magazines like *Macmillan's Magazine* and the *Cornhill*, established in 1859 and 1860, were upmarket challengers to older publications such as *Blackwood's*, selling for a shilling as opposed to two shillings and sixpence, and in the case of the *Cornhill* offering single-column pages and illustrations by eminent artists.

Blackwood's strategy was to issue the expensive three-volume edition at the conclusion of the magazine serial, followed at a carefully judged interval by a two-volume reprint retailing for twelve shillings, and after another interval by a one-volume edition selling for six shillings. He was known for the speed at which he introduced the two-volume edition, the success of which was regarded as an important barometer of future success.

Scenes of Clerical Life

George Eliot's first four publications with Blackwood, *Scenes of Clerical Life* (1858), *Adam Bede* (1859), *The Mill on the Floss* (1860) and *Silas Marner* (1861), were produced using this strategy, with important variations. The 'Clerical Scenes', as Lewes and Blackwood referred to them, were serialised anonymously in *Blackwood's Magazine* from January to November 1857. George Eliot had originally intended to write two more tales, but became discouraged by Blackwood's cool response to the early numbers of 'Janet's Repentance'. In consequence the *Scenes* were too short to fill the standard three volumes, and were issued in two volumes selling at twenty-one shillings. A first edition of 1,000 copies was printed, of which Mudie took 350. Sales of the two-volume edition were sluggish, although the monthly numbers of the magazine continued to sell well. Through Lewes she indicated her willingness to sell the translation and reprint rights to Trübner for £50 (*L*, 2: 481). A second edition, selling for twelve shillings, was published in July 1859, and a third in April 1860. Sales of these editions were boosted by what had by that time become the runaway success of *Adam Bede*. As would become customary with George Eliot's novels, Harper & Brothers of New York paid a fee for the right to bring out an American edition shortly after the first British one, and the firm of Tauchnitz, in Germany, paid for the licence to issue a copyright edition in English for European consumption.

Adam Bede

With *Adam Bede* Blackwood was able to put in place his strategy for maximising circulating library sales while generating additional revenue through cheaper reprints. The result was a triumph. The novel went through more editions and sold more copies during George Eliot's lifetime than any of her other works. Over 3,000 copies were sold in the first three months following publication on 1 February 1859. A total of seven printings were made in the first year alone. As Carol Martin observes, the distinction between 'edition' and 'impression' was often blurred in this rapid production process, but a certain amount of type was reset for each printing. In June 1859 a two-volume 'fourth edition' was published, selling for twelve shillings, followed by four further resettings between July 1859 and June 1860, identified as the 'fifth' to the 'eighth' editions. None of these 'editions' was stereotyped. Around 15,000 copies of the three- and

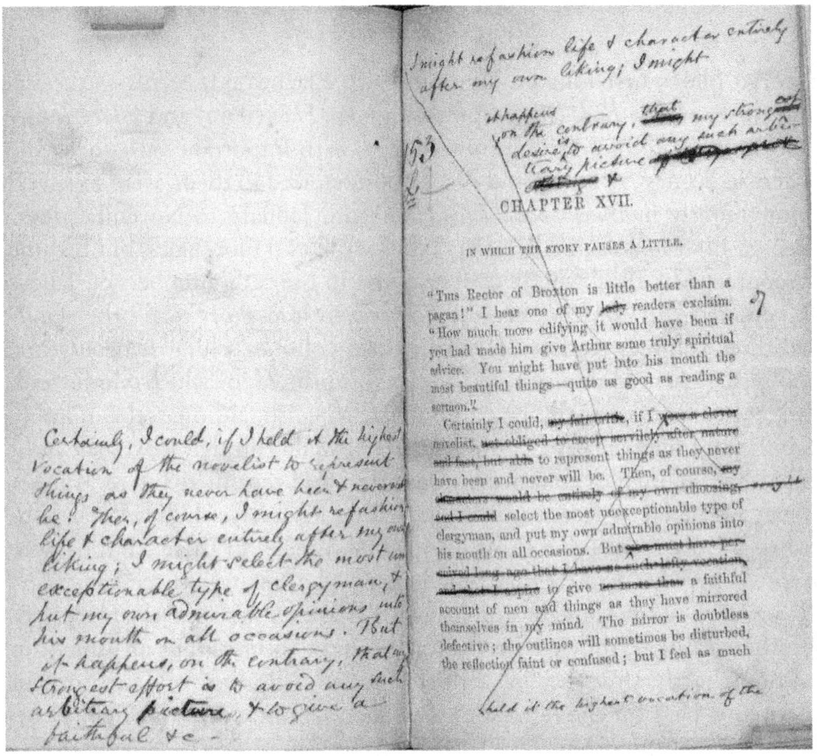

CHAPTER XVII.

IN WHICH THE STORY PAUSES A LITTLE.

"This Rector of Broxton is little better than a pagan!" I hear one of my readers exclaim. "How much more edifying it would have been if you had made him give Arthur some truly spiritual advice. You might have put into his mouth the most beautiful things—quite as good as reading a sermon."

Certainly I could, if I to represent things as they never have been and never will be. Then, of course, select the most unexceptionable type of clergyman, and put my own admirable opinions into his mouth on all occasions. But to give a faithful account of men and things as they have mirrored themselves in my mind. The mirror is doubtless defective; the outlines will sometimes be disturbed, the reflection faint or confused; but I feel as much

Figure 4 George Eliot's revisions of the opening of chapter 17 of *Adam Bede* for the eighth edition.
By permission of Harry Ransom Center, The University of Texas at Austin.

two-volume editions, printed between February 1859 and June 1861, were sold. The novel was translated into more than sixteen European languages.[4] Tauchnitz produced a two-volume copyright edition in 1859 and Harpers paid £30 for the American rights.

By April 1861 Blackwood was contemplating a one-volume edition selling at six shillings, the first volume of a projected 'cheap' edition of her novels. In preparation, George Eliot read through and made substantial corrections to the eighth edition, including a significant revision to chapter 17, 'In which the story pauses a little' (see Figure 4). Three thousand copies of the one-volume edition were printed from stereotyped plates and published on 31 January 1862. According to the firm's ledgers, the plates of this edition were then used for every subsequent reprinting of *Adam Bede* until the Cabinet Edition of 1878.

The Cheap Edition, the first collected edition of her works, was marketed as 'The Works of George Eliot', and included *The Mill on the Floss* (1862) and a third volume comprising *Scenes of Clerical Life* and *Silas Marner*, issued in 1863. The edition went through three printings between 1862 and 1866, a total of 4,500 copies. More significantly, because George Eliot had corrected the texts of all four, and because they were printed from stereotyped plates, the collected edition established the texts of her first four novels.

The Mill on the Floss

Meanwhile *The Mill on the Floss* was published in three volumes on 4 April 1860. 4,000 copies were printed, using stereotype plates cast from the corrected proofs. Subscriptions totalled 3,600 before publication, so a further 2,000 copies were run off. Most of the 6,000 were sold by the end of the year, a success William Blackwood, John's brother, told her had not been equalled since Scott's Waverley novels earlier in the century. She received £3,050 from Blackwood, a further £300 from Harper & Brothers for the American reprint, and £100 from Tauchnitz. Other smaller sums were received for German and Dutch translations.

Blackwood was keen to repeat the successful strategy he had used for *Adam Bede*. A two-volume second edition went to press in November 1860, George Eliot having made some minor corrections to the first edition; 2,000 copies were printed, and published on 1 December. It was not a success. By their original agreement Blackwood paid her £300, a miscalculation which left him out of pocket, as he ruefully confessed (*L*, 3: 368). In preparation for the 'cheap' edition she carefully corrected the two-volume edition, as she had done with *Adam Bede*. The one-volume six-shilling edition of *The Mill on the Floss* was published on 6 December 1862. As was the case with *Adam Bede*, the evidence from Blackwood's ledgers indicates that the electrotype plates of this edition were used for the next sixty years.

Silas Marner

George Eliot was occupied during the autumn of 1860 with her one-volume story *Silas Marner* which was published on 2 April 1861. Its popular success was a pleasant surprise for Blackwood, who initially worried about publishing another short fiction that might not be taken by the libraries. The single volume was deliberately made 'thicker and handsomer' than a volume of an ordinary three-volume novel (*L*, 3: 383), and he calculated that the price of twelve shillings would attract individual buyers. He offered her £800 for an edition of 4,000. The response from both the libraries and the public exceeded expectations. Of the 8,000 copies run off in five separate printings in 1861, fewer than 200 remained at the end of the year. Mudie took 3,000. Harper's brought out an edition in the same year, as did Tauchnitz. She corrected the first edition for the one-volume edition which formed part of 'The Works of George Eliot', published in April 1863. The 1863 plates were used until the text was reset for the Cabinet Edition of 1878. There were more printings of this popular text after her death in 1880 as copyrights expired, including versions with notes for young readers. The Tauchnitz edition in particular had many reprintings.

Romola

George Smith's offer of £10,000 for the copyright and serialisation of *Romola* was unprecedented in a period when 'fancy prices', as Margaret Oliphant termed them, were much talked about. According to Lewes, it was 'the most magnificent offer ever yet made for a novel' (*L*, 4: 17–18). Bradbury and Evans would offer Dickens the same amount for *Our Mutual Friend* in 1864, and in 1880 Longman paid Disraeli £10,000 for *Endymion*, his position as a recent prime minister popularly interpreted as relevant to the extravagant offer. In the end George Eliot settled for £7,000 and the reversion of the copyright after six years. It was still more than twice what she received for *The Mill on the Floss* and scarcely less than her earnings from all her previous works put together. The return of her copyright meant that the novel could be included later in 'any general edition', as she told Blackwood (*L*, 4: 35).

The novel was serialised in fourteen parts in the *Cornhill* from July 1862 until August 1863 with twenty-four illustrations by Frederic Leighton. It was published in three volumes on 6 July, a month before its completion in the magazine, and only four weeks after George Eliot had finished it. According to Andrew Brown, the number of substantive variants between the *Cornhill* version and the first edition suggests that she made corrections for the volume publication.[5] But sales of the three-volume edition could not match the success of *The Mill on the Floss*. Just over 2,000 copies were printed, of which only 1,700 were sold in the first twelve months; 1,300 sets were taken by libraries, 550 of them by Mudie. Harpers issued an American edition reprinted from the *Cornhill* text, and Tauchnitz's continental edition also appeared in 1863.

By September 1865 the edition had been remaindered. Smith then produced a one-volume 'Illustrated Edition', selling for six shillings, which utilised four of Leighton's original illustrations, and had a specially commissioned illustrated title page. Just over half of the 1,500 copies printed were sold in a year. Again, the number of substantive variants between the first edition and the Illustrated Edition indicates that George Eliot corrected the proofs.[6] The stereotyped plates were subsequently used for a 'New Edition' in one volume, this time selling for two shillings and sixpence. This proved a more successful format. The plates were reused on several occasions into the 1870s, with a total of 7,000 copies sold up to 1874 although the copyright had reverted to George Eliot in August 1869. Smith, Elder made one last attempt to capitalise on their investment during her lifetime, producing a Deluxe Edition of two imperial octavo volumes of 1,000 numbered copies in 1880. The edition, retailing for five guineas, sold out within six months.

Felix Holt, the Radical

According to George Smith, George Eliot offered him her next novel, *Felix Holt*, in the spring of 1866, indicating that she expected £5,000 for it. After reading the manuscript he concluded that it would not be a popular success and rejected it. She then wrote to Blackwood, who professed pleasure that she turned to him 'in the first instance' and offered £5,000 for the copyright for six years.[7] Smith's judgement proved correct. The three-volume first edition was published on 14 June 1866. Just over 5,000 copies were printed, of which several hundred remained at the end of the year. More than 300 were still in stock in 1873. In December George Eliot corrected the first edition in preparation for the publication of a two-volume edition, which sold for the usual price of twelve shillings. This proved a real disappointment: 2,100 copies were printed, of which fewer than 800 had been sold as late as 1876. Blackwood strongly suspected that the cheaper Tauchnitz editions were competing with the English two-volume ones, and hesitated to agree terms with Tauchnitz for *Felix Holt*. He made no plans for a cheap one-volume edition, but included the novel in the Illustrated Edition of George Eliot's fiction in 1869.

The Spanish Gypsy and *The Legend of Jubal*

The next book-length publication was George Eliot's long poem *The Spanish Gypsy*, which she had begun as early as 1865 but only completed in

1868. Blackwood issued it in one volume selling for ten shillings and sixpence with a print run of 2,000. She was paid £300. Lewes proposed that there should be a new 'edition' each time the previous one sold 1,000 copies. As a result there were some sixteen reissues, using the original stereotype plates, between 1868 and 1886. She made corrections to the volumes up to 1874. The 1868 American edition, published by the Boston firm of Ticknor & Fields, was also popular. A volume of poems, *The Legend of Jubal*, was published in 1874.

Middlemarch and *Daniel Deronda*: a radical experiment

The comparative failure of *Felix Holt* hardened Blackwood's resolve to challenge the circulating libraries by more innovative forms of publication. The firm turned its energies to the radical experiment of issuing *Middlemarch* in eight five-shilling parts at two-monthly intervals, followed by a four-volume edition selling for two guineas, or forty-two shillings. Blackwood offered Eliot and Lewes the choice of a fee of £6,000 on the first 4,000 copies sold or a 40 per cent royalty on both part and volume publication. They opted for the royalty. He professed himself 'sanguine that we shall run a great coup' (*L*, 5: 183). Having threatened a boycott, Mudie took 1,500 copies of Book I and 1,000 of Book II. W. H. Smith took 1,000 copies of Book I. By December 1872, when all eight books had appeared, the total sale was 6,000 copies of Book I and 5,000 of each of the remaining seven. Lewes was disappointed in the figures, having prophesied a sale of two to three thousand more of each of the parts. George Eliot earned £4,000, plus fees for rights in America, Canada and Australia. She was paid for the serialisation in *Harper's Weekly* from December 1871 to February 1873 and in the Melbourne journal the *Australasian* from February 1872 to March 1873. There were more fees for translations into Dutch, German and Russian. The continental English version was published not by Tauchnitz but by Asher & Co. of Berlin, at Lewes's instigation. They paid her a royalty of £327 on a printing of 2,000, more than Tauchnitz's usual terms.

The subscription for the eight parts bound into four volumes was not large. Blackwood proposed a cheaper edition of four volumes selling for a guinea or twenty-one shillings. The initial print run was 1,000. With four additional printings in 1873, the total sale of the edition was close to 3,000 copies.

There was one further and crucial edition. Joseph Langford, manager of the Edinburgh office, proposed a one-volume edition selling at seven shillings and sixpence. George Eliot was given an opportunity to make corrections and alterations. On this occasion she was entirely in charge of the proofs, a task normally shared with Lewes, who was preoccupied with the publication of *Problems of Life and Mind*. Among the changes was an important alteration to the final two pages that eliminated specific comment on the attitude of Middlemarch society to Dorothea's marriage to Casaubon in favour of the resonant statement that the 'determining acts of her life were not ideally beautiful. They were the mixed result of young and noble impulse struggling amidst the conditions of an imperfect social state' ('Finale'). This one-volume edition of 1874 established the text of the novel which was used for the Cabinet Edition and subsequently. The sales at the end of 1874 exceeded 10,000, beyond everyone's expectation, 'wonderful out of all whooping', as George Eliot told Blackwood (*L*, 6: 75).

The *Middlemarch* formula was repeated for *Daniel Deronda*. The novel was issued in eight monthly parts from February 1876 until September. She adjusted the length of some of the parts at the proof stage, in consultation with Blackwood. A four-volume reprint was issued at a guinea, which had a poor sale, but the one-volume reprint at seven shillings and sixpence, similar to that of *Middlemarch*, was more successful, selling more than 5,000 copies, with reprintings continuing up to 1902. As with *Middlemarch*, she was paid a royalty of 40 per cent on each part. Harpers paid her an unprecedented £1,700 for the American rights plus serialisation in *Harper's New Monthly Magazine*. She was paid a fee again for serialisation in the *Australasian*, for the Tauchnitz edition, and for Dutch and German translations. By the end of 1879 her total earnings on the novel exceeded £9,000.

The final publication during her lifetime was *Impressions of Theophrastus Such*, a collection of essays published in 1879. Blackwood issued them in a single volume selling at ten shillings and sixpence. Most of the 6,000 copies printed were sold during the year. As a final gesture before his death in October, Blackwood raised her royalties from the £875 agreed to £1,000.

Collected editions

The success of his early experiment with a collective edition, the three-volume 'Works of George Eliot' of 1862–3, no doubt prompted Blackwood to think of further collections as more novels were added to the list. The Illustrated Edition of 1867–70 consisted of the first four novels together with *Felix Holt*, issued first in sixpenny numbers and then in single volumes at three shillings and sixpence. The numbers were a failure, but the three-and-sixpenny volumes were the basis for the New or Stereotyped edition, to which *Romola*, *Middlemarch* and *Daniel Deronda* were added later as volumes six, seven and eight. These went on being reprinted into the second decade of the twentieth century.

The purpose of cheap collective editions as they emerged in the 1840s was to increase sales to individual purchasers, particularly the railway travelling public. It was only later in the century that publishers conceived of commemorative collected editions, but here too their purpose was as much commercial as sentimental. It was probably with both in mind that late in 1877 Lewes proposed the Cabinet Edition of ten titles in nineteen volumes to be published monthly in 1878–9. Blackwood's ten-year lease on the first five novels had come to an end in 1876, and he was anxious to renew it, with the addition of the last three novels, confident that sales in the next decade would be much greater than in the last (*L*, 6: 297n).

The new collective edition would use the plates of the stereotyped edition, with wider margins and new covers. George Eliot herself was enthusiastic, proposing a 'rich olive green' cover which would provide a contrast with the gold and black lettering. The edition began with *Romola*, which she pronounced 'handsome – and handy', the last a reference to its size (*L*, 6: 422–3, 435). The nineteen volumes, including two volumes of poetry, appeared at monthly intervals in 1878–9, with *Impressions of Theophrastus Such* added in 1880. The addition of *Essays and Leaves from a Notebook* in 1884 and Cross's *George Eliot's Life* in 1885 made the eventual total thirteen titles in twenty-four volumes.

Collective editions continued to be produced after George Eliot's death. The plates from the Cabinet Edition were used for Blackwood's Standard Edition, in twenty-one volumes in 1895, with cheaper paper and bindings. The stereotyped plates were used again in the New Cabinet Edition of 1913. The American market was flooded with posthumous collective editions after her death.

Twentieth-century editions of individual novels reflected the gradual recuperation of her academic reputation from the 1940s onward, with Penguin and Oxford University Press's World's Classics series taking the lead from the early 1960s in producing paperback editions with scholarly introductions and explanatory notes. There were analogous American editions as well. This process culminated with the commissioning of the authoritative Clarendon Edition of the novels published by Oxford University Press under the general editorship of Gordon Haight in 1980. An edition of the complete shorter poems was published in two volumes in 2005, followed by *The Spanish Gypsy* in 2008, both edited by A. G. van den Broek.

The editions of George Eliot's works both conformed to and resisted publishing trends in her lifetime. She had missed out on part publication, in which both Dickens and Thackeray published the majority of their novels, which was on the wane by the mid 1850s. She produced her first six works of fiction at a point when magazine serialisation was at its peak. Finding its demands unpalatable, she preferred the three-volume library editions or 'three-deckers' that had dominated nineteenth-century fiction publishing since the days of Scott. At the end of her career, with the help of an independently minded publisher and her ever-resourceful partner, she successfully challenged the very system she had earlier endorsed, publishing in a format that encouraged book-buying rather than library borrowing. Scarcely more than fifteen years after her death, the three-volume novel, which she had once so enthusiastically espoused, came to the end of its useful life.

NOTES

1 *Victorian Novelists and Publishers* (London: Athlone, 1976), p. 1.

2 The others were Chapman and Hall, Bradbury and Evans, Macmillan, Richard Bentley and Longman. Of the seven, only Longman had been in business at the beginning of the nineteenth century (Sutherland, *Victorian Novelists and Publishers*, pp. 1–3).

3 Margaret Oliphant, *Annals of a Publishing House: William Blackwood and His Sons, their Magazine and Friends*, 2 vols. (Edinburgh and London: William Blackwood and Sons, 1897), vol. II, p. 458.

4 Carol A. Martin, *Adam Bede*, p. lv. See William Baker and John C. Ross, *George Eliot: A Bibliographical History* (New Castle, DE and London: Oak Knoll Press and The British Library, 2002), pp. 78–92, for details of translations, as well as for more detailed bibliographical and other information about George Eliot's works. Each volume in the Clarendon Edition (see p. xix) provides a comprehensive textual history for the novel in question.

5 Andrew Brown (ed.), *Romola* (Clarendon edn, Oxford University Press, 1993), p. lii.

6 Ibid., p. lvi.

7 Leonard Huxley, *The House of Smith Elder* (London: Smith, Elder, 1923), p. 103; *L*, 4: 240–1. Smith's and Blackwood's accounts of who was approached first do not tally.

CHAPTER 4

Genre

Nancy Henry

George Eliot is best known as a realist novelist, but over the course of her career she produced work in every major literary genre except drama. Her first significant publication was a translation of German biblical scholar David Strauss's *Life of Jesus* (1846), and she also translated Ludwig Feuerbach's *The Essence of Christianity* (1854). As an editor and journalist in London, she wrote short book reviews and review essays for the periodical press. Her first important works of fiction were linked stories, and she also wrote two freestanding short stories or novellas. Most importantly, she experimented in a variety of poetic forms from sonnets and dialogues to the epic narrative poem *The Spanish Gypsy* (1868). Though she failed to complete the drama she aspired to write, her poem 'Armgart' (1871) is structured as a drama in five scenes. Her last and most experimental work is a collection of essays unified by a first person narrator. *Impressions of Theophrastus Such* (1879) revives and reinvents the classical tradition of character sketching based on the *Characters* of Theophrastus (*c.* 372–287 BCE) and anticipates Modernist fragmentation in form as its characters, unmoored from plot, are viewed through the eyes of the narrator – a modern Theophrastus. Recognition of the extent of George Eliot's writing in a variety of genres provides us with a completer understanding and appreciation of her overall literary achievement.

In the 1840s, George Eliot published in the provincial newspaper the *Coventry Herald and Observer* most notably 'Poetry and Prose from the Notebook of an Eccentric' (1846–7), essays that are difficult to place generically and involve a double narration by the character Macarthy and the friend who publishes his papers posthumously. In 1849, she reviewed J. A. Froude's controversial novel *The Nemesis of Faith* in the *Herald and Observer*. It was not until she was asked to review R. W. Mackay's *The Progress of the Intellect* for the *Westminster Review* (January 1851) that her work began to reach a wider audience. In 1851 she moved to London, lodging in the home of publisher John Chapman and thus entering the cultural and intellectual centre of the English publishing world.

At this time, literary reviews and journal articles, as well as much serialised fiction, appeared anonymously. The intention and effect of this convention was to make each journal speak as if in a single voice and to de-emphasise the individual author. Using the pronoun 'we' rather than 'I', authors could express their opinions freely within the agenda of the particular journal. But no censure meant no credit for their contributions, which editors had the right to alter to bring into line with the policies of the journals. Those within the tight London literary circles might know who wrote the articles, but many readers did not. The practice eventually came to an end, influenced by the establishment of the *Fortnightly Review* in 1865, a journal G. H. Lewes edited from 1865 to 1866. Rosemary Ashton writes that the plan of the *Fortnightly* was to give 'contributors complete freedom from editorial interference or party adherence. To this end all articles would be signed – an innovation in English periodical history.'[1] The only journal articles signed 'by George Eliot' appeared in the *Fortnightly*.

From 1851 to 1854, George Eliot edited the *Westminster* without pay or acknowledgment, gaining experience and exerting influence without formal recognition. During the same period, she was mastering the form of the short review, publishing frequently in Lewes's journal, the *Leader*. Though her editorial role ended when she left for Germany with Lewes in 1854, she continued to write for the *Westminster* and from 1855 to 1856 was responsible for its 'Belles Lettres' section, which reviewed contemporary literature. Like many journalists, George Eliot wrote reviews to earn money, but writing them was also a valuable intellectual exercise for her. These pieces reveal her extensive reading and her skills as a critic. Reviewing taught her to go straight to the heart of a book's content, and there are consistencies and continuities in her analyses that make these pieces interesting to students of her fiction. For example, her review of Volume III of John Ruskin's *Modern Painters* in 1856 contains a statement that was to be reiterated in her own writing: 'The truth of infinite value that he teaches is *realism* – the doctrine that all truth and beauty are to be attained by a humble and faithful study of nature, and not by substituting vague forms, bred by imagination on the mists of feeling, in place of definite, substantial reality.'[2]

Her longer review essays in the *Westminster* offer statements of the realist aesthetic she was formulating prior to her career as a novelist. 'The Natural History of German Life' (July 1856) is a serious consideration of the sociological analyses of German peasantry by Wilhelm Heinrich von Riehl.

'Silly Novels by Lady Novelists' (October 1856) is a caustic and humorous critique of inferior and unrealistic novels by women. Both essays show her expanding an argument, as well as displaying her knowledge and asserting her opinions about what fiction should do. In the essay on Riehl, she wrote: 'The greatest benefit we owe to the artist, whether painter, poet, or novelist, is the extension of our sympathies' (*Essays*, 270). Under cover of anonymity, she developed an authoritative voice that foreshadows the narrative voice of her fiction. In these pieces, she speaks at once as herself and also as a type – the literate reviewer of the London periodical press. This persona comments in 'Silly Novels', for example: 'We may remark, by the way, that we have been relieved from a serious scruple by discovering that silly novels by lady novelists rarely introduce us into any other than the very lofty and fashionable society' (*Essays*, 303). As she made the transition to fiction, traces of this voice persisted, embodied in an implicitly masculine narrator who, especially in her early works, claimed to know the characters about whom he was writing.

The pseudonym 'George Eliot' was first used when *Scenes of Clerical Life* appeared in two volumes at the beginning of 1858, the three component stories having been published anonymously in *Blackwood's Edinburgh Magazine* the previous year. Given the dominance of the novel, it is easy now to overlook the fact that short fiction was an important Victorian genre and a mainstay of the burgeoning periodical press. Charles Dickens wrote a number of short stories and published those by others in the journals he edited, *Household Words* (1850–9) and *All the Year Round* (1859–70). Additionally, novels were often serialised in periodicals, allowing readers to follow the multiple plots as they developed week by week or month by month. Book publication would follow the completion of the serialisation. The novel series, which continued the characters from one book to the next, was another emerging sub-genre in the mid nineteenth century and included Anthony Trollope's Barsetshire series (1855–67) and Margaret Oliphant's 'Chronicles of Carlingford' (1862–76). George Eliot never linked her novels in this way, but because of its focus on the history of a place, *Scenes of Clerical Life* has more in common with the novel series than it does with Victorian story collections that are unified by a frame narrative to explain the grouping of otherwise unrelated tales, such as Gaskell's *Round the Sofa* (1859), Trollope's *An Editor's Tales* (1870) and Sheridan Le Fanu's *In a Glass Darkly* (1872).

George Eliot followed *Scenes* with her first novel, *Adam Bede* (1859), and then with *The Mill on the Floss* (1860). In these novels, she used her narrative voice to articulate and theorise the realist aesthetic she practised.

While Dickens in *Oliver Twist* (1837) and Gaskell in *Mary Barton* (1848) had relegated statements about their realist agenda to prefaces, George Eliot incorporated her comments within the fiction itself, for example in her famous chapter 17 of *Adam Bede*, breaking the frame in an experimental gesture that distinguished her work and established her position as an innovator in realist fiction.

Silas Marner (1861) and *Romola* (1863) departed from her previous works in distinctive ways. *Silas Marner* is a realistic representation of rural England in the early nineteenth century, but the short novel has a fable-like quality and a moral about the supreme importance of human bonds that seems more easily encapsulated than those of her longer novels. *Romola* was a self-conscious departure from her tales of rural England and marks a turning point in her career as a novelist. Its setting in fifteenth-century Florence and its serialisation in the *Cornhill Magazine* places it in a tradition with other fiction of the period, such as Harriet Beecher Stowe's *Agnes of Sorrento* (1861–2), also set in fifteenth-century Italy and serialised in the *Cornhill*. But *Romola*'s heavily researched, dense allusiveness, made it a unique contribution to the sub-genre of historical novel as established by Sir Walter Scott and his imitators (such as G. P. R. James), as well as by Bulwer Lytton, author of *Rienzi, The Last of the Roman Tribunes* (1835), which George Eliot read in preparation for writing *Romola*. In some respects, all her novels are historical: *Middlemarch* is as much a historical novel as *Romola*, if more subtly so for being set in nineteenth-century England. Both works fulfil George Eliot's requirements for what the historical imagination should do. She wrote in a fragmentary essay, 'Leaves from a Notebook' (published posthumously in 1884), that the historical novel should show: 'How triumphant opinions originally spread – how institutions arose – what were the conditions of great inventions, discoveries, or theoretic conceptions – what circumstances affecting individual lots are attendant on the decay of long-established systems' (*Essays*, 446).

George Eliot took breaks from writing her novels to write short fiction, including 'The Lifted Veil', published in *Blackwood's Edinburgh Magazine* in July 1859, and 'Brother Jacob', written in 1860 but not published in the *Cornhill* until July 1864. These works show what she was able to do when freed from her self-imposed mandate to represent the real and the probable. 'The Lifted Veil' is unique for its supernatural premise. Narrated by the central character, Latimer, who has the power to hear the thoughts of others as well as to foresee his own death, this foray into the newly emerging genre of science fiction ends with what seems like a futuristic experiment in which a woman is brought back to life by a blood transfusion.

As short fiction, it is anomalous: neither ghost story nor detective story, it seems to represent George Eliot's dark broodings about the limits and dangers of the sympathy she was advocating in her novels. Knowing rather than imagining what others think turns out to be a kind of torture. 'Brother Jacob' does not stretch the bounds of the probable, but its sarcasm and unpleasant characters allowed her to relax the demand that readers sympathise with her characters. In this underappreciated work, she played on themes from *Silas Marner*, such as stolen gold coins, conflict between brothers, and the desire to escape a past life and identity. At one point titled 'The Idiot Brother', the story of the self-interested confectioner David Faux is light in tone and dark in its overall view of human behaviour. These two stories rounded out a volume with *Silas Marner* in the Cabinet Edition of her works (published by Blackwood's in 1878). These literary experiments allowed her to expand her imagination beyond the confines of the strict realism to which she adhered in her novels.

George Eliot is not known as a poet, but writing poetry was important to her for reasons that shed light on overall attitudes towards literary genres in the mid-nineteenth century. Critics have wondered why she persisted in writing and publishing in a form that seemed unsuited to her particular talents (Poetry, 1: xxvii–lii). The answer is at once personal and broadly cultural. On the one hand, her poetry allowed her to do things she could not do in her fiction: adopt mythical characters, develop single themes and experiment in metrical forms of language. On the other hand, she may have retained some of her culture's lingering suspicion of novels as a lower form of art than poetry. While Scott, her sentimental favourite, produced popular verse and fiction, George Eliot's fellow realists Dickens, Thackeray, Gaskell and Trollope showed little interest in writing poetry. Nor did the major poets of the mid-Victorian period – Tennyson, the Brownings and Matthew Arnold – write novels. The authors she most admired, from Dante to Shakespeare, Milton and Wordsworth, were poets. Whether she wanted to attain the greatness of these authors, thereby exceeding the accomplishments of other novelists, or simply to explore her own imaginative and linguistic capabilities, she passed through a period in the late 1860s and early 1870s in which she particularly sought to develop her poetic skills.

In addition to a lifetime of reading poetry, George Eliot studied aesthetics, from Aristotle's *Poetics* to the essays collected in Joseph Haslewood's *Ancient Critical Essays upon English Poets and Poesy* (1815). She also read contemporary studies of prosody, including James J. Sylvester's *The Laws of Verse* (1870).[3] Only her near contemporaries – those writing in the age of the novel's primacy – discuss the differences between novels and poetry and between those who wrote in these distinct genres. John Stuart Mill, for example, insisted: 'So much is the nature of poetry dissimilar to the nature of fictitious narrative, that to have a really strong passion for either of the two, seems to presuppose or to superinduce a comparative indifference to the other.' He elaborated: 'The truth of poetry is to paint the human soul truly; the truth of fiction is to give a true picture of life.'[4] Poet Letitia E. Landon (L.E.L.) thought that poetry had its origins in 'higher impulses speaking so strongly of some spiritual influence of a purer order than those of our common wants and wishes'.[5] This spirituality (specifically belief in God) is the main element that in 1885 Rose Elizabeth Cleveland found wanting in George Eliot's poetry (Poetry, 2: 253–67).

If George Eliot's poetry did not imply a higher than human power, it deepened her exploration of humanism, asking questions about the origins of poetry and the role of the poet in society. In another fragmentary essay, 'Notes on Form in Art' (1868), she speculates that 'the funeral or marriage sing-song, wailing or glad, with more or less violent muscular movement & resonance of wood or metal made the rude beginnings of lyric poetry' (*Essays*, 435–6). This physical origin of poetry in the sound of human work, as well as in the sounds of nature, is the subject of her poem 'The Legend of Jubal' (1870). In this biblically inspired myth of her own creation, she imagines the invention of music as derived from 'The clear-winged fugue of echoes vanishing; | And through them all the hammer's rhythmic ring' (Poetry, 1: 50). Her archetypal artist Jubal transforms his primitive society, realising that 'This heart of music in the might of sound, | Shall forthwith be the share of our race' (Poetry, 1: 52). In a comment on the immortality of art, as opposed to the artist, Jubal becomes a celebrated figure but dies scorned by those who prefer to believe in the myth rather than reality of music's creator.

From the chapter epigraphs or 'mottoes' that she wrote for *Felix Holt* (1866), *Middlemarch* (1871–2) and *Daniel Deronda* (1876), to her various experiments in lyric and longer narrative verse, George Eliot's poetry is worth studying in itself, as well as for the ways in which writing it may have influenced these late works, which took the genre of the novel in new directions. The period of intensive poetry writing in the late 1860s was a transitional one. She felt the need to exercise and extend her linguistic powers and to think in broad, even mythical terms. Following this immersion in poetry, she wrote her most mature, expansive and linguistically complex novels. *Middlemarch* and *Daniel Deronda* may owe their thematic scope – as well as the greatness of their prose – to the poetry that preceded their composition.

All of George Eliot's narrative voices are in a sense characters. In addition to her novels, she wrote occasional pieces, such as 'Address to Working Men' (published in *Blackwood's Edinburgh Magazine* in January 1868), a political essay in the voice of the fictional Felix Holt, and the four 'Saccharissa' essays, whimsical pieces unusual in being published under a pseudonym other than George Eliot (*Pall Mall Gazette*, March–May 1865). Her last book represents a unique experiment in narrative voice, combining contemporary social commentary and character sketching. *Impressions of Theophrastus Such* draws on all of her previous prose writings in a uniquely self-conscious meditation on authorship, elevating 'culture' – that is, the writing that is preserved and handed down from generation to generation – to an almost religious status, anticipating late nineteenth-century nationalism and the importance of distinctive national cultures. Her narrator Theophrastus is concerned with the 'debasing' of the 'moral currency', and the transgressions of egoism, hypocrisy, greed and prejudice. These are all themes found in her novels, but the difference of *Impressions* lies in its form. Fragmented, densely allusive and preoccupied with the value of the writing that will represent Victorian England to future generations, the work anticipates the Modernist poetry and prose of the next century by authors such as Gertrude Stein, Virginia Woolf, T. S. Eliot and James Joyce.

In the section on 'Story-Telling' in 'Leaves from a Notebook,' George Eliot observed that early poetry used 'primitive instruments of thought': 'The desire for orderly narration is a later, more reflective birth' (*Essays*, 445). While she experimented with poetry, as well as short stories and essays, Eliot nonetheless recognised that the realist novel was the most significant and representative art form of her time. It is this genre to which she contributed most significantly and for which she is rightly best remembered.

NOTES

1 *G. H. Lewes: A Life* (Oxford University Press, 1991), p. 224.
2 Rosemary Ashton (ed.), *George Eliot: Selected Critical Writings* (Oxford World's Classics, Oxford University Press, 1991), p. 248.
3 On Eliot's reading in English prosody, see Poetry, 2: 165–71.
4 Mill, 'What is Poetry?' (1833), *Broadview Anthology of Victorian Poetry and Poetic Theory*, concise edn (Peterborough, ONT: Broadview, 2000), pp. 562, 564.
5 Landon, 'On the Ancient and Modern Influence of Poetry' (1832), in *Broadview Anthology of Victorian Poetry*, p. 556.

CHAPTER 5

The biographical tradition

Margaret Harris

Biographers of George Eliot face an exquisitely difficult challenge, encapsulated in an obituary comment: 'she herself was her greatest work'.[1] The pen name 'George Eliot', chosen when she began to publish fiction by the woman who otherwise wished to be known as Marian Lewes, has been charged with significance both by its bearer and by others. As a consequence, biographies have tended to be preoccupied with the distinction between the cerebral writer and the dependent woman.

Who was George Eliot? There was speculation from the outset. When George Eliot was introduced to the reading public as the author of *Scenes of Clerical Life* on its book publication in 1858, it was assumed that the name was that of a clergyman. Reviewers of both *Scenes* and *Adam Bede* proceeded on this assumption, with no suspicion that 'George Eliot' was a pseudonym, let alone that the author was a woman. The reasons for Marian Lewes's adoption of a pen name are obvious. She was known in literary circles for her work as a journalist and translator, but also as the partner of George Lewes. Assumed to be an apostate because of the translations from German of D. F. Strauss's *Life of Jesus* and Ludwig Feuerbach's *The Essence of Christianity*, and marked even more scandalously by her liaison with Lewes, she had greater reason than other women entering the literary marketplace to seek the protection afforded by a male pseudonym.

Her identity was not revealed even to her publisher until February 1858, when *Scenes* was being favourably reviewed, though John Blackwood appears to have had his suspicions. Another who may have penetrated the disguise was Charles Dickens, given a sly locution in his letter of thanks for a copy of *Scenes* in January 1858: 'If they originated with no woman, I believe that no man ever before had the art of making himself mentally so like a woman since the world began' (*J*, 293). Barbara Bodichon was not in doubt, claiming that the reviews of *Adam Bede* 'instantly made me internally exclaim that is written by Marian Evans, there is her great big head and heart and her wise wide views' (*L*, 3: 56).

This much is now commonplace. What is less apparent is how little factual biographical information about Marian Evans or George Eliot was in circulation in her lifetime, at least in print. Identification of people and places in the vicinity of Nuneaton and Coventry with situations in the fiction began with the publication of *Scenes*. By the time of publication of *Adam Bede* in 1859, speculation about the identity of George Eliot was rife especially once the would-be clergyman Joseph Liggins claimed authorship (Haight (1968), 281–91). The resulting publicity caused George Eliot to 'come out' to her friends, including the unsuspecting Coventry-based Brays and Sara Hennell – who soon reported 'Mr Evans of Griff has been heard to say, after reading Adam Bede – "No one but his Sister could write that book"' (*L*, 3: 98). That there was no longer a secret at least about the gender of the author is apparent in reviews of *The Mill on the Floss* in 1860. Greater frankness about the open secret of George Eliot's relationship with Lewes was apparent in American publications than in British ones, and at his death in 1878 there were guarded references to it in obituaries.

It was a conscious decision on George Eliot's part to withhold biographical information from the public domain. She resisted the prospect of a biography of Lewes, declaring, 'Biographies generally are a disease of English literature' (*L*, 7: 230) – notwithstanding that Lewes' *Life of Goethe* (1855) remains his best-known work, and that they read a good deal of biography, including Gaskell's *Life of Charlotte Brontë.* She was emphatic that '[t]he best history of a writer is contained in his writings – these are his chief actions' (*L*, 7: 230). In one way this statement is a platitude, but in other respects it is particularly pertinent to the case of George Eliot herself.

Only with her obituaries did more biographical information emerge, though as Charles Kegan Paul commented, 'of outward events her life had few'.[2] The most significant new data concerned her writing life, and in this connection the obituaries by Alexander Allardyce in *Blackwood's Edinburgh Magazine* (February 1881) and Mark Call in the *Westminster Review* (July 1881) are especially notable. Both draw on publishers' records to identify her *Westminster Review* contributions of the 1850s in the one case, and in the other to trace the incredibly important relationship with her principal publisher, especially her warm friendship with the estimable John Blackwood. In preparing the biography of his wife, John Cross made considerable use of the firm's papers, including sales ledgers as well as correspondence, which round out his delineation of George Eliot the writer.

George Eliot's Life as related in her letters and journals, arranged and edited by her husband J. W. Cross was eventually published in three volumes by

Blackwood in January 1885, though Cross was at work already within weeks of her death on 22 December 1880. As the full title spells out, his principal resource was the copious documentation available to him, though he also took advice from friends and relations. Cross knew George Eliot only in her last decade, and needed help from those who had known her longer to establish accurate information.

While Cross was at pains to get facts right, he needed to tread carefully, constrained as he was by the scandals of George Eliot's career. *George Eliot's Life* plays down personal relationships, especially that with Lewes, and – unsurprisingly – contains no indication of its subject's intense relationships with John Chapman and Herbert Spencer, nor of her friendships with women. Cross's treatment of her loss of faith was expanded after the first edition by a judicious account supplied by a Coventry friend and pupil, Mrs John Cash (née Mary Sibree), which traces George Eliot's concern in her early adult years about 'a *theoretic* severance of religion from morality' deriving from her reading of Scott's novels, to her strenuous engagement with scriptural criticism.[3]

The work sold well, but its reception was mixed: Gladstone famously declared it 'a Reticence in three volumes', and William Hale White called for 'future work' in which 'the salt and spice will be restored to the records of George Eliot's entirely unconventional life'.[4] These comments were reiterated by many others, though reviewers for the most part complimented Cross on his execution of what was recognised to be a difficult task. Despite contemporary disappointment, and subsequent revelation of Cross's scholarly shortcomings, the influence on subsequent accounts of George Eliot's life and work of this assemblage of material cannot be overestimated.

Cross declared in his preface that 'The life has been allowed to write itself in extracts from her letters and journals' (Cross, 1: v). The disingenuousness of this claim was demonstrated by Gordon Haight, who showed how Cross conflated letters and edited out what he considered unseemly passages (*L*, 1: xiii–xv). Yet in round figures, 1,400 of the 1,500 pages in the three volumes are George Eliot's words. Apart from linking passages, Cross's commentary is confined to the opening section and the final chapter, and shapes the novelist's career according to tropes of the romantic artist. His 'Introductory Sketch' explicitly identifies George Eliot's early experiences with those of Maggie Tulliver in *The Mill on the Floss* and of Theophrastus Such in her final work, making heavy use of organic metaphors: 'Her roots were down in the pre-railroad, pre-telegraphic period – the days of fine old leisure – but the fruit was formed during an era of

Figure 5 John Walter Cross (1840–1924), George Eliot's husband and biographer, is seated on the right.

extraordinary activity in scientific and mechanical discovery' (Cross, 1: 10). It is more than likely that Cross was at least subliminally conditioned by his wife to cast her in a particular generic image of the artist. Consider his report of the way she composed: she claimed 'a "not herself"' took possession of her, and specifically instanced the scene between Dorothea and Rosamond in chapter 81 of *Middlemarch* (3: 424–5). Jerome Beaty's analysis of the manuscript completely deconstructs this claim to romantic inspiration, and details the 'process of evolution and discovery' involved in crafting the sequence.[5]

Cross's 'authorised' *Life* was preceded by another book-length biography. The poet Mathilde Blind's study for the short-lived 'Eminent Women' series came out in 1883. This book uncompromisingly takes up the cudgels for George Eliot as a woman writer. Blind defines as 'specifically feminine' her 'unparalleled vision for the homely details of life', acknowledging her masculine grasp of abstract philosophical ideas together with 'instinctive processes of the imagination'.[6] Although Blind used documentary sources, including some not published by Cross, her account relied a good deal on interviews with George Eliot's family and Coventry friends: she met with Isaac Evans, the Brays and Sara Hennell, and others, including 'a certain William Jacques (the original of the delightfully comic Bob Jakins [*sic*] of fiction)' who 'remembers carrying her pick-a-back on the lawn in front of her father's house'.[7]

George Eliot was admitted also to the 'English Men of Letters' series, where Leslie Stephen's study appeared in 1902, following his sonorous *Cornhill* obituary in February 1881 and his entry for 'CROSS, MARY ANN or MARIAN' in the *Dictionary of National Biography* in 1888. Stephen is a particularly interesting and influential witness, who comes close to articulating the proposition that underlay many obituaries and other accounts, that George Eliot's works enact a virtue lacking in her life. His argument for preferring her early work to the later novels is that in moving from her childhood experiences she compromised her distinctive feminine strength ('The combination of an exquisitely sympathetic and loving nature with a large and tolerant intellect') by engaging with 'the philosophical tendencies which were shared by none of her contemporaries'.[8] He allows her a range of intellectual accomplishments, but not a critical intellect. It is in the sense that he sees her characters – especially but not only Maggie Tulliver – as versions of herself that he reads her fiction as 'implicit autobiography'.[9]

Stephen's opinions in some degree rely on the identification of George Eliot with the Warwickshire countryside that had begun with *Scenes of*

Clerical Life. Before long, the author tacitly acknowledged these associations when illustrations for the Stereotyped Edition of her works in 1867 included such vignettes as 'Shepperton Church, As It Was' – recognisably Chilvers Coton. Publications identifying 'real' places and people in the works followed. Given George Eliot's reticence, this elision of the boundary between real and invented was welcomed by those writing about her, the more so because the rural scenes were picturesque. The tendency to dilate on 'homes and haunts' was taken up in obituaries, some of which were illustrated. Barely two weeks after her death, 'Reminiscences of George Eliot' in the *Graphic* carried two full pages of pictures of Nuneaton scenes with captions referring to their counterparts in the novels, while Charles Kegan Paul's tribute carried a number of images of places where she had lived, and her grave (see Figure 18).[10]

It was only with the growth of 'celebrity' reporting from the 1880s on that a fuller sense of George Eliot's personality and demeanour emerged. She described such articles as 'low gossip about [an author's] private life and personal appearance' (*L*, 6: 163). It was reminiscences in the vein of 'A Week with George Eliot'[11] that were to fill out the austere outlines drawn by Cross, though few of them tap so informal a vein as this from Lucy Clifford:

> [T]here was George Eliot with a ring of chairs round her, just as on the Sunday afternoons of old; but instead of philosophers, poets and other Victorian giants sitting on them, there were dolls; and through an open window – it was early spring-time – came the sound of merry voices.
>
> 'Charles's children are in the garden,' she explained, smiling, but with a sad little shake of her head, 'they've brought their children to see me,' nodding to the dolls.[12]

K. K. Collins has recently proposed that about forty such recollections constitute 'nothing less than a canon of reminiscence: the basis, along with her letters and journals, of our current perceptions of George Eliot's distinctive personal character'.[13] Think of Charles Bray's phrenological reading of her head, with its resonant judgement 'She was not fitted to stand alone'; Henry James 'in love with this great horse-faced blue-stocking'; and what Collins calls 'the most often quoted and reprinted recollection of GE [*sic*]', F. W. H. Myers's account of her pronouncement on 'the words *God, Immortality, Duty* … how inconceivable was the first, how unbelievable the second, and yet how peremptory and absolute the third'.[14] Collins's compilation of nearly 200 accounts from 150 people constitutes a biographical narrative of particular value, principally because of their variety. They offer a spectrum of perspectives on George Eliot in person, qualifying reverential assumptions, and building up nuanced testimony for instance about the rituals of her receptions at 'The Priory', together with descriptions of her warmth and sincerity. Many accounts tell of her low and melodious voice: here is one which startlingly particularises her manner of speaking: 'Little, indeed, did she ever say, and what she did say was (as they phrase it in Scotland) *in print*: every word clean cut and perfectly enunciated.'[15] She remains mostly sedentary, though clearly placing store by outdoor exercise (including tennis in her later years) as well as concerts and exhibitions. We learn that 'She was very fond of blue', but nothing of her tastes in food.[16]

Such descriptions of her animate the handful of visual images that survive (she was notoriously reluctant to be painted or have photographs taken). These include an oil painting made by her Swiss friend François D'Albert-Durade in 1849; a photograph by John Edwin Mayall in 1858, of which her friend Mme Belloc (Bessie Rayner Parkes) commented that it gave 'the only real indication left to us of the true shape of the head, and of George Eliot's smile and general bearing'; (see Figure 1)[17] Samuel Laurence's drawings of 1860; the Frederic Burton drawing of 1865 – engraved by Paul Rajon in 1884 for Cross's *Life* (see Figure 2); and some sketches probably made without her knowledge by professional artists such as George Du Maurier and amateurs like Princess Louise.

It was well into the twentieth century before any fresh biographical impulse was apparent, with a cluster of publications in the later 1920s and early 1930s. Some of this activity is attributable to the next generation of Lewes's descendants, especially his granddaughter Elinor (Mrs Carrington Ouvry), who gave access to material not previously drawn on. Arthur Paterson's *George Eliot's Family Life and Letters* (1928) accords Lewes his place in the daily life of the more famous George, while Anna T. Kitchel's *George Lewes and George Eliot: A Review of Records* (1933) is notable for its recuperative attention to Lewes's various writings. Anne Fremantle's book in 1933 breaks the mould cast by Cross: it was first to draw on John Chapman's diaries, and the first major re-interpretation of George Eliot's career, developing a Freudian reading of her as rebel. Focused discussion of George Eliot as intellectual was initiated by Pierre Bourl'honne's *George Eliot: essai de biographie intellectuelle et morale, 1819–1854, influences anglaises et étrangères* (1933).

By mid century, a new champion held the field. *George Eliot and John Chapman: With Chapman's Diaries* (1940) led off Gordon S. Haight's inimitable contributions to the study of George Eliot. In documenting and discussing her relationship with Chapman, he revealed a sexual secret not

Figure 6 Gordon S. Haight (1901–85), Professor of English at Yale from 1933, photographed in 1938. His work on George Eliot, especially his edition of her letters in nine volumes (1954–78), is indispensable.

Reproduced by permission of Manuscripts & Archives, Yale University Library. Office of Public Affairs, Yale University. Photographs of Individuals (RU686).

mentioned by Cross. Haight followed through with his nine-volume edition of *The George Eliot Letters* (1954–78), a magisterial work that includes selections of material from Lewes's letters and diaries, Blackwood's records, and other sources, together with exemplary explanatory apparatus. His 1968 biography was anti-climactic, effectively summarising the narrative developed more amply in the *Letters*, and readily endorsing Cross's presentation of George Eliot's congenital emotional dependence. The two champions reveal curious affinities.

Only in the 1990s was there a move in biographies of George Eliot from re-interpretation of existing information to active new research, in which Rosemary Ashton was pre-eminent. She began with a biography of George Henry Lewes (1991) that expanded knowledge especially about his family and early years, and gave him his due as an author and intellectual in his own right. The companion *George Eliot: A Life* (1996) was a landmark, respectful of Haight's work, but going beyond it to set out the dense intellectual, social and literary contexts of which George Eliot was part. These contexts were further amplified in a biography of John Chapman, *142 Strand: A Radical Address in Victorian London* (2006), which places him and his business at the centre of a stage previously dominated in scholarship by George Eliot. Ashton's work is complemented, for instance, by the intensive examination of George Eliot's intellectual life based on a reconstruction of her reading provided by Avrom Fleishman in *George Eliot's Intellectual Life* (2010), which in its turn complements earlier work such as

Valerie Dodd's *George Eliot: An intellectual life* (1990). Other biographies of recent decades have addressed George Eliot as in some way representative of her age: Kathryn Hughes (1998) bills her as 'the last Victorian', Frederick Karl (1995) as 'voice of the century'.

Meanwhile, publication of substantial new documentation further thickens descriptions of George Eliot's life. *The Journals of George Eliot*, edited by Margaret Harris and Judith Johnston (1998), prints complete versions of material selectively presented by Cross and Haight, constituting what is in effect a new text by her. *Autobiography of a Shirtmaker*, the journal kept by an acolyte, Edith Simcox, has also been published in full.[18] This remarkable contemporary document is among the most extended, though partial, accounts of the novelist's later years. Simcox could see the attraction of John Cross before others did, but as Gillian Beer stresses, 'of all her later women friends Edith Simcox is the only one who could offer equal intellectual engagement'.[19]

Most telling is a move back to intensive reading of George Eliot's life through her writing that comes full circle to the reflection of the *Athenaeum* obituarist, 'she herself was her greatest work'. He was drawing attention to the way her demonstrable accomplishments in science, philosophy and history, as well as music and the visual arts, were supplemented by 'width of sympathy and acuteness of observation' in her writing. Readers now interrogate her texts with different assumptions and practices. Rosemarie Bodenheimer's illuminating reading of the letters discloses new dimensions to an understanding of George Eliot's actions, nowhere more powerfully than in the argument that in her fifties George Eliot 'increasingly allowed herself to be identified with her own narrative voice', as a source of wise counsel and guidance.[20] Bodenheimer concludes:

> Her reluctance to confront any direct form of autobiographical writing was of a piece with the fundamental instinct to perform her self-understanding through outward projections. George Eliot must have known – as she knew so much about herself – that her only real opportunity for evoking the many-sided truths of her inward experience lay in the imaginative activity of fiction making.[21]

Partly in reaction to Bodenheimer, but principally as a flowering of her own long and deep relationship with George Eliot, Barbara Hardy has provided what she describes as 'a kind of anti-biography' in *George Eliot: A Critic's Biography*, which demonstrates different ways to read the life in the novels.[22] She attends to imagery and language in George Eliot's writing in all genres, and in the writing of some of her friends too, in order 'to focus on lived moments often ignored in the broad narrative sweep of biography, and fictional moments neglected in theme-and-pattern-seeking criticism'.[23] Time and again Hardy's discussion brings us up short, undermining easy generalisations about George Eliot's emotional dependence with insights into reciprocal need, or about rootedness as an absolute for her by demonstration of the ways her art thrived on foreignness. Barbara Hardy once again does the inestimable service for her author of reading her close and hard, coming to grips with the issues of negotiation of life experience in art that challenged George Eliot, and continue to challenge her biographers and critics alike.

NOTES

1 *Athenaeum* (1 January 1881), 21.
2 *Harper's New Monthly Magazine* (May 1881), 912. See also K. K. Collins, *Identifying the Remains: George Eliot's Death in the London Religious Press* (Victoria, BC: ELS Editions, 2006), especially pp. 15–19.
3 *George Eliot's Life*, 3 vols. (1885; Cabinet edn, Edinburgh and London: William Blackwood and Sons, 1885), vol. 1, p. 395.
4 E. F. Benson, *As We Were: A Victorian Peep-show* (London: Longmans, Green, 1930), p. 111; *Athenaeum* (28 November 1885), 702. Hale White rectified the deficiency in his depiction of George Eliot as Theresa in his quasi-autobiographical *The Autobiography of Mark Rutherford* (1881).
5 *'Middlemarch' from Notebook to Novel: A Study of George Eliot's Creative Method* (Urbana, IL: University of Illinois Press, 1960), pp. 122–3.
6 Mathilde Blind, *George Eliot* (London: W. H. Allen, 1883), pp. 5–6.
7 Ibid., p. 16.
8 Leslie Stephen, *George Eliot* (London: Macmillan, 1902), pp. 201, 200.
9 Ibid., p. 201.
10 *Graphic* (8 January 1881), 27–30; *Harper's New Monthly Magazine* (May 1881), 912–23.
11 *Temple Bar*, 73 (1885), 226–32. One of a number of reminiscences by Matilda Betham Edwards, novelist and close friend of Barbara Bodichon, this describes a Christmas holiday on the Isle of Wight.
12 'A Remembrance of George Eliot', *Nineteenth Century*, 74 (1913), 117.
13 K. K. Collins (ed.), *George Eliot: Interviews and Recollections* (Basingstoke: Palgrave Macmillan, 2010), pp. xvii–xviii.
14 All included in Collins, *George Eliot: Interviews and Recollections*, pp. 15–16, 79, 155–6.
15 Ibid., p. 192.
16 Ibid.
17 Bessie R. Belloc, 'Dorothea Casaubon and George Eliot', *Contemporary Review*, 65 (February 1894), 213.

18 Constance M. Fulmer and Margaret E. Barfield (eds.), *A Monument to the Memory of George Eliot: Edith J. Simcox's 'Autobiography of a Shirtmaker'* (New York and London: Garland, 1998).
19 'Simcox, Edith', in John Rignall (ed.), *Oxford Reader's Companion to George Eliot* (Oxford University Press, 2000), p. 390.
20 Rosemarie Bodenheimer, *The Real Life of Mary Ann Evans: George Eliot Her Letters and Fiction* (Ithaca, NY: Cornell University Press, 1994), p. 233.
21 Ibid., p. 267.
22 Barbara Hardy, *George Eliot: A Critic's Biography* (London: Continuum, 2006), p. xi.
23 Ibid., p. 147.

CHAPTER 6

Afterlife

Margaret Harris

The Victorian novelists most present in the popular imagination of the early twenty-first century are Charles Dickens, the Brontës collectively, and Thomas Hardy, largely because their works have been adapted frequently for stage, film and television. Such commodification via modern media technology underpins their celebrity status – a status which George Eliot has never attained. For each George Eliot adaptation there have been tens of the works of Dickens and the Brontës. Moreover, she is not connected with a particular place: 'Dickens's London' is a by-word; literary pilgrims began to travel to Haworth from the 1850s; while 'Hardy's Wessex', centred on Dorchester, is substantially his creation. George Eliot has eluded such placement: while her association with the countryside around Coventry is recognised, 'George Eliot Country' is not.

George Eliot lives principally on university curricula and in academic publications. This situation is analogous to that of her lifetime: thus while the very successful *Adam Bede* was quoted in Parliament soon after it appeared (*L*, 3: 39), the novel did not achieve the success by imitation that attended either *The Pickwick Papers*, of which five theatrical adaptations were performed during its serialisation in 1836–7, or *Jane Eyre*, dramatised within months of its October 1847 publication. George Eliot's reception was distinguished by the emergence of a significant readership which valued her intellectual strength, moral seriousness and complexity, and in large measure it has been this facet of George Eliot as a phenomenon that has determined her afterlife. Tim Dolin aligns the revival of George Eliot's critical stocks from the mid twentieth century with the emergence of new forms of readership identified principally with the academy, and specifically with the professionalisation of criticism in universities in English-speaking countries.[1] Literary scholars have not been alone in their attention to George Eliot. In a perpetuation and modification of the sibylline image of her later years, philosophers now engage with her work in debating the nature of morality, as well as turning to it for illustrations of moral dilemmas.[2]

The Blackwood franchise

Brand 'George Eliot' was the most effectively managed business conducted by a major Victorian novelist, after the 'Charles Dickens' industry largely fostered by Dickens himself. The credit for its success during her lifetime is mainly attributable to the house of William Blackwood and Sons, her loyal principal publisher, and to George Henry Lewes as her wily agent and manager. But the daughter of Robert Evans did not lack business acumen, and George Eliot herself contributed actively to marketing decisions about matters like serialisation, and the timing and format of reissues.

After her death, the firm continued to nurture the brand. William, the Blackwood of the day, was forbearing with the widowed John Cross in the course of his protracted labours on *George Eliot's Life* (1885), and was rewarded by strong sales. Meanwhile, Charles, the eldest of Lewes's sons, actively assumed his responsibilities as sole executor and residual legatee, keeping an eye on receipts, but also preparing a selection of published and unpublished material by George Eliot, *Essays and Leaves from a Notebook*, for publication in 1884. After Charles's death in 1891, his widow Gertrude took over, guided by William Blackwood, who shrewdly managed issues of new editions (including collected editions) as the copyrights of individual novels expired from the late 1890s on. In death as in life, George Eliot's earnings supported the extended Lewes family. Moreover, David Finkelstein in *The House of Blackwood: Author-Publisher Relations in the Victorian Era* (2002) has shown how important George Eliot was to the Blackwood balance sheet down to World War I; and there is no doubt that the fact that her works were reliably in print, in English (including colonial) and American editions, held off the early twentieth-century decline in her reputation.

Locale

'A human life, I think, should be well rooted in some spot of a native land', George Eliot reflected in *Daniel Deronda* (ch. 3). Her early fiction especially was 'well rooted' in the Warwickshire countryside and the towns of Nuneaton and Coventry she knew as a girl and young woman, but she did not live there during her fiction-writing career – indeed, did not visit from 1854 when she went to live with Lewes, though in 1862 she made a donation to support the Coventry workers suffering from the cotton famine occasioned by the American Civil War (*L*, 4: 72).

Paradoxically, of course, the secret of her pseudonym was penetrated in part because settings and people in her early works were identified. From the 1880s on, images of places represented in her novels were published in works such as Charles Olcott's *George Eliot: Scenes and People in her Novels* (1910), which included moody photographs of the Red Deeps and other places connected with her life and works. This book is a prime example of the heightened interest in literary geography that developed in the early twentieth century and was integrally related to the phenomenon of literary tourism. As with Hardy's Wessex, the geography of 'George Eliot Country' depends on a reader's knowledge of the fates of fictional characters in relation to local topography, and the desire to verify reading experience by reference to actual places.[3] Over time, the rural landscape of 'George Eliot Country' has been encroached on by heavy industry: by World War I, Coventry had become the hub of the British automotive industry, and because of this suffered severe bomb damage in World War II.

Both Coventry and nearby Nuneaton, her birthplace, celebrated the centenary of her birth in 1919. A centrepiece of the Nuneaton celebration, held in July, was a pageant and a procession, together with lectures, literary competitions and a fancy dress ball. The pageant was performed in the open air in the grounds of Arbury Hall (the Cheverel Manor of *Scenes of Clerical Life)*, opening with a prologue from one Amyntas (a name derived from the Greek 'amyntor', defender), and centring on *Silas Marner*'s Rainbow Inn as the community centre. Tableaux from other novels were followed by an apotheosis of George Eliot herself, with Amyntas proclaiming:

> And thus to genius is our tribute paid.
> Now on this spot your flowers and laurels lay.
> Behold, George Eliot who inspired our play.[4]

This George Eliot celebration followed hard upon celebration of peace, its mixture of nostalgia and nationalism explicitly acknowledging changes in the area because of the war and increasing industrialisation.

The Coventry event coincided with George Eliot's birthday on 22 November, and concentrated on lectures, an exhibition of memorabilia, a musical recital with readings from her works and a dramatisation of *Adam Bede* (performed in Nuneaton). An appeal for funds to erect a more permanent memorial eventually resulted in a George Eliot Alcove in the

Coventry Library, opened in 1927. Overall, the centenary celebrations gained limited purchase in the attempt both to recognise George Eliot as a local celebrity, and to co-opt her artistic fame in the interests of the image of a community undergoing a redefinition of identity. (It may be pertinent that George Eliot is Warwickshire's second most famous author, after Shakespeare, and Coventry's second most famous woman, after Lady Godiva.) The national press paid little attention to the centenary.

By contrast, the centenary of George Eliot's death in 1980 was accorded more widespread recognition. Ironically, the author who resisted having her likeness taken was depicted on a series of English postage stamps, 'Famous Authoresses', along with Charlotte and Emily Brontë, and Mrs Gaskell [*sic*]. Thanks to the initiative of the George Eliot Fellowship, established in 1930 and based in Coventry, a memorial stone was set in Westminster Abbey where she had been denied burial. The Fellowship now conducts an annual wreathlaying ceremony there, and organises other events in Coventry and Nuneaton including a wreathlaying at a memorial in the grounds of the Nuneaton George Eliot Memorial Garden, opened in 1952, close to the Nuneaton Museum and Art Gallery which houses a small collection of memorabilia, including Eliot's piano and one of her dresses. The Fellowship also organised the erection of a bronze statue of George Eliot in Newdegate Square, Nuneaton, in 1986. From 2007, Fellowship events have included sesquicentennial celebrations of the publication of her works, with activities including a dramatised version of the work of the year. The University of London hosts a conference on the relevant work. The Fellowship publishes one of the two specialist George Eliot journals, both annuals (the other is *George Eliot–George Henry Lewes Studies)*: but *Brontë Studies* comes out four times a year, and there are several Dickens journals.

Despite this local energy, George Eliot has never been assimilated into the heritage industry. The most likely moment was the mid 1990s, following the 1994 BBC-PBS mini-series of *Middlemarch*: patronage increased for coach tours of 'George Eliot Country' with refreshments at Griff House (her home in childhood and early womanhood, by then part of the Beefeater restaurant chain). But the series was filmed on location at Stamford in Lincolnshire, over forty miles away. Round Coventry, material traces of the author are most readily to be found in placenames and commodities. By the late nineteenth century there were George Eliot bicycles and motorcycles, with other incongruities following, in the form of mundane products like George Eliot flour and pickles. There are now three schools whose names commemorate George Eliot and her work, together with hospitals and street names. And there is the George Eliot Hotel in Nuneaton, formerly The Bull, and held to be the original of The Red Lion in 'Janet's Repentance'.

Further afield, she is distinguished by being one of two women (the other is Florence Nightingale) represented on a monument to Queen Victoria in Dalton Square, Lancaster, erected in 1907. The stone plinth supporting the Queen's statue carries 'very interesting bronze reliefs of groups of Victorian worthies', including artists as well as 'writers, scientists (Darwin), politicians, reformers (Shaftesbury), explorers, etc.'.[5] George Eliot is on the west face, with (among others) Dickens and Thackeray, Darwin and Faraday.

Adaptations

There have been notable adaptations of George Eliot's works, not all popular successes. John Picker drolly comments that 'publishers and parodists do not appear to have rushed out many *Madam Bedes* or *Shomalas* to meet popular demand'.[6] *Adam Bede, Junior: A Sequel* was advertised by the devious London publisher Thomas Cautley Newby in October 1859, causing considerable consternation to the Lewes household – but the book seems never to have been published. Sequels to her last novel, *Daniel Deronda*, did in fact eventuate, one in *Punch's Pocket Book for 1877*; and a novel, *Gwendolen; or, Reclaimed. A Sequel to George Eliot's Daniel Deronda*, by Anna Clay Beecher, was published in Boston in 1878. The ideology of this extraordinary narrative is floridly anti-Semitic. Mirah dies in childbirth in Cairo, where Daniel's fervour for Jewishness has been shaken. After many complications and journeys, he is 'reclaimed for England, Christendom, and, of course, Gwendolen'.[7] As Picker reminds us, perhaps the most important 'sequel' is Henry James's *Portrait of a Lady* (1881). In working through the moral and psychological subtleties of the situation of his central character, James was responding to both *Middlemarch* and *Daniel Deronda*.

Dramatisations have been more frequent. An unauthorised adaptation of *Adam Bede* was produced at the Surrey Theatre in 1862, its plot premonitory of the kinds of change evident also in subsequent adaptations. Hetty's child turns out to have been taken by gypsies, while Hetty and Arthur were married all along. Lewes entertained ideas of dramatising *Deronda*, and referred to Sir William Gilbert's *Dan'l Druce, Blacksmith* as partly derived from *Silas Marner* (*L*, 8: 303). This work has been most adapted, presumably because of the engaging central motif of the miser

Figure 7 Still from the set in Florence for *Romola*, directed by Henry King (1924), with (left to right) Dorothy Gish (Tessa), Ronald Colman (Carlo Bucellini), Henry King, unknown, Lillian Gish (Romola).

Courtesy of www.doctormacro.com.

redeemed by love of a child. The earliest film version was D. W. Griffith's *A Fair Exchange* (1909), and there were at least five more silent films of it. Giles Foster's *Silas Marner* (1985), starring Ben Kingsley, originally made for television, is the film of a George Eliot text that has had the most critical and popular success.

Other stage versions include an *Adam Bede* in Nuneaton in 1890, with a different version performed in 1919 for the George Eliot centenary (nearly thirty years on, the same actors played Adam and Arthur!). The 1919 version omitted the last book of the novel, and ended with Hetty dying in Arthur's arms. More recently a new kind of adaptation has emerged, dating from Geoffrey Beevers's *Adam Bede* (1990), which confronts the challenge of dramatising George Eliot's omniscient narration by distributing passages of it among the characters who deliver it direct to the audience. In her powerful adaptation of *The Mill on the Floss* (1994), made for the Shared Experience Theatre Company, Helen Edmundson occasionally has the whole cast act as a wordless chorus. Three actors play Maggie, with Second and Third Maggie sometimes commenting on their younger self, First Maggie.

Adaptation for film also presents the challenge of dealing with omniscient narration. In silent film, there was little room for manoeuvre: the action had to be presented visually, with interpretative prompts from the intertitles. Inevitably, subtleties of character and situation in the work being adapted were elided, though the films could create powerful effects. A case in point is the full-length *Romola*, directed by Henry King (1924), pre-eminent among the silent versions of George Eliot's novels (see Figure 7). The iconic Lillian Gish played Romola, with her sister Dorothy as Tessa, temperamental opposites in the film as in life. Ronald Colman appears as Carlo Buccellini, a sympathetic artist character created for the film, to whom Romola ends up married once the perfidious Tito (William Powell) is out of the way. Gish as so often played a victim, appearing fragile but in fact strong, and there is an extraordinary recognition scene – a motif of many of her films – when she realises that her husband Tito has fathered Tessa's child. Gish was heavily involved in the production, and her passion for authenticity rivalled George Eliot's own. Seventeen acres of sets were constructed on location in Florence: it is perhaps unsurprising that the film did not recoup production costs. It also suffered from some of the defects of the novel, being described in the *New Yorker* review as 'a beautiful and tiresome thing'.[8]

The first George Eliot talkie was a British production of *The Mill on the Floss* in 1937, with an American director, Tim Whelan, and script by the poet John Drinkwater (who altered the ending by having Philip go to warn Maggie of the approaching flood, brought about by a burst dam, and they drown together). The cast included a number of well-known actors, including some – like Geraldine Fitzgerald as Maggie, and James Mason as Tom – whose careers were yet to blossom. Despite its blue ribbon team, the film had only a moderate reception.

The most important adaptations have been for television. Here the British Broadcasting Corporation has an honourable sustained record of producing both radio and television serialisations. Radio has favoured *Adam Bede*, *The Mill on the Floss* and *Silas Marner*, though recently there has been also 'The Lifted Veil'. There have been occasional full-length television versions in addition to Giles Foster's *Silas Marner* – *Adam Bede* (again Giles Foster, 1991) and *The Mill on the Floss* (1965, 1978, 1997). The mini-series of *Middlemarch* (1994, also 1968) and *Daniel Deronda* (1970 and 2002) stand out. The 1994 *Middlemarch* was a major event – for BBC costume drama, and to some extent also for the 'high culture' mini-series.[9] Virginia Woolf's declaration that *Middlemarch* is 'one of the few English novels written for grown-up people' was widely used in advertisements, 'to promote the relaunched classic serial as sophisticated television'.[10] A co-production with the Boston Public Broadcasting System, it had a budget in excess of £6 million for the six episodes, and in one week the Penguin edition of the novel topped the best-seller list. There was much to admire: casting of an unknown, Juliet Aubrey, as Dorothea; a young actor on the way up, Rufus Sewell, as Will, with Robert Hardy (Grandcourt in the 1970 *Daniel Deronda)* as Mr Brooke – and so on. The script was by Andrew Davies, who went on to adapt *Pride and Prejudice* for the wildly successful mini-series the following year. The challenge of omniscient narration was met by introducing some passages of it into dialogue (thus a modified version of the 'other side of silence' passage in chapter 20 is spoken by Dorothea), and by directorial choices of camera shot and gesture. This *Middlemarch* was a phenomenon in its own terms, with considerable cultural significance. Tim Dolin goes beyond my description of it as 'an intelligent, conservative "reading" of the novel for John Major's Britain', arguing for it as 'an audacious defence of the role of television itself – the role of a national television institution more specifically – in the national cultural life of John Major's Britain'.[11]

'Incalculably diffusive'?

The reactions of other writers to George Eliot are a study in themselves. She is sometimes invoked as a notation or metaphor: thus in Virginia Woolf's *To the Lighthouse* (1927), Minta Doyle's loss in a train of the last volume of *Middlemarch* emblematises the irrelevance of Victorian certainties to the modernist generation.[12] In recent years, neo-Victorian fiction has set about disrupting stereotyped assumptions concerning the period, with Dickens and Collins the principal stimuli. Peter Carey's take on *Great Expectations* in the full-blown 'writing back' of *Jack Maggs* (1997) is a prime example. In Carey's earlier neo-Victorian novel, *Oscar and Lucinda* (1988), George Eliot is a monitory offstage character, a friend of Lucinda's mother who sends a doll to her god-daughter in Australia. Elements of Maggie Tulliver are transposed onto Lucinda: but Lucinda does not drown, she lives on to run a factory.

During the later part of her career and the decades immediately after her death, 'George Eliot' became a by-word for sententiousness, to the extent, Leah Price argues, that 'sententiousness finally replaced sex as the scandal admirers needed to explain away'.[13] Elaine Showalter discusses the particular consideration of how George Eliot is read by other authors in terms of the 'anxiety of influence' among women writers down to Margaret Drabble, proposing that her immediate successors were intimidated, while later writers reference the sufferings of George Eliot's heroines in depicting those of their own characters.[14] Yet the example of George Eliot has been affirming for some women, and the freighted detail of Minta Doyle's carelessness is far from representing Woolf's own attitude to the senior author. In her famous essay for the 1919 centenary, Woolf broke the mould of the monumental figure mocked by some of her contemporaries and offered potent testimony to George Eliot's uncompromising quest for 'more knowledge and more freedom'.[15] Forty years later, from a different cultural tradition, the philosopher Simone de Beauvoir wrote explicitly about George Eliot's formative influence on her. Beauvoir's *The Second Sex* (1948) is now held up as the foundational text of second-wave feminism, and her *Memoirs of a Dutiful Daughter* (1958), Elaine Showalter proposes, 'is clearly a structured homage' to *The Mill on the Floss*.[16]

George Eliot remains a presence to be reckoned with, not only as a tutelary text. The 'fine issues' of her life and work run in many channels, 'like that river of which Cyrus broke the strength', and, like the acts of Dorothea Ladislaw, are 'incalculably diffusive' (*M*, 'Finale'). George Eliot's legacy, however, is a potent one, constantly visited, revisited and revisioned.

NOTES

1 Tim Dolin, *George Eliot* (Oxford World's Classics, Oxford University Press, 2005), pp. 219 ff.

2 E.g. Jonathan Dancy in *Moral Reasons* (Oxford: Blackwell, 1993), pp. 70–1, deploys the 'men of maxims' passage from *The Mill on the Floss*, in arguing his influential case for moral particularism. In *The Moral of the Story: An Anthology of Ethics through Literature* (Oxford: Blackwell, 2005), Peter Singer (with Renata Singer) gives extracts from *Middlemarch* in three separate sections: 'Who Am I?', 'Love, Marriage and Sex' and 'Rules, Rights, Duties, and the Greater Good'. Thanks to Moira Gatens for these references.

3 Nicola J. Watson, *The Literary Tourist: Readers and Places in Romantic and Victorian Britain* (Basingstoke: Palgrave Macmillan, 2006), esp. pp. 13–14 and 169–75.

4 Margaret Harris, 'The George Eliot Centenary of 1919', *The George Eliot Review*, 38 (2007), 38.

5 Nikolaus Pevsner, *The Buildings of England: Lancashire*, vol. II, *The Rural North* (Harmondsworth: Penguin, 1969), p. 157.

6 John M. Picker, 'George Eliot and the Sequel Question', *New Literary History*, 37 (2006), 365.
7 Ibid., p. 375.
8 Charles Affron, *Lillian Gish Her Legend and Her Life* (New York: Scribner, 2001), pp. 177–8.
9 There is now an extensive literature on the 1994 *Middlemarch*, e.g. Dolin, *George Eliot*, pp. 234–44. Dolin also provides a digest of film and television adaptations, pp. 270–1.
10 Woolf, *Times Literary Supplement*, 20 November 1919, repr. in Gordon S. Haight (ed.), *A Century of George Eliot Criticism* (London: Methuen, 1966), p. 189; Dolin, *George Eliot*, p. 238.
11 Harris, 'George Eliot on Stage and Screen', *Arts: The Journal of the Sydney University Arts Association*, 24 (2002), 36; Dolin, *George Eliot*, p. 243.
12 Dolin, *George Eliot*, p. 216.
13 *The Anthology and the Rise of the Novel* (Cambridge University Press, 2000), p. 153.
14 *A Literature of Their Own: British Women Novelists from Brontë to Lessing* (Princeton University Press, 1977), pp. 103–32, and 'The Greening of Sister George', *Nineteenth-Century Fiction*, 35 (1980), 292–312.
15 *TLS*, 20 November 1919, in Haight (ed.), *A Century of George Eliot Criticism*, p. 189.
16 Showalter, 'Greening', p. 301.

PART II

Critical fortunes

CHAPTER 7

Critical responses: to 1900

Juliette Atkinson

'That an author should be able to produce a series of works so good in so very peculiar a style, is as remarkable as anything that has occurred in the history of English literature in this century.'[1] Under the pseudonym 'George Eliot', the author discussed in this 1861 review had published four works of fiction in as many years, and enjoyed extraordinary success since the publication of her first novel, *Adam Bede*, in 1859; the 'peculiar' style was principally her realist depiction of humble rural life. By 1861, however, dissident notes were heard, partly due to the increasing philosophical dimensions of her fiction and partly due to the revelation that 'George Eliot' was an atheist living out of wedlock with a married man. It was principally the former consideration that led critics to treat her differently from other novelists: they responded to her not simply as a novelist but as a moral sage. George Eliot, plagued by artistic insecurities and sensitive to criticism of her private life, was wary of her critics, although her partner George Henry Lewes sought to shield her from their harsher judgements. For George Eliot, 'private criticism has more chance of being faithful than public' since critics 'must by all means say striking things' (*L*, 3: 322).

Reactions to *Scenes of Clerical Life* on its publication in two volumes in 1858 did not immediately secure George Eliot's fame, though in many ways it laid the ground for later responses to her work. A *Saturday Review* article is broadly representative of these first reactions. Describing the author as someone 'who can paint homely every-day life and ordinary characters with great humour and pathos', it tried to pinpoint the nature of her 'Dutch' realism. The reviewer laid particular emphasis on the writer's power of sympathy, which fed into the evident mastery of dialogue, and greatly contributed to the overall charm of the stories. Further, the tales 'betray a philosophic culture', but the precise nature of George Eliot's unorthodox ideas had not yet been revealed, enabling the reviewer to conclude that the work is 'religious, without cant or intolerance'. The handful of critics who reviewed the work agreed that the elusive 'George Eliot' had introduced a new element into English fiction by boldly disregarding 'circulating-library principles' and using a style that 'showed little or no family resemblances with that of any living author'.[2]

George Eliot's distinction was confirmed with the publication of *Adam Bede*, which prompted *The Times* to declare: 'It is a first-rate novel, and its author takes rank at once among the masters of the art.'[3] It earned her enthusiastic letters from Jane Carlyle and Charles Dickens, Queen Victoria recommended it, and it was quoted in Parliament – success indeed for a novel which its author had feared was 'too quiet and too unflattering to dominant fashions ever to be very popular' (*L*, 3: 191).

It was precisely George Eliot's realism that provoked discussion. The close observation of rustic life offered a 'steady protest against exclusiveness',[4] and 'something we have not had before'.[5] The characters and environment seemed 'so true' that the novel 'has found its way into hands indifferent to all previous fiction'.[6] Readers agreed that the principal charm of the novel resided with Mrs Poyser, a 'really humorous creation'.[7] Given later representations of George Eliot as a moralist, it is striking to note how important humour was in securing her popularity. With some prescience, E. S. Dallas wrote that Mrs Poyser 'is the firstling of the author's mind, which he is not likely to surpass'. Indeed, for the rest of her career, reviewers complained that George Eliot failed to produce a character to rival her.[8] George Eliot's realism also attracted two, somewhat paradoxical, criticisms. On the one hand, there was dissatisfaction with the novel's final volume, which transgressed realism by venturing into melodrama. On the other hand, the novelist shared rather too much about the female body – realism became objectionable when it involved an 'almost obstetric accuracy of detail'.[9] The novel's apparent 'truthfulness' had a further consequence: it encouraged readers to discern links between the work and its author. Reviewers were confident that they knew with whom they were dealing: 'evidently a country clergyman'.[10] Readers came closer to unmasking Mary Ann Evans by mapping Warwickshire scenes and personalities onto the novels. Since it was assumed that 'what is so vividly reported is taken from life', George Eliot was initially admired as an autobiographical novelist.[11]

She would never again experience such success. 'George Eliot's' reputation was affected by the discovery in the latter part of 1859 that behind the pseudonymn was not the expected clergyman but a woman who had translated German philosophical critiques of Christianity and lived, unmarried, with George Lewes. Many readers and critics were alienated. Ironically, reviewers had praised *Adam Bede*'s wholesome nature, although some, such as the *Times* critic, sensed that the novel provided 'a secular rendering of the deepest sentiment of Christianity'.[12] The change of tone once her identity was revealed is illustrated by the *London Quarterly Review*, which denounced *Adam Bede* as a work of 'artistic skill which hides its evil beneath its good'.[13] Henceforth, George Eliot's reviewers would rarely forget that they were dealing with the translator of Feuerbach.

Responses to *The Mill on the Floss* (1860) reflect this wariness. Critics held that it showed 'no falling off nor any exhaustion of power' but was unlikely to prove as popular as its predecessor.[14] George Eliot's realism continued to provoke conflicting reactions. Reviewers agreed that 'her description of child-life is unique', but found aspects of the novel 'sordid'.[15] Nevertheless, greater efforts were made to understand her art. E. S. Dallas dwelt on the narratorial interruptions and consolidated the depiction of George Eliot as a moralist by concluding that she seeks 'not merely to amuse us as a novelist, but, as a preacher, to make us think and feel'.[16] Again the weakness of the final volume was noted, most feeling that it had been inadequately prepared – a view with which the author concurred. The *Spectator*, however, insisted that the work presented a compelling unity as 'the epic of a human soul, traced through childhood, development, and temptation'.[17] Stephen Guest met with almost uniform disapproval, and the implausibility of Maggie's fascination with him has remained a common criticism.

Matters of artistic integrity were overshadowed by concerns with the novel's morality. The discovery that they were dealing with a female author encouraged critics to compare George Eliot with her most formidable predecessors. Some were complimentary (the scenes at Dorlcote Mill offer 'minute manner-painting worthy of Miss Austen')[18] but others used these comparisons to formulate a protest against improprieties in female fiction. The *Saturday Review* warned that 'Currer Bell and George Eliot, and we may add George Sand, all like to dwell on love as a strange overmastering force … But we are not quite sure that it is quite consistent with feminine delicacy to lay so much stress on the bodily feelings of the other sex.' Nor was passion the only tendentious area: 'because they occur, it does not follow that spiritual doubts and conflicts are a proper subject for a novelist'.[19]

After the 'sordid' environment of *The Mill on the Floss, Silas Marner* (1861) came as a relief, and earned enthusiastic praise. R. H. Hutton was struck by the 'intellectual impress which the author contrives to give to a story of which the main elements are altogether unintellectual', and he was not the only one to acknowledge the work's Wordsworthian quality.[20]

Though it was a slighter work than *Adam Bede*, critics found new reason to marvel at George Eliot's portrayal of humble life. Praise for the Rainbow Inn scene approached that accorded to the characterisation of Mrs Poyser. The *Saturday Review* felt that here George Eliot excelled Dickens, and that the humour was 'of the same kind as that displayed in the comic passages of Shakespeare's historical plays'.[21] Five years later, Henry James commented that *Silas Marner* probably held 'a higher place than any of the author's works. It is more nearly a masterpiece; it has more of that simple, rounded, consummate aspect, that absence of loose ends and gaping issues, which marks a classical work', and this view endured.[22]

As Mathilde Blind later commented, *Romola* (1863) marked 'a new departure in George Eliot's literary career. From the present she turned to the past, from the native to the foreign, from the domestic to the historical.'[23] *Romola* also marked a change in her publication methods, since for the first time she attempted serial publication, in the *Cornhill.* She struggled to meet her deadlines, and her fears that her literary methods were unsuited to this format were justified: the *Athenaeum*, for example, advised that 'those who have read *Romola* in its monthly course should begin the story afresh, now that it is complete and appears in a connected form'.[24] The portrait of Savonarola was widely praised, but most concurred that the novel 'smells of the lamp', in Henry James's phrase.[25] R. H. Hutton offered the most considered analysis, arguing that George Eliot 'has Sir Walter Scott's art for revivifying the past, – but not Scott's dynamical force in making you plunge into it', for which 'she compensates by a deeper and wider intellectual grasp'.[26] Yet, as Hutton accurately predicted, *Romola* would never be her most popular novel.

A common view was that with *Romola*, George Eliot strayed too far from the material for which she had become celebrated, and critics expressed their approval that, with *Felix Holt, the Radical* (1866), she had 'come back to those studies of English life, so humorous, so picturesque, and so philosophical'.[27] The relief was expressed through enthusiastic claims: 'hitherto Miss Austen has had the honour of the first place among our lady novelists, but a greater than she has now arisen'.[28] *Felix Holt* also prompted Henry James's first review of George Eliot. He made the first of many complaints about what he regarded as her problems with structure, but also celebrated her 'humanity', which 'colors all her other gifts – her humor, her morality, and her exquisite rhetoric'. James nodded to George Eliot's sage-like properties by commenting that 'it is so new a phenomenon for an English novelist to exhibit mental resources which may avail him in other walks of literature'.[29] John Morley joined in the praise, but perceptively warned that readers were wrong to celebrate George Eliot as the creator of 'quaint-speaking souls' and of the 'photographic reproduction of the life of midland dairies', because such emphases would lead to a misunderstanding of the fundamental nature of her novels.[30]

It was not, however, a novel with which readers were next presented, but a dramatic poem: *The Spanish Gypsy* (1868). Despite one rhapsodic review in *St James's Magazine*, which claimed that with the exception of Tennyson and Browning 'no poet of the present day has given us a work of such completeness', the response was lukewarm.[31] *The Spanish Gypsy* confirmed for many the growing intrusion of the intellect in George Eliot's work: Matthew Browne complained that 'the intellectual ground-work … shows, far too plainly, under the colouring of passion and the movement of the story', though Henry James conceded that the work came 'very near being poetry'.[32] Most were forced to conclude that 'there is a wide difference still … between the poet and the prose writer, even when that prose holds some of the finest attributes of the highest order of poetry'.[33] Critics had accepted George Eliot's invitation in *Scenes of Clerical Life* to see 'the poetry and the pathos' of everyday life; *The Spanish Gypsy* established that her poetry did lie above all in her prose.

Middlemarch (1871–2) showed George Eliot once again moving into new territory. Edith Simcox announced that '*Middlemarch* marks an epoch in the history of fiction … chiefly as giving a background of perfect realistic truth to a profoundly imaginative psychological study'.[34] Sidney Colvin was 'afraid of exaggerating the meaning such work will have for those who come after us, for the very reason that we feel its meaning so pregnant for ourselves'.[35] Critics adapted to this novelty by using a new language to analyse her work, abandoning their usual descriptions of her charming portrayals of everyday life. Sidney Colvin turned to scientific discourse: George Eliot has given the novel a new 'psychological instrument', and there is in *Middlemarch* 'a profound sense of the importance of the physiological conditions in human life'; Caleb's portrayal is 'a complete physiognomical study in the sense of Mr. Darwin'.[36]

Henry James followed suit: *Middlemarch*, he declared, 'sets a limit, we think, to the development of the old-fashioned English novel'. His awareness of the novel's groundbreaking qualities did not imply unqualified admiration. James was unable to perceive the novel's carefully built unity, with its parallels between the trajectories of Dorothea and Lydgate, and found that it was 'a treasure-house of details, but it is an indifferent whole'.[37] George Eliot had also again failed to provide a convincing love interest for her heroine. The weakness of Will Ladislaw, a 'woman's man', was all the more perplexing in comparison with the depiction of Rosamond and Lydgate's relationship, of which James wrote that 'there is nothing more powerfully real … in all English fiction, and nothing certainly more *intelligent*'. Overall the novel strained at the limits of fiction writing: George Eliot is seen as 'really philosophic', a quality that held 'corresponding perils', above all that of 'loss of simplicity'.[38] Colvin had also conceded that some of her language could be dismissed as 'intellectual slang'.[39] These criticisms illustrate the lines along which opinions were forming, with her earlier 'charming' novels being pitted against her later 'intellectual' works.

This evolution continued with *Daniel Deronda* (1876). Reviewers were again broadly united in their praise and criticism: Gwendolen, 'this throbbing, bleeding heart, torn by the thwarting circumstances we all know to our pain',[40] appeared all the more magnificent alongside the 'prig' Deronda.[41] James's 'Daniel Deronda: A Conversation', in which three characters work out their differences, dramatises the ambivalence the novel provoked.[42] Some supporters, such as James Picciotto, defended the novel on artistic and philosophical grounds, while most found fault with the Jewish portions: George Saintsbury's doubts that 'the mystical enthusiasm for race and nation' could offer 'stuff for prose fiction to handle' were widely shared.[43] R. E. Francillon warned that readers would not meet in the novel 'the natural historian of real life, whom we know and have known for twenty years': he was unusual in venturing that the novel would slowly but surely secure for George Eliot 'deeper and higher fame than the works with which it does not enter into rivalry'.[44]

However, ambivalence over *Daniel Deronda* did little damage to her status as the most important living English novelist. Reviewers used the novel to reflect on her career. Saintsbury saw it as a 'fresh variation' on a theme that had informed all her novels, namely the conflict of duty and desire, while the *Academy* reviewer pointed out that her work repeatedly explored 'why egotism is a term of reproach'.[45] Critics also demonstrated how far they had come from their initial unease with George Eliot's morality: talk of impropriety had been replaced by discussion of her 'grandeur'.[46] They were even capable of calmly assessing her religious humanism: R. R. Bowker concluded that 'as unreligious in the personality of her novels as Shakespeare the dramatist, George Eliot is always dealing with the most profound of practical religious questions'.[47]

Critics continued to take stock of George Eliot's entire oeuvre in reaction to her final work, *Impressions of Theophrastus Such* (1879). Writing in the *Edinburgh Review*, William Mallock boldly pronounced her 'the first great *godless* writer of fiction that has appeared in England'.[48] Critical engagement with her ideas reflected a disappointment with her formal achievements in a work which, according to George Saintsbury, had been 'spoilt by an insufficient attention to form and an insufficient recognition of its necessity'.[49] Theophrastus exemplified the problem: 'there is either too much or too little of Mr. Such' or, as the *Examiner* critic opined, 'he is merely used as a peg on which to hang many wise and witty remarks'.[50] Praise (then as now) was predominantly reserved for 'Looking Backwards', which seemed to offer further proof that her genius lay above all in capturing the charm of her childhood environment. The *Saturday Review* concluded that if *Theophrastus* 'cannot be said to add to its author's literary reputation, it does not detract from it'.[51]

George Eliot's death in 1880 enabled open comment on her life. In particular, Lewes's role could be discussed, with opinion wavering as to whether any of her novels 'would have been written or even planned without the inspiriting influence of his constant encouragement', as Edith Simcox argued, or whether, as James proposed, they 'would have got themselves written'.[52] The dual scandals of her atheism and her unconventional union were not forgotten. She was refused burial in Westminster Abbey on the grounds that it would be inappropriate for a woman 'whose life and opinions were in notorious antagonism to Christian practice in regard to marriage, and Christian theory in regard to dogma'.[53]

Biographical speculation did not entirely overshadow discussions of George Eliot's works. Leslie Stephen's 1881 obituary insisted on the magnitude of her achievement: 'in losing George Eliot we have probably lost the greatest woman who ever won literary fame'. Stephen echoed earlier descriptions of *Middlemarch* by suggesting that 'the works of George Eliot may hereafter appear as marking the termination of the great period of English fiction which began with Scott'.[54] In many ways his article represents the response to George Eliot immediately after her death, not least in confirming the division between her early and later works. For Stephen, 'the sphere which she has made specially her own is that quiet English country life which she knew in early youth'. From *Romola*, he felt, 'the reflective faculties have been growing at the expense of the imagination', and works such as *Middlemarch* are 'painful' more than 'charming'.[55]

George Eliot's reputation as a moralist was consolidated in 1885 by J. W. Cross's humourless and expurgating biography of his wife, which severely damaged her reputation with the next generation. Increasingly, her image as a dour moralist took hold, her novels out of tune with *fin-de-siècle* fashions for aestheticism, naturalism and Decadent literature. In 1890, W. E. Henley published a damaging piece in which he mocked the Victorian 'Novel-with-a-Purpose' and aligned himself with those who held that George Eliot had carried what he called 'the "Death's-Head Style" of art a trifle too far' – a phrase that stuck.[56] Henley's often misogynistic attack prefigures early twentieth-century responses. In 1895, George Saintsbury observed that 'for some years past George Eliot, though she may still be read, has more or less passed out of contemporary critical appreciation'.[57] It would take more than fifty years for her reputation to recover.

NOTES

1 'Silas Marner', *Saturday Review* (13 April 1861), 369.
2 'A New Novelist', *Saturday Review* (29 May 1858), 566–7.
3 [E. S. Dallas], 'Adam Bede', *The Times* (12 April 1859), 5.
4 [Anne Mozley], 'Adam Bede and Recent Novels', *Bentley's Quarterly Review* (June 1859), 434.
5 'Adam Bede', *Saturday Review* (26 February 1859), 250.
6 [Mozley], 'Adam Bede', 434.
7 'Adam Bede', *Saturday Review*, 250.
8 [Dallas], 'Adam Bede', 5.
9 'Adam Bede', *Examiner* (5 March 1859), 149.
10 'Adam Bede', *Saturday Review*, 250.
11 [Mozley], 'Adam Bede', 436.
12 [Dallas], 'Adam Bede', 5.
13 *London Quarterly Review* (July 1861), 302.
14 'The Mill on the Floss', *Saturday Review* (14 April 1860), 470.
15 [E. S. Dallas], 'The Mill on the Floss', *The Times* (19 May 1860), 10.
16 Ibid.
17 'The Mill on the Floss', *Spectator* (7 April 1860), 331.
18 Ibid.
19 'The Mill on the Floss', *Saturday Review*, 470–1.
20 'Silas Marner', *Economist* (27 April 1861), 455.
21 'Silas Marner', *Saturday Review* (13 April 1861), 369.
22 'The Novels of George Eliot', *Atlantic Monthly* (October 1866), 482.
23 *George Eliot* (London: W. H. Allen, 1883), p. 148.
24 'Romola', *Athenaeum* (11 July 1863), 46.
25 'George Eliot's Life', *Atlantic Monthly* (May 1885), 675.
26 'Romola', *Spectator* (18 July 1863), 2265.
27 John Morley, 'Felix Holt', *Saturday Review* (16 June 1866), 723.
28 [E. S. Dallas], 'Felix Holt', *The Times* (26 June 1866), 6.
29 *Nation* (16 August 1866), 128.
30 Morley, 'Felix Holt', 723.
31 'George Eliot's "Spanish Gypsy"', *St James's Magazine* (April 1868), 478.

32 Browne, 'George Eliot as a Poet', *Contemporary Review* (July 1868), 391; James, *North American Review* (October 1868), 622.
33 [Edwin Paxton Hood], 'George Eliot as a Poet', *Eclectic Review* (September 1868), 223.
34 'Middlemarch', *Academy* (1 January 1873), 1.
35 'Middlemarch', *Fortnightly Review* (19 January 1873), 142.
36 Ibid., 144.
37 'Current Literature', *Galaxy* (March 1873), 424.
38 Ibid., 428.
39 Calvin, 'Middlemarch', 144.
40 [R. R. Bowker], 'Daniel Deronda', *International Review* (January 1877), 70.
41 Oscar Browning, *Life of George Eliot* (London: Walter Scott, 1890), p. 148.
42 'Daniel Deronda: A Conversation', *Atlantic Monthly* (December 1876), 684–94.
43 Picciotto, 'Deronda the Jew', *Gentleman's Magazine* (November 1876), 593–603; Saintsbury, 'Daniel Deronda', *Academy* (9 September 1876), 254.
44 'George Eliot's First Romance', *Gentleman's Magazine* (October 1876), 411, 412.
45 Saintsbury, 'Daniel Deronda', 254; 'Notes and News', *Academy* (5 February 1876), 120.
46 [R. H. Hutton], 'Daniel Deronda', *Spectator* (9 September 1876), 1331.
47 [Bowker], 'Daniel Deronda', 69.
48 'Impressions of Theophrastus Such', *Edinburgh Review* (October 1879), 562.
49 'Impressions of Theophrastus Such', *Academy* (28 June 1879), 557.
50 Ibid., p. 556; 'George Eliot's New Work', *Examiner* (7 June 1879), 740.
51 '*Impressions of Theophrastus Such*', *Saturday Review* (28 June 1879), 805.
52 Simcox, 'George Eliot', *Nineteenth Century* (May 1881), 783; James, 'George Eliot's Life', 677.
53 T. H. Huxley to Herbert Spencer, 27 December 1880, in Leonard Huxley (ed.), *Life and Letters of Thomas Henry Huxley*, 2 vols. (London: Macmillan, 1900), vol. II, p. 19.
54 'George Eliot', *Cornhill Magazine* (February 1881), 152.
55 Ibid., 155 and 164.
56 *Views and Reviews: Essays in Appreciation* (London: D. Nutt, 1890), p. 130.
57 *Corrected Impressions* (London: William Heinemann, 1895), p. 171.

CHAPTER 8

Critical responses: 1900–1970

Juliette Atkinson

Although George Eliot's novels continued to be widely read in the early twentieth century, she was either condemned or ignored by most critics, and it was not until the middle of the century that she gained a strong foothold in academic circles. At the beginning of the century, American critics witnessed this depreciation with some surprise; William Crary Brownell described it in 1900 as 'one of the most curious of current literary phenomena'. Brownell rather simplistically attributed her fall to the fickle nature of the reading public, who had experienced 'a surfeit of psychological fiction since George Eliot's day'. While Brownell felt that this decline was undeserved, he did not propose a wholesale rehabilitation. He discerned a rigidity in her work, stemming from the fact that her characters 'do a tremendous lot of thinking' and, more damagingly, claimed that 'she has no style'.[1] Brownell's allegiance to French stylists and his quest for 'fine' passages in George Eliot's works suggest why he found it so difficult to make sense of her work.

Brownell was countered by another American, Henry Houston Bonnell, in *Charlotte Brontë, George Eliot, Jane Austen: Studies in Their Works* (1902), from which George Eliot emerges as his favourite of the three novelists. Although Bonnell offered few comments on the structure of the novels, he gave unprecedented attention to her language, and argued that 'one has the frequent feeling in reading George Eliot that in this happily selective ability the one correct word is found to describe what must otherwise be described only by circumlocution'. Conversely, he is more ambivalent about her moral preoccupations, which he sees as a form of 'bondage' from which 'the untroubled masters of the objective method – the Balzacs and Scotts … are alone free'.[2] George Eliot's themes and style were rarely appreciated together.

The same year saw the publication of Leslie Stephen's study of George Eliot in the *English Men of Letters* series. The work reiterates his pleasure in her early works and disappointment in the later novels. Stephen's insistent portrayal of her as an author who had 'a full share of the feminine docility' is often irksome, but he also offers some thoughtful comments, for example by suggesting that George Eliot resisted depicting contemporary life because she thought 'of the world chiefly as the surrounding element of sordid aims into which her idealists are to go forth'. Stephen noted approvingly: 'The combination of an exquisitely sympathetic and loving nature with a large and tolerant intellect is manifest throughout.'[3] His study convinced Edith Wharton that George Eliot was only suffering the 'momentary neglect' that was 'the lot of all great writers'. He did not succeed, however, in converting George Meredith, who wrote to Stephen that he 'could not have refrained from touches on the comic scene of the Priory' where 'an erratic woman' was 'worshipped as a literary idol and light of philosophy'.[4]

As the century progressed, the iconoclastic spirit exemplified by Lytton Strachey's *Eminent Victorians* (1918) grew stronger. Largely because of exaggerations concerning her moral preaching, George Eliot, more than any other novelist, became the scapegoat for modernist frustrations with the Victorians. With something like glee, Ford Madox Ford noted in 1911 that 'here was an authoress almost omnipotent in her power to charm at once the great multitude and the austere critic of her time … Yet, to the great bulk of educated criticism to-day, George Eliot has become a writer unreadable in herself and negligible as a critical illustration'.[5]

The debunking continued with Edmund Gosse's 1919 centenary article. He had seen George Eliot in London, a 'large, thickset sybil, dreamy and immobile, whose massive features, somewhat grim when seen in profile, were incongruously bordered by a hat'. Echoing Ford, Gosse insists that the world has forgotten 'what a portentous thing was the contemporary fame of George Eliot. It was supported by the serious thinkers of the day, by the people who despised mere novels, but regarded her writings as contributions to philosophical nature'. Gosse is not altogether wrong in dwelling on George Eliot's sage-like qualities, but misrepresents the manner in which her contemporaries engaged with her novels: many saw their more intellectual aspects as weaknesses. By misunderstanding this response, he ends up mimicking her nineteenth-century critics. Like them, he stresses that her 'early imaginative writings … had a freshness, a bright vitality', which relied on 'their felicity of expressed reminiscence'. Also like them, he deems that 'her failure … began when she turned from passive acts of memory to a strenuous exercise of intellect'. Such judgements led him to characterise *Middlemarch*, famously, as a 'remarkable instance of elaborate mental resources misapplied, and genius revolving, with tremendous machinery, like some great water-wheel, while no water is flowing underneath'.[6] Such responses typify the myth that had grown around George Eliot, and stood in the path of a more even-handed analysis of the novels.

'To read George Eliot attentively is to become aware how little one knows about her.'[7] Virginia Woolf's reconsideration in the *Times Literary Supplement* (1919) signals the extent to which portrayals of her such as those by Meredith and Gosse had obscured the real nature of her achievements. The essay offers comparatively little detailed analysis of the novels themselves, and even suggests that there is a quality in George Eliot's works, particularly the early novels, that resists critical discussion. George Eliot seems to deliver 'so spontaneously' the 'flood of memory and humour' that 'it leaves us with little consciousness that there is anything to criticise. We accept; we feel the delicious warmth and release of spirit which the great creative writers alone procure for us.'[8] Although such comments seek to rehabilitate her, they offer little space for an analysis of her art. Woolf's famous comment that George Eliot's power 'is at its highest in the mature *Middlemarch*, the magnificent book which with all its imperfections is one of the few English novels written for grown-up people' is offered with no further explanation, to counter the preference of critics, including her father, Leslie Stephen, for the earlier works. For Woolf, if you 'confine George Eliot to the agricultural world of her "remotest past" ... you not only diminish her greatness but lose her true flavour'.[9] Woolf's initial concern is to convince her contemporaries that there is 'no trace of pomposity' here, before the works themselves can be scrutinised.

Above all, however, the essay was important in showing the potential for a feminist reading of George Eliot's life and work. Woolf recognises that the myths surrounding George Eliot personally had become the biggest obstacle to her appreciation, and works hard to replace the notion of 'the elderly celebrated woman, dressed in black satin, driving in her victoria', with a narrative that underscores the unconventionality and bravery of the novelist.[10] George Eliot's heroines fit into this narrative, and Woolf was one of the first critics to pay them close attention. She acknowledges that 'those who fall foul of George Eliot do so, we incline to think, on account of her heroines' who 'bring out the worst of her, lead her into difficult places, make her self-conscious, didactic, and occasionally vulgar'. Yet Woolf pleads for them, sensing a close identification between the author and Janet, Dinah, Maggie, Romola and Dorothea. George Eliot, uneasy about this projection, 'disguised them in every possible way' but faltered in the representation of their lovers because she herself had been excluded

Figure 8 The iconoclastic critic F. R. Leavis (1895–1978; charcoal drawing by Robert Sargent Austin, 1934) included George Eliot in his influential *The Great Tradition* (1948). © National Portrait Gallery, London.

from the drawing rooms of good society. These flawed portrayals are the result of 'the ancient consciousness of woman, charged with suffering and sensibility, and for so many ages dumb', which has 'brimmed and overflowed'. Although Woolf noticed, as later feminists would, that George Eliot emerged far more 'triumphant' from such struggles than her heroines, she laid the ground for a feminist appraisal of the much-maligned novelist.[11]

That Woolf's essay did not have an immediate impact on George Eliot's reception is illustrated by Oliver Elton's discussion in *A Survey of English Literature, 1830–1880* (1920). Elton, like Woolf, was intrigued by the intensity of the reaction against George Eliot, but remained cautious. His limitations as a critic become apparent when he describes *Middlemarch* as 'a precious document for the provincial life of that time, vaguely astir with ideas, but promptly sinking back into its beehive routine'. Elton's analysis is more perceptive when discussing the harshness with which she treats so many of her characters, who are 'scourged out of all proportion', but he quickly relapses into generalisations, such as the comment that her sympathy with suffering is 'true to the better habit of her sex, even if it will not do for our rougher one'.[12] Critical rehabilitation of George Eliot would have to wait a little longer.

The turning point came with F. R. Leavis's *The Great Tradition* (1948). (See Figure 8.) There had been earlier attempts to challenge modernist caricatures, such as Lord David Cecil's 1935 endeavour to make a case for the importance of the 'intellectual' rather than the charming George Eliot. Lord David offered the unfashionable judgement that George Eliot is 'nearer to us in form and subject than the other Victorians', but also deemed that 'the virtues of her admiration, industry, self-restraint, conscientiousness, are drab, negative sort of virtues; they are school-teachers' virtues'.[13] Crucially, however, he implied that if George Eliot were to become palatable again, it was necessary to make sense of the moral and philosophical aspects of her work. This is precisely what Leavis sought to do.

The main originality of the study lies in its measured celebration of aspects of George Eliot's novels that were usually perceived as weaknesses. Leavis questions the 'accepted view' that 'the great George Eliot' is 'the novelist of reminiscence'.[14] While he concedes the charming nature of her early novels, he warns of the dangers of using charm as an indicator of her power: 'at the risk of appearing priggish one may suggest that there is a tendency to overrate charm. Certainly charm is overrated when it is preferred to maturity.'[15] The later novels had finally found their champion.

Leavis proposed a canon of the English novel spanning from Jane Austen to George Eliot, James, Conrad and D. H. Lawrence, with the later inclusion of Dickens. These novelists are defined in opposition to writers such as Flaubert for whom '"form" and "style" are ends to be sought for themselves'. Moreover, 'far from having anything of Flaubert's disgust or disdain or boredom, they are all distinguished by a vital capacity for experience, a kind of reverent openness before life, and a marked moral intensity'. For Leavis, this involves the novelists' capacity to enter objectively into their characters' experiences. Consequently, he is harsher towards those heroines with whom George Eliot seemingly over-identified in order to compensate for her own frustrations. Leavis approvingly quotes T. S. Eliot's dictum that 'the more perfect the artist, the more completely separate in him will be the man who suffers and the mind which creates'. Unusually, Leavis locates the beginning of her maturity in *Felix Holt*: 'it is in the part of *Felix Holt* dealing with Mrs Transome that George Eliot becomes one of the great creative artists. She has not here, it will be noted, a heroine with whom she can be tempted to identify herself.' Gwendolen is another heroine of this kind, and stimulates such enthusiasm in Leavis that he dismisses the Jewish portions of *Daniel Deronda* and reinvents the work as a novel entitled *Gwendolen Harleth*: 'So much pride and courage and sensitiveness and intelligence fixed in a destructive deadlock through false valuation and self-ignorance – that is what makes Gwendolen a tragic figure.'[16]

Despite building his analysis on the separation of her own desires and her creations, Leavis's appreciation is undoubtedly influenced by the appeal he finds in George Eliot herself, and specifically her 'noble and ardent nature'. He proposes that 'what she says of Dorothea might have been said of herself: "Permanent rebellion, the disorder of life without some loving reverent resolve, was not possible to her."' The moral note in his critical approach resounds in his conclusion, in which he presents George Eliot as 'fortifying and wholesome', a writer who might do much to correct the excesses of the mid twentieth-century – an advertisement that conceivably discouraged as many readers as it attracted. Leavis's study is by no means uncritical of George Eliot – for example, he concurs with many earlier critics by describing Stephen Guest as a 'significant lapse' on the author's part. By celebrating those aspects of George Eliot that had recently been dismissed as off-putting, however, Leavis brought new attention to her later novels, and encouraged others to see her as a novelist with the same 'depth and reality' as Tolstoy.[17]

In 1948, Asa Briggs declared that George Eliot was 'only in the process of being discovered'.[18] Leavis gave a new impetus to the study of her work, but in the 1950s it was form, rather than morality, that became the focus of attention. In many ways, this was the most daring approach yet, for even among her admirers, structure and aesthetic considerations were rarely considered her strengths. The major project which helped to shift the nature of this academic interest was Gordon Haight's publication of George Eliot's letters between 1954 and 1978. The letters nuanced J. W. Cross's stern portrayal of his wife, and brought out a more complex picture of the novelist. Given the common notion that her early novels were profoundly autobiographical, it was illuminating to discover, as Geoffrey Tillotson noted in a review of the first three volumes, that 'for all the uses to which George Eliot put the experience of Mary Ann Evans, she did not use the material which was most obviously rich'.[19] Thomas Pinney's edition of her essays in 1963 extended the understanding of George Eliot's methods and aesthetic creed.

A new wave of studies confirmed that George Eliot had survived the early twentieth-century onslaught on her reputation. Although they did not all tackle form (John Holloway's *The Victorian Sage* (1953), for example, argued that she offered a rare example of the female sage), most

Figure 9 Barbara Hardy (born 1924; photograph by Bassano, 1974): a key figure in the post-World War II critical rehabilitation of George Eliot.

responded to the new, broader, academic interest in the creative processes of novelists. Dorothy Van Ghent included a discussion of George Eliot in *The English Novel: Form and Function* (1953), and argued that in *Adam Bede* 'the movement is one of a massive leisureliness that gathers up as it goes a dense body of physical and moral detail, adding particle to particle and building layer upon layer with sea-depth patience'.[20] It was Barbara Hardy, however, who put technique centre stage (see Figure 9). *The Novels of George Eliot* (1959) is announced as being 'chiefly concerned with her power of form', since the 'engrossing realistic interest of her human and social delineation' had obscured the manner in which she shaped her narratives.[21] Hardy's study brings out the unity within and between the novels in terms of overarching preoccupations, such as the use of a tragic form applied to ordinary, rather than extraordinary, heroes and the 'classifying division into egoist and altruist'. The unity of George Eliot's style is also emphasised, with recurrent imagery such as that of currents and light being traced. Indeed, George Eliot's 'formal subtlety is something which places her in a special relation to the writing of our own century … because it finds an expression for themes which are close to the themes of novelists and poets of our time'.[22] Other studies consolidated the awareness of her technical achievements, such as Jerome Beaty's *'Middlemarch' from Notebook to Novel* (1961) and W. J. Harvey's *The Art of George Eliot* (1961), which argued that her novelistic techniques, especially her use of the omniscient narrator, are more complex than had been thought.

Having survived the attacks of the 1920s, undergone the moral-oriented criticism of the 1930s and 1940s and structural and formal analysis of the 1950s, George Eliot studies now splintered off into diverse paths. These included attempts to trace the influence of George Eliot's intellectual circle on her novels, such as Bernard J. Paris's discussion of her religious and philosophical ideas and U. C. Knoepflmacher's analysis of her religious humanism, both published in 1965. George Eliot was one of the six novelists considered by the deconstructionist J. Hillis Miller in *The Form of Victorian Fiction* (1968), which identified the omniscient narrator as a key convention of Victorian novelists who, in reaction to a 'loss of belief in God's transcendence', were 'unwilling to accept the notion so prevalent in fiction after Conrad and James that no comprehensive view of society is possible'.[23] Although different in their orientations, these later studies demonstrate a new desire to explore how George Eliot's stylistic choices are determined by, but also influenced, her belief system, and in turn how both can further illuminate the nineteenth-century novel.

NOTES

1 *Scribner's Magazine* (December 1900); repr. in W. C. Brownell, *Victorian Prose Masters* (New York: Charles Scribner's Sons, 1901), pp. 99, 100, 101, 120.
2 Henry Houston Bonnell, *Charlotte Brontë, George Eliot, Jane Austen: Studies in Their Works* (New York: Longmans, Green, 1902), pp. 230, 132.
3 Leslie Stephen, *George Eliot* (London: Macmillan, 1902), pp. 16, 203, 201.
4 'George Eliot', *Bookman* (May 1902), 247; Meredith to Leslie Stephen, 18 August 1902, in C. L. Cline (ed.), *The Letters of George Meredith*, 3 vols. (Oxford University Press, 1970), vol. III, p. 1460.
5 'English Literature of Today: I', *The Critical Attitude* (London: Duckworth, 1911), pp. 55–7.
6 'George Eliot', *London Mercury* (November 1919); repr. in Edmund Gosse, *Aspects and Impressions* (London: Cassell, 1922), pp. 1, 2, 4, 14.
7 Virginia Woolf, 'George Eliot', *Times Literary Supplement* (20 November 1919), 657–8; repr. Gordon S. Haight (ed.), *A Century of George Eliot Criticism* (London: Methuen, 1966), p. 183.
8 Ibid., pp. 185–6.
9 Ibid., pp. 187, 188.
10 Ibid., p. 184.

11 Ibid., pp. 187, 189.
12 Oliver Elton, *A Survey of English Literature, 1780–1880* (New York: Macmillan, 1920), vol. IV, pp. 265, 271–2.
13 *Early Victorian Novelists: Essays in Revaluation* (London: Constable, 1935), pp. 291, 327.
14 *The Great Tradition: George Eliot, Henry James, Joseph Conrad* (London: Chatto and Windus, 1948), pp. 40, 33.
15 Ibid., p. 35.
16 Ibid., pp. 8–9, 54–5, 109.
17 Ibid., pp. 78, 123–5.
18 '*Middlemarch* and the Doctors', *The Cambridge Journal*, 1 (1948), 749.
19 'The George Eliot Letters', *The Sewanee Review*, 63 (1955), 497.
20 *The English Novel: Form and Function* (New York: Holt, Rinehart and Winston, 1953), p. 173.
21 *The Novels of George Eliot* (London: Athlone, 1959), pp. 1, 5.
22 Ibid., pp. 115, 233.
23 Bernard J. Paris, *Experiments in Life: George Eliot's Quest for Values* (Detroit, MI: Wayne State University Press, 1965); U. C. Knoepflmacher, *Religious Humanism and the Victorian Novel* (Princeton University Press, 1965); J. Hillis Miller, *The Form of Victorian Fiction* (London: University of Notre Dame Press, 1968), pp. 31, 119.

CHAPTER 9

Critical responses: 1970–present

Juliette Atkinson

Barely had the early twentieth-century view of George Eliot as haughty and inartistic been successfully challenged when her novels were once more under attack. The Victorian novel as a whole was put under intense scrutiny in the 1970s by feminist, Marxist, and postcolonial critics, but George Eliot was dealt with more harshly than most. This was partly because of the pre-eminent status that nineteenth-century critics had granted her, but above all because the boldness of her personal choices did not seem to tally with the ideologies displayed in her novels. Feminist critics of the 1970s bitterly reproached her for her failure to demonstrate greater female solidarity. In *Sexual Politics* (1970), Kate Millett was disappointed that George Eliot 'lived the revolution … but did not write of it'.[1] Lee Edwards, even more dismayed, declared in 1972 that *Middlemarch* 'can no longer be one of the books of my life'. By marrying Dorothea to Will Ladislaw, George Eliot had refused to represent 'that world she forced into existence when she stopped being Mary Ann Evans and became George Eliot instead'.[2] The trajectories of George Eliot's heroines were all the more unsatisfactory when compared to those of Charlotte Brontë's angry protagonists, celebrated by Sanda Gilbert and Susan Gubar in *The Madwoman in the Attic* (1979). Against such rebellious figures, George Eliot's heroines displayed what Elaine Showalter called 'self-sacrificing masochism'.[3] Maggie Tulliver in particular provoked complaints, as Elizabeth Weed's '*The Mill on the Floss* or the Liquidation of Maggie Tulliver' illustrates. 'Why is such an attractive character', Weed asks, 'abandoned to a death by flood', which 'precludes all possibility of Maggie's resolving her dilemma in exclusively human terms?'[4]

Others resisted the 'role model' argument, maintaining that George Eliot's commitment to realism meant that she set out not to represent ideal, but rather representative female lives. For Zelda Austen, 'the feminist's insistence that literature show women as more than bride, wife and mother is admirable, but it can't be applied to novels that were written when most women were either brides, wives, mothers, or dependent spinsters'.[5] Kathleen Blake's emphasis was different: she defended *Middlemarch* as 'a great feminist work' that represented 'the cramping narrowness of a woman's prospect'.[6] Blake, somewhat problematically, even defends Dorothea's remarriage by arguing that it enables her to prepare the way for the Reform Bill. In 1980, Showalter softened her earlier position in an essay that addresses the excesses of a decade of arguments. The essay, which reminds critics that George Eliot remained 'a presence in women's lives and imaginations', was a timely plea for moderation.[7]

It is perhaps surprising to note that *Daniel Deronda*'s Gwendolen Harleth had to wait until the 1980s before she attracted serious feminist attention. Shirley Foster places marriage at the centre of George Eliot's personal and fictional preoccupations. In the novels, marriage is presented as a space for both men and women to demonstrate their powers of sympathy, with the consequence that it becomes an 'emblem of social cohesion'. Gwendolen regards this emblem with scepticism, and seeks to manipulate, rather than submit to, traditional roles, but in the end the author 'seems uncertain what to do with her'.[8] Gillian Beer finds greater strength in Gwendolen; abandoned by Deronda, who 'first succours and then violates' her, she reasserts her independence, insisting, 'Don't be afraid. I shall live.'[9] Both critics note that in Deronda's mother, the Princess Halm-Eberstein, George Eliot portrays a gifted woman who rejects marriage and motherhood for her career. Foster argues that she ultimately condemns the Princess for her 'inability to respond from the heart', but Beer points to the energy of the portrayal of 'the passional, declarative woman, essentially creative, and freed from the ordinary conditions of living as a woman'.[10]

The debate did not stop there. Elizabeth Langland amplified the case against George Eliot in 1995 by tracing how the novels 'efface the productive tensions generated by women's contradictory class and gender placements', and in the process belittle 'the life of a lady', such as Rosamond's. By declaring 'the invisibility of servants' in *Middlemarch* to be 'startling', Langland perpetuates the critical tradition of reproaching George Eliot for what her novels fail to include.[11] Impatience with such reproaches, however, has become increasingly felt. In 1996, Mark Turner and Caroline Levine invited critics to 'broaden the debate about Eliot and gender, to move beyond the task of establishing Eliot definitively as either feminist or anti-feminist'.[12] The response, however, has been rather muted. Tracey S. Rosenberg observed in 2007 that 'feminist research on Eliot ... has slowed to a crawl', and no recent study has sought to contradict her.[13]

Marxist criticism, and more generally the scrutiny of George Eliot's engagement with class, has focused predominantly on the difficulty she experienced in balancing the representation of communities and individuals. For Raymond Williams, George Eliot's works form part of an evolution in the English novel ranging from Austen to Hardy that 'brings into focus a persistent rural disturbance hitherto unrepresented in fiction'. However, he identifies a tendency to talk of 'the Poysers, the Gleggs, and the Dodsons' in the plural 'while the emotional direction of the novel is towards separated individuals'. George Eliot, aware of the problem, 'extends the plots of her novels to include the farmers and the craftsmen' but 'finds it difficult to individuate working people'. Nevertheless, Williams values the early novels, where one can find 'the development that matters in the English novel'.[14] Terry Eagleton rephrased this as a tension between 'two forms of mid-Victorian ideology: between a progressively muted Romantic individualism, concerned with the untrammelled evolution of the "free spirit", and certain "higher", corporate ideological modes'. George Eliot insists on the significance of 'rural petty-bourgeois' life to her readers while apologising 'for choosing such an unenlightened enclave as the subject matter of serious fiction'; she senses the potentially stifling nature of such communities, but also wishes to celebrate the value of their 'humble yet nourishing soil'. Like Williams, Eagleton mitigates his reproaches by suggesting that this 'indeterminacy', best exemplified in *Middlemarch*, is a reason for her enduring worth.[15]

Such early generosity towards the fluidity of George Eliot's ideological perspectives was gradually superseded by a more negative appreciation of her engagement with class issues. In most cases, the philosophical dimension of the novels is seen to be at fault. Daniel Cottom maintains that her moral vision ultimately enforces the bourgeois status quo. By depicting individuals 'undergoing the process of enlightenment', she transforms their experiences into a 'fable of universal truth', which marginalises the significance of class and politics.[16] For others, on the contrary, George Eliot is profoundly motivated by ideology. Deirdre David argues that she embodied the role of the intellectual partly to identify with the landowning aristocracy. More frequently, George Eliot is seen as attempting to preserve bourgeois hegemony. Nancy Armstrong holds that, like many other novelists, she saw that the middle-class environment could empower women. In a similar manner, Margaret Homans finds that, by making the characteristics of the middle class appear 'natural', 'Eliot's early novels universalise the British middle class and, in doing so, align themselves with other efforts to consolidate middle-class hegemony'. By the end of *Adam*

Bede, for example, the aristocracy has been trivialised, and the middle class has become the 'natural rank'.[17]

Discussion of George Eliot's most overtly political novel, *Felix Holt, the Radical*, has maintained the idea that her philosophical vision is ultimately irreconcilable with a political perspective. Catherine Gallagher reads the novel as a prefiguration of Arnold's *Culture and Anarchy*, and states that in the 1860s 'Eliot seemed to have become acutely aware of a larger crisis in … liberalism' and used the novel to probe the realism and social vision of her earlier work.[18] Gallagher and others see the vagueness of Felix's strategies and the difficulty of gaining his perspective on events as a sign of George Eliot's unease with the value of political action. Similarly, Evan Horowitz stresses the novel's disillusion with the possibility of radical change, to such an extent that it takes on the characteristics of conservatism. The novel 'dramatises the … futility of trying to overcome alienation by way of political reform', which could have potentially catastrophic consequences; for George Eliot, any solution had to eschew 'mere political reform in favor of something broader'.[19] So far, politically oriented studies of George Eliot have concluded that her interests lay elsewhere.

Although George Eliot escaped the kind of censure suffered by Jane Austen for her (non)treatment of imperialism in *Mansfield Park* and the scrutiny of Charlotte Brontë's depiction of the 'other' in *Jane Eyre*, postcolonial criticism has not ignored her. Unsurprisingly, *Daniel Deronda* has dominated such discussions. In 1979, Irving Howe ventured explanations for George Eliot's mysterious decision to present her readers 'with so ponderous, so *unEnglish* a theme as the proto-Zionism to which the hero of the novel commits himself'. These include a protest against English 'smugness', a return to her 'youthful religious enthusiasm' and a sense of the narrative potential in the Jewish movement 'toward national regroupment'.[20] The following year, Edward Said agreed that George Eliot uses 'the plight of Jews to make a universal statement about the nineteenth century's need for a home'. However, the colonising conclusion of the novel lays her open to attack: her understanding of the 'peoples of the East' is vague, and she is mistaken in believing that Zionism may offer 'a dramatic lesson for mankind', ignoring in the process that Eastern populations would be threatened by Deronda's project.[21]

Later critics have proved more reluctant to isolate the Jewish sections of the novel. Carolyn Lesjak dwells on the strong parallels between the Zionist plot and the experience of Gwendolen, whose early fantasies are coloured with the language of imperialism, but who in turn is subjected to Grandcourt's colonising desires. Nevertheless, the portrayal of 'the other' remains problematic. Lesjak agrees with Said that 'even in its most stereotypical form', George Eliot's depiction of the Jewish characters overshadows that of 'the peoples of the East', who are given no individuality. Having condemned colonialism through Gwendolen, George Eliot reasserts the value of a national, and even imperial, project through Deronda.[22] Susan Meyer takes this further in *Imperialism at Home* (1996) by proposing that Gwendolen's desire to become 'a queen in the East' is projected onto Deronda, leaving her disempowered. For Meyer, the 'final suppression of feminist impulses in *Daniel Deronda* is accompanied by … an *increase* in imperialist sentiment and an endorsement, by way of proto-Zionism, of racial separatism'.[23]

However, critics have increasingly taken issue with the notion that George Eliot's novels pursue an imperialist ideology. Bernard Semmel justifies her interest in the Zionist project, and more broadly in the theme of inheritance, by exploring her intellectual and personal feelings of alienation from society.[24] In *George Eliot and the British Empire* (2002), Nancy Henry draws on the nineteenth-century literature of empire together with George Eliot's letters and journals to throw new light on how Victorian novelists conceived of the British Empire. *Daniel Deronda*, Henry insists, is shown to be 'as much philanthropic as nationalistic'.[25] Alicia Carroll's *Dark Smiles: Race and Desire in George Eliot* (2003) partakes of the same impulse and argues that George Eliot is not 'unreflectingly supportive of the values of empire'. Carroll points to the strong presence of the 'other' in the novels (for instance, the gypsies in *The Mill on the Floss*) which serves to introduce the exotic into English provincial life. Though this position in itself is not unproblematic, the study is symptomatic of a growing desire to step away from the controversies surrounding George Eliot, and to recontextualise the novels.[26]

Indeed, while feminist, Marxist and postcolonial criticism of George Eliot has repeatedly expressed frustration that her works did not live up to the unconventionality of her life, another important strand of research has sought to trace her engagement with some of the most innovative scientific and philosophical thought of her time. Such is the emphasis of Gillian Beer's groundbreaking *Darwin's Plots* (1983), which explores how Victorian novelists, and George Eliot in particular, absorbed Darwinian concepts and language. *Middlemarch* displays affinities with *The Origin of Species* (1859), with its discussions of taxonomy and diversity and its preoccupation with the 'web of affinities'. *Daniel Deronda*, in turn, contains echoes of Darwin's *The Descent of Man* (1871), which 'shifted the focus of evolutionary debate on to man's specific inheritance and future'.[27] Sally

Shuttleworth's *George Eliot and Nineteenth-Century Science* (1984) further probes her 'organic conception of society', and places particular emphasis on how the ideas of Auguste Comte and George Lewes influenced her use of scientific and philosophical concepts.[28] In 2004, Janis Maclarren Caldwell shifted attention to the discussion of medicine in *Middlemarch.* Caldwell argues that the novel reflects contemporary debates about whether doctors should rely on the patients' own reports of their illnesses, or whether their own physical examinations should prevail, which finds a parallel in the novel's depiction of the balance between emotional engagement and detachment.[29] In 2006, Michael Davis turned to the impact of psychology on George Eliot, and suggested that, for her, 'the mind has potential both as a positive ethical force and as a source of radical, perhaps destructively egoistic, isolation'.[30]

Research into George Eliot's scientific influences has not been matched by an equal scrutiny into the less fashionable area of religion. Nevertheless, Peter Hodgson's *Theology in the Fiction of George Eliot* (2001) queries the longstanding view that she was 'a nonbeliever who used religion to achieve certain aesthetic, psychological, political or moral effects', and contends that although she moved 'beyond evangelicalism and the religion of humanity toward something new', she remained profoundly imbued with a sense of 'mystery'.[31] In *George Eliot and the Conflict of Interpretations* (1992), David Carroll usefully brings together many of these different strands. He stipulates that George Eliot had a 'special awareness of the crisis of interpretation which the Victorians were experiencing … As an intellectual of formidable learning she was fully aware of the latest developments in a whole range of intellectual disciplines undergoing radical change … As a novelist she could deploy her fictions to domesticate these revolutionary ideas in the lives of ordinary people'. Carroll relates this project to her attempts to grapple with 'nineteenth-century hermeneutics'.[32]

The process of placing George Eliot back in the context of nineteenth-century developments has lately stretched to include technology. Richard Menke's *Telegraphic Realism* (2008) and John Condon Murray's *Technologies of Power in the Victorian Period* (2010) share this interest. For Menke, the nineteenth-century novel 'could begin imagining itself as a medium and information system in an age of new media'. Menke focuses on 'The Lifted Veil' to explore how George Eliot reflected on her own methods as a realist novelist through the development of new technologies, and in particular photography.[33] Murray argues that 'the encroachment of technology into the Victorian public sphere transformed how people communicated in the mid-nineteenth-century', and considers how *Felix Holt* depicts Felix's resistance to seeking means of reform through new technologies rather than through a broader historical discourse.[34] Overall, criticism has become wary of evaluating George Eliot according to her affinities with post-Victorian ideologies and of isolating her from the contemporary factors that influenced her, producing a more contextual approach that has been further enabled by the publication of her journals in 1998.[35] The result has been a greater willingness to see such contexts and her realist aesthetic as inextricably linked.

The creation over the last forty years of two specialist journals, *George Eliot–George Henry Lewes Studies* (1982–) and *The George Eliot Review* (1970–), and the growing range of critical companions to her work testify to her secure place inside university walls. However, George Eliot has not received anything like the popular enthusiasm accorded Austen and the Brontës. Unlike them, she has not generated a tourist industry; nor has Hollywood so greedily adopted her, despite a very successful television mini-series of *Middlemarch* in 1994 and other adaptations for screen and stage. Cultural studies have given considerably less attention to George Eliot than to other major Victorian novelists, though one study has sought to bring out her own response to popular culture: Susan Rowland Tush's *George Eliot and the Conventions of Popular Women's Fiction*.[36]

During her lifetime, reviewers found it hard to resist weaving speculations about George Eliot's life into discussions of her work; later readers and critics continued to prefer those works which they assumed were the most autobiographical. A century and more after her death, it is interest in George Eliot's biography that still attracts the widest audience. Gordon Haight's *George Eliot: A Biography* (1968) was for a long time the authoritative work. By making extensive use of the letters which he had edited, Haight corrected some of the distortions of Cross's 1885 *George Eliot's Life*, although he resisted offering a new interpretation of George Eliot for a modern readership.[37] Subsequent biographers such as Rosemarie Bodenheimer and Kathryn Hughes offer more searching accounts of George Eliot's complex psychological and emotional make-up, while Rosemary Ashton's *George Eliot: A Life* (1996) emphasises the literary and intellectual milieu in which she moved and out of which the novels emerged.[38] Together, they strip away the forbidding image of George Eliot circulated by her contemporary and modernist readers, and capture for a modern audience the boldness of her life and work.

NOTES

1 *Sexual Politics* (New York: Doubleday, 1970), p. 139.
2 'Women, Energy, and *Middlemarch*', *The Massachusetts Review*, 13 (1972), 238, 236.
3 *A Literature of Their Own: British Women Novelists from Brontë to Lessing* (1977; London: Virago, 2009), p. 133.
4 '*The Mill on the Floss* or the Liquidation of Maggie Tulliver', *Genre*, 11 (1978), 427.
5 'Why Feminists are Angry with George Eliot', *College English*, 37 (1976), 552.
6 'Middlemarch and the Woman Question', *Nineteenth-Century Fiction*, 31 (1976), 285, 291.
7 'The Greening of Sister George', *Nineteenth-Century Fiction*, 35 (1980), 310.
8 Shirley Foster, *Victorian Women's Fiction: Marriage, Freedom and the Individual* (Beckenham, Kent: Croom Helm, 1985), pp. 193, 213.
9 Gillian Beer, *George Eliot* (Brighton: Harvester, 1986), pp. 226, 224.
10 Foster, *Victorian Women's Fiction*, p. 198; Beer, *George Eliot*, p. 211.
11 *Nobody's Angels: Middle-Class Women and Domestic Ideology in Victorian Culture* (Ithaca, NY: Cornell University Press, 1995), pp. 183, 199.
12 'Introduction', *Women's Writing*, 3.22 (1996), 95–6.
13 'The Awkward Blot: George Eliot's Reception and the Ideal Woman Writer', *Nineteenth-Century Gender Studies*, 3 (Spring 2007), www.ncgsjournal.com [accessed 21.09.2010].
14 'The Knowable Community in George Eliot's Novels', *NOVEL*, 2 (1969), 255, 258, 261, 268.
15 *Criticism and Ideology: A Study in Marxist Literary Theory* (1976; London: Verso, 2006), pp. 111, 114–15.
16 *Social Figures: George Eliot, Social History, and Literary Representation* (Minneapolis: University of Minnesota Press, 1987), pp. 71, 30.
17 David, *Intellectual Women and Victorian Patriarchy: Harriet Martineau, Elizabeth Barrett Browning, George Eliot* (Ithaca, NY: Cornell University Press, 1987); Armstrong, *Desire and Domestic Fiction: A Political History of the Novel* (Oxford University Press, 1987); Homans, 'Dinah's Blush, Maggie's Arm: Class, Gender, and Sexuality in George Eliot's Early Novels', *Victorian Studies*, 36 (1993), 156, 161.
18 'The Failure of Realism: *Felix Holt*', *Nineteenth-Century Fiction*, 35 (1980), 376.
19 'George Eliot: the Conservative', *Victorian Studies*, 49 (Autumn 2006), 9.
20 'George Eliot and the Jews', *Partisan Review*, 46 (1979), 359, 363–4.
21 *The Question of Palestine* (London: Routledge Kegan Paul, 1980), pp. 62, 64.
22 *Working Fictions: A Genealogy of the Victorian Novel* (London: Duke University Press, 2006), p. 129.
23 *Imperialism at Home: Race and Victorian Women's Fiction* (Ithaca, NY: Cornell University Press, 1996), p. 160.
24 *George Eliot and the Politics of National Inheritance* (Oxford University Press, 1994).

25 *George Eliot and the British Empire* (Cambridge University Press, 2002), p. 117.
26 *Dark Smiles: Race and Desire in George Eliot* (Athens, OH: Ohio University Press, 2003), p. 20.
27 *Darwin's Plots: Evolutionary Narrative in Darwin, George Eliot and Nineteenth-Century Fiction* (1983; Cambridge University Press, 2000), pp. 156, 170.
28 *George Eliot and Nineteenth-Century Science: The Make-believe of a Beginning* (Cambridge University Press, 1984), p. x.
29 *Literature and Medicine in Nineteenth-Century Britain from Mary Shelley to George Eliot* (Cambridge University Press, 2004).
30 *George Eliot and Nineteenth-Century Psychology: Exploring the Unmapped Country* (Aldershot: Ashgate, 2006), p. 3.
31 *Theology in the Fiction of George Eliot: The Mystery Beneath the Real* (London: SCM Press, 2001), p. 13.
32 *George Eliot and the Conflict of Interpretations: A Reading of the Novels* (Cambridge University Press, 1992), p. 3.
33 *Telegraphic Realism: Victorian Fiction and Other Information Systems* (Stanford University Press, 2008), p. 3.
34 *Technologies of Power in the Victorian Period* (Amherst, NY: Cambria, 2010).
35 Margaret Harris and Judith Johnston (eds.), *The Journals of George Eliot* (Cambridge University Press, 1998).
36 *George Eliot and the Conventions of Popular Women's Fiction. A Serious Literary Response to 'Silly Novels by Lady Novelists'* (New York: Peter Lang, 1993).
37 *George Eliot: A Biography* (Oxford University Press, 1968).
38 Ashton, *George Eliot: A Life* (London: Hamish Hamilton, 1996); Bodenheimer, *The Real Life of Mary Ann Evans: George Eliot, Her Letters and Fiction* (Ithaca, NY: Cornell University Press, 1994); Hughes, *George Eliot: The Last Victorian* (London: Fourth Estate, 1998).

PART III

Cultural and social contexts

CHAPTER 10

Class

Ruth Livesey

In 1881 John Ruskin wrote a series of essays on the state of fiction in the later nineteenth century and decided that one – recently deceased – author was the consummation of its 'foul' nature. George Eliot's novels were, he argued, a form of Cockney literature 'developed only in the London suburbs, and feeding the rows of similar brick houses': her characters were the 'sweepings-out of a Pentonville Omnibus'; 'the personages ... picked up from behind the counter and out of the gutter; and the landscape by excursion train to Gravesend'.[1] Ruskin's 'Fiction – Fair and Foul' was an attempt to redirect the literary and artistic trends of realism; developments supported by his earlier work which George Eliot had reviewed with enthusiasm in 1856.[2] But by the latter part of the century, to Ruskin at least, such realism had become associated with representing the lower orders of society, immorality and the titillation of a mass readership.

Ruskin's dismissal of George Eliot's work is written in a language of class fraught with anxiety about social mobility, mass literacy and mass culture. Pentonville was a lower-middle-class suburb in London; those riding on the omnibus would have been people not wealthy enough to own a carriage or hire a cab – shop girls, clerks, skilled artisans, higher servants, for example; a literate but not particularly well-educated crowd. The essay suggests that George Eliot's novels lack beauty and the right kind of truth because both the author and the characters she depicts are drawn from the ugly world of modern urban living for the masses: the daily life and imagination of workers and the lower-middle class. By the time Ruskin wrote his essay, the granting of the vote to the majority of working-class men in 1867 and the introduction of mass elementary education in 1870 had fuelled anxieties that beauty and culture were threatened by popular desire for less demanding forms of entertainment. Rather awkwardly, George Eliot stands in Ruskin's account as a suburban modern novelist, selling cheap thrills to a lower-class (and mostly female) readership about, for example, two young people 'forgetting themselves in a boat'.[3]

Ruskin's attack on George Eliot is revealing in its mismatch to what her novels actually do in terms of class. Her social origin was that of the rising, self-sufficient, lower middle class or skilled artisans; a background echoed in her fond portrait of Caleb Garth, the land surveyor in *Middlemarch* (1871) and the mixed fortunes of the Dodson and Tulliver families in *The Mill on the Floss* (1860). But George Eliot's works avoid the tendencies Ruskin ascribes to them: the representation of modern urban life and the sense that class limits and determines experience and imagination. Rather, the near-historical and provincial settings of her earlier works detail rural working life but do not represent a mass of individuals confined to a common identity through that labour. The relations between different orders of society in a modernising society become an increasing concern in her later fiction. *Middlemarch* and, especially, *Daniel Deronda* (1876) move closer to the contemporary era and depict a more mobile society in which new money and old landed wealth dine and play at the same table. The divide between the traditional landed gentry of the Brookes and the Chettams and the new manufacturing wealth of the Vincys and Bulstrodes, for instance, is carefully underscored in *Middlemarch*, where the supposedly radical Mr Brooke 'always objecting to go too far, would not have chosen that his nieces should meet the daughter of a Middlemarch manufacturer unless it were on a public occasion' (*M*, ch. 10). These later novels acknowledge the separation formed by different sorts of social environment and insist on the need to communicate despite these divisions. All of this leads to an odd paradox when it comes to considering George Eliot's works in relation to class: on the one hand, her fiction provides some of the most carefully observed portrayals of distinctions between different social orders in the nineteenth century; on the other, class – as it is understood by Marxist literary critics and social historians – scarcely comes to the surface in her novels.

Class in nineteenth-century Britain, according to the influential social historian E. P. Thompson in *The Making of the English Working Class* (1963), is not a set social classification, but an active process – the 'making' of a self-conscious class – that results from the identification of collective common experience within a group as against another group in society. 'We', the workers, for instance, realise that our experience of factory labour gives us common cause against 'them', the property-owning classes, at base thanks to the economic organisation of capitalism. It is this formation of conscious class identities that fuels the movement of social change in Marxist analyses. George Eliot's works feature relatively little in such critical accounts of Victorian literature and culture, largely because her fiction seldom depicts class consciousness or conflict.[4] Oppositional identities are represented as a threat to the organic unity of society in George Eliot's works: the duty of the modern novelist is to open out the boundaries of class consciousness; to feel with the lives of others. The inward effects of inheriting a certain position in society are carefully mapped in her fiction, but class is often represented as a more recent social and economic imposition that overlays the hierarchies of nature.

Before she published her first works of fiction, George Eliot dismissed the 'modern generalisation' that 'all social questions are merged in economical science, and that the relations of men to their neighbours may be settled by algebraic equations'. In her essay 'The Natural History of German Life' (1856), she is explicit that she embraces a different means of analysing the state of '"the people", "the masses", "the proletariat", "the peasantry"'. Rejecting both economic generalisations and romantic idealisation, she calls for a 'natural history' of the working classes, revealing their 'real characteristics' to those outside their ranks (*Essays*, 268). In George Eliot's critical work and the fiction that followed it, collective abstractions such as class are shown to be deceptive and limiting. Her narrative interest in the mode of natural history, as opposed to abstract generalisations, leads to representations of the interplay between character, heredity and environment. Diagrammatic classifications by type are displaced by pictures of individual particularities.

In 'The Sad Fortunes of the Reverend Amos Barton' (1857), George Eliot's earliest study of this sort, Barton is depicted as a lower-middle-class man out of his fitting environment. 'Nature' has given him a strong opinion of himself as a preacher, but he would have been better to remain in the hereditary sphere of his father, as an 'excellent cabinetmaker and deacon of an Independent church', where faulty English and constant sniffing would not have prevented him being 'a shining light in the Dissenting circle of Bridgeport' (*SC*, 'Amos', ch. 2). In what seems at first a clear statement of social conservatism, against the upward mobility of the lower orders, Barton is shown to be a misfit as a country clergyman, a 'tallow dip … plebeian, dim, and ineffectual' taken from the kitchen where it belongs and stuck in a silver candlestick in the drawing room (ch. 2). The pathos and comedy of Barton's narrative is in great part that he does not recognise or feel this social displacement: he is entirely unconscious of the way in which his class origin is patent to his peers (and the implied reader) and the parishioners of rural Shepperton.

Yet to label George Eliot as a social conservative opposed to class mobility would be to miss the emphasis on exceptionalism evident in her early fiction; the way in which 'Nature' distributes gifts unevenly, endowing some with talents that make them stand out from the social class into which they are born, determining, over time, shifts in social standing. The sad fortunes of Amos Barton are in part due to the fact that Nature has not given him quite enough of a gift to rise free from his hereditary order, unlike, for example, Adam Bede:

> He was not an average man. Yet such men as he are reared here and there in every generation of our peasant artisans – with an inheritance of affections nurtured by a simple family life of common need and common industry, and an inheritance of faculties trained in skilful courageous labour: they make their way upward, rarely as geniuses, most commonly as painstaking honest men. (*AB*, ch. 19)

A careful scrutiny of the natural history of any rural neighbourhood, the narrator implies, will throw up such exceptions, growing out of the peasant environment to rise beyond it and enrich a whole community; individuals who cannot be reduced to a fixed identity of class over time. Society, in George Eliot's fiction and social analysis, is never static but in a constant process of change, in which some slip 'a little downward, some [get] higher footing' (*M*, ch. 11). Her social conservatism lies in the fact that such change is depicted as an organic process in which different social groups are interdependent, not in conflict and opposition, despite the hitches and tension as misfitting individuals struggle to find their places. Adam Bede, for instance, makes his employers richer, but is represented as a free agent and proud owner of his skilled labour, not an exploited proletarian. When the old squire tries to pay Adam only a guinea for a commission Adam priced at one pound thirteen shillings, Adam refuses the exchange and gives the screen in question as a gift to the squire's daughter rather than take less than his 'regular price' (*AB*, ch. 21). It might seem a minor incident in the novel, but it speaks volumes in terms of contemporary representations of the working classes at the mid nineteenth century.

The contrast between *Adam Bede* (1859) and one of the best-known nineteenth-century novels of working-class industrial life shows how George Eliot's novel unravels oppositional urban class relations. Elizabeth Gaskell's *Mary Barton* (1848) shares much with *Adam Bede*: a beautiful, vulnerable working-class girl prone to vanity and romance; a respectable, hard-working admirer, bound to rise on his own abilities; the son of the local magnate who absent-mindedly tries to seduce the young woman and gets in a fight with his rival; murder; a trial, and a last-minute reprieve. While the factory employees, John Barton and Jem Wilson, in mid-nineteenth-century Manchester are subject to the whims and needs of their masters, Adam can walk away from Squire Donnithorne confident in his freedom to contract more labour elsewhere. John Barton's unstable employment and union activities constitute his sense of oppression in opposition to the factory-owning Carsons; Jem Wilson's fight with young Harry Carson over Mary and subsequent trial permanently damage his employment prospects, which can only be resurrected by emigration. But Adam Bede remains to prosper, and it is the upper-class young squire, Arthur Donnithorne, who is displaced to military service in the colonies. *Adam Bede* replays the cross-class seduction plot of *Mary Barton* that had a long association with Radical melodrama and attacks on the unjust privileges of wealth. By changing the setting from urban industry to rural artisans and workshops, from the mid nineteenth century to 1799, George Eliot's novel redirects the reflex plotting of class blame and insists on sympathy for the individual in his or her particular context.

When the modernising industrial city does feature in George Eliot's work, as in *Silas Marner* (1861) or *Middlemarch*, the narrative moves action into a more variegated rural landscape, where labourers, professional men and the landed gentry encounter each other on a daily basis. As Josephine McDonagh has noted, *Silas Marner* shifts its protagonist from the industrial modernity and massed working class of Lantern Yard to rural Raveloe, 'aloof from the currents of industrial energy and Puritan earnestness', reversing the pattern of urban migration that characterised the nineteenth century:

> the rich ate and drank freely ... and the poor thought the rich were entirely in the right of it to lead a jolly life; besides, their feasting caused a multiplication of orts [leftovers], which were the heirlooms of the poor. Betty Jay scented the boiling of Squire Cass's hams, but her longing was arrested by the unctuous liquor in which they were boiled. (*SM*, ch. 3)[5]

In Raveloe, the narrator implies, oppositional class does not exist: it is an interdependent world of rich and poor, with mutual interests; the appetite for the good things in life sated by ham stock and a sight of the dancing. This is not a high-Tory lament for a lost world, however. George Eliot was quick to condemn the 'aristocratic dilettantism' of social reformers who idealised peasant life and called for a return to the '"good old times" by a sort of idyllic masquerading, and to grow feudal fidelity and veneration as we grow prize turnips' ('Natural History', *Essays*, 272). Squire Cass is a neglectful landlord, and the villagers know that and comment on his family's shortcomings. The workers drinking at the Rainbow in

Silas Marner, like the working-class patrons of Mrs Dollop's Tankard in *Middlemarch*, are an articulate, if not very well-informed, chorus to the action of the landed and middle classes. In both cases, the employments of the drinkers shape contributions to the discussion: a 'meditative shoemaker' at the Tankard, for example, quotes from a newspaper to illuminate a Middlemarch scandal; the barber has gathered his news on the subject from shaving a clerk working for one of the parties involved (ch. 71). The workers, in this representation, share a social space, but their being and conscious selves are shown as individuated organic growths rooted in daily customs, rather than a mass identity shaped by a common economic position. I would argue that Eppie's rejection of the Casses' offer to adopt and legitimate her as a proper lady is not a Radical gesture of class solidarity against the neglectful squirearchy, as some earlier critics have suggested.[6] It is another illustration of George Eliot's continued interest in the way in which environment and daily occupations nurture a deep-rooted affection for the known and near, as opposed to class resentment and a desire for the abstract goods of social elevation. Social identity, in this account, is an organic growth over time and in a particular place, not a manifestation of economic relations.

George Eliot's depiction of this sort of 'humble' existence provoked the ire of Ruskin and other early critics of her work, and it is important not to underestimate how radical it was to claim such lives as subject matter for serious art at the time. As in *The Mill on the Floss*, however, the narrow vision associated with such an artisanal and lower-middle-class environment is placed under the microscope by the narrator for an implied readership of higher social class, broader education and experience:

> You could not live among such people; you are stifled for want of an outlet towards something beautiful, great, or noble; you are irritated with these dull men and women … I share with you this sense of oppressive narrowness; but it is necessary that we should feel it, if we care to understand how it acted on the lives of Tom and Maggie – how it has acted on young natures in many generations, that in the onward tendency of human things have risen above the mental level of the generation before them, to which they have been nevertheless tied by the strongest fibres of their hearts. (*MF*, book 4, ch. 1)

George Eliot's ethical realism insists here and, most famously, in chapter 17 of *Adam Bede*, on cultivating the 'secret of deep human sympathy'; a sympathy that requires that social generalisations, such as class, are set aside in favour of individual emotions. 'We' need to feel with 'them'. But this effort to feel with others is an ethical imperative precisely because social differences create chasms of experience that can only, according to George Eliot, be surmounted through the imaginative power of art. The implied reader is from one class, the loving, illiterate Dolly Winthrop in *Silas Marner*, or those old women scrubbing carrots in the Dutch paintings the narrator commends in *Adam Bede*, from another altogether. George Eliot's pattern of setting her fiction in the just-historical period of her own, or her parents' youth, back into a rural landscape is a means to stage relations between the classes impossible in modern city life, where workers and employers lived increasingly divided and differentiated lives. Contemporary class relations are, in this sense, ever present in her fiction in the narrative mode that invokes them to set them aside. It is this duality that makes her most explicitly political novel, *Felix Holt, the Radical* (1866), so productively unstable when it comes to considering class.

Felix Holt opens on 1 September 1832, just after the passage of the first Reform Act, and its concerns are tied to debates current in the mid 1860s when George Eliot was writing the novel, on further extending the franchise – Parliamentary voting rights – to the mass of working-class men. Democracy was often represented as a fearsome prospect at the time, in which the sheer number of uneducated new voters might, as she put it (in the guise of Felix Holt's 'Address to Working Men', published in January 1868 after the passing of the second Reform Act), 'throw the classes who hold the treasures of knowledge – nay, I may say, the treasure of refined needs – into the background' *Essays*, p. 426. Throughout the novel, Felix Holt's speeches work to undo class conflict and rapid social change. This is particularly evident in chapter 30, in which a working-class trades unionist's speech, peppered with references to the power relations of 'us', working men, and 'them', the aristocrats, is countered by Felix's language of individual ethics: the need for right 'feeling' and the strength of universal, educated 'public opinion' (*FH*, ch. 30). Felix asserts, 'I am a working man myself, and I don't want to be anything else', yet what makes this novel stand out from George Eliot's earlier works is that this expression of class identity has become an elective affinity: a conscious choice (ch. 30). Felix's inheritance and gifts have already offered him the prospect of a social rise in class as a 'doctor on horseback' before he turns his back on university in favour of an apprenticeship to a watchmaker in order to educate his fellow workers (ch. 43). In a similar vein, Esther's renunciation of her claim to Transome Court and Harold Transome in favour of life with Felix Holt is depicted as a far more intellectually conscious act than Eppie's loving attachment to what she has always known in *Silas Marner*.

Class consciousness is therefore more visible in *Felix Holt* than in any other of George Eliot's works; but class in this novel has also become something more deeply engrained through birth and heredity than it appeared in her earlier works. It is not just the outgrowth of a certain environment or pursuing a particular kind of labour, but is an inherited part of the self – as with Esther's delicate distaste for the smell of tallow candles – that should be acknowledged.[7] *Felix Holt* the novel underlines the embodied and durable nature of class, while Felix Holt the protagonist insists that the class system is like the co-dependent parts of a living body, and to be conscious of class, according to Holt, means to work within your class of birth towards its improvement, rather than claim rights to power against the established order. Small wonder, then, that nineteenth-century Radicals like Joseph Jacobs believed the language of class in this novel meant that it would be more appropriately entitled, 'Felix Holt, the Conservative, not even a Tory Democrat'.[8] Class determines so much in *Felix Holt*, but Felix argues that class opposition needs to be set aside.

The threat to high culture embodied by the 1867 Reform Act was something feared by both Ruskin and George Eliot. But whereas Ruskin increasingly despaired of life dominated by the passengers on the Pentonville omnibus, George Eliot imagines how exceptional individuals may choose to remain with their people and use this sense of belonging to infuse modern society with culture and right feelings. Class – as birth, inheritance, or simple economic determination varying over time – becomes an unstable means to pursue this in *Felix Holt*. *Daniel Deronda* (1876), the most contemporary of all George Eliot's major works, thus uses ethnic identity, rather than class, to explore the tensions of modern mass culture and to imagine resistance to modern moral corruptions in preserving deep-rooted social differences.

NOTES

1 'Fiction – Fair and Foul v', *Nineteenth Century*, 10 (1881), 521.
2 [George Eliot], 'Art and Belles Lettres', *Westminster Review*, 65 (1856), 626.
3 Ruskin reports this as all one young lady can say about a novel she has recently read: the allusion is clearly to Maggie Tulliver and Stephen Guest in Eliot's *The Mill on the Floss:* 'Fiction – Fair and Foul i', *Nineteenth Century*, 7 (1880), 951.
4 A notable exception is Terry Eagleton's *Criticism and Ideology* (London: Verso, 1978), pp. 102–61.
5 Josephine McDonagh, 'Space, Mobility, and the Novel: "the spirit of place is a great reality"', in Matthew Beaumont (ed.), *Adventures in Realism* (Oxford: Blackwell, 2007), pp. 50–67.

6 See, for example, Q. D. Leavis's introduction to the original Penguin Classics edition, repr. as an appendix in David Carroll (ed.), *Silas Marner* (Harmondsworth, 2003), pp. 208–39.

7 See Janice Carlisle, 'The Smell of Class: British Novels of the 1860s', *Victorian Literature and Culture*, 29 (2001), 1–19.

8 Joseph Jacobs, *Literary Studies* (1895), quoted in Hilda Hollis, 'Felix Holt: Independent Spokesman or Eliot's Mouthpiece?', *ELH*, 68 (2001), 155–77.

CHAPTER II

Dress

Clair Hughes

Dress is one of the most obvious markers of order and change, especially in the new middle-class world of nineteenth-century England. It expresses individual taste within social limits, it is a measure of ambition and respect, but it can also betray, deceive and seduce. In fiction dress is rarely described in full: too much detail can be distracting. George Eliot acknowledged 'excess in this effort after artistic vision' – a vision that contained densely detailed accounts of historical costume – as 'a fault in "Romola"' (*L*, 4: 97). 'Attitudes to clothes', Barbara Hardy says of *Middlemarch*, 'rather than the actual clothes are important',[1] but 'the faithful representing of commonplace things' was an article of faith for George Eliot (*AB*, ch. 17). In 'Silly Novels by Lady Novelists', written in 1856, she targets those novelists who 'conduct you to true ideas of the invisible [by] … a totally false picture of the visible'. The 'feelings, faculties and flounces' of their 'perfectly religious' heroines are bogus and implausible (*Essays*, p. 300).

Dress is also always over-determined, open to a variety of readings and therefore an ambiguous guide to character. The contrast between Dorothea Brooke and Rosamond Vincy in *Middlemarch*, for example, is often seen as that between a noble woman and a modish coquette. High-minded women, we assume, are not interested in dress, but they play key roles in George Eliot's fiction. What style can be found that represents their fine qualities without sinking into clichés of Puritanism? And is a concern with appearance so despicable? But as Ellen Moers has pointed out, George Eliot's approach is more nuanced: Dorothea Brooke has 'the most stunning wardrobe in Victorian fiction'.[2]

The first of the *Scenes of Clerical Life*, 'The Sad Fortunes of the Reverend Amos Barton', is set in rural society of the 1830s. Countess Czerlaski settles near the Barton family and cultivates the acquaintance of Amos. His status requires that his family be dressed 'with gentility from bonnet-strings to shoe-strings' on a meagre stipend ('Amos', ch. 1). Dining with the Countess, his wife Milly is 'graceful in a newly-turned black silk', an image that suggests beauty but also penury, for an old gown has been altered to show a less worn side. She silently envies the Countess's silk dress 'of pinkish lilac hue' and lace accessories, and longs for the Countess's balloon sleeves (ch. 3) – at their widest around 1835 and rightly known as *imbecile* sleeves. This detail dates the scene and makes its point by setting Milly's timeless black against the Countess's stylishness, while in no way mocking Milly's yearnings.

Adam Bede, set in 1799, paints a picture of pre-industrial England in the solid detail of Dutch genre art: Dolly has 'a dark-striped linen gown, [and] red kerchief'; Adam 'leather breeches, and dark-blue worsted stockings' (*AB*, ch. 1). Dutch art sets the general tone, but Hetty Sorrel, the novel's coquettish heroine, is all French Rococo. George Eliot's treatment of Hetty has been called harsh, but attention to dress-description reveals that it is Dinah Morris, the 'noble' woman of *Adam Bede*, who is presented in negatives and drained of life: 'no book in her ungloved hands', in a 'long white dress … almost like a lovely corpse', and a cap grim enough 'to frighten the crows' (chs. 2, 15, 18).

Despite attacks on Hetty's eyelashes and intellect, George Eliot in fact paints an entrancing portrait of her. 'It is of little use for me to tell', she begins – and then *does* go on to tell how lovely is 'the contour of her pink-and-white neckerchief, tucked into her low plum-coloured stuff bodice' (ch. 7). Hetty's real and fantasy selves are evoked before a mirror: her stays 'were not of white satin – such as I feel sure heroines [of Silly Novels?] must generally wear – but of a dark greenish cotton' (ch. 15). She dreams she is Arthur Donnithorne's bride, 'feathers in her hair … sometimes in a pink dress, sometimes in a white one' (chs. 22, 15). 'Visible' Hetty is lovelier even than her dream: 'if ever a girl looked as if she had been made of roses, that girl was Hetty' (ch. 18). When she dresses up in Dinah's Quakerish clothes she looks incongruous rather than noble. Dinah herself wears grey for her wedding to Adam: a compromise that softens but lends little life to her image compared to that of the tragically frivolous Hetty.

In 1860 George Eliot began fashioning Maggie Tulliver, a very different heroine. In *The Mill on the Floss* Maggie embodies the hopes of a woman who is both intelligent and sensual, but Maggie's 'passionate longings for all that was beautiful' are never realised (*MF*, book 3, ch. 5). The first adult image of her is in an 'old lavender gown' and 'hereditary black silk shawl', for the Tullivers have fallen on hard times (book 5, ch. 1). George Eliot stresses Maggie's physical attraction to and for the opposite sex; her pretty cousin Lucy artlessly wonders 'what witchery it is in you, Maggie, that makes you look best in shabby clothes'. Maggie spots a double-edged compliment, and spurns Lucy's offer of a brooch: 'won't that mar the charming effect of my consistent shabbiness?' (book 6, ch. 2).

Maggie refuses a pink dress to replace Aunt Glegg's dingy blue: an exercise in renunciation that Eliot's noble women are prone to (*MF*, book 5, ch. 5). Still, Lucy and Aunt Pullet contrive to dress Maggie for social events. She appears in a borrowed 'white muslin of some soft-floating kind' which sets off her 'simple, noble beauty', without compromising her principles, and is a contrast to 'the more adorned and conventional women around her' (book 6, ch. 9).

Because dress is rarely their primary concern, novelists often draw on stereotypes for their descriptions. Stephen Guest is first drawn to Maggie in black brocade cut to expose her shoulders – a cliché of coquetry. But George Eliot's use of the stereotype is not simple. It is proper Aunt Pullet who has altered her own dress to make Maggie seductive, but Maggie's poverty and *gaucherie* disturb the cliché, evoking black's other connotations of thrift, self-effacement and even death. After her escapade with Stephen, gossip imagines Maggie decently married in a dress of 'maize-coloured satinette' (book 7, ch. 2) – an image so nasty that her actual fate seems almost an honourable alternative. Self-fashioning involves aesthetic choices, and Maggie's are constantly thwarted – her clothes are loans or gifts. In dress, as in other respects, Maggie's aspirations are defeated.

In her earlier works, George Eliot accurately recreated dress codes of her own times, inflecting them for artistic purposes. In undertaking a recreation of life in Renaissance Florence in *Romola*, her quest for authenticity became burdensome. Her wish to make a fable of the novel, where event and detail have symbolic weight, is impeded by her exhaustive researches. To convey period colour she refers to garments and textiles by their specific names, with explanatory phrases. But a surfeit of *luccos*, *becchettos*, *scarsellas* clogs the text. The black dress-notes of the novel, however, seen mainly on the treacherous Tito, effectively chart the trajectory of Savonarola's harsh rule in Florence and reinforce a sense of impending tragedy.

Tito's 'wives', Romola and Tessa, are most interesting in the context of our concerns here. Tito is attracted to Tessa's blue eyes and peasant's red hood before he meets Romola, the scholarly aristocrat he marries to further his career. Romola wears a 'gown of black rascia', her golden hair 'confined by a black fillet' (*R*, ch. 5). The contrast is both social and aesthetic, and our sympathies hover between the two. With Romola, George Eliot plays on the associations of black, white and grey – the palette she used for Dinah and will employ again with Dorothea Brooke. At her marriage to Tito, we see Romola 'like a tall lily' in white and gold; 'the white mist of her long veil … fastened on her brow by a band of pearls' (ch. 20). Despite George Eliot's researches, this is an anachronism. White was not yet the bridal colour, and veils were not adopted for weddings until the early nineteenth century.[3] George Eliot may well have known this but felt readerly expectations overrode strict accuracy; in any case, it was what she needed for her fable's aesthetic and symbolic structure.

Romola's relations with Tito deteriorate when she discovers a dagger-proof vest, his 'garment of fear'. Turning sadly to her wedding dress, she sees lying beneath it the grey stuff of a Franciscan habit, which she puts on. The harsh cloth hurts, but she feels a 'scorn of that thing called pleasure which made men base … which now made one image with her husband' (ch. 36). Each has now a dress-'other', not an opposite but an evolution of the self; ambition has turned to crime, idealism to self-mortification.

Tessa, on the other hand, looks what she is: 'a simple contadina' in 'her gown of dark green serge, with its red girdle … the string of red glass beads round her neck' – less a coquette than an affectionate child. She is repeatedly seen in plain stuffs and strong colours (it is tempting to associate her colours of red, green and white with the Italian flag, symbol in 1863 of Garibaldi's newly unified nation). Only her jewellery changes. Where garnets that replaced beads marked Hetty Sorrel's fall, Tessa acquires 'a fine gold ring' (ch. 33). However fine it looks, it marks the sham marriage into which Tito has tricked her.

Romola flees Florence dressed as a Franciscan, the Dominican Savonarola's enemy; for she has rejected his credo as she has Tito's. Grey has been a rejection of Dominican black and bridal white; with the deaths of Savonarola and Tito her choices are freed, but there are no more accounts of her appearance. Romola is seen finally with Tessa, beside whose bright solidity and lively children she subsides into wan saintliness, another grey Dinah.

If the use of dress adds complexity and interest to the earlier novels, it is in *Middlemarch* that it reaches its most important deployment. The novel opens with Dorothea prevaricating over some gems to which she soon succumbs. Critics are rarely sensitive to the role of dress in literature, but several cultural historians have discussed the novel's clothes. Ellen Rosenman argues that George Eliot assigns detailed sartorial comment to the lower classes: Dorothea, as one of the elite, promotes an aesthetic of 'underdetailing'.[4] Kate Flint relates the book's concern with dress to the Midlands textile industry: she sees Dorothea as an inversion of Rosamond's materialism, citing Dorothea's declaration to Ladislaw, that she can 'live quite well' on 'seven hundred-a-year – I want so little – no new clothes' (ch. 83)[5] – though in fact this was a substantial sum in the 1830s, the period in which the novel is set.

Dress charts Dorothea's quest for identity: hesitations, renunciations, exaggerations, but also 'stunning' outfits in simple white and grey, such as the one she wears during her honeymoon in Rome. Posed in front of a sculpture of Ariadne in the Vatican, she is in 'Quakerish grey drapery... one beautiful ungloved hand pushing backward the white beaver bonnet which made a sort of halo to her face' (*M*, ch. 20). Dorothea's dress may be Quakerish, but her bonnet of costly beaver is clearly of fashionable dimensions. At the same time its shape lends a spiritual aspect to her appearance, appropriate to the place and a contrast to the pagan Ariadne. George Eliot thus places Dorothea both within and outside time.

Dorothea's self-fashioning, if inconsistent and theatrical, is essentially outward-looking: she wishes to make life, everybody's life, beautiful. In contrast, Rosamond Vincy's solipsism, shaped by an indulgent upbringing, assumes her entitlement to the latest fashions and to the world's admiration: she is her own unchanging standard of a perfect lady. Acquisition – whether of quilled bonnets, embroidered collars or fine furnishings – is what drives Rosamond, whereas Dorothea's development sheds superfluities. We know life will start improving for Dorothea when Celia removes her overblown widow's cap.

The search for an authentic expression of self culminates when, after a sleepless night, Dorothea looks out of her window and sees an ordinary family and its dog in the fields, and realises she must rejoin 'that involuntary, palpitating life'. She asks Tantrip, her maid, to lay out her new dress and bonnet, and in so doing sheds her tragedy-queen mourning, those 'hijeous weepers' (*M*, ch. 80). The putting-on of fresh garments to signal change has time-honoured resonances, but it is also the gesture of a woman – of Rosamond, of Mrs Bulstrode, or of Celia – who senses the pleasures of dress as well as its significance in the eyes of the world. She fashions an identity and finds love: finds what she wants, even if it's not all *we* want for her. The harsh truth, as George Eliot saw it, was that society as yet held little hope for the inchoate dreams of Maggie or Dorothea.

To Gwendolen Harleth, the ambitious heroine of *Daniel Deronda*, the future already looks sterile: 'We must stay where we grow ... plants ... are often bored, and that is the reason why some of them have got poisonous' (*DD*, ch. 13). Poisonous colours and gems are linked to Gwendolen as black is to Tito. The novel opens with Deronda watching her at the gaming table: does her beauty augur good or evil? She is Lamia, 'a Nereid in sea-green robes and silver', a 'serpent … all green and silver; images so toxic that readers can be in little doubt (ch. 1). Impressions worsen when, after losses, Gwendolen sells 'the ornament she could most conveniently part with', turquoises that had been her father's (ch. 2). Deronda contrives to return the jewels to her and the ties of affection they represent revive, linking her to Deronda and her nobler self, and modifying our initial image of her.

Jewellery, the traditional gift of male to female, becomes a kind of currency, 'a system of exchange', Peter Brooks says, 'in which Gwendolen is absolutely imprisoned'.[6] The wearing, the acquisition, the gift of gems is an action of moral consequence for George Eliot. The motif was introduced in *Adam Bede*, developed in *Romola* and culminates in *Daniel Deronda*. If less subject to fashion, jewellery, like dress, signals taste and status – but being stones, jewels are also cold and lifeless.

Gwendolen's life, George Eliot says, 'moves strictly in the sphere of fashion' (*DD*, ch. 6), and generalised references to crinolines offer a fashion context. Gwendolen's image achieves its fullest beauty at the archery contest, where she meets and flirts with Grandcourt. Her image, in 'white cashmere with its border of pale green' and green-feathered hat, is very different from that first reptilian impression (ch. 11). In a woodland context green signals youth and energy. With the gold star of victory on her breast, she is Diana triumphant.

The gloomy city setting in which we then see Mirah is a contrast so abrupt that it almost fractures the narrative. There is little 'noble' in Deronda's first sight of her all in black by the Thames, evidently suicidal. Such women were common sights, he owns; but struck by her 'delicate beauty', he rescues her and installs her with the Meyricks. Here she is re-clothed several times but always to emphasise her insubstantial, sombre aspects. Her borrowed dress is too big, falling round tiny soft slippers.

Gwendolen's moment of nobility in black is delusory. Learning that Grandcourt has a mistress, she decides to turn down his proposal – in a black silk dress: 'Black is the only wear when one is going to refuse an offer' (ch. 27). But she in fact accepts him and his diamonds, sent to her by his mistress. Although she shrinks from the gems – they 'had horrible words clinging and crawling about them' – Grandcourt forces them on her. To others, 'they were brilliants that suited her perfectly'; to Deronda, seeing through Gwendolen's 'fine raiment', they represent 'the poor soul within her sitting in sick distaste' (ch. 35).

Figure 10 *The Fair Toxophilites* depicts one of the archery contests fashionable in the second half of the nineteenth century, at which young elite women like Gwendolen Harleth were able to display their persons and their dress to best advantage. Dress and headgear could be elaborate as archery was an essentially static affair.

The Fair Toxophilites, 1872, by William Powell Frith (1819–1909).

Royal Albert Memorial Museum, Exeter, Devon, UK/The Bridgeman Art Library. Nationality/copyright status: English/out of copyright.

By displaying her turquoise necklace Gwendolen betrays her feelings for Deronda and, 'in her splendid attire … a white image of helplessness', she submits to Grandcourt's fury (ch. 36). White metamorphoses here from positive to negative, from victory to defeat; Mirah's black moves in the opposite direction. In black silk 'such as ladies wear', she triumphs at her concert; Gwendolen, 'in poisoned diamonds', applauds a success she herself had once hoped for (chs. 39, 45). The two women thus retain their dress contrasts but their situations are reversed. After Gwendolen's moment of choice in black, she is stifled under furs, rich stuffs and jewels. Mirah, once one of the dispossessed, attains professional success, economic independence and Deronda's love – still in unrelieved black. Accepted orders of meaning are reversed: black becomes the new white, the colour of purity, youth and victory. Immaculate Mirah has all that George Eliot denied her noble heroines until now – or so it would seem.

She has everything, that is, but credible life for the reader. Mirah's last outfit is a resumption of her first suicidal black. George Eliot had despised 'perfectly dressed, perfectly religious' heroines, but here she imposed on her perfectly noble woman perfectly colour-free, flounce-free anti-fashion – an inverted version of the cliché she had striven to avoid. When she shoehorned her heroines into minimalist garb of this kind, she denied them a human – a Victorian – expression of their dreams. Victorian love of decoration added to surfaces all kinds of ornament into which ambition and fantasy could be read. An early reader begged for more of Hetty's silks and earrings (*J*, 101), and it is Maggie's thwarted longing for beauty that we most easily recall as well as Dorothea's 'stunning' if idiosyncratic style.

I would suggest, however, that in reaching for a style of monochrome simplicity George Eliot is ahead of her time. She is in search of a tailor to undertake for women that modernisation of dress already achieved by men. Anne Hollander argues that 'male dress was always essentially more advanced than female', and by 1800 male wear had been pared back into what it is today, the body-defining, tailored three-piece suit, a chic blend of Puritan plainness and the countryman's simple stuffs. Such an idea seems to lie behind George Eliot's soft white, pious grey and uncompromising black; but dressing is picture-making, and in 1870 there was no corresponding fashion image for women. By 1890 a new female clerical class could find dark ready-made costumes that had, as Hollander says, 'their own modern virtue'.[7] Coco Chanel later fashioned tweed, flannel and jersey into the 'poor look' that would subvert the whole idea of fashion as display. Coco Chanel and George Eliot may seem an unlikely couple, but then 'everything in George Eliot', Henry James said, 'will bear thinking of'.[8]

NOTES

1 Barbara Hardy, 'The Surface of the Novel: Chapter 30', in Barbara Hardy (ed.), *Middlemarch: Critical Approaches to the Novel* (London: Athlone, 1967), p. 166.
2 Ellen Moers, *Literary Women* (London: The Women's Press, 1986), p. 194.
3 Ann Monserrat, *And the Bride Wore …* (London: Gentry Books, 1973), p. 11. See also Clair Hughes, *Dressed in Fiction* (Oxford and New York: Berg, 2005), pp. 157–85.
4 Ellen Rosenman, 'More Stories about Clothing and Furniture', in C. L. Krueger (ed.), *Functions of Victorian Culture in the Present* (Athens, OH: Ohio University Press, 2002), pp. 48–51.
5 Kate Flint, 'Materiality in *Middlemarch*', in Karen Chase (ed.), *Middlemarch in the 21st Century* (Oxford University Press, 2006), pp. 69–70. See also Andrew Miller, *Novels Behind Glass* (Cambridge University Press, 1995), pp. 192–203, and Hughes, *Dressed in Fiction*, pp. 89–113.
6 Peter Brooks, *Realist Vision* (New Haven, CT: Yale University Press, 2005), p. 104.
7 *Sex and Suits* (New York: Kodansha International, 1994), pp. 6, 80, 143.
8 Henry James, *Literary Criticism: American Writers; English Writers* (New York: Library of America, 1984), p. 991.

CHAPTER 12

Education

Elizabeth Gargano

In a vivid scene in *The Mill on the Floss*, Maggie Tulliver and her brother Tom romp in the study of Tom's teacher Mr Stelling, knocking over Stelling's massive reading stand, the symbol of his oppressive authority. The moment is playfully subversive: Maggie's hair 'twirl[s] about like an animated mop' as the children's 'revolutions round the table' – revolutions in two senses – topple the reading desk and send it 'thundering down with its heavy lexicons to the floor' (*MF*, book 2, ch. 1). Throughout the novel's extensive school scenes, both Maggie and Tom display rebellious feelings towards Mr Stelling and his unimaginative attempts to drill his male pupils in Latin grammar. Yet, tellingly, Tom and Maggie rebel for opposite reasons, Tom because he loathes the classical education forced on him by his father's desire for upward mobility, and Maggie because she longs for the education in classical languages denied her by her gender. Rich in ambiguity, the brief scene evokes a number of George Eliot's concerns about contemporary educational practices: the tyranny of educational conventions, the arbitrary impact of gender and class assumptions on teaching, and the need for an innovative and individualised pedagogy.

Like many of her contemporaries, George Eliot sometimes suggests that educational reform offers the key to the reformation of society as a whole. At the same time, she expresses doubts about the value of current educational practices, proposing that conventional schooling often blunts latent abilities rather than cultivating them. Her conviction that education must be tailored to individual needs and talents leads her to statements and positions that may seem contradictory. Committed to offering women a university education, she also critiques university teaching in *The Mill on the Floss*, *Middlemarch* and *Daniel Deronda*. In 'Address to Working Men' (1868), purportedly written by her fictional working-class character Felix Holt, she argues that unions should require members to send their children to school (*Essays*, 428). Yet she also agrees with her friend Mrs Nassau Senior 'about the superiority of that home education which calls out the emotions in connection with all the common needs of life' (*L*, 6: 47). Ultimately, for George Eliot, education should 'propagate the true gospel that the deepest disgrace is to insist on doing work for which we are unfit – to do work of any sort badly' (*L*, 6: 425). Given her view that education entails an individual process of self-discovery, any institutionalised method or standard pedagogy can become suspect. Repeatedly in her essays, correspondence and fiction, she attacks the notion that 'we are to have one regimen for all minds' (*MF*, book 2, ch. 1). If such a view seems self-evident today, it must be remembered that George Eliot lived in a time of intense debate about educational purposes and processes, when numerous groups and individuals became invested in endorsing a single system or method.

Throughout the nineteenth century, educational reform was at the centre of a passionate public conversation in England. As small property holders, artisans and labourers gained the right to vote in a series of legislative acts over the course of the century, greater access to education appeared ever more urgent. For many, expanding religious education

268.—DOUBLE CLASS-ROOM, SHEWING DUAL ARRANGEMENT OF DESKS.

Figure 11 As chief architect for the School Board of London, E. R. Robson was responsible for the design of hundreds of schools in London after the Elementary Education Act of 1870. 'Double Class-Room, shewing dual arrangement of desks' is from his *School Architecture; Being Practical Remarks on the Planning, Designing, Building and Furnishing of School-Houses* (1874), which encapsulated the principles he espoused.

offered the answer. As the loose network of existing parish schools extended its reach, dissenting academies also proliferated, reflecting debates about the role of religious doctrine in schooling. Yet the greatest changes would be wrought by the establishment of government schools. At the beginning of the century England had no national school system, little public funding of education, no nationwide standards for evaluating teachers and teaching, and no mandatory school attendance. By the end of Victoria's reign, all these reforms would be in place. The Revised Code of 1862 wrought a major change in the educational scene, requiring schools in receipt of government funding to submit to inspections and to follow mandated educational standards. Another series of milestones, the Education Acts of 1870, 1876 and 1880, established local school boards, moved towards secularising education, and finally made elementary education compulsory.

As legislators set standards for both teachers and students, the very definition of education was also in flux, along with its perceived purposes and agenda. For centuries, educators had seen their primary function as preparing pupils for a specific social role, whether related to rank, profession or gender. Now, a new idea was in the air: the notion that each individual required a different education, adapted to his or her specific interests and innate intellectual talents. In part a legacy of the Romantic movement's emphasis on individuality, this new conception of individualised education was also influenced by the novel theories of continental educators and philosophers. Jean-Jacques Rousseau's educational treatise *Emile* (1762) questioned the conventional methods of rote instruction and memorisation, advocating an experiential education involving gardening and games, as well as thought-provoking conversations with an adult mentor. Although Rousseau tended to dismiss the notion of an intellectual education for girls and working-class boys, the Swiss educator Johann Pestalozzi (1746–1827) strove to adapt Rousseau's methods to educate children of all classes and both genders. While traditional views would continue to dominate public policy in England, the ideal of a radically individualised education made its way from the continent into English intellectual circles. Pestalozzi inspired numerous English admirers, from the writer Maria Edgeworth, who argued for a more rigorous female education in *Letters for Literary Ladies* (1795), to the social philosopher Herbert Spencer, George Eliot's longtime friend. Sympathetic to the new theories (and also mindful that a continental education was often less expensive), her partner George Lewes sent his sons to the Hofwyl School in Switzerland, whose founder was a follower and former student of Pestalozzi.

In sum, Victorian debates about education revealed deep political and ideological divisions. An expanded educational system, it was becoming clear, carried the potential for eroding class boundaries and remaking society in a new image. A commitment to education as an engine of social reform became the hallmark of the intense, stimulating and sometimes acrimonious public debates of the day, carried on in Parliament, in educational treatises, journals and newspapers, and even in the pages of memoirs and novels. Works of literature both reflected and affected the educational scene, often stimulating further controversy. When Dickens's *Nicholas Nickleby* (1838–9) attacked the notorious Yorkshire boarding schools as holding facilities for unwanted children, readers reacted with horror, and numerous schools in the region, good as well as bad, were forced to close. Similarly, Charlotte Brontë's grim portrait of Lowood School in *Jane Eyre* (1847), where half-starved girls fell victim to an epidemic fever, elicited angry responses from supporters of the Cowan Bridge School, on which Lowood was allegedly based.

Like Dickens, Brontë and numerous other Victorian novelists, George Eliot weaves critiques of current pedagogy and educational agendas into the fabric of her fiction. She explores working-class education in *Adam Bede* and *Felix Holt, the Radical*, and satirises 'the education of a gentleman', consisting largely of an 'arduous inacquaintance with Latin', in such works as *The Mill on the Floss* and 'Janet's Repentance' ('Janet', ch. 2). Questioning the effectiveness of higher education in *Middlemarch* and *Daniel Deronda*, she also portrays intelligent women like Maggie Tulliver who suffer from the lack of it. A diverse array of teachers populates George Eliot's fiction. Reflecting the limited opportunities for female employment in the Victorian era, a preponderance of her female protagonists work as teachers for at least brief periods of time. In fact, the necessity of teaching often presents itself as a sort of moral test, one embraced, though not always happily, by strong-minded women. Maggie Tulliver, Esther Lyon in *Felix Holt*, Mary Garth in *Middlemarch* and Dinah Morris in *Adam Bede* all spend time teaching young children, with varying degrees of enthusiasm and success. In *Daniel Deronda*, the impoverished Mirah Lapidoth welcomes the chance to support herself by offering music lessons, while Gwendolen Harleth, appalled by the prospect of teaching, retreats into an incompatible marriage that proves disastrous.

Although many of the teachers in George Eliot's fiction seem lacklustre or incompetent, a clear picture of good teaching emerges. Regarding teaching as 'delightful', Mary Garth's mother Susan conducts a dame school in her kitchen for neighbourhood children, as well as her own offspring (*M*, ch. 40). Some critics have questioned the effectiveness of Mrs Garth's teaching, performed in between household chores; yet judging by results, her own children appear exceptionally well educated. Bartle Massey, the village schoolmaster in *Adam Bede*, teaches children by day and working men by night. Irascible with unmotivated pupils, he seems endlessly patient with those who desire to learn, even when they stumble. Massey demonstrates his genuine vocation, not only through his formal instruction, but also through his enduring moral influence on his pupil Adam Bede long after Adam has left the classroom.

George Eliot herself was deeply influenced by some of her teachers, most notably the evangelical Maria Lewis at Mrs Wallington's School, who helped to shape her early intellectual and spiritual outlook. Like many middle- and upper-class girls of her day, she attended a local dame school before being sent to boarding school to complete her education. She studied at three successive boarding schools, each more demanding than the last, before returning home at the age of sixteen to nurse her dying mother. Recognised by her teachers as an exceptionally gifted student, she began translating Maria Edgeworth's fiction into French at the age of thirteen, foreshadowing her talent for languages and her later career as a translator. Despite the demands of nursing her mother and, later, managing her father's household, she continued her education at home, with extensive reading in history, theology, poetry and science, while also learning German and Italian with the help of a tutor.

A decade before she published *Scenes of Clerical Life*, her first extended work of fiction, George Eliot wrote, 'I think "Live and teach" should be a proverb as well as "Live and learn." We must teach either for good or evil' (*L*, 1: 242). The statement epitomises the centrality of education in her thought, as well as her conviction that teaching others is a risk as well as a responsibility; she remained sceptical that education could ever be an objective purveyor of truth. 'It is folly to talk of educating children without giving their opinions a bias', she affirmed. 'This is always given whether weak or strong, not always … a permanent one, but one instrumental in determining their point of repose' or basic orientation towards life (*L*, 1: 91). Over the years, she came to view her writing as a form of teaching. Characteristically, she strove to educate her readers, not through injunctions or bald assertions, but rather through an imaginative experience of identification and sympathy. 'My function', she wrote in an often-quoted letter, 'is that of the *aesthetic*, not the doctrinal teacher' (*L*, 7: 44).

George Eliot's fictions frequently draw a contrast between the limitations of formal education and the rich possibilities of what she portrays as a more authentic self-education, directed by the goals and talents of the individual learner. For her, one danger of formal education is that it can so easily become commodified, reduced to a mere matter of economic exchange. 'I'll not throw away good knowledge on people who think they can get it by the sixpenn'orth, and carry it away with 'em as they would an ounce of snuff,' Bartle Massey asserts (*AB*, ch. 21). In a similar vein, George Eliot writes in *Felix Holt* that '[a]ll life' seems 'cheapened' when a young student discovers that earning a degree does not require 'bring[ing] his powers to bear with memorable effect', but merely paying out 'the sum (in English money) of twenty-seven pounds ten shillings and sixpence' (*FH*, ch. 43). In *The Mill on the Floss*, the young Tom Tulliver is caught between the mercenary motives of his father and his teacher, Mr Stelling. While Stelling teaches chiefly to supplement his income as a clergyman, Mr Tulliver hopes that an elite education will secure his son wealth and social status. Similarly, *Middlemarch*'s Fred Vincy is sent to university to rise in the world; after graduating, he considers becoming a clergyman because his expensive education has equipped him for no other occupation. With no spiritual vocation, however, he chooses instead to work for the surveyor and land agent Caleb Garth. Although Fred's apprenticeship to Garth offers a more useful education for a man of his practical bent, his father laments that he has 'thrown away [his] education, and gone down a step in life' (*M*, ch. 56).

Like *Middlemarch*, *Daniel Deronda* reflects George Eliot's interest in the movement for university reform, which called for such diverse changes as lowering the cost of education, de-emphasising rote learning, and expanding the science curriculum. George Eliot and Lewes had various university connections, including a long-term friendship with Mark Pattison, Rector of Lincoln College, Oxford. While George Eliot was at work on *Daniel Deronda*, Lewes wrote to Pattison that his essay 'Philosophy at Oxford' was 'particularly pleasing to Mrs Lewes because confirming something she has written in her new book' (*L*, 5: 202). Pattison had denounced the emphasis on academic prizes that encouraged cramming for examinations in place of genuine philosophical exploration. George Eliot's depiction of Daniel's flawed university education would translate Pattison's logical analysis of Oxford's failings into narrative terms, embodying its argument within the rhetoric of fiction. At Cambridge, the sensitive and serious Daniel consistently disappoints his tutors: 'Everyone … agreed that he might have taken a high place if his motives had been of a more pushing sort'. Instead of 'regarding [his] studies as instruments of success', Daniel 'hamper[s] himself with the notion' that they should help him acquire knowledge and gain wisdom (*DD*, ch. 16). Like Fred Vincy, Daniel finds a more fulfilling education only after he leaves university – in his case, when he learns about and explores his Jewish heritage.

If, as George Eliot suggests, male students frequently endured an inappropriate or uninspired formal education, their female counterparts faced a worse plight: a paucity of rigorous secondary training and exclusion from the university system. As early as 1792, Mary Wollstonecraft's *A Vindication of the Rights of Woman* had taken aim at 'the present corrupt state of society', in which lack of education 'enslave[s] women by cramping their understandings'.[1] In an essay of 1855, George Eliot cites approvingly Wollstonecraft's contention that women should be educated for skilled professions. In contrast, she maintains, a woman trained only in ladylike accomplishments is 'fit for nothing but to sit in her drawing-room like a doll-Madonna in her shrine' ('Margaret Fuller and Mary Wollstonecraft', *Essays*, 205). This statement foreshadows her later portraits of characters like Rosamond Vincy and Gwendolen Harleth, both flawed by an education centred on ladylike accomplishments. Although of a different class, *Adam Bede*'s Hetty Sorrel is also victimised by her narrow education. Instructed in such delicate accomplishments as lace-mending and discouraged from seeking out any practical occupation, she is strikingly ignorant about the world and consequently vulnerable to the blandishments of her seducer.

In her pamphlet *Women and Work* (1857), George Eliot's friend Barbara Bodichon deplored most women's lack of 'a professional education' and advocated that women find careers not only as governesses, but also as school inspectors, physicians, engravers, watchmakers, accountants, nurses and operators of the new technology of the electric telegraph.[2] Along with Emily Davies, Bodichon founded Girton College, the first attempt to offer women a liberal and classical education equal to men's. George Eliot supported their efforts, contributing money to the college, as well as advice about the new curriculum to be offered. The 'better Education of Women', she affirmed, 'is one of the objects about which I have *no doubt*' (*L*, 4: 399). In 1878, when the University of London accepted women candidates for all of its degrees, she wrote jubilantly to Bodichon, 'no doubt you are rejoicing too' (*L*, 7: 6). George Eliot admired Bodichon's activism while making it clear that she herself sought a different path, offering private support while also exploring the controversies surrounding female education in her fiction. As Gillian Beer asserts, Victorian 'reviewers of *Middlemarch* were in little doubt about the book's intended topic: it was the nature and the education of women, and the question of society's responsibility for women's difficulties'.[3]

Middlemarch's naive heroine Dorothea Brooke conflates her quest for self-education with the ideal of ministering selflessly to the needs of a male scholar. She marries Casaubon in hopes of becoming his assistant and 'saving [his] eyes' by reading to him in classical Greek, a language she has yet to learn. George Eliot frankly reveals the ground of Dorothea's desire to help: 'she had not reached the point of renunciation at which she would have been satisfied with having a wise husband; she wished, poor child, to be wise herself' (*M*, ch. 7). Although, as Laura Green notes, Dorothea imagines her impending marriage as 'the highest sort of higher education', the pedantic Casaubon is incapable of teaching her what she yearns to know.[4]

By contrast, in *Romola*, the title character serves as the selfless amanuensis of her blind father, a scholar frustrated by his lack of recognition. After her father's death and her husband's betrayal, Romola indulges in a short-lived fantasy of becoming a self-supporting scholar. By the novel's close, she is once again using her knowledge to assist a male figure, in this case her husband's illegitimate son Lillo, now her ward: 'My father … taught me a great deal', she informs him. 'That is the reason why I can teach you' (*R*, ch. 73).

Whether excluded from university education like Dorothea or forced to endure an unsatisfying university curriculum like Daniel Deronda, George Eliot's most sensitive and thoughtful protagonists at least attempt to take their education into their own hands, recognising that they bear a measure of responsibility for determining what they need to learn. Writing to her friend John Sibree about the prospect of his studying abroad, the young George Eliot romanticised his projected journey as an intellectual adventure, involving introspection and self-development in preparation for life: 'O the bliss of having a very high attic in a romantic continental town, such as Geneva – far away from morning callers[,] dinners and decencies; and then to pause for a year and think "de omnibus rebus et quibusdam aliis," and then to return to life and work for poor stricken humanity and never think of self again' (*L*, 1: 261). George Eliot's mature fictions would temper this youthful optimism by illustrating the perils of the intellectual life, from Romola's frustrated yearning to the dreary failure of Casaubon. Yet they also retain a deep respect for self-education, embodied in her depiction of that blissful 'high attic', an image of space and solitude where, in the mildly ironic words of the Latin quotation, one can think 'of all things, and something more besides'.

NOTES

1 Mary Wollstonecraft, *A Vindication of the Rights of Woman* (1791; Miriam Brody (ed.), Harmondsworth: Penguin, 1971, rev. 1992), p. 104.
2 Barbara Leigh Smith Bodichon, *Women and Work* (New York: C. S. Francis, 1859), p. 18.
3 Gillian Beer, *George Eliot* (Bloomington, IN: Indiana University Press, 1986), p. 147.
4 Laura Green, '"At once narrow and promiscuous": Emily Davies, George Eliot, and *Middlemarch*', *Nineteenth-Century Studies*, 9 (1995), 1.

CHAPTER 13

Etiquette

Judith Flanders

Retrospectively, Victorian social life appears an elaborate dance, one where everyone knew the steps and carefully followed the prescribed pattern. In reality, it was precisely because everyone did not know the steps – because the steps were constantly evolving – that the rules needed to be so firmly laid out. One indicator of this fluidity was the number of magazine articles and advice books that oracularly pronounced on the eternal verities of etiquette. The rules were important, not because everyone could (or wanted to) follow them, but because while appearing to define 'us' and erecting barriers against 'them', they in fact permitted social movement. Society was hierarchical, but it was also porous. The rules, therefore, acknowledged a society that was open to anyone with sufficient income who was happy to accept certain strictures of behaviour.

Etiquette, therefore, was an indication of status. What was 'done', or 'not done', was regularly updated in magazines and manuals, but at any given time most people were in little doubt about the parameters of acceptable behaviour. George Eliot rarely detailed the dance of social life in her fiction – for her and her contemporary readers it was part of the wallpaper, the background against which her characters operated, a given. It is only at a distance in time that the details of the wallpaper need to be picked out once more, in order to understand fully the world the characters operate in.

For women, marriage was the event that precipitated all adult social life. With luck, a suitable marriageable candidate emerged among the family's friends. A man was expected to provide for his wife, from the first day of marriage, an economic status exactly equal, if not superior, to that she had enjoyed under her father's roof. It was tacitly understood that this was unattainable for most; hence the prolonged engagements that occupy so much fiction of the period. Thus the first obligation for a man was to reflect on his financial status and prospects.

Should he not know a suitable woman, an introduction to a prospective candidate had to be arranged. Introductions were serious business: 'Those who undertake such an office … are … expected to be scrupulously careful in performing it, and to communicate all they happen to know affecting the character and circumstances of the individual they introduce.'[1] The introducer was taking on a social responsibility: 'If he disgraced himself … you share … in his disgrace.'[2] If the suitor's finances and family background (checked, respectively, by the father and mother of the candidate) were compatible, he was introduced into the family circle, where the relationship could flourish or wither without compromising the girl. If things went well, the next step was to speak to the girl's father, and only then, if the proposal was welcomed, to the girl herself.

The wedding ceremony appears to have been less central to the nineteenth century than to our own: in fiction, in diaries and letters, weddings are given proportionately less space than other rites of passage, and for much of the century a trip to the parish church with parents and one or two close friends appears to have been the norm for most couples. Though versions of 'the marriage plot' concern George Eliot in much of her fiction, she rarely depicts a wedding ceremony. Dorothea's first marriage famously occurs offstage: chapter ten of *Middlemarch* ends: 'Not long after the dinner-party she had become Mrs Casaubon, and was on her way to Rome.' Weddings that are described – like those of Adam and Dinah (*AB*, ch. 55) and Eppie and Aaron (*SM*, 'Conclusion') – are communal occasions. It was only gradually that the elaborate and formal ceremonies of the prosperous classes came to be perceived as the norm. For them, on the morning of the wedding, the groom despatched bouquets for the bride and her bridesmaids, together with presents. After the ceremony, wedding favours – sprigs of blossom with ribbons, or leaves and acorns, prepared by the bridesmaids – were worn by the bridesmaids and the groom's attendants, as well as the servants of the bride's family (and the horse pulling their carriage), as they returned to the bride's family home for the wedding 'breakfast' at midday.

The following day the bridesmaids returned to the bride's family house to despatch wedding-cards, earlier supplied by the groom. These folded cards, announcing that a wedding had taken place, had the groom's name on the outside and the bride's maiden name inside. The bride was expected to consider her new social status and decide which of her acquaintances no longer fitted in: those who did not receive cards understood that social relations had been severed. Or, more gently, a wedding-card was sent, but without the bride's new address, indicating that she did not wish to be called upon by the recipient. Those who received cards with an address understood that they were expected to pay a formal call after the wedding trip.

This was only one of several social situations in which a call was mandatory. The others were after a dinner party or any sort of entertainment; during an illness; and after a death. These 'morning' calls were paid between three and five p.m. (morning originally meaning anything before dinner). A call, with visitors making only light, impersonal conversation, never exceeded half an hour, and fifteen minutes was more acceptable. If another visitor arrived, the first was expected to take her leave. Women did not remove their shawls or bonnets, and men carried their hats and sticks into the morning room, to indicate that they would not stay long. Visiting cards were essential. Ladies' cards were 3½ inches (9 cm) deep, with the woman's name – Mrs Joseph Bloggs – in the centre, and her address at the lower left. Men's cards were larger, with the man's title and last name – Mr Bloggs – centred, his home address at the lower left, his club on the right. If daughters paid calls with their mother, this was indicated by turning down the right-hand corner of their mother's card (boys did not pay calls). Women paying calls on a husband and wife left their own card, and one of their husband's; calling on a widow, they left only their own.

Callers asked at the door if the mistress of the house was at home, and left a card if she was not, or not 'receiving'; or they handed their card to the servant, saying, 'For Mrs X', which indicated that they did not want to visit. Any call had to be returned within a week, and like returned with like – if a card had been left, a card was left; if a visit had been paid, a visit was expected. If a more socially prominent woman returned a card with a visit, this was complimentary; if she returned a visit with a card, it was a snub. Visiting-books were used to keep everything straight. They resembled ledgers, with columns for the name of the caller, the date, whether it was a visit or a card, and when the visit/card was returned. Many women had 'days' when they were 'at home', which meant one could, without rudeness, be 'not at home' on other days. At 'The Priory' in the 1860s and 1870s, for example, George Eliot's 'at home' day was Sunday. Cards only were left in houses of illness or death, and many obligations could be wiped off in one afternoon. Marion Sambourne, the very sociable wife of the *Punch* cartoonist Linley Sambourne, recorded of a typical afternoon: 'After lunch called at Mrs Baines … Mrs Smiles (too ill to see anyone) Mrs Sington (little girl v. ill) Marion Pollock (out) Mrs Kemp (had tea there)

Mrs Eykyn (out) and Mrs V. Cole … tea there … card at Miss Winthorp's and enquired after Dr Harcourt, little better.'[3] Three visits, two teas and six cards left, three of which were illness-related, in one two-hour stretch.

Tea, by the time Marion Sambourne went calling, was in the late afternoon. What time people ate, what the meals were called and how they were served were all status indicators, and all changed over the century. Dinner was originally a meal eaten in the middle of the day, while supper was served early in the evening, followed by tea before bed. By mid century, when most middle-class men no longer worked near or at home, dinner migrated to five or six p.m., after office hours, and only the working classes continued to eat dinner in the middle of the day. The rich ate dinner ever later, as a sign of leisure; this was mimicked by the upper middle classes, and then the middle classes. As dinner moved later, tea was brought forward to fill the gap between luncheon and dinner. By the 1880s, upper- and middle-class tea consisted of small sandwiches and cakes, while those with less money ate a 'meat' or 'high' tea, which included some animal protein – meat, fish (frequently potted or preserved) or an egg.

A formal dinner party adhered to an intricate ritual. Invitations were sent three weeks before the event, in the name of the hostess and her husband; a reply within twenty-four hours was expected. By the end of the century, dinners were fixed between 7.30 and 8.30 p.m.; arriving more than 15 minutes after the time indicated was rude. General introductions were not performed; the host took each man to the woman he was to partner at dinner and introduced them singly. Precedence was a serious matter – see, for instance, the discussion of precedence in seating at Arthur Donnithorne's birthday feast (*AB*, ch. 23). Many books were available to arbitrate on which professions took precedence over which (clergy, armed forces, the law), as well as giving rankings within professions. At Cambridge, for example, precedence was given to heads of colleges based on the foundation date of each college; regius professors from their subject (divinity first), then by chair foundation dates. Women took their position from their fathers and then later their husbands. The host escorted the woman of the highest rank to the dining room, followed by pairs in order of precedence, ending with the hostess, escorted by the man of highest rank, followed by any single men. At the table, the most prominent man sat on his hostess's right, the next in rank on her left, while the same took place for women next to the host; this continued down to the middle of the table, where the least significant guests were seated.

Until the 1850s and 1860s, dinner was served *à la française*: food was placed on the table before the guests appeared, with a tureen of soup at one end, a large fish at the other. (At parties this would be two sorts of soup, clear and thick, mild and spicy, or white and brown, followed by two fish.) The master and mistress served, with a servant to pass, and the guest on the hostess's right assisting her. These dishes were accompanied by 'corner' or side-dishes of sweetbreads, cutlets, stews, curries – food that required no carving – that were passed by the guests, who served each other. The men were expected to serve wine to those around them: 'Will you take a glass of wine with me?' was the formal phrase used. After the first 'remove', a joint of meat and a fowl were placed at the head and foot, with corner and side-dishes of vegetables, starches and further hashed or stewed foods. The second remove produced a sweet and a savoury dish for the head and foot of the table, and corner and side-dishes of more savoury dishes as well as jellies, trifles and sweet dishes. At grand parties, this was followed by cheese, celery and radishes, before 'dessert' (meaning fruit and nuts) followed. At this point the hostess rose, and the women left the room, the door being held by the man sitting nearest to it. Young men of low status might be told, 'You must find it very boring; I'm sure you would prefer to join the ladies,' and this was not a matter of choice. The women, reaching the drawing room, would, if necessary, now be introduced to one another. The men left behind replenished their wine, and possibly ate 'zests' – anchovy toast, devilled dishes or other spicy items.

No one was expected to eat, or even taste, every dish: the point of service *à la française* was to offer choice. One guide to correct behaviour warned that the fanciest dinner should last only two hours, which shows that the guests were not steadily chomping their way through twenty-odd dishes.[4] Some hostesses routinely gave 'second-day dinners' the night after a large dinner party: they asked fewer people, from among their less prestigious friends, who were served the leftovers that were the result of the display element of service *à la française*. By the 1880s, service *à la russe* had entirely replaced service *à la française*. The new system is our own: the meal was carried in dish by dish, served by a servant in 'courses' rather than removes. Less food was needed, as there was no longer any choice, making dinners much cheaper.

As display was reduced at meals, so it increased in another sphere of Victorian etiquette, mourning and mourning dress. The height of the period of elaborate mourning was *c.* 1860–80 and, as always, the rules retrospectively appear rigid, but in fact altered over time, and according to social status, with the poor and middle classes only making token adherence to guidelines established by the most prosperous. Yet the number of magazine articles setting out changing rules as though they were immutable was a sure indication that most people did not automatically know what 'Second wives [mourning] for the parents of the [husband's] first wife' should wear.[5]

Every aspect of life was touched by mourning, and its accoutrements were expected to be used from the day of the funeral, although for sudden death it often took longer to obtain the necessary items. The letters notifying friends and relatives of the death were written by a family member on black-bordered paper, sent in a black-bordered envelope, the thickness of the border calibrated to the position of the deceased, his relationship to the writer, and the time that had passed since the death. Sometimes, for recipients in poor health, regular envelopes were used to obviate the anxiety a black border brought. Otherwise using insufficiently thick borders, or decreasing the size of the borders too soon, was considered to indicate lack of feeling. A family in mourning was expected to give up all social life; calls were paid on them, but cards only were left, and the family saw only relations and the closest friends. Men soon returned to work, wearing their regular clothes with a black tie, and black arm- and hatbands. Women were more constrained, both in the types of clothes that were permitted, and in their social interaction.

For them, if a new black dress was financially viable, one was bought or made. For the prosperous, black alone was not enough to indicate their grief: the fabric had to be bombazine or crape, both fabrics with a dull finish. Glossy fabrics such as silk were inappropriate for the first period of mourning. If it was affordable, the entire wardrobe was dyed or a black wardrobe purchased, right down to the underwear (with black ribbons). Only a white indoor cap, collars and cuffs relieved the inky blackness. But many middle-class women found this expenditure impossible, and settled for black outerwear and 'best', while their daily clothes were simply old dresses dyed over. 'Deep', or 'first', mourning lasted a year, and a widow wore heavy crape for a year and a day (so she should not seem to be rushing to discard it); jewellery, apart from diamonds and pearls, or made from the hair of the deceased, was not worn. The widow removed some of the crape for 'second' mourning, and six to nine months later, with 'ordinary' mourning, any black fabric became acceptable, together with white, perhaps even with ribbons (black, of course), and jet jewellery. This is the progression observed by Dorothea Casaubon after her night vigil (*M*, ch. 80). At the end of two years, half-mourning began (one famous London shop specialising in mourning clothes called its half-mourning section the 'Mitigated Affliction Department'). Lilac, purple and grey were the colours of half-mourning-dress.

This was the standard pattern for widows mourning husbands, but there were endless variations: women mourning children wore first mourning for only six months; in an interesting indication of their respective importance, women mourning in-laws wore mourning for eighteen months. There were many lesser periods: parents mourning a son- or daughter-in-law's parent wore only ordinary mourning, and only for a month, while a second wife mourning the sibling of a first wife endured a mere six weeks in ordinary mourning.[6]

Many, however, rebelled at these infinitesimal gradations even at the height of the devotion to all things mourning. In *The Mill on the Floss*, Mrs Glegg warns that if her husband failed to leave her sufficient money she would 'cry no more than if he had been a second husband' (book 1, ch. 12); while in *Middlemarch*, Dorothea's maid Tantripp announces: 'if anybody was to marry me flattering himself I should wear those hijeous weepers [long white streamers attached to a widow's cap] two years for him, he'd be deceived by his own vanity, that's all'. Yet even she accepts that 'There's a reason in mourning … and three folds [of crape] at the bottom of your skirt … is what's consistent for a second year' (ch. 80).

Tantripp says what most people understood: as with all forms of etiquette, there were rules, and then there was what people really did.

NOTES

1 Anon., *Etiquette of Courtship and Matrimony: with a complete guide to the forms of a wedding* (London: Routledge, Warne & Routledge, *c.* 1865), pp. 8–9.
2 From an etiquette manual of the 1860s, cited in Leonore Davidoff, *The Best Circles: Society, Etiquette and the Season* (London: Croom Helm, 1973), p. 41.
3 Shirley Nicholson, *A Victorian Household*, rev. edn (Stroud: Sutton, 1994), p. 54.
4 Lady Jeune, *Lesser Questions* (London: Remington, 1894), p. 62.
5 *Sylvia's Home Journal*, cited in Alison Adburgham, *Shops and Shopping, 1800–1914: Where, and in What Manner, the Well-dressed Englishwoman Bought her Clothes*, rev. edn (London: George Allen & Unwin, 1981), p. 64.
6 'A Member of the Aristocracy', *Manners and Rules of Good Society, or, Solecisms to be Avoided* (London: Frederick Warne, 1887), pp. 222–8. Many books give similar but not identical prescriptions. Analogous codes applied to funerals: Thias Bede is interred with dignity but little ceremony before the usual church service on a Sunday (*AB*, ch. 18), while Peter Featherstone leaves copious written instructions for his elaborate funeral (*M*, ch. 34).

CHAPTER 14

Families and kinship

Josie Billington

George Eliot's lifetime saw the evolution of the English family into its modern 'nuclear' form, shaped by pressures exerted in a newly industrial age. On the one hand, an increase in mechanised production meant that work formerly undertaken by the family in its home environment was transferred to public locations (offices and factories); the male's wage-earning activities were separated from his wife's and children's domestic ones, and the model of the Victorian family became a structure of fragmented yet related networks.[1] On the other hand, the widespread dislocation from older traditions and institutions occasioned by unprecedented social and economic change itself contributed to the ideal of home and family as a refuge from the Malthusian chaos of the Victorian world and as a preserver of sustaining values. Concurrently, the function of the primary roles of family and society – mother, father, daughter, son – were being shaken and reviewed as the Christian worldview which had stabilised and guaranteed their meanings was dismantled both by growing political controversy around 'the Woman Question' and by the shift in scientific and intellectual paradigms engendered by Darwinian evolutionary theory. George Eliot's writing on family was taking place when its foundations were being revised in radical ways. Darwin's *The Origin of Species* (1859) proposed that humanity's heritage was not Paradise Lost, as recorded in *Genesis*, but evolutionary process.

Her most penetrating study of family, *The Mill on the Floss*, is a novelistic contribution to contemporary debates surrounding that institution. Published in 1860 and thus definitively 'Victorian', the novel is nonetheless set in the pre-Victorian era of George Eliot's own childhood and concentrates on the ante-industrial extended family model. This focus is clearly signalled in several of the titles considered for *The Mill on the Floss* during its composition. 'Sister Maggie', for example (referring to the novel's heroine, Maggie Tulliver), is a social as well as familial identifier and mode of address which (like 'brethren') belongs to an older, more settled world in which family relations were the basis and type of small-scale community ties. In the novel itself, 'The Tullivers' (another of the working titles – *L*, 3: 243–9) refers as much to a lineage, mindset and culture (often comically opposed to that of the 'Dodsons') as it does to the family who own, occupy and work the mill. Paradoxically, an older, more stable paradigm allows the novel to focus on the significance of the traditional *idea* of family in a post-religious age. Moreover, though often regarded as George Eliot's most autobiographically nostalgic novel, *The Mill* runs counter to Victorian idealisation of the family, by presenting the family not as a shelter from the outside world but as an obstacle to it. Family is a medium of limitation as palpably as is marriage in the author's later works. Most of the 'excesses' of behaviour attributed to the heroine Maggie Tulliver by her family – and the extended social family of St Ogg's in which she lives – are represented as the overflow of repressed intellectual and creative energies, most emphatically through the contrast between Maggie and her brother Tom. The 'naughtiness' that Mrs Tulliver criticises in her daughter she finds completely 'natural' in her son, Tom, and while Mr Tulliver enjoys the cleverness of Maggie – 'she's twice as 'cute as Tom' – he also wishes it away – 'Too 'cute for a woman I'm afraid' (book 1, ch. 2). Where unimaginative and conventional Tom is 'a man … and can do something in the world' (book 5, ch. 5), his vitally intelligent sister has no such opportunity for fulfilment in activities external to family – formal education, work, vocation. Her ambitions are expressed instead in intellectual, religious or emotional yearnings, as her talent seeks to discharge itself upon something commensurate with the needs of her burgeoning personality. Only orphaned Jane Eyre offers so complete a study of how deep the external constraints upon nineteenth-century woman penetrated, and no other Victorian heroine demonstrates that phenomenon entirely from within the bosom of a loving family.

But family is not simply a metonym for patriarchy in this novel. Maggie's sense of 'oppressive narrowness', asserts the narrator at the centre of the novel:

> has acted on young natures in many generations, that in the onward tendency of human things have risen above the mental level of the generation before them, to which they have been nevertheless tied by the strongest fibres of their hearts. The suffering, whether of martyr or victim, which belongs to every historical advance of mankind, is represented in this way in every town, and by hundreds of obscure hearths. (book 4, ch. 1)

Maggie's struggle belongs not to herself alone, but to a wider determining system, recognisably derived from Darwin's model of evolutionary development, whereby the very progress of the human species – the emergence of its 'fittest' for survival – is a result of the tensions created by familial and generational conflict. True to George Eliot's 'scientific' dictum of tracing 'great' human developments in 'the smallest things', the novel microscopically lays bare the complexity of this process as it is manifested at hearth level (book 4, ch. 1). For example, the catastrophe of the novel is Mr Tulliver's financial ruin (caused partly by his own obstinacy, partly by the wily tenacity of a shrewder business rival) which leaves him dangerously ill and the family at the mercy of the bailiffs. As Mrs Tulliver's 'feeble faculties' focus pitifully on the loss of her prized domestic possessions, Tom, for his part, is urged by the 'double stimulus' of the Dodsons' refusal to save his mother from shame and 'the sense that he must behave like a man and take care of his mother' to assert the 'natural strength and firmness of his nature'. The event which allows Tom's nature to emerge at its maximum practical best produces a Maggie whose situation renders her even more useless than her gender already makes her.

> The implied reproaches against her father – her father, who was lying there in a sort of living death – neutralised all her pity for griefs about table-cloths and china; and her anger on her father's account was heightened by some egoistic resentment at Tom's silent concurrence with her mother in shutting her out from the common calamity. She had become almost indifferent to her mother's habitual depreciation of her, but she was keenly alive to any sanction of it, however passive, that she might suspect in Tom. (book 3, ch. 2)

Apparently incidental words disclose Maggie's pity here, virtually buried as they are amid her 'mingled anger and grief': that the reproaches against her father are 'implied' rather than explicit; that the resentment which increases her fury is 'egoistic' more than it is just; that Tom's complicity with their mother is 'passive' more than vindictive are Maggie's implicit recognitions as much as they are the narrator's. George Eliot's characteristically subtle use of free indirect discourse is finely tuned to Maggie's more hidden heart fibres as well as to those 'keenly alive', and shows that there is a better Maggie here, as involuntarily and lovingly loyal to one parent's pain as to the other's. Yet Maggie, no more than her mother, can work free of 'habitual' emotional responses.

George Eliot's most famous statement of how 'mingled' are the biological and habit-formed logic of family love appeared in her first novel, *Adam Bede*.

> Family likeness has often a deep sadness in it. Nature, that great tragic dramatist, knits us together by bone and muscle, and divides us by the

> subtler web of our brains; blends yearning and repulsion; and ties us by our heartstrings to the beings that jar us at every movement. We hear a voice with the very cadence of our own uttering the thoughts we despise; we see eyes – ah! so like our mother's – averted from us in cold alienation; and our last darling child startles us with the air and gestures of the sister we parted from in bitterness long years ago. The father to whom we owe our best heritage – the mechanical instinct, the keen sensibility to harmony, the unconscious skill of the modelling hand – galls us and puts us to shame by his daily errors. (ch. 4)

The family relations idealised by her readership are here presented as symptomatic of a design flaw in human biological technology. Family likeness is the indubitable physical evidence of primary ties continuing beyond the complete loss of – or lapse into merely residual – personal significance; while, even thus, it is evolution's jarring reminder of family *difference.* George Eliot's most shockingly sudden illustration of this twist of natural law occurs in the opening chapter of *Felix Holt, the Radical* where Mrs Transome awaits the return after a long absence of her son Harold, 'the one great hope of her years':

> She heard herself called 'Mother!' and felt a light kiss on each cheek … Three minutes before, she had fancied that, in spite of all changes wrought by fifteen years of separation, she should clasp her son again as she had done at their parting; but in the moment when their eyes met, the sense of strangeness came upon her like a terror. (ch. 1)

'Hope' proves the wrong preparation for the moment when all hope is extinguished by the very physical proximity for which Mrs Transome has yearned. But it is not simply distance that has turned her son, she will realise, into a political radical in alienating betrayal of her own traditional conservatism. For that career path is itself a symptom of genetic loyalty to the biological father, of whom Mrs Transome has concealed all knowledge from her son: 'the likeness to herself was no longer striking, the years had overlaid it with another' (ch. 1). In a brilliant, Hardyesque tragic irony, Mrs Transome's secret literally stares her in the face – in the features of the son she treasures. Yet in George Eliot's work, irony is characteristically tempered by 'deep sadness' at the recognition that human beings, in their most primary relationships, are programmed to fall away from a unitary ideal even while continually preserving the memory of that oneness at the level of physical being – finding it 'knitted' into bone, muscle and heartstring. Humans are fallen creatures biologically 'tied' nonetheless to prelapsarian wholeness. So in Romola's often resentful sense of duty to her blind and aged father – whose 'likeness' of feature she bears while, as his reader and amanuensis, she also replaces his lost physical functions of hand and eye – there remains an uncorrupted hope, even 'belief': 'she hastened to lay the book on his lap, and kneeled down by him, looking up at him as if she believed that the love in her face must surely make its way through the dark obstruction that shut out everything else' (ch. 5). The father's irascibly borne affliction seems a literal symptom of his incapacity to see his own 'best heritage' tenderly put to use in his own behalf; the daughter's faith in love's power to penetrate, rather than simply compensate, for her father's blindness, shows an improvement on that 'best' which, however, can only increase her silent sense of gall and shame.

These failures of coherence between biology and evolved character strengthen the case for the greater efficacy of surrogate familial relationships in George Eliot's novels, which often provide more freedom and better fortune. When, for example, Romola – orphaned, widowed and childless – takes on a maternal role in relation to the inhabitants of a plague village and fulfils the role of father in relation to her husband Tito's illegitimate children by Tessa, she helps make amends for the instances of dereliction of parental duty which abound in the novel. So also in George Eliot's secular version of a Christian parable – the novella *Silas Marner* (written when *Romola* was already in gestation) – a type of the prodigal son, alienated (albeit unjustly) from home and family, is returned first to himself and thence to his adoptive community, Raveloe, where he brings up an abandoned infant girl as his own. 'As the child's mind was growing into knowledge, his mind was growing into memory: as her life unfolded, his soul, long stupefied in a cold narrow prison, was unfolding too, and trembling gradually into full consciousness' (*SM*, ch. 14). A reciprocally nurturing relationship, born of contingency rather than consanguinity, nonetheless corrects the biological malfunctioning which has left both deserted by blood relatives. In *The Mill on the Floss*, it is Philip, not Tom, who responds to Maggie's 'unsatisfied intelligence and … beseeching affection' (book 2, ch. 5). Together, they become 'brother and sister in secret' (book 5, ch. 4) in mutual fulfilment of emotional need: thus Philip – 'if you had had a brother like me, do you think you should have loved him as well as Tom?' (book 2, ch. 6); and Maggie – 'What a dear good brother you would have been Philip … You would have loved me well enough to bear with me, and forgive me everything. That was what I always longed that Tom should do' (book 5, ch. 3). Kinship substitution is written into the very syntax of this intercourse – where 'you [Maggie] should have loved me [Philip]' and 'You [Philip] would have loved me [Maggie]' is grammatically dependent on the conscious displacement of Tom, but still shadowed by what remains 'unsatisfied' by natural ties. These right feelings are demonstrably not in the right places. Yet this ideal shadow or 'might have been' still provides the model for the compensatory friendship which replaces that of natural kinship, just as the latter's syntax still rests on the deep grammar and primary you/me identity of brother–sister bonds and family love. In the case of Silas Marner, also, past 'memory' of family love makes possible his nurturing role in relation to little Eppie who occasions it: 'he had a dreamy feeling that this child was somehow a message come to him from that far-off life: it stirred fibres that had never been moved in Raveloe – old quiverings of tenderness' (ch. 12).

The evidence of George Eliot's oeuvre taken as a whole, in fact, is that such prototype family models are crucial to the success of mature relationships. 'When a marriage is conducted on a different basis [to the pseudo-sibling one], and the husband is nothing like a brother', the results are disastrous:[2] the failed marriages of Rosamond Vincy and Lydgate and Dorothea and Casaubon in *Middlemarch*; Dempster's abusive treatment of his wife in 'Janet's Repentance'; Tito's duplicity in *Romola*; Grandcourt's tyranny in relation to Gwendolen Harleth in *Daniel Deronda*. Conversely, those disasters are redeemed by relationships which (like that of Maggie and Philip) at once imitate sibling relationships and demonstrate their deficiencies. It seems another sad irony of the familial system that 'those who sit with us at the same hearth, are often the farthest off from the deep human soul within us … and in our moments of spiritual need, the man to whom we have no tie but our common nature, seems nearer to us than mother, brother or friend' ('Janet', ch. 16). Thus, in Dorothea's appeal to Lydgate from her own desperate marriage – 'Think what I can do' – Lydgate hears a 'cry from soul to soul', bespeaking their sharing of 'the same embroiled medium, the same troublous fitfully-illuminated life' (*M*, ch. 30), which is altogether missing from his wife Rosamond's icy rejection of his plea that they 'think … together' to address their domestic debt (ch. 58). Likewise, it is Dorothea who must do for Lydgate and Rosamond what they cannot do for one another or for themselves: Dorothea's trust in Lydgate, when his good character is impugned and his marriage and career fail, 'changes the lights' for him and (like a tiny miracle inside mundanity and waste) 'recovers' to him his real self (ch. 76); while the example and 'energy' of Dorothea's generosity surprise even Rosamond into a sisterly union in sorrow which transcends the narrow egoism of sexual jealousy:

'for a minute the two women clasped each other as if they had been in a shipwreck' (ch. 81). When Daniel becomes the insistent monitor and safeguard of Gwendolen's better self that she hardly knows she has, the sense of kinship is felt as a 'pressure' which hovers outside and above them: 'They both stood silent for a minute, as if some third presence had arrested them' (*DD*, ch. 36).

It is in these fleeting instances of 'common' fellowship that George Eliot's characters most completely embody the ideas of Ludwig Feuerbach, the philosopher whose work the author translated and whose influence she unequivocally acknowledged. In *The Essence of Christianity*, Feuerbach argued that religion was the result of an urgent need in humankind to objectify, in the form of a perfect transcendental being, the very best qualities and feelings of humanity itself. The virtues of charity, mercy, pity and moral judgement which humans had projected onto God were qualities and needs which belonged to humans themselves. The task for a secular world was to see that, as human nature was its highest value, so the love of humans for one another must be its first and highest law. Love honours and guarantees shared humanity while enjoining morally right thinking and conduct for the sake of the species: 'The other is my *thou* … my *alter ego*, man objective to me, the revelation of my own nature, the eye seeing itself.'[3] This is why when Dorothea believes in Lydgate or Daniel watches over Gwendolen as her externalised conscience, they embody secular versions of grace, as if substituting for the lost 'presence' of a witnessing and loving divinity. For Feuerbach as for George Eliot, all relations – of child and parent, husband and wife, brother and friend – were 'religious' because all potentially contributed to what is called in the 'Finale' to *Middlemarch* 'the growing good of the world'. Yet that large vision of human kinship which in George Eliot's work seeks to rescue and mend a world without God still has its foundation in the family piety of moments like this in *The Mill on the Floss*, where Mr Tulliver retracts his demand for the money owed to him by his brother-in-law: 'It had come across his mind that if he were hard upon his sister, it might somehow tend to make Tom hard upon Maggie at some distant day, when her father was no longer there to take her part' (book 1, ch. 8). For all Maggie's sense of limitation, the family is not against the individual but against egoism – the failure of 'I' to recognise 'thou'. The model of the wider human family which is offered by George Eliot's fiction as an evolutionary 'advance' on its biological paradigm also helps to recover the primary meaning and ideal value of the latter for a newly secular age.

NOTES

1 For a comprehensive overview see Philip Davis, *The Victorians* (*Oxford English Literary History*, vol. 8, 1830–80; Oxford University Press, 2002), pp. 13–54.
2 Valerie Sanders, *The Brother–Sister Culture in Nineteenth-Century Literature: from Austen to Woolf* (Basingstoke: Palgrave, 2002), p. 105.
3 Ludwig Feuerbach, *The Essence of Christianity*, trans. Marian Evans (1854; New York: Harper, 1975), p. 158.

CHAPTER 15

Gender and the Woman Question

Kyriaki Hadjiafxendi

George Eliot's career coincided with the campaign for improvement in women's rights which came to prominence in the 1850s and launched a high-profile public debate over the role and status of women, commonly referred to as 'the Woman Question'. However, her reluctance to engage directly with the vexed debates over the economic, political and legal status of women caused both suspicion of and disappointment with the gender politics of her work. This essay explores the controversial character of George Eliot's attempts to widen women's sphere, after her own fashion. Her uncertainty about the aims of nineteenth-century feminism played an important role in her wariness about the impact of direct forms of political commitment.

In a letter of 12 July 1877, George Henry Lewes describes a conversational exchange which reflects, in a number of contrary ways, George Eliot's awkward, individualistic, yet deep-seated understanding of the Woman Question:

> The other day at dinner Madonna [George Eliot] was talking with Bright about woman's suffrage, and the Princess Louise interposed with, 'But you don't go in for the superiority of women, Mrs Lewes?' 'No.' – 'I think,' said Huxley, 'Mrs Lewes rather teaches *the inferiority of men*.' (*L*, 6: 394)

This anecdote demonstrates George Eliot's association with a liberal intellectual elite for whom women's suffrage and other improvements in women's rights were a *cause célèbre*. Despite her reluctance to associate her name with female suffrage, she was close to several of the leaders of the growing nineteenth-century feminist movement, and in particular the Langham Place group – Barbara Leigh Smith, Bessie Rayner Parkes and Emily Davies – who campaigned from the 1850s onwards for the legal reform of women's property rights as well as for greater employment and educational opportunities. In 1854, she went so far as to sign and pass on to her friend, Sara Hennell, a copy of Leigh Smith's petition to support

Lord Cranworth's Married Women's Property Act, which was being contested throughout the 1850s. As the Divorce and Matrimonial Causes Act of 1857 began the slow process of opening up divorce proceedings, a woman's suit could not be brought on the basis of adultery alone but had to be compounded by abuse, incest or bigamy. It was not until 1870 that the first Married Women's Property Act would be passed to allow married women to hold property in their own name or to sign contracts.

George Eliot explored the vulnerability of women in marriage throughout her literary work, from *Scenes of Clerical Life* (1858) to her last novel *Daniel Deronda* (1876). She sympathised with the efforts of female educationalists like Jane Senior (*L*, 6: 46–7), Elizabeth Malleson (*L*, 5: 346) and Elizabeth Phelps (*L*, 6:317–19) to set up organisations such as Working Women's Colleges. She encouraged women's experimentation with the arts (*L*, 6: 108), medicine (*L*, 5: 209–10) and mathematics (*L*, 9: 300). Why then did Princess Louise doubt her commitment to promoting 'the superiority of women'? The fact that the question was asked indicates that even during her lifetime the strength of her commitment to women's rights was under scrutiny. Huxley's response is telling because, for George Eliot, gender could never be reduced to the Woman Question. With her commitment to a relational understanding of gender equality, she understood female enfranchisement as both a gender and a gendered question. For her the Woman Question was an already loaded term which made women, rather than patriarchal structures, the problem.

Contemporary scholars continue to grapple with George Eliot's reluctance to pronounce upon the Woman Question. Kate Flint, for example, asks 'why do many of her views concerning women, and the choices faced by women in her writings, seem to lack the boldness that might be expected – even desired – of her?'.[1] She echoes the complaints of second-wave feminists from the 1960s and 1970s such as Kate Millett and Ellen Moers who criticised George Eliot for neither giving her female characters a lifestyle as 'radical' as the one she shared with Lewes, nor carrying through her conventional personal choices into a public commitment to feminism.[2] Yet the dynamic of her relationship with Lewes is more complex than is sometimes realised. His reference to her by the pet name of Madonna in the anecdote quoted earlier conjures up associations of asexuality and ideality that are more disconcertingly traditional than might be expected given their intellectual and professional partnership.

Lewes's careful protection of George Eliot led to complaints of her being cosseted away from the pragmatics of life. Margaret Oliphant was one woman novelist to wonder, half-critically, half-enviously, 'Should I have done better if I had been kept, like her, in a mental greenhouse and taken care of?' – looked after by 'a caretaker and worshipper unrivalled – little nasty body though he [Lewes] looked.'[3] Lewes's ideological construction of George Eliot as a sibylline figure contributed to the mistrust of her social alienation which, together with her silence on the Woman Question, was seen as part of a more general political disengagement.

Oliphant's double-edged comment suggests that George Eliot's withdrawal from public life was a strategy that contributed to her literary success as a female author. Similarly, while George Eliot's use of a male pseudonym could be linked to the conservative notion of separate gendered spheres of public and private, her separation of her life from her work was an attempt to mediate her relationship with her readers. The sex of 'George Eliot' was always a key element in her reception, both confirming and confusing essentialist Victorian preconceptions regarding the gendered stylistics of writing. While Mrs Blackwood, Margaret Oliphant and W. M. Thackeray thought that 'George Eliot' was a man, Charles Dickens was convinced that 'he' was a woman because of the 'womanly touches' that a man did not have the art of making (*L*, 2: 424).

In the most generous interpretation, George Eliot's apparent lack of political activism stemmed from her artistic commitment. Tellingly, she makes her most forceful feminist strictures against Victorian gender inequalities and double standards in her pronouncements on the subject of fiction writing. It is here that she is at her most uncompromising. Her unwillingness to involve herself in practical agitation in support of the pursuit of a new legal dispensation for women was actually because of her conjoined commitment to her art and professional career. In early 1858, she turned down an offer from Bessie Rayner Parkes to contribute to the *English Woman's Journal* (1858–64), a newly founded periodical (to which she subscribed, however) intended to be the principal feminist campaign vehicle for issues such as women's property rights and employment opportunities.

George Eliot was at pains to explain to Parkes that her refusal to write for the *Journal* had nothing to do with its feminist aims but was due to the fact that she could not 'shilly-shally' about her new commitment, the writing of books:

> My negative about the writing has no special relation to the 'Englishwoman's Journal' but includes that and all other Reviews … I have given up writing 'articles,' having discovered that my vocation lies in other paths. In fact *entre nous*, I expect to be writing *books* for some time to come … It is a

> question whether I shall give up building my own house to go and help in the building of my neighbour's garden wall. (*L*, 2: 431)

George Eliot's dedication to fiction writing as her chosen vocation – implicitly a more rewarding calling than the unsigned reviewing she undertook in the first part of her career – marks her single-minded pursuit of her own professional, creative and personal self-fulfilment. Although in keeping with the aims of the emergent feminist movement in terms of widening woman's sphere, the individualism that motivated her pursuit of intellectual pleasure through her writing is open to the charge of misogyny because of its circumvention of feminist collectivity.

A letter of 4 October 1869 sets out the scope and limits of George Eliot's political engagement with the Woman Question. Her equivocation about egalitarian feminist politics is only partially tempered by her unwavering belief in the importance of female education, in this case through her support for Girton College:

> I feel too deeply the difficult complications that beset every measure likely to affect the position of women and also I feel too imperfect a sympathy with many women who have put themselves forward in connexion with such measures, to give any practical adhesion to them. There is no subject on which I am more inclined to hold my peace and learn, than on the 'Women Question'. It seems to me to overhang abysses, of which even prostitution is not the worst. Conclusions seem easy so long as we keep large blinkers on and look in the direction of our own private path.
>
> But on one point I have a strong conviction, and I feel bound to act on it, so far as my retired way of life allows of public action. And that is, that women ought to have the same fund of truth placed within their reach as men have; that their lives (i.e. the lives of men and women) ought to be passed together under the hallowing influence of a common faith as to their duty and its basis. And this unity in their faith can only be produced by their having each the same store of fundamental knowledge. It is not likely that any perfect plan for educating women can soon be found, for we are very far from having found a perfect plan for educating men. But it will not do to wait for perfection. (*L*, 5: 58)

George Eliot shared Barbara Bodichon's enthusiasm when London University opened all its degrees to women in 1878 (*L*, 7: 6). At the same time, she envisaged complexities and unintended consequences from female empowerment that her more radical contemporaries struggled to comprehend. She considered the benefits of alleviating prostitution and the sexual double standard to be set against unspecified dangerous consequences of reform. Her view that change should take place gradually contrasts with more impassioned treatment of the Woman Question by other woman writers. George Eliot's heroines may suffer frustrations similar to those of Charlotte Brontë, but they do not utter such audible cries as Jane Eyre's 'women feel just as men feel; they need exercise for their faculties, and a field for their efforts'.[4] The New Woman's casting aside of the sexual and social constraints of the past at the *fin-de-siècle* is a long way from George Eliot's incrementalism.

Taking herself to be an exception rather than the rule, George Eliot believed that mid-Victorian society did not provide the conditions under which women could easily find vocational or professional fulfilment. Doubting the tone of political certainty that characterised some of her contemporaries' questioning of the ideology of separate spheres, she could not see how the Parliamentary Acts promoting social and legal equality could transform Victorian women's existence in the short term. However, as she put it in a letter to John Morley in 1867, two years before John Stuart Mill's influential treatise *On the Subjection of Women*, 'I would certainly not oppose any plan … to establish … an equivalence of advantages for two sexes, as to education and the possibilities of free development' (*L*, 4: 364).

The deficiencies of women's education permeate her novels, as well as her reviews and poetry, which focus on the aesthetic, economic and moral constraints imposed upon middle-class women. In the last essay she wrote before embarking on writing fiction in 1856, she argued that women's education in social accomplishments put them in an unequal position to men, who were educated within a utilitarian culture that privileged reason over feeling. This is an idea that she reworked through the siblings Maggie and Tom Tulliver in *The Mill on the Floss* (1860), as well as in her 'Brother and Sister' sonnets (1869), which make the obvious point that gender inequality originates from boys' and girls' different schooling. Recently, Isobel Armstrong has pointed out that George Eliot's poems are 'preoccupied with women's artistic work, professionalism, celebrity, and consistently raise the question not only of women and the public sphere but seem also to be enquiring if a female public sphere is possible'.[5]

In *Middlemarch* (1872), the limitations of female education, and its consequent psychological and emotional damage, are poignantly unfolded through their contrasting impact upon the lives of Dorothea Brooke and Rosamond Vincy. At the beginning of the novel, Dorothea, fresh from her liberal education in Switzerland, idealistically embarks on a project to improve the lot of the local poor by building model cottages. However, when she tries to inspire Sir James Chettam with her plans, he pays only lip service to them as part of his attempted courtship. In Dorothea,

George Eliot created a heroine who not only has the 'impressiveness' of 'a fine quotation from the Bible', but who is also on a quest for her own 'ideal of life' in marriage, to give her access to the kind of knowledge she is denied as a woman (*M*, ch. 1). Unable to imagine herself as Abraham's self-sacrificing wife Sara, Dorothea's thirst for knowledge and grand designs for social change lead to her ill-fated match with Casaubon, the older scholar-priest who is busy working on his all-encompassing but hopelessly flawed publishing project, the 'Key to All Mythologies'.

Dorothea's experience parallels yet is also antithetical to that of Rosamond Vincy. Rosamond is educated at Mrs Lemon's, an institution where 'the teaching included all that was demanded in the accomplished female – even to extras, such as the getting in and out of a carriage' (*M*, ch. 11). Rosamond is the star pupil in skills of 'mental acquisition and propriety of speech, while her musical execution was quite exceptional' (ch. 11). Her education in genteel 'feminine' accomplishments is ruthlessly utilitarian in that it is wholly geared to the ultimate aim of acquiring a husband. Whereas Dorothea naively disregards all other considerations except for her desire for knowledge, Rosamond is uninterested in Lydgate's intellectual achievements except for the lustre they will add to her prospective marriage. Tellingly, George Eliot also shows Lydgate and Casaubon to be disenchanted by their marriages. For both, their misplaced scholarly endeavours, which focus on discerning one singular, universal answer rather than on understanding the interconnected nature of knowledge, are part of a broader patriarchal worldview that is linked to their desire for wives who fulfil the prevailing ideology. Lydgate, for example, relies 'much on the psychological difference between what for the sake of variety I will call goose and gander: especially on the innate submissiveness of the goose as beautifully corresponding to the strength of the gander' (ch. 36). Almost mercilessly, George Eliot shows up their deficiencies; indeed, their frustrations help to drive both Casaubon and Lydgate to premature graves. Dorothea learns that her grand ideals cannot but be tempered by the reality of the patriarchal social order and her position within it. Yet the end of the novel suggests that she still has agency through her small, selfless, diffusive works of sympathy in everyday life, by means of which 'knowledge passes instantaneously into feeling, and feeling flashes back as a new organ of knowledge' (ch. 22). George Eliot's lauding of sympathy as an antidote to the effects of social determinism captures a key aspect of her authorship which is integral to understanding her complex engagement with gender and the Woman Question: namely, her status as a realist writer. *Middlemarch* is here instructive in that her 'Study of Provincial Life' aims to demonstrate that there is no person 'whose inward being is so strong that it is not greatly determined by what lies outside it' ('Finale').

What are the consequences of this overarching commitment to the determining effect of material and social circumstances? Like Maggie in *The Mill on the Floss*, Dorothea learns of her interconnectedness to the world outside herself, yet this knowledge comes at a price in that she cannot escape the limitations of women's conventional roles. Her aspirations to achieve grand schemes – after the model of Spanish mystic and founder of religious communities, St Theresa of Avila (1515–82) – have been modified by circumstances. Dorothea ends supporting her new husband, Will Ladislaw, in his career as a Member of Parliament striving to improve the public good. The narrator poignantly reflects: 'Many who knew her thought it a pity that so substantive and rare a creature should have been absorbed into the life of another, and be only known in a certain circle as a wife and mother. But no one stated exactly what else that was in her power she ought rather to have done' ('Finale').

George Eliot's commitment to a realist aesthetic based on capturing the slow, organic unfolding of the everyday arguably works against the portrayal of grand, revolutionary gestures that might take forward the Woman Question. While Dorothea's fate exemplifies the political limits of George Eliot's realism, her quest for a kind of art capable of extending sympathy needs to be considered in terms of her commitment to what she saw as its ethical and social potential. For George Eliot as for Lewes, the power of the artist stems from the ability to create scenes in which characters and readers can feel themselves in the position of 'the other'.[6] As E. S. Dallas discerned in his review of *Felix Holt, the Radical*:

> The secret of her power is to be found in the depth and the range of her sympathies. She gets to the heart of her characters, and makes us feel with them, care for them, like to know about them. Even if they are stupid people who lead dull lives, she has the happy art of making us take an interest in their story and wish to hear it out.[7]

George Eliot's ethical and aesthetic attachment to sympathy needs to be understood as part of her attempt to overcome the gendered dichotomy between reason and emotion. Her questioning of her contemporaries' preconceptions about the gendering of writing was undermined partly by the inherent contradiction of trying to reconcile these binary opposites. Yet in spite of how frequently the ethics of sympathy break down in her literary work, she held to the belief that it had long-term potential for socio-political reform, and sympathy became the means through which she tried to resolve the battle of the sexes. It is perhaps in her attempt to develop through sympathy a cognitive aesthetic of feeling that the most dynamic aspect of her engagement with gender and the Woman Question lies. In a letter, she argued:

> My function is that of the *aesthetic*, not the doctrinal teacher – the rousing of the nobler emotions, which make mankind desire the social right, not the prescribing of special measures, concerning which the artistic mind, however strongly moved by social sympathy, is often not the best judge. (*L*, 7: 44)

Perhaps both the strength and weakness of George Eliot's quest for a cognitive aesthetic of feeling, by which she attempted to turn emotion into knowledge, and sympathetic identification into critical understanding, is its lack of immediate social applicability. Her political disengagement from the Woman Question is correspondingly liable always to be regarded with frustration. For better and for worse, George Eliot refused to be bound by the terms of its vexed debates over the economic, legal and socio-political status of women.

NOTES

1 Kate Flint, 'George Eliot and Gender', in George Levine (ed.), *The Cambridge Companion to George Eliot* (Cambridge University Press, 2001), p. 160.
2 Kate Millett, *Sexual Politics* (New York: Doubleday, 1970), p. 139; Ellen Moers, *Literary Women* (Garden City, NY: Doubleday, 1976), p. 194.
3 Elisabeth Jay (ed.), *The Autobiography of Margaret Oliphant: The Complete Text* (Oxford University Press, 1990), p. 15.
4 Charlotte Brontë, *Jane Eyre* (1847; Sally Shuttleworth (ed.), Oxford World's Classics, Oxford University Press, 2000), p. 109.
5 Isobel Armstrong, 'Preface', in Kyriaki Hadjiafxendi (ed.), *The Cultural Place of George Eliot's Poetry*, Special Issue of *George Eliot–George Henry Lewes Studies*, 60–1 (2011), 4.
6 George Henry Lewes, 'Of Vision in Art' (July 1865), in Rosemary Ashton (ed.), *Versatile Victorian: Selected Writings of George Henry Lewes* (London: Bristol Press), p. 239.
7 E. S. Dallas, 'Review of *Felix Holt, the Radical*', in Stuart Hutchinson (ed.), *George Eliot: Critical Assessments* (Mountfield: Helm Information, 1996), p. 221.

CHAPTER 16

Historiography

Joanne Wilkes

A preoccupation with history, and especially the growing tendency to fix on the interpretation of the past as a vital source for understanding the present, was identified during the first third of the nineteenth century by two writers who were to become two of the period's most influential thinkers. In 1830 Thomas Carlyle (1795–1881), an author George Eliot much admired, declared in his essay 'On History' that 'the Past is the true fountain of knowledge', such that people 'do nothing but enact History' and 'say little but recite it'; for, he asks, 'what is all Knowledge but recorded Experience, and a product of History?'[1] A year later John Stuart Mill (1806–73) observed that comparing the present age with former ages and ages yet to come had become the 'dominant idea' of his own age.[2]

The words of Carlyle and Mill came at a time of great political turbulence in Britain, when campaigns for reform of the electoral system were at their height. The central demand was for an extension of the suffrage, so that more middle-class and urban-dwelling men would be enfranchised, thus (it was thought) reducing the political power of the rurally based aristocracy and gentry. But this impulsion towards change, which resulted in the Reform Bill of 1832, simultaneously encompassed a wider discontent with the status quo, and was the prelude to working-class demands for greater political power.

Such developments reflected a widespread experience – not only at this pressure point, but also before and after – of social changes that were unprecedentedly rapid, and often disconcerting and disruptive. Mechanical inventions had led to the creation of factories and factory work, transforming the landscape as well as employment practices. As manufacturing expanded in towns and cities, too, at the expense of rurally based employment, there was a significant shift of population from country to urban areas, with attendant problems of overcrowding, social dislocation and bad hygiene. Also significant was the development of the railways, which further transformed the landscape, and made travel between different parts of the country far easier and quicker than ever before.

These social changes are well known; their relevance here is that they fostered the increasing importance attached to investigating the past, a preoccupation which continued through the nineteenth century. Where change was so swift and so bewildering, people believed that comprehending the past could provide some anchorage, some sense of the salient events and trends that had led to the present: perhaps some guidance, therefore, for the future.

George Eliot's novels, apart from *Daniel Deronda*, are set a generation or more before the time of writing. The historical setting is clear in *Romola*, where the events take place in the fifteenth century; nowadays, however, the fact that the other novels relate to the past is not so obvious. But *Adam Bede* and *Silas Marner* are set around the turn of the nineteenth century, while 'Mr Gilfil's Love Story' from *Scenes of Clerical Life* takes us back into the last decades of the eighteenth century. The late 1820s into the 1830s – that period of notable political turbulence – was of particular interest to George Eliot, and was one she explored from the vantage point of a generation later. This period is the setting of 'Amos Barton' and 'Janet's Repentance' (from *Scenes of Clerical Life*) and *The Mill on the Floss*, as well as of the later novels *Felix Holt, the Radical* and *Middlemarch*, which pay much attention to the implications of political reform.

Mill's comments in 'The Spirit of the Age', nevertheless, pointed not only to social changes, but also to a crucial revolution in 'the human mind'.[3] Intellectual developments over George Eliot's lifetime were significant as regards the conceptions of history which influenced her writing. Especially important in her case was 'Higher Criticism', which examined the Bible, and particularly the life of Christ, as products of human history rather than of divine revelation. Her labour in translating D. F. Strauss's *The Life of Jesus* (1846) and Ludwig Feuerbach's *The Essence of Christianity* (1854) consolidated her shift from the Anglican faith of her youth, and was supplemented by that of the Positivist theories of the French writer Auguste Comte and his 'Religion of Humanity'. For George Eliot, the overall implication of these intellectual trends was that the focus of human beings' aspirations and activities should be the welfare of their fellow men and women.

Historical criticism of the Bible, together with other contemporary intellectual movements (notably, of course, the theory of evolution), contributed to the prevalent interest in history, even when they did not undermine people's Christian faith. Yet George Eliot's fiction not only examines the past, but does so without any underlying belief in the Providential ordering of events. Developments in the lives of her characters, or in the periods between their lives and the time of writing, cannot be attributed to the guidance of any plan of divine origin, as is the case in the novels of contemporaries such as Dickens and Charlotte Brontë. This circumstance has generated much critical interest in the issue of how George Eliot's fiction treats causality. How far, for example, do her novels bear out her declaration, in her early review (1851) of R. W. Mackay's *The Progress of the Intellect*, that we must recognise 'the presence of undeviating law in the material and moral world', that is, the 'inexorable law of consequences' (*Essays*, 31)? How much control does the individual have over his or her own life? And what forces govern larger historical developments, the transition from one period to the next?

These questions were explored on a philosophical scale by a German theorist of history well known to George Eliot, G. W. F. Hegel (1770–1831), who had also been an influence on both Strauss and Feuerbach. According to Hegel, history as events (*res gestae*) was a mixture of interconnected mental and physical developments governed by Spirit (*Geist*), a free entity that he saw as opposed to Matter. The course of history shows the mind's progress towards perfect self-consciousness and towards awareness of the interconnection between self and world. Spirit in its present form, too, still encompasses all its pre-existing stages. In Hegel's view, the role of history as written (*historia rerum gestarum*) is crucial, since it offers a people a representation of their own image. Moreover, since the past is organically linked to the present, expressing a coherent interpretation of this connection for the benefit of present readers is a vital task for the historian.[4]

Hegel's conceptions of history, then, suggested that its course was fundamentally progressive, but that links with the past were always implicit in the present. Nineteenth-century British treatments of history, however, were often quite politicised. A focus on valorising the past tended to reflect a politically conservative orientation, while the 'Whig' view of history stressed political progress, conceived of as the gradual extension of political liberties. The extent to which George Eliot's novels imply that historical change is generally progressive is a complex one, and has been the subject of much critical debate. So some sense of the British intellectual context of her time is useful.

The key thinkers of a conservative orientation were Edmund Burke (1729–97) and Samuel Taylor Coleridge (1772–1834). Burke's *Reflections on the Revolution in France*, although published in 1790, remained well known through the next century, and influenced Coleridge's 1830 treatise, *On the Constitution of Church and State*. Burke opposed the Revolution, partly because it aimed to effect a radical and violent transformation of society by uprooting and destroying long-established customs and institutions. These customs and institutions were by no means perfect, he argued, yet they possessed some beneficial aspects, not least the feelings they were capable of arousing; the destruction of some elements, moreover, put the rest at risk. Hence what was desirable was gradual growth, a notion based on a conception of society as an organism. This 'organic' view of society was also central to the theories of Coleridge.

This way of conceptualising society is especially evident in a passage from an essay George Eliot wrote in 1856 (just before she began to publish fiction) – 'The Natural History of German Life'. Reviewing two books by the German cultural historian W. H. von Riehl that focus on the history of the German peasantry, she criticised the tendencies of social theorists to idealise the working classes and to promote radical social change on that basis. By contrast, she praises Riehl for recognising that European society is '*incarnate history*', and thus cannot be disengaged from this history without destroying its 'social vitality'. This is because what 'has grown up historically can only die out historically', and

> [t]he external conditions which society has inherited from the past are but the manifestation of inherited internal conditions in the human beings who compose it; the internal conditions and the external are related to each other as the organism and its medium, and development can only take place by the gradual consentaneous development of both. (*Essays*, 287)

The other major trend in British historiography, the politically liberal or Whig approach, while neither advocating radical change nor unmindful of the views of Burke and Coleridge, was more sanguine about the progressive development of British society. The leading figure here was Thomas Babington Macaulay (1800–59), formerly a prominent Whig politician: the successive volumes of his *History of England* appeared in 1848 and 1855, and were immensely popular. Macaulay's stance, as he expressed it at the beginning of his *History*, was that 'the history of our country during the last one hundred and sixty years is eminently the history of physical, of moral, and of intellectual improvement'.[5] So, as well as tracing what he saw as the expansion of political liberty, Macaulay included in his account several set-pieces where he compared a scene as it appeared in the present very favourably with the same scene as he imagined it in the late seventeenth century.

Macaulay's *History* was based on copious research, plus extensive travels throughout England. A significant development in nineteenth-century historiography was the emphasis on detailed and wide-ranging research. This included consulting original archival sources, an activity pioneered, like so much else, by German historians. In Britain official records became more organised and accessible over the century, while history gradually became more of a professional scholarly discipline. Whereas University chairs in history at Oxford and Cambridge had once been held by gifted amateurs, and the subject was not included in the regular curriculum, in 1873 History at Oxford became a separate subject from Law, and at Cambridge it was severed from Moral Sciences in 1875. The appointment of William Stubbs to the Regius Chair of History at Oxford in 1866 was a watershed, because of his scholarly editing of eighteen medieval texts for the Rolls series, and the later publication of his monumental *Constitutional History of England* (1874–8).

The focus on detailed research reflected, too, a concern that the lives of people in the past should be registered as embedded in that past, and thus as affected by its conditions – that is, not seen solely through the lens of the present. The greatest German historian of the nineteenth century, Leopold von Ranke (1795–1886), was adamant that the historian should strive to be impartial, avoiding the temptation for the prejudices of the present to colour his approach to the past. For George Eliot, it was important not to idealise the past so as to lambast the present as a sad falling-off – something she criticised Charles Kingsley for doing in his novel *Westward Ho!*, set in the Elizabethan period (*Essays*, 127). Nor, however, should we consider the past in a 'smiling survey of human folly', she wrote during the composition of *Romola*, her most comprehensively researched novel (*L*, 3: 437). There were similarities between people of the past and those of the present, but in order to perceive 'identity of nature under variety of manifestation', she argued in her review of Mackay, the historian's mind had to possess a 'susceptibility to the pleasure of changing its point of view, of mastering a remote form of thought' (*Essays*, 29). What her novels constantly do is invite readers to enter into the circumstances and mental parameters of characters living in the past, to comprehend the differences between these figures and themselves, and then to perceive what they and these characters may actually have in common.

George Eliot's research for *Romola* was such that her partner G. H. Lewes remarked that she had come to know 'immensely more' about fifteenth-century Florence than any other writer on the subject (*L*, 3: 474).

Such a comment points to the conscientiousness of her approach to history – but also to the permeable boundary between history and fiction at the time. The key figure here was Sir Walter Scott (1771–1832). His novels are set in historical periods ranging from the recent past (like most of George Eliot's), such as *Waverley; or, 'Tis Sixty Years Since* (1814), *Guy Mannering* (1815) and *Redgauntlet* (1824), to those set back in the Middle Ages, such as *Ivanhoe* (1819) and *Quentin Durward* (1823). Scott's novels were extremely popular throughout the nineteenth century, and probably contributed more than any historical work to readers' assumptions about British history. Scott was in fact a major influence on Macaulay: although Macaulay's *History* concentrated on political developments, he essayed in his third chapter a social panorama of English life in the late seventeenth century, having learned from Scott (as he had put it back in 1828), that the historical developments that had the greatest impact on most people were not political or military events.[6] He also modelled his vivid and dynamic style on Scott, so that his *History* owed part of its success to its 'novelistic' qualities.

George Eliot was an enthusiast for Scott's novels, from the time when, in her youth, they contributed to unsettling her evangelical fervour because he was 'healthy and historical' (*L*, 9: 330), and she cites them often in her fiction, letters and essays. In particular, his novels suggested ways of demonstrating how the thoughts, feelings and behaviour of characters might be conditioned by historically specific circumstances, while at the same time be recognised by readers as resembling their own.

The specifics of historical circumstances and of historically located communities were important to George Eliot, a concern she owes partly to Scott. As the essay on Riehl shows, she was very dubious about generalisations, and praised the German historian for his personal and detailed familiarity with the various communities he wrote about. It is notable, for example, that, although *Adam Bede* and *Silas Marner* are both set in rural areas in the early years of the nineteenth century, the people of Hayslope in *Adam Bede* show some awareness of public events, whereas the Raveloe villagers of the later novel are much more isolated and hence uninformed, while old-fashioned superstitions linger there too.

Another aspect of contemporary historiography which is important in considering George Eliot's novels is the issue of how far significant changes can be attributed to the actions and influence of individuals. The notion of 'laws' governing historical developments, suggested in her review of Mackay, was an increasingly prevalent one: if the physical and natural sciences manifested the operation of laws, then might this also be the case with the social sciences? Such an assumption tended to downplay the impact of individual 'great men'. On the other hand, Carlyle, especially in his *On Heroes, Hero-Worship and the Heroic in History* (1841), championed the achievements of individuals, declaring that 'the history of what man has accomplished in this world is at bottom the History of the Great Men who have worked here'.[7]

George Eliot's novels do not deal with 'great men' in the sense of the renowned individuals of history, except for Savonarola in *Romola.* But they do focus on fictional individual men, and, scanning the recent past, the novels pose questions about the role played in historical change by men of talent and strong ethics, such as Adam Bede, Felix Holt, and Caleb Garth in *Middlemarch* – imagined as figures possibly representative of other obscure but conscientious workers for the benefit of their communities. And in a figure like *Middlemarch*'s Tertius Lydgate, George Eliot investigates the reasons why the potential for good and progressive achievement may remain unfulfilled.

Finally, one dimension of the past and its actual or potential legacy which was seldom considered in nineteenth-century historiography was the possible contribution of women. George Eliot's novels pay attention to the fates of women, and, since they seem to convey mixed messages, this aspect of her fiction has been a major focus of critical attention since the 1970s. What did Romola achieve in her historical locale? What is implied when Dinah Morris in *Adam Bede* is prevented from continuing her preaching career? If Maggie Tulliver represents the most advanced form of consciousness in St Ogg's, what is the significance of her death at the end of *The Mill on the Floss*? Esther Lyon chooses rightly in rejecting the corrupt Harold Transome for the morally upright Felix Holt, but does this choice exhaust her potential? Most intriguingly, perhaps, what does it mean that Dorothea Brooke in *Middlemarch*, living in that historically resonant period of the Reform movement, ends up living an 'unhistoric' life?

NOTES

1 'On History', *Fraser's Magazine* (1830), repr. Chris R. Van de Bossche (ed.), Thomas Carlyle, *Historical Essays* (Berkeley, CA and London: University of California Press, 2002), p. 4.

2 'The Spirit of the Age – I', *Examiner* (9 January 1831), repr. Ann P. Robson and John M. Robson (eds.), *The Works of John Stuart Mill* (University of Toronto Press, 1986), vol. XXII, p. 228.

3 Ibid.

4 Hegel's thought and its impact on George Eliot are discussed in Valerie A. Dodd, *George Eliot: An Intellectual Life* (Basingstoke: Macmillan, 1990), pp. 120–8; and Avrom Fleishman, *George Eliot's Intellectual Life* (Cambridge University Press, 2010), e.g. pp. 60 and 82.

5 Thomas Babington Macaulay, repr. Charles Harding Firth (ed.), *History of England* (London: Macmillan, 1913), vol. 1, p. 2.

6 'History', *Edinburgh Review*, 47 (1828), 331–67, repr. *The Miscellaneous Writings of Lord Macaulay* (London: Longman, Green, Longman and Roberts, 1860), vol. 1, pp. 275–8.

7 Michael Goldberg *et al.* (eds.), *On Heroes, Hero-Worship, and the Heroic in History* (1841; Berkeley, CA and London: University of California Press, 1993), p. 3.

CHAPTER 17

Industry and technology

Richard Menke

George Eliot wrote at a time when the changes wrought by technologies such as steam engines and the electric telegraph had reshaped everyday life in Great Britain and were becoming dramatically visible in the landscape of cities and the countryside. Her biography suggests her interest and experience with new technologies, from her railway journeys and visit to the 1851 Great Exhibition in London – an international showcase for modern manufacturing and commerce – to a special tour of Bell's new London telephone office in 1878, after which she pronounced the telephone 'very wonderful, very useful' (*L*, 7: 16n).

During most of George Eliot's lifetime, the innovation that seemed to make life modern was above all steam power. In the early eighteenth century, Thomas Newcomen had invented an engine in which steam condensation created a vacuum to move a piston. A half-century later, James Watt designed vastly improved and more efficient engines, and over the next decades he and others continued to increase their power and flexibility, so that steam power found more and more uses in mining, manufacture (including printing) and transportation. Cotton cloth production became the signature application of steam in manufacturing, especially after the adoption of the power loom in the early nineteenth century. Yet other industries such as iron production also expanded rapidly in the age of steam, and even traditional industries such as glass manufacture grew quickly.[1] In *Middlemarch*, Will Ladislaw satirically claims to be working on a painting that will represent the conqueror Tamburlaine as an allegory for the power of 'the world's physical history' – that is, 'earthquakes and volcanoes' (as Dorothea suggests) but also 'migrations of races and clearings of forests – and America and the steam-engine' (ch. 22).

Industrial change could represent not just dizzying economic expansion but also human misery: dangerous factory work, with low wages and irregular employment, and dire conditions for workers in overcrowded cities. Most famously, there was the plight of the handloom weavers, their craft rendered obsolete by use of the power loom, which could be run by poorly paid, unskilled operators – a situation that inspired sabotage and machine breaking. Moreover, industrial growth supplanted the seasonal rhythms of agriculture with the boom-and-bust cycles of the nineteenth-century economy, and brought confrontations between labour and capital. In 1848, the philosopher and economist John Stuart Mill found it 'questionable' whether 'all the mechanical inventions yet made have lightened the day's toil of any human being'. Although innovations had permitted 'manufacturers and others to make large fortunes' and had 'increased the comforts of the middle classes', Mill concluded that their effect on labour was to allow 'a greater population to live the same life of drudgery and imprisonment'.[2]

The growth of industrial manufacturing coalesced with other changes in agriculture, demographics and economic ideologies, and helped produce the sense of a distinctly modern daily life in Britain, even outside London (now the largest city in history) and the industrial districts clustered in the North, the Midlands and Scotland. Furthermore, during George Eliot's lifetime a variety of astonishing technologies were invented or improved for widespread use: gas lighting, the daguerreotype and paper photography (she never liked photographs of herself), the railway, the electric telegraph, the sewing machine, brilliant aniline dyes, the Bessemer process for making steel. By the 1870s, the methodical development of new technologies such as the telephone, phonograph and incandescent lighting demonstrated how invention itself had become a systematic, industrialised process.

Daniel Deronda – with the casual use of railways, steamships and telegrams that aids its cosmopolitan plot – and *Impressions of Theophrastus Such* are set in 'this age of steam' (*DD*, ch. 15), while *Romola* imagines pre-industrial life in Renaissance Florence. But apart from these works, George Eliot's major fiction turns again and again to the era that has come to be called the Industrial Revolution, and to a region associated with it. *Scenes of Clerical Life*, *Adam Bede*, *Silas Marner*, *The Mill on the Floss*, *Felix Holt* and *Middlemarch* are set in the late eighteenth or early nineteenth century, in the English Midlands where Mary Anne Evans was born and raised. In a broad sense, we might identify one of George Eliot's great subjects in these works as the moral crises generated as modernity makes itself felt in the Midlands. Yet, despite her commitment to treating individual lives alongside social developments, the alterations brought by the era's industrial and technological changes might at first glance hardly seem to impinge on much of this fiction.

Silas Marner is a handloom weaver whose story spans the time when the power loom relegated a labouring elite to unemployment and penury. In *Middlemarch*, the curate of Lowick complacently assures Dorothea that the parish includes 'no looms here, no Dissent' from the Church of England (ch. 9); Silas's occupation and religious background are bywords for social unrest. In real life, Silas's work on linen would have insulated him from the power loom's impact. But in historical terms, there is ample reason why in the century's 'early years' wandering weavers might strike rural observers as 'pallid undersized men … remnants of a disinherited race', as Silas Marner's opening sentence declares (ch. 1).

Silas Marner highlights the weaver's work, especially 'the monotony of his loom and the repetition of his web', and sends him from a Northern industrial town, where he is part of the religious and artisanal community of Lantern Yard, to exile in the village of Raveloe (ch. 14). This scenario could sketch out a story about the human effects of industrialism and technology. But Silas's banishment is not economic but personal; he has been wrongly blamed for a theft, betrayed by a friend, and traduced by the drawing of lots in which God was supposed to reveal the guilty. In the story's final pages, an elderly Silas makes a return visit to Lantern Yard only to find the place and its inhabitants vanished, replaced by 'a large factory' (ch. 21). Yet even this development confirms not the industrial transformation of towns and trades so much as the supplanting of Silas's bitter past by living ties to his adopted daughter Eppie.

In other works, too, George Eliot seems to presuppose the impact of industry or technology but to sidestep the specific issues they might raise. *Felix Holt, the Radical* is often considered her version of the early Victorian 'industrial novel', fiction that sought to represent class conflict in a Britain of factories and trade unions. But in *Felix Holt*, that Britain seems to exist largely in the periphery, especially when compared to works such as Elizabeth Gaskell's *Mary Barton* (1848) and *North and South* (1854–5) or Charles Dickens's *Hard Times* (1854). Felix renounces medical study and class mobility not by working in a factory or mine but by mending watches. And *Felix Holt*'s social plot, along with its working-class riot (an industrial novel's characteristic climax), revolves around not industrial conflict but the first election after the 1832 Reform Bill. In the plot of George Eliot's industrial novel, the Industrial Revolution hardly seems to register.

Set just before the action of *Felix Holt*, *Middlemarch* incorporates the 'infant struggles of the railway system' to reach the town but carefully presents a society just on the verge of that change (*M*, ch. 56). As a textile manufacturer, Mr Vincy is 'one of those who suck the life out of the wretched handloom weavers in Tipton and Freshitt', quips Mrs Cadwallader (ch. 34). Speechifying before Middlemarch's 'weavers and tanners', Mr Brooke inanely assures them: 'It won't do, you know, breaking machines' (ch. 51). But the main plots of *Middlemarch* seem little troubled by the fate of the weavers, or the new dye that rots Mr Vincy's silk; the novel might almost echo Rosamond Vincy's reply to worries about the dissolution of Parliament and 'machine-breaking everywhere': 'what can that have to do with my marriage?' (ch. 36). Yet at the deepest level, *Middlemarch* asserts the connections between industry and the lives of characters in its famous invocations of the web, an image that describes not only an organic society but a woven textile – or a railway network.

If we didn't know that an industrial revolution was happening in the Midlands and North of England in the early nineteenth century, it might be difficult to discover this from the tale of Silas the weaver, the 'industrial' concerns of *Felix Holt* or the web of *Middlemarch*. These works might remind us that the concept of the Industrial Revolution was widely popularised only after George Eliot's time, by Arnold Toynbee's *Lectures on the Industrial Revolution in England* (1884). Before Toynbee, British writers by no means took it for granted that there was a particular historical development called the Industrial Revolution with a specific setting, significance and effects.[3] Furthermore, in the early nineteenth century the word 'industry' itself retained some overtones of 'effort' or 'industriousness', although its dominant sense was confirmed by the coinage of 'industrialism' by the philosopher and historian Thomas Carlyle. And the term 'technology', which links innovation to science, was unusual enough in mid-Victorian Britain for George Wilson, the holder of the country's first technology professorship, to use his inaugural lecture to define the word, claiming that he could only find it in a single dictionary; the commoner term would have been 'industrial (or 'useful') arts'.[4]

Rather than treating industrial change as having created a revolution, some of the most influential writers of George Eliot's time centred their social criticism on the abstract idea of the machine as a symbol of contemporary life. In their work, issues of technology or industry often seem secondary to the invocation of 'machines' and 'machinery' as figures for what Carlyle in his 1829 essay 'Signs of the Times' had dubbed 'The Mechanical Age', an era of standardisation and contrivance in material production and human affairs alike. Matthew Arnold's *Culture and Anarchy* (1869) echoes this critique, decrying reliance on material tokens of progress – 'coal' and 'railroads' but also 'wealth', 'freedom' and even 'religious organisations' – as so much 'faith in machinery'.[5]

George Eliot's work seems largely removed from such broad attacks on social machinery. Instead, her fiction treats the period soon to be called the Industrial Revolution as a critical transition to modernity, emphasising the vital relationships between the present and the vanished past, as well as the practical integration of new advances into daily life. Her upbringing would have reinforced her sense of this integration. The Arbury Estate, where her father worked as manager and where she was born, included farms but also a coal mine; handloom weavers worked in the Arbury villages.[6] A passage from Cross's *Life* may overstate the split but aptly suggests its result: 'Her roots were down in the pre-railroad, pre-telegraphic period – the days of fine old leisure – but the fruit was formed during an era of extraordinary activity in scientific and mechanical discovery. Her genius was the outcome of these conditions' (Cross, 1: 10). In Eliot's fiction, industrial change at most appears as revolutionary in retrospect, in part because its transformations are inextricably bound with the lives of characters and communities. *Silas Marner* illustrates this approach when it reveals a transformed industrial town, and the disappearance of an entire labouring community, as the corollary for a weaver's changed emotional life.

A similar intertwining of machinery and emotion marks *The Mill on the Floss*, a novel named for a setting that is also a classic piece of industrial equipment. Maggie and Tom's uncle Deane credits steam power as the essential force of modernity. Yet his reflections interweave steam's physical power with its implications for daily life:

> the world goes on at a smarter pace now than it did when I was a young fellow. Why, sir, forty years ago, when I was much such a strapping youngster as you, a man expected to pull between the shafts the best part of his life, before he got the whip in his hand. The looms went slowish, and fashions didn't alter quite so fast ... It's this steam, you see, that has made a difference: it drives on every wheel double pace, and the wheel of fortune along with 'em. (book 6, ch. 5)

Deane's views tie the power of steam to generational change and to the lives of the young as they make their way in the world – that is, to the defining concerns of a *Bildungsroman* such as *The Mill on the Floss*.

Earlier in the novel, uncle Deane speculated about how 'business' at Dorlcote Mill 'might be increased by the addition of steam-power', for one of the characteristic uses of steam was to supplement wind- or water-power at existing factories and mills (book 3, ch. 7). *The Mill on the Floss* echoes this paradigm on a larger scale. Steeped in images of water from its opening line to its last catastrophe, the novel nevertheless represents the intense psychology of its characters in terms of steam and heat: Tom seems 'as close as an iron biler' as he sits 'a-lookin' at the fire' (book 6, ch. 4); after visiting the inside of the mill, Maggie's 'dark eyes flash out with new fire' (book 1, ch. 4). The novel explains its focus on the Tullivers by comparing the 'histor[ies] of unfashionable families' to the coarse industries and painful work that sustain upper-class life:

> good society, floated on gossamer wings of light irony, is of very expensive production; requiring nothing less than a wide and arduous national life condensed in unfragrant deafening factories, cramping itself in mines, sweating at furnaces, grinding, hammering, weaving under more or less oppression of carbonic acid – or else, spread over sheepwalks, and scattered in lonely houses and huts. (book 4, ch. 3)

In the final encounter between the unfashionable Tullivers and 'huge fragments' of 'wooden machinery', *The Mill on the Floss* follows out the terms of this comparison (book 7, ch. 5).[7]

As George Eliot recognised, the new technologies of her time shaped not only the 'production' of society but also how one observes it. 'Janet's Repentance' (the final story in *Scenes of Clerical Life*) contrasts the sight of the fictional Milby 'more than a quarter of a century' ago, when a coach passenger would have found 'a dingy-looking town, with a strong smell of tanning up one street, and a great shaking of handlooms up another', with its appearance to a modern observer who views Milby from a 'handsome railway station' and under 'brilliant gas-light' (ch. 2). Similarly, *Felix Holt* sets the novel's scene through an imaginary stagecoach ride across the Midlands, contrasting this obsolete mode of movement with a hypothetical technology even more modern than the railway: 'Posterity may be shot, like a bullet through a tube, by atmospheric pressure from Winchester to Newcastle' (*FH*, 'Introduction'). The technologies that shape our observations and George Eliot's narrations can also operate on a level subtler than gaslight or long-distance transport. *Middlemarch* does not merely mention Lydgate's stethoscope and microscope as evidence of his progressive medical views but also uses them to provide metaphors for circulation, interpretation and narrative. In a fragment written as the opening for a late novel, George Eliot recurred to the turn of the previous century and to 'Central England' but presented this favourite setting through an old technology of vision and a new technology for hearing – the telephone at which she had marvelled: the 'story … is a telescope you may look through a telephone you may put your ear to'.[8]

But if George Eliot's earlier fiction looked back and saw industry and technology interwoven with human life, her late work could articulate the modern fear that our technological advances may outstrip us. In 'Shadows of the Coming Race', Theophrastus Such answers a friend's assurance that all painful work 'will soon be done by machinery' with the worry that machines that can act for us and sense for us will soon learn to think for us, even to repair themselves and reproduce (*TS*, ch. 17). Since 'each new invention casts a new light along the pathway of discovery, and each new combination or structure brings into play more conditions than its inventor foresaw', might our own ingenuity make humanity technologically obsolete (ch. 17)?

NOTES

1 Charles More, *Understanding the Industrial Revolution* (London: Routledge, 2000), p. 7.
2 John Stuart Mill, *Principles of Political Economy*, in J. M. Robson (ed.), *Collected Works of John Stuart Mill* (London: Routledge and University of Toronto Press, 1965), vol. III, pp. 756–7.
3 Economic historians still debate the term's value. While D. C. Coleman in *Myth, History, and the Industrial Revolution* (London: Hambledon, 1992), treats the Industrial Revolution as a powerful 'myth', Joel Mokyr and others defend the usefulness of the concept in Mokyr (ed.), *The British Industrial Revolution: An Economic Perspective*, 2nd edn (Boulder, CO: Westview, 1999).
4 George Wilson, *What Is Technology? An Inaugural Lecture Delivered at the University of Edinburgh on November 7, 1855* (Edinburgh: Sutherland, 1855).
5 J. Garnett (ed.), Matthew Arnold, *Culture and Anarchy* (1869; Oxford World's Classics, Oxford University Press, 2006), p. 8.
6 Tim Dolin, *George Eliot* (Oxford World's Classics, Oxford University Press, 2005), p. 47.
7 This reading is argued more fully in Tamara Ketabgian, *The Lives of Machines: The Industrial Imaginary in Victorian Literature and Culture* (Ann Arbor, MI: University of Michigan Press and University of Michigan Library, 2011), pp. 124–38.
8 William Baker, 'A New George Eliot Manuscript,' in Anne Smith (ed.), *George Eliot: Centenary Essays and an Unpublished Fragment* (London: Vision, 1980), p. 10. John Picker connects this passage to George Eliot's interest in sound, aural communication and acoustic technologies in *Victorian Soundscapes* (Oxford University Press, 2003), p. 109.

CHAPTER 18

Interiors

Judith Flanders

It was the great historian of manners, the sociologist Norbert Elias, who first suggested, in his study of the court of Louis XIV, that we can understand social relationships by examining the places in which people lived.[1] Charles Dickens had internalised this idea a full century earlier than Elias: the homes of his characters are essentially expressions of their characters. But, noted D. H. Lawrence: 'It was [George Eliot] who started putting all the action inside';[2] she made visible the invisible world inside the heads of her characters. And certainly those with an interest in the physical homes of fictional characters will find scanty gleanings in her novels – novels of piercing realism only glancingly furnished.

By the time of the Great Exhibition, in 1851, it was generally accepted that one's quality of life could be judged by the number and type of possessions one owned. This was a nineteenth-century idea. (The first use of the phrase 'standard of living' that I have located is a newspaper report of 1825, pre-dating the first citation in the *Oxford English Dictionary* by half a century.)[3] John Ruskin, no fan of what would later be called consumption, extrapolated its ideas in his advocacy of the Pre-Raphaelite painters and their minute observation of daily life.

And *Adam Bede* (1859) can partly be read as the realism of the Pre-Raphaelite painters rendered into prose. Yet while daily life, and the natural world, are recorded with fidelity, George Eliot painted the homes of the characters with an impressionistic lightness. Hall Farm, home of the Poysers, is described less by its furnishings than by its cleanliness. Lisbeth Bede's kitchen, too, is described by its condition, not by its contents. It is 'soiled', 'untidy' and has 'objects out of place' after the sudden death of her husband: dirt and untidiness are standard Victorian tropes to indicate something very wrong morally. Dr Southwood Smith, in *Recreations of a Country Parson*, written two years after *Adam Bede*, had no doubt that

> [a] clean, fresh, and well-ordered house exercises over its inmates a moral, no less than a physical influence, and has a direct tendency to make the members of the family sober, peaceable, and considerate of the feelings and happiness of each other; nor is it difficult to trace a connexion between habitual feelings of this sort and the formation of habits of respect for property, for the laws in general, and even for those higher duties and obligations the observance of which no laws can enforce.[4]

It was the Methodist John Wesley who is generally thought to have first pronounced that 'Cleanliness is next to Godliness'. Dinah's assistance to the Bede household must be read in this context, as must the focus on status (clean/dirty) over objects at Hall Farm. The elision is seen too in George Eliot's own life, when she wrote, 'I think, after all, I like a clean kitchen better than any other room – not just any kitchen, of course, but a *clean* one' (*L*, 4: 109).

The furnishings of Mr Irwine's study, by contrast, are delineated in slightly more detail, although some of those details seem better suited to George Eliot's vantage point of 1859 than the fictional date of 1799. For the depiction of fifteenth-century Florence in *Romola* (1863), such details were obsessively researched. Here, however, the changes over sixty years appear greater from our perspective than they seemed at the time. The rector's study has a 'great glass globe with gold fish in it', which stands on a pillar, and he sits in an easy chair upholstered in crimson damask (*AB*, ch. 16). Both these objects are unlikely at the turn of the nineteenth century. It was only in the 1830s that 'wardian cases', the precursor to both the terrarium and the aquarium, first appeared. A few aquariums, as luxury items among the aristocracy, appeared earlier, but it is implausible that a country rector, thirty years before, would have been so advanced. Even less likely was his red damask easy chair. Upholstered furniture was then a rarity: it was in the 1820s and 1830s that coil-spring upholstery began to appear, and the love of red was later still, becoming really popular only in the 1850s and 1860s. Although Jane Eyre (1847) admires Thornfield Hall's crimson sofas, that colour in furnishings was then confined generally to the upper classes. It was two decades later that the artist (and subsequently arts administrator) Charles Eastlake, in his *Hints on Household Taste* (1868), noted that by now many households had 'crimson curtains, crimson sofa, crimson everything'.[5]

Just as in *Adam Bede* the Poyser household is described to the reader through its cleanliness, so in *Middlemarch* (1871–2) the Vincy household is depicted not by its objects, but by the times meals are taken, and how

The Priory—Drawing-room.

Figure 12 'The Priory – Drawing-Room', engraving from *George Eliot's Life* by J. W. Cross. The room was decorated by the fashionable designer Owen Jones when George Eliot and George Lewes bought the house in 1863.

the family behaves towards its servants. Stone Court has a single repeated tag, to its 'wainscoated parlour', to establish its old-fashioned, dark mood (*M*, ch. 25). Rosamond's own house is treated almost entirely as a reflection of social status: its furnishings will establish her sense of place in the world. The house she wants to take on her marriage is simply 'very large' and 'will take a great deal of furniture – carpeting and everything, besides plate and glass' (*M*, ch. 36). Lydgate soon bitterly comprehends the central importance of house and household: 'what can a woman care about so much as house and furniture? a husband without them is an absurdity' (*M*, ch. 64).

The expense of a new house and furnishing that sets much of the Lydgate–Vincy narrative in motion was well understood by the novel's readers, and by the author. In 1863 George Eliot and Lewes purchased a forty-nine-year lease of 'The Priory', a house north of Regent's Park in

London, for £2,000. The drawing room and the dining room (the two rooms that were generally understood to represent the public face of the house) were decorated for them by their friend Owen Jones, the architect and designer (see Figure 12). Jones had long been interested in interiors and the display of objects – at the Great Exhibition he had been in charge of the overall organisation and display of goods, as well as the decoration of the building. From the 1840s, Jones also produced designs for tiles and wallpaper, and the drawing room at 'The Priory' had a specially designed paper for the walls (rather unfortunately, as it turned out: in the course of the move, the piano tuner was sick over the wall and the new carpets, and the paper had to be re-manufactured as there was none of the one-off design left – *L*, 4: 112). While George Eliot was clearly happy with the results, 'enjoying the prettiness of colouring and arrangement', and the rooms being 'altogether charming and comfortable', she wrote, 'I have made a vow never to think of my own furniture again, but only of other people's' (*L*, 4: 124, 118, 116).

She has little more to say in her fiction. *Middlemarch* presents three views of house *vs* home: there is Quallingham, the home of Lydgate's titled family, which is never described, but is thought of by Rosamond, and presented to the reader, as house-as-status; there is the Garths' house, 'a homely place … rambling, old-fashioned', undescribed in its interiors, except insofar as it is filled only with furniture of no value – 'all the best furniture had long been sold' (ch. 24); and, in the middle, there is Rosamond's house, a house that is so much not hers that it is introduced to the reader as 'Mrs Bretton's house', and is filled with furniture not loved, but purchased, and soon to be sold.

In *Daniel Deronda* (1876), the idea of house-as-status is expanded: 'it is always worth while to make a little sacrifice for a good style of house' like Offendene, says Mr Gascoigne at the very outset. Offendene once 'sufficed for dowager countesses', and 'No one need be ashamed of living [t]here' (*DD*, ch. 3). Yet as we have by now learned to expect, the descriptions of Offendene and the other houses that play such an important part in marking the status gradations of George Eliot's characters are of the most general. Offendene simply has 'sombre furniture and faded upholstery', and a bedroom that is identified merely by a colour scheme (ch. 3). Ryelands is 'a much finer place … larger in every way' (ch. 35), Quetcham is a 'beautiful place' (ch. 9), and the Meyricks' Chelsea home is identified by its 'miniature rooms' (ch. 18). Gadsmere's drawing room has one of the fullest descriptions, having a 'square projecting window', a 'low black cabinet … old oak table … [and] chairs in tawny leather' (ch. 30).

The house-as-status was part of the fabric of the culture. In 1843 Sarah Stickney Ellis, the educationalist, temperance campaigner and author of conduct books, wrote that it was 'scarcely necessary … to point out … the loss of character and influence occasioned by living below our station'.[6] (It may not have been necessary, but it was important enough that she did so anyway.) Trying too hard was equally bad, while living beyond one's means was simply immoral. The greatest good was knowing one's place in the world, and having one's house reflect that place precisely. Thus, decorating one's house was not a matter of taste, but a matter of respectability; conforming to current norms was an indication of acceptance of that responsibility. Nearly fifty years later, this was still a theme that needed to be aired. Mrs Panton's *From Kitchen to Garret: Hints for Young Householders* was successful enough to go through eleven editions in a decade. And she was blunt: 'In starting to buy the furniture [to set up home on marriage] … let us consider not what is handsome or effective or taking to the eye, but what is suitable to [the husband's] position.'[7]

What was suitable for whom depended on income primarily, on family background and status as a secondary consideration. Eliot's tenant farmers are in the main relatively prosperous. Her middle-class characters rarely have precise income figures attached to them. And her upper-class characters speak of money in a way that would make the middle classes widen their eyes. In *Middlemarch*, the rector wants to marry on an income of more than £1,000 a year, and yet his intended's family were against the match: 'nobody could see anything in me'. If Dorothea gives up Casaubon's money, she will be 'so poor' on her private income of £700 a year, plus Ladislaw's earnings (*M*, ch. 84). In reality, these incomes made both the rector and Dorothea more prosperous than many, if not most, of their gentry coevals. Gwendolen Harleth, whom Sir Hugo thinks is so badly treated by her late husband's will, has 'only' £2,000 a year 'and a house in a coal-mining district' (*DD*, ch. 64).

Most people were not in this high-income bracket, and did not inherit houses. For them, renting a house was a much more sensible option than buying, giving the opportunity of moving as circumstances altered, to larger or smaller houses in more or less fashionable neighbourhoods. Firm figures are impossible to come by, but a general estimate puts home ownership at about ten per cent of the population.[8] Ownership was of less importance than occupancy and display.

The size of the house mattered, and the neighbourhood, but the main focus was on the interior rather than exterior. Georgian balconies vanished in the Victorian age, and windows were covered with layers of curtains and blinds, turning attention inward. Furnishings were a private matter, and public displays of what should be kept in the home were more than out of place: they were disturbing. This is the subtext running through the Larchers' sale in *Middlemarch*. The townspeople are, in effect, prying into the Larchers' home life, while they, in turn, are to be condemned. They are selling their goods, after all, not because of financial reverses, but because Larcher has been so successful that he is buying a 'mansion' ready furnished 'in high style': he is, in fact, moving above his sphere (*M*, ch. 60). Similarly in *The Mill on the Floss*, George Eliot stresses the auctioneer's scanty 'tincture' of education (book 1, ch. 3), while Mrs Tulliver mourns not just that her 'chany' (china) is being sold, but that it is being 'sold *i' that way*' (book 3, ch. 3, my italics). This is in contrast to the Garths, who had to sell their good furniture because of financial reverses; by doing so, they had also lost social caste. Mr Trumbull, the auctioneer, is presented as entirely vulgar, as one who sells private items in public must of necessity be: he says 'recherchy' for 'recherché', 'connoiss*ures*' for 'connoisseurs' (*M*, ch. 60). George Eliot here follows a long line of fictional rejection of public auctions of household goods. In 1815 Walter Scott's Guy Mannering thinks it is 'disgusting … to see the scenes of domestic society and seclusion thrown open to the gaze of the curious and the vulgar'; half a century later, Trollope's Archdeacon Grantly is merely disappointed when Major Grantly wants to marry a curate's daughter from a family beneath them socially; but he is horrified when the Major's possessions are auctioned to finance the marriage.[9]

A marriage, of necessity, needed financing. By mid century, a three-bedroom house for a family with two servants (thus, the middle of the middle class), could be completely furnished for under £600, thought one advice writer.[10] It is an indication of the financial comfort of the Leweses that in 1871, they made renovations to 'The Priory' that cost £505, spending an unnamed further sum on bookshelves and other furniture (*L*, 4: 144; Haight (1968), p. 432). And, after the success of *Middlemarch*, they purchased a Broadwood piano, a mirror, a Persian rug (Haight (1968), p. 459) and, like Lydgate, a 'dinner-service' that was 'expensive, but that might be in the nature of dinner-services. Furnishing was necessarily expensive' (*M*, ch. 36). Early in the Victorian period, the furnishings for a middle-class drawing room would include horsehair sofas, ottomans, upright chairs, stools, and a variety of tables: console tables, work tables, sewing tables, occasional tables and, most importantly, a round table for the centre of the room. Easy chairs were beginning to appear, usually horsehair, but sometimes upholstered at the upper end of the market, and there were standard easy chairs and 'ladies' chairs', with more upright backs and lower arms, to accommodate women's skirts. In the 1860s, when crinolines appeared, these became ever more necessary.

How to decorate this essential room changed as the furnishings did. By the 1860s the chintzes and upholsteries which had earlier been confined to the upper classes had expanded down the economic scale, and by the end of the century, as H. G. Wells noted ruefully of the lower-middle-class room of his 1870s childhood, 'something was hung about or wrapped round or draped over everything'.[11] Mrs Panton presented herself as writing for the upper middle classes, not for the son of a shopkeeper, as Wells was, but in fact she echoed this love of fabric embellishment at the end of the century, suggesting that pianos and music stools should each be covered with fringed fabrics; the cupboard to store the sheet music should also be covered by a cloth, while fabric-covered armchairs should have further embroidered-fabric antimacassars.[12]

The mantelpiece was also draped. A simple mantel might have a clock, candlesticks, a few ornaments, vases and spills (long twists of paper to light the fire). Gradually, the proliferation of display objects saw mantels extended by boards and covered by fabric and a draped valance, and embellished with a fringe.

The light, airy Georgian windows were now covered by muslin to prevent outsiders peering in; then by curtains in rep or damask, with fringes, tie-backs and pelmets; frequently, venetian or roller blinds were a third layer of protection against the outside. In *Daniel Deronda*, George Eliot's stress on the lack of curtains and blinds in Sawyer's Cottage is an indication of its lack of status, its utter unfitness for Mrs Davilow (*DD*, ch. 24).

Of course, what was once fashionable soon fell out of fashion. 'I can conceive nothing more terrible than to be doomed to spend one's life in a house furnished after the fashion of twenty years ago,' worried Robert Edis, an architect and author of *Decoration and Furniture of Town Houses* (1881).[13] But while being old-fashioned was condemned, things that were obviously new were equally bad. In Wilkie Collins's *Basil* (1852), the falsity of a woman is asserted by elision with her parents' drawing room, in which 'Everything was oppressively new.'[14] These people were emotionally related to Dickens's Veneerings in *Our Mutual Friend*, 'bran-new people in a bran-new' house.[15]

Dickens's devastatingly brilliant superficial characters mirror their devastatingly brilliant sham-surface name. They are perceived from the outside in, moving objectifications seen mirrored in their houses. George Eliot, by contrast, moves outward, examining her houses through the lens of her characters, subjectifying these inanimate objects. For her, interiors were only interior.

NOTES

1 Norbert Elias, *The Court Society*, trans. Edmund Jephcott (Oxford: Basil Blackwell, 1983).
2 Cited in G. H. Ford, *Dickens and His Readers: Aspects of Novel Criticism Since 1836* (Princeton University Press, 1955), p. 182.
3 The phrase 'standard of living' is used in 'Combinations', *Morning Chronicle* (8 October 1825), 4.
4 Cited in Adrian Forty, *Objects of Desire: Design and Society, 1750–1980* (London: Thames and Hudson, 1986), pp. 108–9. Dr Smith's connection to Eliot was not only in shared attitudes to hygiene as morality. His granddaughter Gertrude Hill later married G. H. Lewes's son Charles.
5 Cited in Asa Briggs, *Victorian Things* (Harmondsworth: Penguin, 1990), p. 277.
6 Sarah Stickney Ellis, *The Wives of England, Their Relative Duties, Domestic Influence, and Social Obligations* (London: Fisher, Son & Co., [1843]), p. 219.
7 Cited in Briggs, *Victorian Things*, p. 244.
8 For example, F. M. L. Thompson, *The Rise of Respectable Society: A Social History of Victorian Britain, 1830–1900* (Cambridge, MA: Harvard University Press, 1988), pp. 168–9.
9 Walter Scott, *Guy Mannering* (London: Simpkin, Marshall, 1829), p. 136; Anthony Trollope, *The Last Chronicle of Barset* (1866/7; Oxford World's Classics, Oxford University Press, 2001), p. 606.
10 J. H. Walsh, *A Manual of Domestic Economy* (London: G. Routledge, 1857). For an analysis of Walsh's figures, see J. A. Banks, *Prosperity and Parenthood: A Study of Family Planning among the Victorian Middle Classes* (1954; London: Gregg Revivals, 1993), pp. 49–50.
11 H. G. Wells, *Tono-Bungay* (1909; New York: Duffield, 1909), p. 60.
12 Mrs [Ellen] Panton, *Homes of Taste. Economical Hints* (London: Sampson Low, Marston, Searle, and Rivington, 1890), pp. 76–7.
13 Robert R. Edis, *Decoration and Furniture of Town Houses* (London: C. Kegan Paul, 1881), pp. 17–20.
14 Wilkie Collins, *Basil* (1852; London: Chatto and Windus, 1890), p. 61.
15 Adrian Poole (ed.), Charles Dickens, *Our Mutual Friend* (1865; Harmondsworth: Penguin, 1997), p. 118.

CHAPTER 19

Landscape

John Rignall

Reviewing the third volume of John Ruskin's *Modern Painters* in April 1856, Marian Evans referred to the 'intense interest in landscape which is a peculiar characteristic of modern times'.[1] That interest was one she shared, as can be seen by her early familiarity with the landscape painting of W. Clarkson Stanfield, Thomas Roberts and Thomas Creswick (*L*, 1: 248) and her knowledge of the work of J. M. W. Turner and lesser artists like Helen Allingham.[2] Her familiarity with landscape painting could colour her response to scenes she encountered, so that she could describe 'a stroll along the banks of the Trent' on a visit to Newark in terms of 'seeing some charming quiet pictures – Frith landscapes' (*J*, 133); and her interest in the subject was to manifest itself in the fiction she wrote as George Eliot.

An interest in landscape was in part a product of the growing urbanisation of nineteenth-century society, a process in which she herself had participated by moving to London in the early 1850s, so that the landscape of the English Midlands that is central to most of her novels represents the world of her childhood and upbringing which she had left behind. In her writing that world thus often takes on the lineaments of a Wordsworthian landscape of memory,[3] as it does most plainly in certain passages of narratorial reflection in *The Mill on the Floss*. Declaring that 'we could never have loved the earth so well if we had had no childhood in it', the narrator describes walking in a wood on a 'mild May day, with the young yellow-brown foliage of the oaks between me and the blue sky, the white star-flowers and the blue-eyed speedwell and the ground ivy at my feet' and finds these details of the natural world, and the 'furrowed and grassy fields, each with a sort of personality given to it by the capricious hedgerows', to be 'the mother tongue of our imagination, the language that is laden with all the subtle inextricable associations the fleeting hours of our childhood left behind them' (*MF*, book 1, ch. 5). Landscape familiar from childhood is both evoked in language and likened to a language in its power to arouse and articulate the workings of the imagination.

This nexus of landscape and memory, language and imagination, was later to appeal strongly to Marcel Proust, for whom *The Mill on the Floss* was a favourite novel; and it was anticipated earlier in George Eliot's critical writing, where the natural landscape served as a touchstone of the poetic imagination. In her demolition of Edward Young, 'Worldliness and Other-Worldliness: The Poet Young' (1857), his failings as a poet are illustrated by his blankness in the face of the natural world: 'Place him on a breezy common, where the furze is in its golden bloom, where children are playing, and horses are standing in the sunshine with fondling necks, and he would have nothing to say' (*Essays*, 369). Landscape is here a figure of life, and although she avoids the sentimentality of attributing a moral power to nature, sardonically remarking in another essay, 'The Natural History of German Life' (1856), that the 'selfish instincts are not subdued by the sight of buttercups' (*Essays*, 270), she identifies the ability to respond to the natural world as a measure of the poetic sensibility.

The Midland landscape of the fiction is not simply Wordsworthian and, as Hugh Witemeyer has shown, in a characteristic description of that landscape in *Middlemarch* when Rosamond and Fred Vincy are riding to Stone Court, there are elements of the eighteenth-century picturesque in the manner of William Gilpin and of the detailed naturalistic precision advocated by Ruskin.[4] This 'pretty bit of midland landscape' is pictured with attention to the 'little details' that 'gave each field a particular physiognomy, dear to the eyes that have looked on them from childhood', and the description picks out painterly features like the 'stray hovel, its old, old thatch full of mossy hills and valleys with wondrous modulations of light and shadow such as we travel far to see in later life' (*M*, ch. 12). But with her commitment to realism as set out in 'The Natural History of German Life', George Eliot shares with Ruskin a suspicion of the merely picturesque since for her it ignores the extent to which landscape is a construction, a product of human labour and a place of often arduous work. When the narrator of *The Mill on the Floss* reflects critically on how 'good society' is sustained by the unregarded toil of working people, that 'wide and arduous national life' is to be seen not only in factories and furnaces but also in the landscape, 'spread over sheepwalks, and scattered in lonely houses and huts on the clayey or chalky corn-lands, where the rainy days look dreary' (*MF*, book 4, ch. 3). Distance may lend enchantment to the view – 'What horrors of damp huts, where human beings languish, may not become picturesque through aerial distance', as the narrator of *Daniel Deronda* tartly observes (*DD*, ch. 14) – but the novelist's characteristic practice is to dismantle the picturesque by moving from the distant perspective to the revealing close-up. Although an observer, 'under the softening influence of the fine arts which makes other people's hardships picturesque', might have found Dagley's homestead in *Middlemarch* 'a sort of picture which we have all paused over as a "charming bit"', the details the narrator singles out – the chimneys choked with ivy, the grey worm-eaten shutters, the mouldering garden wall – point to the general 'depression of the agricultural interest' and show up Mr Brooke's particular failings as a landlord (*M*, ch. 39).

Bearing the imprint of human labour and social conditions, landscape serves for George Eliot as a witness to history, a point that she spells out most clearly in her final work *Impressions of Theophrastus Such* where, in 'Looking Backward', she considers 'our native landscape' as 'one deep root of our national life and language' (*TS*, ch. 2). Adopting the persona of Theophrastus, an unsuccessful bachelor writer in middle age who has made the same journey from the Midlands to London that she has, she has him look back at the landscape of his childhood and reflect on its connection to the course of English history:

> Our national life is like that scenery which I early learned to love, not subject to great convulsions, but easily showing more or less delicate (sometimes melancholy) effects from minor changes. Hence our midland plains have never lost their familiar expression and conservative spirit for me; yet at every other mile, since I first looked on them, some sign of world-wide change, some new direction of human labour has wrought itself into what one may call the speech of the landscape – in contrast with those grander and vaster regions of the earth which keep an indifferent aspect in the presence of men's toil and devices. (ch. 2)

The contrast between the undramatic landscape of the Midlands and 'grander and vaster regions of the earth' carries a distant echo of Ruskin's reflections on 'Mountain Beauty' in the fourth volume of *Modern Painters* which she had reviewed in the *Westminster Review* in July 1856, and it is accompanied by a similar evaluation of the human above the sublime. Where human activity in those latter regions, such as a caravan creeping across 'the unresting sameness of the desert', seems insignificant in the face of the vastness of nature, the landscape of the English Midlands shows nature and mankind in sympathetic balance and co-operation:

> But our woodlands and pastures, our hedge-parted corn-fields and meadows, our bits of high common where we used to plant the windmills, our quiet little rivers here and there fit to turn a mill-wheel, our villages along the old coach-roads, are all easily alterable lineaments that seem to make the face of our Motherland sympathetic with the laborious lives of her

> children. She does not take their ploughs and waggons contemptuously, but rather makes every hovel and every sheepfold, every railed bridge or fallen tree-trunk an agreeably noticeable incident; not a mere speck in the midst of unmeasured vastness, but a piece of our social history in pictorial writing. (*TS*, ch. 2)

This sense of landscape as imprinted with the history of its inhabitants and as a witness to the long continuities of English life is widely shared in the nineteenth century. It looks back in particular to one of her favourite novelists, Walter Scott, and forward to such writers as Thomas Hardy, with his awareness of how the land bears the traces of centuries of unrecorded life, and Rudyard Kipling, who conjures up a vision of England and English history from the Sussex countryside in *Puck of Pook's Hill* (1906). But if there is a Whiggish suggestion in the passage from *Theophrastus Such* that the course of English history is uniquely privileged in its unbroken evolution, and a matter for celebration, that view is challenged and qualified by her own pictorial writing of the landscape in the novels, which presents a more complex and differentiated view of social history.

In her most elaborate exercise in writing the landscape, the 'Author's Introduction' to *Felix Holt, the Radical*, the device of an imaginary coach journey across the Midlands 'five-and-thirty years ago' allows her to register the contrasting features of both the countryside and its social history. The beauty of the natural scene is acknowledged, but with an underlying awareness of how it may be at odds with social needs and social progress. When we are told that 'everywhere the bushy hedgerows wasted the land with their straggling beauty', the discreetly discordant 'wasted' implies, with whatever degree of irony, the sceptical reservation of a mind aware of the value of agricultural production, while the description of the hedgerows as 'the liberal homes of unmarketable beauty' spells out the tension between the beauties of nature and the needs of political economy. The same hedgerows can also throw into relief the often benighted nature of the human lives adjacent to them: 'Such hedgerows were often as tall as the labourers' cottages dotted along the lanes, or clustered into a small hamlet, their little dingy windows telling, like thick-filmed eyes, of nothing but the darkness within' (*FH*, 'Introduction'). But in contrast to such backwardness there are 'trim cheerful villages too', the description of which may owe as much to Victorian genre painting as to the author's memories of the world of her childhood:

> there was the pleasant tinkle of the blacksmith's anvil, the patient cart-horses waiting at his door; the basket-maker peeling his willow wands

Figure 13 Vignette by Myles Birket Foster for the title page of Blackwood's 1874 one-volume edition of *Middlemarch.*

> in the sunshine; the wheelwright putting the last touch to a blue cart with red wheels; here and there a cottage with bright transparent windows showing pots of blooming balsams or geraniums, and little gardens in front all double daisies or dark wallflowers. (*FH*, 'Introduction')

These scenes recall paintings by Myles Birket Foster, who had published a book of *English Landscapes* with similar subjects in 1863 and who was later to provide the vignette for the one-volume 'Cheap Edition' of *Middlemarch* (1874) which George Eliot found charming (*L*, 6: 45; see Figure 13).

The Midland landscape of *Felix Holt* offers even more striking contrasts in that it juxtaposes rural and industrial scenes. 'In these midland districts', we are told, 'the traveller passed rapidly from one phase of English life to another', so that the journey becomes a journey through time as well as space. 'But as the day wore on the scene would change', and the changes suggest not just the passage of the sun but the course of social history: 'the land would begin to be blackened with coal-pits, the rattle of the handlooms to be heard in hamlets and villages'. The journey proceeds from a seemingly pre-industrial England to a world of mining and manufacturing, of dissenting chapels and 'of riots and trades-union meetings' and 'the recent initiation of railways' (*FH*, 'Introduction'). The landscape as seen from the coach thus comes to illustrate the condition of England in a way which may owe something to Ruskin, though it is unburdened by what she termed 'his wrathful innuendoes against the whole modern world' (*L*, 7: 295). At the same time it anticipates the work of later observers of the landscape who reflect on its connection to national culture, such as the rural essayist Richard Jefferies, the poet Edward Thomas and the novelist Ford Madox Ford.[5]

Although the light goes out of the landscape as the journey proceeds, there is no pessimistic presumption of decline in the succession of phases of English life. Change may be problematic but it is not inconsistent with a belief in the positively evolutionary course of English history. A darker understanding of human history is not excluded from George Eliot's fiction but it tends to be articulated in terms of landscapes that are foreign rather than English, like Latimer's premonitory vision of Prague in 'The Lifted Veil': 'a city under the broad sunshine, that seemed to me as if it were the summer sunshine of a long-past century arrested in its course … scorching the dusty, weary, time-eaten grandeur of a people doomed to live on in the stale repetition of memories' ('LV', ch. 1). The emphasis on the inorganic, the 'blackened statues … along the unending bridge' and the broad river like 'a sheet of metal', denies history the life and capacity for change implied in the benignly evolving landscape of the English Midlands. For the novelist the foreign landscape has the advantage of distance, allowing her to stand back from the richly imagined English provincial world, as she does, for instance, in *The Mill on the Floss*, and reflect upon history and man's relationship to nature in general terms by comparing the landscapes of the Rhône and the Rhine. The contrast of dreary ugliness and romantic beauty they present is also a contrast between two visions of human life and history. The 'dead-tinted, hollow-eyed, angular skeletons of villages on the Rhone', ruined by its floods, convey an oppressive sense that much of human life 'is a narrow, ugly grovelling existence' condemned to 'be swept into the same oblivion with the generations of ants and beavers', while the 'ruins on the castled Rhine, which have crumbled and mellowed into such harmony with the green and rocky steeps, that they seems to have a natural fitness, like the mountain pine', speak of 'the grand historic life of humanity' and summon up 'the vision of an epoch' (*MF*, book 4, ch. 1). These contrasting views of hostility and harmony between man and nature, and of history as meaningless flux or meaningful continuity, could both be distilled from the fictional Floss and the lives of the Tullivers, but articulating them in general terms through the device of the foreign landscape abstracts them from the fictional action, which is thus left open to interpretation in different ways.

The landscapes of the early fiction, particularly *Adam Bede*, which George Eliot described to her publisher as 'a country story – full of the breath of cows and the scent of hay' (*L*, 2: 387), are predominantly pastoral. The village of Hayslope with its 'grey steeple looking out from a pretty confusion of trees and thatch and dark-red tiles' is explicitly framed as a 'picture' to the eye of the traveller who surveys the 'typical features of this pleasant land' (*AB*, ch. 2). The description moves from the horizon formed by 'huge conical masses of hill' protecting 'this region of corn and grass against the keen and hungry winds of the north' and 'with sombre greenish sides visibly speckled with sheep', through a line 'of hanging woods, divided by bright patches of pasture or furrowed crops', to 'a foreground which was just as lovely – the level sunlight lying like transparent gold among the gently-curving stems of the feathered grass and the tall red sorrel' (ch. 2). The carefully composed picture is idyllic but the traveller has come to this pleasant land from the harsher country to the north, 'a bleak treeless region, intersected by lines of cold grey stone', and the narrative that follows is committed to a realism that knows the limitations of the idyllic setting (ch. 2). The seductively easy pastoral life of Hayslope plays its part in Hetty Sorrel's fatal seduction, and her inner agony when she sets out on her desperate journey is, like the crucifix in the smiling foreign landscape, a reminder of what may lie 'hidden among the sunny fields and behind the blossoming orchards' (ch. 35). Pastoral landscape can also be a site of suffering.

The relationship between landscape and the inner life is examined more fully in *Adam Bede* when Adam, Dinah and Seth define their different natures by describing the landscapes they prefer. Dinah, for instance, reveals her Puritan temperament and fund of compassion for the poor by preferring the bleak hills of Stonyshire to the undulating landscape of Loamshire 'rich in corn and cattle' (ch. 11). While George Eliot is aware from her reading of Ruskin of the dangers of the pathetic fallacy, of sentimentally attributing human emotions to nature, she is adept at using nature in the form of landscape to illumine human emotions. Thus in *Middlemarch* Dorothea's emotional development is conveyed by what she sees, or sometimes fails to see, from her windows. Returning from her honeymoon, her dawning sense of the bleakness of the married life before her is suggested by the view from her boudoir of 'the long avenue of limes lifting their trunks from a white earth, and spreading white branches against the dun and motionless sky' (*M*, ch. 28). And at the moral crisis of her life it is the landscape seen from her bedroom window, the road and the fields beyond with the emblematic figures of working men and women and 'far off in the bending sky ... the pearly light', that makes her feel 'the largeness of the world and the manifold wakings of men to labour and endurance' and prompts her to act in the interests of others (ch. 80). Here inner and outer, view and vision, the realistic and the symbolic, are fused in a landscape which, in combining the working world with the moral life, defines the characteristic terrain of George Eliot's fiction. Landscape for her is always and only significant for its relation to human activity and human consciousness.

NOTES

1 *Westminster Review*, 65 (1856), 631.
2 Hugh Witemeyer, *George Eliot and the Visual Arts* (New Haven, CT and London: Yale University Press, 1979), pp. 10–11.
3 Christopher Salvesen, *The Landscape of Memory: A Study of Wordsworth's Poetry* (London: Edward Arnold, 1965), pp. 19–22.
4 Witemeyer, George Eliot and the Visual Arts, p. 127.
5 Simon Grimble, *Landscape, Writing and 'The Condition of England' – 1878–1917, Ruskin to Modernism* (Lewiston: Edwin Mellen, 2004), pp. 9–33.

CHAPTER 20

Language

Melissa Raines

Victorian novelist Anthony Trollope once wrote of the literary style of his friend George Eliot, 'she lacks ease'. He then went on to expand his comment by saying, 'In *Daniel Deronda* … there are sentences which I have found myself compelled to read three times before I have been able to take home to myself all that the writer has intended.'[1] Trollope had a high regard for George Eliot, putting her second only to Thackeray in his estimation of the greatest writers of the age. Yet his sense of frustration with her language is something that is often shared by other admirers. Her novels are not easy to read because they are not meant to be easy: her works are substantial in length, but the sentences are crafted with almost poetic sensibility and demand a similar kind of attention. The level of care George Eliot takes with her language is linked fundamentally to her passionate love of words themselves, but this is only one determining aspect of her grammatical complexity. Her study of foreign languages, her interest in the historical development of language and in its geographical variants, and her active engagement with nineteenth-century scientific thought are also central to her complicated syntax. The aim of George Eliot's grammatical complexity, whether represented through the faithful rendering of working-class dialect or the minute shifts of complicated passages of free indirect speech, is to 'express *life*' and, through its expression, to inspire sympathy ('Natural History', *Essays*, 288).

George Eliot wrote her novels in a period when the politics of language was becoming increasingly contentious and the study of language was in a state of flux. The nineteenth-century population shift from rural to urban locations and the resulting rise in inter-class contact were partly responsible for the amplified urgency of the debates surrounding the state of the English language in this period. Because language was seen as an indicator of class and social position, there was an increased drive, in some branches of society, for standardisation, accompanied by an increased anxiety about the use of anything deemed as substandard. Simultaneously, academic considerations of the secular basis for the foundations of language itself were turning the examination of its historical evolution into a science. George Eliot's early engagement with the blossoming field of philology allowed her to develop a theory of language that pre-dated her novels: like philologist R. C. Trench, she firmly believed that words had the potential to be 'boundless stores of moral and historic truth'.[2] Language was both the vehicle through which history was recorded and a documentation of historical change – a multi-layered map of human development. Her intense respect for 'the subtle ramifications of historical language' would remain central to her view of the moral power of her fiction (*Essays*, 288). Furthermore, her utilisation of the geographical and temporal flexibility of the English language – her commitment to embracing regionalisms and to pushing words beyond their current meanings – are challenges at both the grammatical and the philosophical level.

The many languages of Marian Evans

George Eliot was not just gifted in English: she was an accomplished linguist even before she became George Eliot. Marian Evans began learning French before she was ten and would also eventually study German, Italian, Latin, Greek, Spanish and Hebrew. She translated two texts by the philosopher Spinoza from their original Latin, and her fluent knowledge of German is demonstrated in her translations of Strauss and Feuerbach. When translating, she made meticulous efforts to remain true to both the style of the author and the nuances of the original language of the work. Her letters during the translation of Strauss are riddled with confessed uncertainties over small phrases, so much so that at one point she feels obliged to apologise to a friend by writing, 'I never stickle for a word or a phrase unless it express an idea that cannot be equally well conveyed by another' (*L*, I: 189). It is almost as if the experience of translating another's work becomes a kind of sympathetic foreshadowing of her later care with language in her own novels.

Clearly, Marian Evans's growing breadth of linguistic expertise was sustained by the depth of her love of language. For this was a woman who as a teenager could write, 'I am violently in love with the Italian fashion of repeating an adjective or adverb and even noun to give force to expression. There is so much more fire in it than in our circumlocutory phrases' (*L*, I: 107). In this gushing admission, coupled with the heightened awareness of other languages and speech patterns, we see the beginnings of George Eliot the realist writer. But Evans's realist convictions also forced her to struggle with her words. Thus she writes in 1858, 'Words are very clumsy things – I like less and less to handle my friends' sacred feelings with them. For even those who call themselves "intimate" know very little about each other – hardly ever know just *how* a sorrow is felt, and hurt each other by their very attempts at sympathy or consolation' (*L*, 2: 464–5). By 1858, she had already published *Scenes of Clerical Life* as George Eliot, and was actively writing her first full novel, *Adam Bede*, but even literary achievement could not rid her of doubt or ensure that her sentences would always shape themselves to her exacting standard. In reading her letters about the process of writing and translating, it is possible to see even more clearly what we discern from the process of reading her realist novels. Writing is emotionally and intellectually challenging for George Eliot, but necessarily so. As she says, 'Writing is part of my religion, and I can write no word that is not prompted from within' (*L*, 2: 377).

Dialect and realism

Elizabeth Deeds Ermarth argues that George Eliot's 'grasp of the fundamental differences between languages' is vital not only to the intricate construction of her syntax, but to her sympathetic perception of individual ways of 'mapping the world'.[3] Hence a heightened familiarity with individual differences becomes a pathway to greater understanding. One way in which George Eliot's thorough knowledge of other languages is apparent in her prose style is in her skill in rendering the dialects of her own language – especially those of the rural working-classes in the early part of the nineteenth century. She wrote in an early essay, 'Art is the nearest thing to life; it is a mode of amplifying experience and extending our contact with our fellow-men beyond the bounds of our personal lot. All the more sacred is the task of the artist when he undertakes to paint the life of the People' ('Natural History', *Essays*, 271). She clearly felt that subtle historical and geographical differences were part of the art and power of language, and she uses the art and power of the Warwickshire dialect of her childhood throughout her works. In *Adam Bede* and *Silas Marner* particularly, she highlights those differences by allowing the uneducated characters to speak in their own voices and to struggle through difficult intellectual thoughts on their own terms. What results is a language that is poetic and compelling.

A contemporary reviewer wrote of *Silas Marner*, 'One of the most striking features in this striking tale is the strong intellectual impress which the author contrives to give to a story of which the main elements are altogether unintellectual, without the smallest injury to the verisimilitude of the tale'.[4] George Eliot's choice to stay largely within the language of her lower-class characters not only affords them respect, but also helps to show her readers that things which do not match middle-class conceptions of eloquence are not for that reason unworthy of being said. This is expressed most vividly through the character of Dolly Winthrop, the sensible housewife who befriends Silas. She explains the process of working through a difficult thought by saying:

> it got twisted back'ards and for'ards, as I didn't know which end to lay hold on. But it come to me all clear like, that night when I was sitting up wi' poor Bessy Fawkes, as is dead and left her children behind, God help 'em – it come to me as clear as daylight; but whether I've got hold on it now, or can anyways bring it to my tongue's end, that I don't know. For I've often a deal inside me as 'll niver come out. (*SM*, ch. 16)

The complicated thoughts pulse beneath Dolly's searching expressions, which move 'back'ards and for'ards' throughout the passage – starting with her frustrated confusion, breaking into surprised realisation with the second sentence (beginning fittingly with 'But' to signal the sudden awakening), and then shifting back into doubt as Dolly worries that she will never be able to express what she had realised fully. The reader senses something of Dolly's experience through the rhythmic vacillations of the text, while coming to understand that Dolly's commitment to working through these vacillations is in and of itself an eloquently progressive movement.

Through characters such as Dolly, George Eliot presents her readers with a different way of understanding the world. Her real challenge as a novelist, however, is not only to be able to convey the depth of individual character differences, but also to be able to convey the combined difficulty and necessity of sympathetic connection *across* those differences.

Science and the language of the nerves

George Eliot's quest for this kind of psychological realism is grounded in a language that demonstrates heightened scientific awareness. Although science in the nineteenth century was developing quickly, its language was still accessible to non-specialists. Her interest in a field that was attempting to find a physiological basis for human consciousness most likely would have been stimulated by her extensive reading. Her relationship with George Henry Lewes, who studied and wrote extensively on psychology and physiology, ensured a day-to-day involvement with science that had a profound effect on her complicated language.

Many critics have remarked on the frequency of scientific images in George Eliot's work, particularly the 'often-noted deployment of images of tissues, threads, and vibrations'.[5] There are direct associations with Victorian psychological theory here, for such language was commonly used to describe the structure and functioning of the nervous system. This terminology is often more prevalent in specific passages, usually whenever 'Eliot attempts to explain the effects of crisis'.[6] Examples can be found within narratorial observations on the difficulties of life, as in *The Mill on the Floss*: 'There is something sustaining in the very agitation that accompanies the first shocks of trouble, just as an acute pain is often a stimulus, and produces excitement which is transient strength' (*MF*, book 4, ch. 2). The touches are subtle, but undeniable – 'acute', 'stimulus' and, most significantly, that reference to 'shocks', which are metaphorically linked to the shocks that send an impulse racing along a human nerve fibre. This last image of shocks and currents is even more noticeable in descriptions of intense individual experience. So in *Middlemarch*, Will Ladislaw reacts to Dorothea Casaubon's entrance by 'start[ing] up as from an electric shock' as if 'every molecule in his body' has been affected (*M*, ch. 39). The passionate Dorothea yearns for a purpose in life that is one with her 'full current of sympathetic motive' (ch. 10). And the young doctor, Tertius Lydgate, clashes with his cold wife and is left feeling 'such fibres still astir in him' that 'the shock he received could not at once be distinctly anger; it was confused pain' (ch. 64). The individual words ('shock', 'molecule', 'current', 'fibres') jump out at the reader, but what is most important about the final example is that link between 'anger' and 'pain' – the fact that emotional and physical experience cannot be separated in the initial nervous 'shock'. This link is vital to our understanding of George Eliot's use of scientific language.

Sally Shuttleworth proposes that science does more than merely provide George Eliot with a bank of unique and vivid terminology for literary devices, arguing that 'in constructing her novels she engaged in an active dialogue with contemporary scientific thought'.[7] In short, the novelist's conscious decision to use a language of the nerves becomes a statement about her belief in the physiological underpinnings of emotion. This connection is paralleled in her perceived relationship between the grammar of a sentence and the thought it conveys. The words must become the nerves that are the basis for the thought, and so the syntax must become a complex neuro-physiological journey that maps the thought-process within a character's mind. Because of this tie between the psychological and the physiological, the inner experience is often the focus for George

Eliot. Hence her novels are rife with examples of free indirect speech, or what Dorrit Cohn describes as 'psycho-narration' – the narrator's rendering of character experience.[8] It is when the reader ventures into a character's mind through the narrator that we find the best examples of George Eliot's purposefully convoluted syntax.

In *Daniel Deronda*, Gwendolen Harleth lies awake 'in her little white bed' debating over her decision to marry the wealthy but intimidating Henleigh Grandcourt. The passage begins simply and almost childishly, and then plunges into complexity with a direction-shifting 'But':

> But her state of mind was altogether new: she who had been used to feel sure of herself, and ready to manage others, had just taken a decisive step which she had beforehand thought that she would not take – nay, perhaps, was bound not to take. She could not go backward now; she liked a great deal of what lay before her; and there was nothing for her to like if she went back. But her resolution was dogged by the shadow of that previous resolve which had at first come as the undoubting movement of her whole being. (*DD*, ch. 28)

This passage makes Gwendolen's entirely different 'state of mind' real for the reader, through both its content and its grammatical structure. Gwendolen's troubling reflective thoughts come trickling out through the sentences as if Gwendolen herself cannot quite believe what she has done, and must grasp at that comforting state of innocent ignorance when she could enjoy her girlish sleep. This is because 'she who *had been used* to feel sure of herself' now has been moved to take 'a decisive step which *she had beforehand thought* that she would not take' (emphasis mine). The sentence, like Gwendolen, is out of time with itself, as can be seen through the temporally confused verb phrases. It is not just that Gwendolen does not know her new self, but that she can no longer understand her old one. Thus the clauses within the lengthy sentence writhe and almost twist back on themselves within the verb phrases as Gwendolen attempts to find a time when things did make sense. The only certainty is Gwendolen's wavering admission at the end of the sentence, just after '– nay': the qualifying 'perhaps' is another failed attempt at self-assurance as Gwendolen's intense fear of her future husband overwhelms it. Still scrambling for comfort, Gwendolen looks to the future, telling herself that she cannot 'go backward now'. That second sentence is a sigh of relief after the intricate opening. It reads as if the character has collected herself, so that the steady pulse of the simple series of clauses – so different from the convolutions just before – slows the pulse of Gwendolen's nervous heart. But Gwendolen slips into fear and uncertainty again in the final sentence, where 'previous resolve' haunts her new current 'resolution', and the reader leaves the character with no real sense of who she is becoming.

In this passage, George Eliot is not just telling us that Gwendolen is being pushed frighteningly into adulthood by this new step: she is allowing her readers to think and feel their way into this process through the language – as if the sentences themselves become neural pathways. Indeed, the passage is not entirely dissimilar to Dolly Winthrop's spoken description of her search for a way to express a difficult thought. The reader's experience cannot be Gwendolen's or Dolly's, but the shocks in both passages can be felt, the thought processes can be followed, as we tap into a greater primal consciousness through the nervous wanderings of the sentences. This is what it really means to say that George Eliot's language is always distinctly scientific in form, even if it is not so in word choice. Unsurprisingly, the best explanation for her linguistic merging of emotional depth and scientific theory can be found in her novels. As the Reverend Mr Lyon says in *Felix Holt*, 'I am an eager seeker for precision, and would fain find a language subtle enough to follow the utmost intricacies of the soul's pathways' (ch. 5). Those complicated sentences throughout George Eliot's prose are part of her own search for such pathways.

NOTES

1 Anthony Trollope, *An Autobiography* (1883; Michael Sadleir and Frederick Page (eds.), Oxford University Press, 1950), p. 247.
2 R. C. Trench, *On the Study of Words* (1851; Whitefish, MT: Kessinger Press, 2004), p. 4.
3 Elizabeth Deeds Ermarth, 'George Eliot and the World as Language', in Stephen Regan (ed.), *The Nineteenth-Century Novel: A Critical Reader* (New York: Barnes and Noble, 1971), pp. 320–9, 325.
4 [R.H. Hutton], *Economist* (27 April 1861), 455.
5 Rick Rylance, *Victorian Psychology and British Culture, 1850–1880* (Oxford University Press, 2000), pp. 84–6 and 131.
6 Sally Shuttleworth, *George Eliot and Nineteenth-Century Science: The Make-Believe of a Beginning* (Cambridge University Press, 1984), p. 72.
7 Ibid. p. ix.
8 *Transparent Minds: Narrative Modes for Presenting Consciousness in Fiction* (Princeton University Press, 1978), p. 14.

CHAPTER 21

Law

Kieran Dolin

In *Adam Bede* George Eliot compares her aims as a novelist to the act of giving evidence in a court of law: 'my strongest effort is ... to give a faithful account of men and things as they have mirrored themselves in my mind ... I feel as much bound to tell you as precisely as I can what that reflection is, as if I were in the witness-box narrating my experience on oath' (*AB*, ch. 17). In arguing so deliberately that legal procedure and novelistic realism are analogous, George Eliot suggests something of the importance of law for herself and her society. The complex reality that she so faithfully strives to represent is shaped and structured by laws, and from very early in her career as a novelist she ensured that she correctly understood this framework and its details by consulting lawyer-friends. Thanking one of these, Frederic Harrison, on 9 June 1875, she noted, 'through your kindness I may be able to understand what were the family affairs of my personages – for such understanding is necessary to my comfort, if not to the true relation of that part of their history which I undertake to write' (*L*, 6: 150). George Eliot's goal is not merely to understand legal technicalities and thereby ensure the accuracy of her plots, but to infuse a precise and familiar sense of the legal culture in which her characters live, to represent their relationships, attitudes and actions within a historical and normative continuum. Thus for George Eliot the law is an integral part of the unfolding history of society.

The age of reform

From the early decades of the nineteenth century, Evangelical Christian campaigns for the moral reformation of the individual and society were paralleled by a Utilitarian movement to reform the inherited laws and institutions of Britain. George Eliot came into close contact with this reform movement through her work on the *Westminster Review*, which was a major forum for progressive thought. In the great novel of her maturity, *Middlemarch*, the scope of this movement is suggested through incidental references to the Catholic Emancipation Bill of 1829, the new police and the law reformer Sir Samuel Romilly, as well as through the major plot strands detailing Brooke's involvement in the momentous Reform Bill election campaign and Lydgate's ambitions to reform the practice of medicine. Romilly was a lawyer who took up the challenge of implementing Jeremy Bentham's ideas about the need to rationalise the criminal law, to make it a more effective deterrent. The English legal system and its traditional doctrines had been expounded and justified during the 1760s in Blackstone's *Commentaries*, but in the next generation Bentham scathingly criticised its irrational elements and archaism, and especially its reliance on fictions as an instrument of legal change. He advocated comprehensive new legislation as the only remedy for the accumulation of piecemeal statutes and case law handed down from the past. Such was the criminal law at the end of the eighteenth century, the notorious 'Bloody Code', top-heavy with two hundred capital offences. Romilly and others gradually reformed the penal law and trial procedure. Parliamentary inquiries and statutes became the means of rectifying other parts of the law, including the Poor Law, wills and the court system. Underlying this rationalising and modernising movement was a simple concept that law was the command of a sovereign. Although particular campaigns were contested, the ideal of reform was gradually accepted, and by the end of the century its method had become integral to modern liberal democratic politics.

Writing in the latter half of the century, George Eliot the novelist was working from a position of achieved change. Her characteristic stance of retrospective narration, of setting her stories in an earlier era, enables a reflection on the process of legal as well as social reform. The major crimes of infanticide in *Adam Bede* and theft in *Silas Marner* are subject to the Bloody Code, and the late reprieve whereby Hetty Sorrel's death penalty is commuted to transportation was typical of the pre-reform legal system. By contrast, *Felix Holt, the Radical* and *Middlemarch* are set in the midst of the reformist period. Mr Brooke's anxiety over the appropriate punishment for Dagley the poacher is not only a sign of his vacillating character, but also an attempt to adopt the new rehabilitative ideal in his decision-making as a local justice of the peace (ch. 39). In and around Middlemarch, as in the small town of Milby in 'Janet's Repentance', reform is a talismanic ideal for some, and a vaguely threatening epithet for others, whether it is proposed in the religious, political or medical fields.

George Eliot and the social history of law

In notebooks kept while preparing to write *Middlemarch*, George Eliot cited a comment by the legal evolutionist Sir Henry Maine that the secret of Bentham's success was in giving the nation 'a distinct object to aim at in the pursuit of improvement'. He placed this aspiration in a longer historical process, saying that Bentham 'gave escape to a current that had long been trying to find its way outwards'.[1] Maine pioneered the historical study of law in England, offering an account of the development of legal concepts from the earliest known societies. His evolutionary and anthropological approach attracted George Eliot, who took copious notes from Maine's *Ancient Law*. Drawing on Montesquieu and other continental thinkers, Maine argued that law emerged from community customs, not simply from the edicts of a sovereign. George Eliot had developed a similar insight from her reading of Riehl, as she noted in her essay 'The Natural History of German Life': 'To the mind of the peasant, law presents itself as "the custom of the country", and it is his pride to be well versed in all customs. *Custom with him holds the place of sentiment, of theory, and in many cases of affection*' (*Essays*, 279). This sense that laws are surrounded by a penumbra of custom pervades her writings: in the culture of expectation that surrounds Peter Featherstone's will during his last days, and in the shocked responses of the gentry to the codicil to Casaubon's will, in *Middlemarch* (ch. 49); and in Tulliver's obstinate belief that 'water was water' and that he has customary rights to it in *The Mill on the Floss*, for example (*MF*, book 2, ch. 2). Maine's approach revealed the social functions of various categories of law, such as wills, property and contract, as well as their historical development and cultural differences. He offered his readers the potential of a narrative approach to law, in which change was as important as continuity. George Eliot noted his 'three agencies by which law is brought into harmony with society: Legal Fictions, Equity and Legislation'.[2]

Maine's approach was by no means radical, and in the historically minded Victorian era it was highly influential. Another of George Eliot's lawyer-friends, Mr Justice Bowen, recommended the historical method for the study of law in words that echo some of her own images in *The Mill on the Floss*:

> Law is the application of certain rules to a subject-matter which is constantly shifting. What is it? English life! English business! England in movement, advancing from a continuous past to a continuous future. National life, national business, like every other product of human intelligence and

> culture, is a growth – begins far away in the dim past, advances slowly, shaping and forming itself by the operation of purely natural causes.[3]

Although lacking the astringency of George Eliot's judgement about the narrowness of the Dodsons, this hymn to English law and commerce seems to draw subconsciously on her image of 'this rich plain where the great river flows forever onward' (*MF*, book 4, ch. 1).

Reforming the law of the family

In an unguarded moment during the serialisation of *Middlemarch*, Maine asked George Eliot whether it was going to be a very long novel, overlooking the notorious length of legal cases. In *Ancient Law* Maine had noted 'the rigorous consistency with which the view of a complete legal subjection on the part of a wife is carried on by [the English common law], where it is untouched by equity or statutes'.[4] Under the doctrine of *coverture* husband and wife were regarded as one person at common law. The husband was considered lord and the wife his vassal, her will and her property submerged in his. From the 1850s, many of George Eliot's friends worked to reform these laws. In 1854 Barbara Leigh Smith (later Bodichon) published a pamphlet entitled *A Brief Summary of the Laws in England concerning Women*, and then initiated a petition in support of a Married Women's Property Bill, which George Eliot signed. She also addressed this issue in her essays and reviews. Reviewing the 'Life and Opinions of Milton' in 1855 she compared Milton's advocacy of a more rational divorce law to Caroline Norton's writings on the subject, praising both (*Essays*, 196). Norton's marital travails exposed the limits of the common law with respect to child custody, domestic violence, divorce, and women's property and their earnings in a series of *causes célèbres*, and her accounts of marital unhappiness were complemented for George Eliot by Milton's testimony as a husband. In 1855, when George Eliot wrote this review, a new statute empowering a court to grant divorces was before Parliament. When passed in 1857, it gave husbands greater rights than wives, thus preserving the existing gender order while reforming the law. In 1870 and 1882 Married Women's Property Acts were passed that finally dissolved the doctrine of *coverture*, and gave women rights to buy, sell and own property, to sue and be sued in their own right, and to control their earnings.

George Eliot had a personal interest in these laws, having chosen to live with George Henry Lewes without the sanction of marriage, a decision that left her subject to the social penalty of ostracism. Lewes was unable to divorce his wife, Agnes; like Norton, he was deemed to have condoned his spouse's marital offences. The objectionable effects of these laws had long been known. On 1 June 1848 George Eliot had written to Charles Bray, in connection with the plot of *Jane Eyre*, condemning this 'diabolical law which chains a man soul and body to a putrefying carcase' (*L*, 1: 268). Her own fiction generally abjures gothic excess, in order to explore the reality of legal subjection within marriage: Janet Dempster in *Scenes of Clerical Life* has only a vague idea of how the law might protect her from her husband's violence, and decides not to pursue the matter; and Gwendolen Harleth in *Daniel Deronda* is forced to realise her complete humiliation and 'thraldom' while maintaining a façade of marital devotion (ch. 48). Side by side with such literary representations of mental cruelty in marriage, the Divorce Court judges developed a broader interpretation of the cruelty provisions of the 1857 Act, widening the availability of divorce, and demonstrating the potential for law to respond to changing social attitudes and understandings.

Property in law and life

'There is nothing which so generally strikes the imagination, or engages the affections of mankind, as the right of property', declared Blackstone.[5] In their different ways the Tullivers, father and son, illustrate this dictum. The former is devastated by the loss of his land, while the latter restores it by judicious investment in trading ventures. The demands of capital led to new forms of property, such as patents and shares, and vastly expanded the number of consumer goods. Statutes such as the Companies Act 1862 created and sought to regulate new entities, and reanimated old legal fictions, in this instance corporate personality. Landed property retained its power and aura for the industrial magnates rich enough to afford such traditional estates. The growth of literacy in a rapidly rising population created opportunities for entrepreneurial writers. The literary property of authors was confirmed and its term extended through the copyright amendment law of 1842, agitation for which engaged the energies of Wordsworth, Dickens and other writers. George Eliot and Lewes harvested the benefits of this law, carefully negotiating the terms of her publishing contracts, and prudently preserving the value of her copyrights under her own control.

In an apparent riposte to Blackstone, Mr Vincy asks in *Middlemarch*, 'Who was ever awe-struck about a testator, or sung a hymn on the title to real property?' (ch. 31). And yet it is clear that wills and land did attract George Eliot's imagination, as important elements in realist fiction and as practical concerns of her middle-class economic life. Major legal mechanisms whereby property was inherited or lost, including entails and bankruptcy, were the subjects on which she sought advice from lawyers such as Harrison. The legal structures that emerged in response to Britain's commercial and industrial growth interest George Eliot less than the older forms of property; the bank collapse at the start of *Daniel Deronda* is important for its effect on Gwendolen and her family, but less important than Grandcourt's will or the entail on the Mallinger inheritance. However, George Eliot is not entranced by the intricacies of land law or succession, as Anthony Trollope is, for example. Her imaginative investment is in plots of development, more than inheritance, reflecting her position as a member of the newly dominant middle class, and as a woman from the provinces who succeeded in the metropolitan literary marketplace. In *Middlemarch* and *Felix Holt*, the heroines refuse to succeed to estates that are associated with the misdeeds of the past. The complicated plot of *Felix Holt*, which George Eliot refined through a rich epistolary dialogue with Frederic Harrison, shows an inheritance eroded by self-indulgence and intergenerational conflict. Her metaphor for Casaubon's will, the dead hand, translates a term from medieval law, *mortmain*, meaning land bequeathed to religious and other bodies forever, property controlled from the grave. The law governing land was medieval in origin, and had accumulated centuries of technical complexity. Rationalised systems that centrally registered titles developed elsewhere in the mid nineteenth century, but English lawyers resisted reforms until 1882 and 1922. Land and inheritance were cultural and legal categories that preserved traditional power structures and values. George Eliot's reformist and evolutionary commitments lead her to incorporate inheritance plots, but to question the nature or the value of what is being bequeathed. The estates of Featherstone, Casaubon, Transome and Alcharisi all require their beneficiaries to make difficult ethical choices, implying a gap between law, custom and personal ideas of justice.

At her death George Eliot's own estate was valued at £40,000, and included two houses and a farm originally inherited by Lewes, about which she gave firm directions in respect of the lease and cottages on the farm: 'let there be no pulling down to rebuild, … but only attention to keep the roofs good and make sufficient windows for light and ventilation' (*L*, 7: 159). She was tentative and cautious about the purchase of property, relying on professional advisors, such as Mr Justice Bowen and

J. W. Cross. Cross assisted her in buying a house, and Bowen gave advice on a deed of trust which set up the George Henry Lewes Studentship at Cambridge to assist young researchers in physiology. Her last will and testament was notable for its adroit use of her knowledge of the laws relating to women's property: she set up annuities for several women friends, on terms that ensured their husbands could not claim the money.

When George Eliot first sought legal advice for her plots, she joked about consulting 'hard-headed lawyers' (*L*, 3: 180). Dempster in *Scenes of Clerical Life* and Wakem in *The Mill on the Floss* conform to this conventional image. But when Rex Gascoigne in *Daniel Deronda* proposes that 'the foundations and growth of law make the most interesting aspects of philosophy and history' (ch. 58), he reflects the growth of modern professionalism, and expresses an understanding widely shared in Victorian England.

NOTES

1 John Clark and Victor A. Neufeldt (eds.), *George Eliot's Middlemarch Notebooks: A Transcription* (Berkeley, CA: University of California Press, 1979), p. 204.
2 Ibid., p. 203.
3 'Address to the Birmingham Law Students' Society', qtd in Sir Henry Cunningham, *Lord Bowen: A Biographical Sketch* (London: John Murray, 1897), p. 165.
4 Henry Sumner Maine, *Ancient Law: Its Connection with the Early History of Society and its Relation to Modern Ideas* (1861; London: John Murray, 1906), p. 164.
5 William Blackstone, *Commentaries on the Laws of England* (1762; University of Chicago Press, 1979), book II, chapter I.

CHAPTER 22

Metropolitanism

John Rignall

When, in September 1851, Marian Evans left Coventry to take up permanent residence in London at 142 Strand to work on the *Westminster Review* with John Chapman, she was moving to the greatest metropolis in the world, at that moment proclaiming its pre-eminence as the hub of empire and centre of global trade in the Great Exhibition at the Crystal Palace in Hyde Park. Her move was part of that larger social movement from the land to the cities which took the population of London from just under one million to six and a half million in the course of the nineteenth century. It was in London that she became the novelist George Eliot and where, apart from some lengthy visits to continental Europe and summer months spent writing in the country or, from 1877, at her house in Witley, she was to live for the rest of her days. She led a metropolitan life, but although she enjoyed the rich cultural life of the capital with its theatres and concerts, museums and art galleries, she remained a reluctant metropolitan, her imagination always more at home in the provincial, predominantly rural world of her upbringing, which was the principal inspiration and focus of her fiction. In her letters she frequently disparages London and expresses her relief when she has the opportunity to escape it for the countryside. It was only towards the end of her life that she seemed openly to embrace her metropolitan status. In her last published work, *Impressions of Theophrastus Such* (1879), the persona of the unsuccessful middle-aged writer Theophrastus claims that he belongs to the 'Nation of London', and his words strike a note of authorial confession as he looks back to his rural beginnings and admits that, since then, 'I have learned to care for foreign countries, for literatures foreign and ancient … for the life of London, half sleepless with eager thought and strife, with indigestion or with hunger; and now my consciousness is chiefly of the busy, anxious metropolitan sort' (*TS*, ch. 2).

In her early years in London when she was editing the *Westminster Review*, translating Feuerbach and making a new circle of friends and acquaintances, her letters reveal a life and a consciousness that were, indeed, busy, anxious and metropolitan. Writing to her half-sister Fanny in April 1854 when she was correcting proofs of her Feuerbach translation, she declines an invitation to join Fanny at the sea-side with a mild rebuke:

> But do you imagine me sitting with my hands crossed, ready to start for any quarter of the world at the shortest notice? It is not on those terms that people, not rich, live in London. I shall be deep in proof-sheets till the end of May, and shall only dismiss them to make material for new ones. (*L*, 2: 148–9)

Metropolitan life at this stage is the intellectually strenuous one of trying to make a name and a living for herself by her pen, like the 'hard-run literary man, who is every moment expecting the knock of the printer's boy' that she refers to in a review-article of the time (*Essays*, 139). When she leaves for Weimar with G. H. Lewes later that year she finds its quiet provincial backwardness a welcome escape from the pressures of London life, and in 'Three Months in Weimar' she proclaims its attractions, at least for a short time, for anyone 'weary of English unrest, of that society of "eels in a jar", where each is trying to get his head above the other' (*Essays*, 84). The implication is that she herself can find the metropolitan world of ambitious striving and competitive individualism wearying, and it is striking that when she turned to writing fiction, the dramatic potential of that world, which had inspired novelists like Balzac whom she admired, made no appeal to her imagination.

In the brilliant essays she wrote just before the outset of her career as a novelist she anticipates the course of her fiction by distancing herself from the subject of metropolitan life. In 'Worldliness and Otherworldliness: The Poet Young' (1857), the fatal flaw of abstraction she identifies in her critical demolition of Young's poetry is associated with the townsman's distance from the natural world:

> Indeed, we remember no mind in poetic literature that seems to have absorbed less of the beauty and the healthy breath of the common land-scape than Young's. His images … lie almost entirely within that circle of observation which would be familiar to a man who lived in town, hung about the theatres, read the newspaper, and went home often by moon and star light. (*Essays*, 370)

It is the natural rather than the urban landscape that grounds the poetic imagination in reality. In 'The Natural History of German Life' (1856), another form of abstraction is seen to mar the work of the most metropolitan of contemporary novelists, Charles Dickens. He is our 'one great novelist who is gifted with the utmost power of rendering the external traits of our town population', but he fails to render the inner life, so that 'he scarcely ever passes from the humorous and external to the emotional and tragic, without becoming as transcendent in his unreality as he was a moment before in his artistic truthfulness' (*Essays*, 271). What she deprecates here is the yoking together of opposites and oscillation between extremes that can be understood, in Raymond Williams's terms, as Dickens's strikingly original response to metropolitan existence with all its contradictions, 'to the reality of the new kind of city'.[1] That reality is one that her own novels will not confront.

The principal focus of George Eliot's 'Natural History' essay is on peasant life rather than urban, and it indicates the area in which her own fiction is to pursue the aim of artistic truthfulness by avoiding the sentimental idealisation of 'idyllic literature', which she criticises as having 'always expressed the imagination of the cultivated and town-bred, rather than the truth of rustic life' (*Essays*, 269). Her own imagination may not have been town-bred but it was highly cultivated, and it is from the perspective of a widely read, well-travelled, polyglot metropolitan intellectual that she looks for the truth of rustic life in her novels by recreating the provincial world of her origins. Her metropolitanism is one of language and perspective rather than subject matter, and she writes for those who are as distant from the rural world as she now is. The narrator of *The Mill on the Floss* (1860) assumes that its readers will be familiar with '[j]ourneying down the Rhone on a summer's day' and will share a 'sense of oppressive narrowness' 'in watching this old-fashioned family life on the banks of the Floss' led by the Tullivers and Dodsons (*MF*, book 4, ch. 1). The gap between the experience of a cultivated readership and the life of rural characters is brought into sharp focus by the depth of Mr Tulliver's attachment to the home his family have lived in for generations: 'Our instructed vagrancy, which has hardly time to linger by the hedgerows, but runs away early to the tropics, and is at home with palms and banyans … can hardly get a dim notion of what an old-fashioned man like Tulliver felt for this spot, where all his memories centred' (book 3, ch. 9). The restless, mobile educated mind has no fixed abode, and Tulliver's deep roots in place and past are at odds with the rootlessness of metropolitan modernity. In the urbane language of the metropolitan intelligentsia George Eliot prescribes the limits of its understanding.

The Mill on the Floss, with its problematically tragic ending, is not an idyllic representation of rural life, nor is Maggie Tulliver ever allowed to escape the oppressive narrowness of her origins. George Eliot's own liberating removal to the dynamic world of London, a journey which provides one of the classic plots of the nineteenth-century novel, the story of the young provincial confronting the metropolis, is never exploited by her as a subject for fiction. There is no equivalent in her work to Balzac's *Lost Illusions* (1837–43) or Dickens's *Great Expectations* (1860); and the confusion and excitement of Charlotte Brontë's Lucy Snowe in *Villette* (1853) on first arriving in London lies beyond the experience of Eliot's heroines. In *Middlemarch* Dorothea finally moves to London as Ladislaw's wife, but the event is reported rather than dramatised and the radical change that it involves is only hinted at in her sister Celia's comically baffled question: 'How can you always live in a street?' (*M*, ch. 84). Celia's instinctive recoil is close to the novelist's own experience at the time. After writing the final pages of *Middlemarch* at Bad Homburg in Germany in the autumn of 1872, she travelled home with Lewes via Paris but soon fled from that other great metropolis of modernity 'in horrible disgust with the shops of the Rue de la Paix and the Boulevard' to the provincial quiet of Boulogne, claiming that 'we have an affinity for what the world calls "dull places"' (*L*, 5: 318). She visited Paris on many occasions, but although she overcame her initial dislike of the city (*L*, 8: 333), it never inspired her with unqualified enthusiasm, and its one appearance in her fiction, in the retrospective summary of Lydgate's education in *Middlemarch*, casts it in a questionable light. It may be a centre of learning and the most advanced place to study medicine, but it is at the same time a site of melodrama and emotional excess where Lydgate becomes wildly infatuated with the actress Laure and she murders her husband on stage. In what can be read as a back-handed homage to Balzac, metropolitan life is given something of the lurid colouring – though nothing of the density – of his Parisian novels, which she knew well, and it seems to exist on a different level of reality from the richly imagined provincial world of Middlemarch and stands apart as explicitly alien territory.

Although on this occasion Lewes was 'quite rabid about Paris', he was far more at home in metropolitan life than she was. When she first met him she described him to her Coventry friends as 'Londonish' (*L*, 2: 37), and an early biographer, Oscar Browning who knew them both, claimed that it was only because Lewes was 'a confirmed Londoner' that she lived in London and not abroad.[2] Living on a street was never congenial to her. As she put it in 1861 after moving from suburban Wandsworth to central London, 'I suppose I shall never love London, or believe that I am as well in the streets as in the fields' (*L*, 3: 369). What had pleased her about life in Wandsworth were the 'glorious breezy walks and wide horizons' which prompted her to reflect on her preference 'for a nook quite in the country, far away from Palaces crystal or otherwise, with … hedgerow paths among the endless fields where you meet nobody'. But, she concludes, 'the business of life shuts us up within the environs of London and within sight of human advancement, which I should be so very glad to believe in without seeing' (*L*, 3: 14–15).

In central London she and Lewes kept abreast of 'human advancement' by meeting scientists like T. H. Huxley, Richard Owen and John Tyndall as well as writers and artists, and by attending lectures, plays and concerts, but the pleasure these afforded was often qualified by the conditions of city life. Two Beethoven concerts in April 1861 she described as 'musical treats' while complaining that 'the enjoyment of such things is much diminished by the gas and bad air', which prompts her to conclude 'that London privileges of this sort are not worth the purchase to easily perturbed people like ourselves' (*L*, 3: 404). The price she paid for such metropolitan privileges was the depression that often afflicted her: 'this London life oppresses and *de*presses me so terribly' (*L*, 3: 402), she complained to Barbara Bodichon in 1861, and she returned to the same theme two years later: 'The wide sky, the *not*-London, makes a new creature of me in half an hour. I wonder then why I am ever depressed … I come back to London, and again the air is full of demons' (*L*, 4: 102).

Her 1865 poem 'In a London Drawing Room' gives formal expression to this despondent, depressed vision of London:

> The sky is cloudy, yellowed by the smoke.
> For view there are the houses opposite
> Cutting the sky with one long line of wall
> Like solid fog: far as the eye can stretch
> Monotony of surface and of form
> Without a break to hang a guess upon.
> … No figure lingering
> Pauses to feed the hunger of the eye
> Or rest a little on the lap of life.
> All hurry on and look upon the ground,
> Or glance unmarking at the passers by
> The wheels are hurrying too, cabs, carriages
> All closed in multiplied identity.
> The world seems one huge prison-house and court
> Where men are punished at the slightest cost,
> With lowest rate of colour, warmth and joy. (Poetry, 2: 91)

The monotony of the urban landscape is inimical to the imagination – 'without a break to hang a guess upon' – as is its perpetual motion, and the desolate vision of ceaseless, self-absorbed human hurrying chimes with other famous descriptions of the London streets from Wordsworth onwards. Twenty years earlier Friedrich Engels in *The Condition of the Working Class in England* (1845) found the same phenomenon of people crowding past each other without a glance to be a repellent characteristic of life in Britain's great cities and an illustration of the fundamental principle of contemporary society, its narrow self-seeking and atomised individualism. George Eliot's perspective is not as consciously ideological but her vision of the metropolitan world as a huge prison-house for the punishment of mankind implies a similar critique in different terms. Fifty years later images of yellow smoke and fog will be used to more striking effect in T. S. Eliot's early poetry of urban life, while George Eliot's pedestrians who 'all hurry on and look upon the ground' prefigure the crowd flowing over London Bridge where 'each man fixed his eyes upon his feet' in the 'Unreal City' of *The Waste Land* (1922).[3] In her distaste for a world of monotonous streets the novelist anticipates the later Eliot's fastidious recoil from the spiritual desolation of the modern metropolis.

It is only in her last novel *Daniel Deronda* (1876) that she writes about the contemporary metropolitan world she inhabited, but she does so without the intense imaginative engagement and curiosity of Dickens or Thackeray, Balzac or Flaubert. Daniel himself may bear some slight resemblance to the metropolitan figure of the *flâneur* as he roams the streets of London in search of traces of Jewish life after he has met Mirah, but although we are told that 'he looked into shops, he observed faces' (*DD*, ch. 33), what he sees in his rambling is never brought vividly to life, and his curiosity is in any case confined to what answers his inner needs. Neither the character nor his creator seems to have any more than a peremptory interest in the spectacle of London as the dynamic centre of change. Privileged by his upbringing and education, Daniel is a cultivated metropolitan intellectual but he stands musingly apart from that 'eels in a jar' society as one of those 'young men in whom the unproductive labour of questioning is sustained by three or four per cent on capital that someone else has battled for' (*DD*, ch. 17). In this respect he resembles the rentier protagonist of Flaubert's nearly contemporary novel of Parisian life, *L'Education sentimentale* (1869), which Lewes's journal records George Eliot as reading in June 1875 when she was writing *Deronda*; but where Flaubert uses Frédéric Moreau to explore social and historical reality, Daniel is shown to be engaged in a journey of inner discovery which is only indirectly related to the condition of contemporary society. There are glimpses of London life, in public houses or society drawing rooms, or in interior scenes like the Cohen family's celebration of the Sabbath, but what lies beyond the drawing-room window, the rich spectacle of urban existence to be seen on the streets of a great capital such as Flaubert presents, is barely visible.

The principal characteristic of metropolitan life as it appears in the novel is rootlessness. The narrator's well-known observation that a 'human life … should be well rooted in some spot of a native land' clearly implies that such roots are the prerogative of a rural life where one lives in 'one's own homestead' and can discern 'the face of the earth' (*DD*, ch. 3). That rural life is here no more than an object of nostalgia, and no character is further from such roots than the mercenary Lapidoth, the unprincipled father of the highly principled Mirah and Mordecai, in whom metropolitanism is conflated with a suspect cosmopolitanism. Adept at languages and moving restlessly between London, New York and the cities of Central Europe in pursuit of the money he can only gamble away, he is the rootless product of contemporary capitalism and a creature of the modern metropolis, emerging out of the streets of London to haunt his daughter and fading back into them again after he has stolen Daniel's ring. Daniel's search for his own roots takes him in the opposite direction towards an idealised Jewish community and away from the modern urban world. His projected journey to the East at the end of the novel is a final flight of the novelist's imagination from the metropolitanism that was never able to inspire her.

NOTES

1 Raymond Williams, *The English Novel from Dickens to Lawrence* (London: Chatto and Windus, 1970), p. 28.
2 Oscar Browning, *Life of George Eliot* (London: Walter Scott, 1890), p. 40.
3 T. S. Eliot, *Collected Poems 1909–1962* (London: Faber and Faber, 1963), pp. 13, 65.

CHAPTER 23

Money

Dermot Coleman

In January 1862, George Eliot records in her journal the genesis of a negotiation in which the lure of money eventually drew her into a publishing contract away from the house of Blackwood for the first and only time in her career. 'Mr Smith the publisher called and had an interview with G. He asked if I were open to a "magnificent offer". This made me think about money – but it is better for me not to be rich' (*J*, 108). Although George Smith's 'magnificent offer' was subsequently revised down when she refused to agree to a demanding serialisation schedule in the *Cornhill Magazine*, the £7,000 he eventually advanced for *Romola* was an amount she never exceeded for a new novel. Twelve years later, as the cheaper editions of *Middlemarch*, in which she and Lewes had cleverly negotiated an ongoing royalty interest, were continuing to sell beyond expectations, she turns to Wordsworth to articulate the inviolability of her higher ideals in an increasingly materialistic age: 'I care so much for the demonstration of an intense joy in life on the basis of "plain living and high thinking," in this time of more and more eager scrambling after wealth and show' (*L*, 6: 17).

For better or worse, George Eliot became wealthy through her novels and both secured and added to that wealth by prudent investment in the stockmarket. Her individual progression is exceptional but, in thinking a lot about money and doing so in varied and developing ways, she is representative of her generation. In her records of earnings and outgoings, portfolio valuations and dividend receipts, carefully documented in her letters and journals, she testifies to the increasing pervasiveness of the money economy as industrial capitalism matured in Britain during the nineteenth century. Classical economics in the first half of the century had already reformulated the traditional stores of wealth and value – land and labour – according to their ability to generate financial returns. The symbiotic relationship that the emerging 'science' of Political Economy shared with the moral and social philosophy of Utilitarianism during this period, reached a more telling synthesis in the final decade of George Eliot's life with the emergence of the more mathematically grounded Neoclassical economics. For as Utilitarianism applies a common currency (pleasure or pain) to all moral judgements in relation to their consequences, so, argued the economists of the 1870s and 1880s, all economic value can be derived from a single measure: the monetary price exchange at which marginal utility is satisfied. The ascent of money did not, of course, go unopposed and even prominent economic liberals warned of a growing tendency towards a monist system of values. In so doing they were, to some extent, validating the prophecies of the most vociferous opponent of Political Economy, Thomas Carlyle, whose fundamental complaint from around 1830 onwards was that '[w]e have profoundly forgotten everywhere that *Cash-payment* is not the sole relation of human beings'.[1]

George Eliot bore witness to more than just important shifts in economic theory. Her whole life was framed by a series of monetary landmarks

Figure 14 'Sketches in the Bank of England: Machine for weighing gold' (*Illustrated London News*, 1873).

that crucially shaped collective understandings of the nature and meaning of money. At the time of her birth in 1819, Britain was still adjusting to the restoration of more normal economic conditions after many years of war with France. Most significantly, a series of measures was under way that culminated in the passing of the Act for the Resumption of Cash Payment in 1821. The Act returned sterling to the gold standard and overturned the Bank Restriction Act of 1797, which had suspended convertibility as a necessary wartime measure. The over-issuance of banknotes in the intervening period had served to depreciate the currency and fuel inflation. In the novels, George Eliot satirises the nostalgia of those negligent landowners for whom the economic conditions provided an inequitable but temporary source of prosperity: 'It was still that glorious war-time which was felt to be a peculiar favour of Providence towards the landed interest, and the fall of prices had not yet come to carry the race of small squires and yeomen down that road to ruin for which extravagant habits and bad husbandry were plentifully anointing their wheels' (*SM*, ch. 3). While the so-called Banking School, largely representing the interests of trade and industry, continued to argue against the restrictions on note issuance imposed by gold convertibility, bullionism prevailed. In 1844, the year in which George Eliot began the translation of Strauss's *Das Leben Jesu*, the Bank Charter Act was passed. Its core principle was to limit the issuance of paper currency to underlying gold reserves and it provided the monetary stability that allowed the pound sterling to emerge as the global benchmark currency and the British economy to sustain low-inflationary growth for the rest of George Eliot's life.

Banking and financial crises nonetheless recurred periodically, resulting in occasional temporary suspensions of the Bank Charter Act, which freed the Bank of England to inject emergency liquidity into the money markets. It was in response to one such suspension, following the severe banking crisis of 1857, that George Eliot's friend, Charles Bray, wrote a pamphlet (subsequently summarised in a letter to the *Leader* on 19 December 1857 entitled 'Our Monetary System') in which he reasserts the Banking School's case for the repeal of the Act. George Eliot wrote to Bray on the issue, professing economic naivety – it is, she says, 'a subject of which I know so little'. In fact, she demonstrates a subtle understanding of the cases for and limitations of both fiat and metallic currency systems, even employing technical terms with ease and confidence: 'government security', 'circulating medium', 'intrinsic value' (*L*, 2: 414–15). Above all, the letter indicates that she recognised a crucial aspect of the social meaning of money that goes beyond the economic: that money of any variety relies ultimately on the trust of all its users. In this, George Eliot is articulating the shift Mary Poovey identifies around the middle of the century whereby paper currencies and the writing they contained came to be accepted as representations of fact. Poovey describes this process as one of social 'naturalization' whereby first bank notes and then increasingly abstract instruments 'passed beneath the horizon of cultural visibility'.[2]

The temporal settings of most her novels allowed George Eliot to explore the ethical and social implications of economically related motives and actions at this vanishing point, when both the representational forms in which value was stored and exchanged and the institutional frameworks within which those forms were earned, saved and distributed were at a pivotal stage of transition. In her most fabular tales, *Silas Marner* and *Brother Jacob*, she makes use of the talismanic properties of gold coinage to examine concepts of money-related pathology (hoarding, stealing) and transformation in richly allegorical ways that rely on the period settings. Reflecting on the success of *Silas Marner* in May 1861, she tells Blackwood: 'There can be no great painting of misers under the present system of paper money – cheques bills scrip and the like: nobody can handle that dull property as men handled the glittering gold' (*L*, 3: 411). The transition from concrete to abstract understandings of money is most fully worked in *The Mill on the Floss*, in which Uncle Pullet could 'not see how a man could have any security for his money unless he turned it into land' (*MF*, book 1, ch. 9), while his sister-in-law prefers to hide her money in various places around her house, 'for, to Mrs Glegg's mind, banks and strong-boxes would have nullified the pleasure of property – she might as well have taken her food in capsules' (book 1, ch. 12). Significantly, Tulliver's bankruptcy is brought about by an abstract paper mortgage, over whose transferability he has no control. By contrast, his own contribution towards the repayment of his creditors (which is, of course, greatly accelerated by the addition of his son's more speculative profits) is slowly and tangibly accumulated in a very old-fashioned tin box. The novel correlates the speed with which money is accumulated and multiplied with the movement to abstraction. The prosperity of St Ogg's was built on the physical trading of commodities by 'industrious men of business of a former generation, who made their fortunes slowly' (book 1, ch. 12). Mr Deane and his firm of Guest & Co. represent the conglomerating merchant-house of mid century, whose trading origins were extending into wider financing and banking activities and therefore look forward to the money economy from which George Eliot was writing: 'these days of rapid money-getting' (book 1, ch. 12).

Her own 'money-getting' as a novelist was certainly most rapid. In one of her last essays before she turned to fiction, 'Silly Novels by Lady Novelists' (October 1856), she criticises the detachment from the real world of those 'fair writers' who 'think five hundred a-year a miserable pittance' (*Essays*, 303). George Eliot's contempt for writers she justifiably considered her inferiors is understandable. In the three years prior to the publication of *Adam Bede* in 1859, her annual earnings from reviews and *Scenes of Clerical Life* averaged around £300. By 1864, however, advances and sales on her first four full novels alone had earned her around £15,000 and her wealth continued to grow steadily.[3] To put her earnings in context, an 1868 analysis of income distribution in England and Wales shows that a family earning in excess of £1,000 per year fell within the top 0.5 per cent of the total population.[4] Within ten years of this survey, she was receiving more than £1,000 per year from her stock dividends alone, while her total earnings from *Middlemarch* and *Daniel Deronda* eventually surpassed even Smith's payment for *Romola*. Her early career as a translator, de facto editor and essayist obviously had a radically different economic profile, but her attitude to money in this more straitened period shaped her ambivalence to wealth when it came to her. Indeed to understand her formative concepts of money we must go back further.

Even before George Eliot's adoption of a somewhat stern Evangelicalism in the mid 1830s, the influence of Christian Political Economics would have found its way into the more traditionally Anglican household of the sober, hard-working and financially prudent Robert Evans. By 1841, George Eliot is recording her excitement (*L*, 1: 104) at receiving a six-volume edition of the sermons of Thomas Chalmers, whose influential 'Bridgewater Treatise' (1833) made an explicit and direct connection between moral worth and the providential accumulation of money. Thirty years later, she exposes this connection as ethically untenable through the psychologically penetrating portrayal of the banker Bulstrode, a character whose devotion to the precepts of religiously inspired Political Economy loudly echoes Chalmers's description of the philosophy as 'but one grand exemplification of the alliance, which a God of righteousness hath established, between prudence and moral principle on the one hand, and physical comfort on the other'.[5] Meanwhile, more secular illustrations of economic principles founded on individual responsibility were being popularised during George Eliot's formative years, in the writings of Harriet Martineau, Jane Marcet and others. Marcet's *Conversations on Political Economy* appeared in 1824 and Martineau's *Illustrations of Political Economy* in 1832. As Boyd Hilton has observed, it was they, rather than

Ricardo and Mill, 'who mediated political economy for the masses by placing it in the current of domestic household management'.[6]

George Eliot's family background forged a life-long money ethic characterised by thrift and prudence and underpinned by an abhorrence of debt. A letter to Blackwood in 1859 reveals a tellingly jumbled mixture of values and anxieties: 'I certainly care a great deal for the money, as I suppose all anxious minds do that love independence and have been brought up to think debt and begging the two deepest dishonours short of crime' (*L*, 3: 69). The link between money and independence is one that recurs in her letters and journals, and financial responsibility becomes a critical marker of character and virtue in her fictional creations, particularly her women. This link also aligns her with the hugely popular work of Samuel Smiles, whose *Self Help* (1859) urged all working men to elevate themselves 'by means of individual action, economy and self-denial'.[7] For Smiles, as for George Eliot, the accumulation of money, beyond the attainment of physical comfort, was not an end in itself, but a means of securing independence, respectability and moral enlargement.

While Eliot's continuing 'intentions of stern thrift' (*L*, 3: 118) connect her with the mass of respectable working and middle-class mid-century Britons, her diversion of excess earnings into stocks and bonds places her in a small, albeit expanding, minority of active investors. Income-generating assets were a tangible reality throughout her adult life and, even before her financial success, a bequest from her father brought in much-needed investment income. In 1854, just after her elopement with Lewes, she tells Charles Bray: 'circumstances render it desirable for the trustees to call in £1,500 of my money, which must consequently be placed in the funds until a new investment can be found for it … I only hope he [her brother] will think it worth while to get another investment. For a considerable part of my sister's money he gets 5 per cent' (*L*, 2: 184). She was fully aware that any returns above the benchmark three per cent consols in which her uninvested money sat carried additional risk. Risk premia and excess returns feature prominently and are crucially character-referent in the various investment schemes described in *The Mill on the Floss*. Indeed, Uncle Glegg's exasperated response to his wife's puzzlement at the 'ten or twelve per cent' offered by Tom and Bob Jakin's venture – 'You can't get more than five per cent with security' (book 5, ch. 2), he tells her – points to a level of return that seems to mark the vernacular boundary between secured investment and speculation.

George Eliot made her first stock investment, in the Great Indian Peninsula railway, with her proceeds from *The Mill on the Floss* in 1860 and continued to add to her portfolio up to her death. Each new purchase added diversity to that portfolio and the increasing influence of John Cross as her financial advisor from the early 1870s significantly increased the weighting of US securities, reflecting the knowledge and expertise he had built during his time in New York throughout the previous decade. Cross was a prudent and diligent investor and is likely to have been influential in her decision to reduce the equity component of her portfolio in the final years of her life by switching into safer, lower-yielding debentures. Her last recorded portfolio in 1880, comprising twenty-four diversified holdings, was valued at just over £30,000 and generated an annual dividend income of £1,350. When her will was proved on 8 February 1881, her estate was valued at approximately £40,000.

The breadth of George Eliot's investments was made possible by the substantial new issuance of equity and corporate debt securities in the third quarter of the century, following the introduction of permissive limited liability legislation. Largely because most of her novels were set in earlier periods, she did not directly represent specifically stockmarket speculation until her two final, contemporaneously set works. In *Impressions of Theophrastus Such*, the rapacious Sir Gavial Mantrap devises ingenious mining speculations 'for the punishment of ignorance in people of small means' (*TS*, ch. 16); while in *Daniel Deronda*, the demise of Grapnell & Co. is attributed by Mrs Davilow to 'great speculations … about mines and things of that sort' (*DD*, ch. 21). Such references are part of a trend in these late writings towards more direct critiques of contemporary culture, including frequent and parallel meditations on money and literature. The idealistic Daniel Deronda, as he contemplates what he should actually *do* with his life, is contrasted both with those 'in whom the unproductive labour of questioning is sustained by three or five percent on capital which somebody else has battled for' and with those who have drifted into 'authorship – a vocation which is understood to turn foolish thinking into funds' (ch. 17). George Eliot, who worried during this period that her work was to become 'a mere addition to the heap of books' (*J*, 145), is representing a social process that had somehow come to merge the practices of passive stockmarket investment and literary production – both, as it were, representing the misdirection or under-utilisation of respectively financial and intellectual capital.

While money and finance do not feature as prominently or overtly in George Eliot's work as in that of many of her contemporaries (most notably Trollope and Dickens), such passages illustrate how she wove into the novels subtle and complex examinations of contemporary economic value systems. Often referencing her own particular and sometimes ambivalent position as an artist whose inseparable moral and aesthetic purpose was accompanied by fame and wealth, the novels allowed her to test how money can best be reconciled with both individual ethical development and wider concepts of social good. In her essay 'The Natural History of German Life', written at the very time when she had resolved to attempt her first work of fiction, she reflects on the 'many disintegrating forces' acting on the character of the German peasantry, as described by the influential social historian Riehl. Chief among these forces is the increased dependency on 'ready money' and 'hard cash' which, by overturning traditional practices of barter, reciprocity and localised, informal credit arrangements, had left the peasantry vulnerable to 'the vicissitudes of the market' and driven many into the hands of money lenders. As she concludes: 'Here is one of the cases in which social policy clashes with a purely economical policy' (*Essays*, 281). So direct a critique of theoretical Political Economy recurs throughout her novels and would have been applauded by Carlyle, Dickens and Ruskin. Yet George Eliot, with her personal and professional ties to economic liberalism and her uniquely syncretic mind, gave her examinations of the meaning of money a perspective and nuance that went well beyond that of the great sages. Her novels point the way to an individually and socially determined mean that simultaneously upholds higher values and attempts to integrate them into the market capitalism that, by the end of the century's third quarter, was firmly and irrevocably established.

NOTES

1 *The Works of Thomas Carlyle, Volume X, Past and Present* (1843; London: Chapman and Hall, 1897), p. 146.

2 Mary Poovey, *Genres of the Credit Economy: Mediating Value in Eighteenth and Nineteenth-Century Britain* (University of Chicago Press, 2008), p. 16.

3 Because inflation was generally extremely low for much of the century, absolute price levels in the period during which most of Eliot's novels were set is directly comparable with those at the time of writing. Thus, Nicholas Shrimpton calculates the 'seven hundred a-year' Dorothea Brooke receives from her inheritance had a current-money value of £52,000 in 1831 when *Middlemarch* was set and of £54,000 in 1871 when it was written: '"Even these metallic problems have their melodramatic side": Money in Victorian Literature', in Francis O'Gorman (ed.), *Victorian Literature and Finance* (Oxford University Press, 2007), p. 33.

4 Harold Perkin, *The Origins of Modern English Society* (London: Routledge and Kegan Paul, 1969), p. 420.

5 T. Chalmers, *On the Power, Wisdom and Goodness of God as Manifested in the Adaptation of External Nature to the Moral and Intellectual Constitution of Man* (1853), quoted in G. R. Searle, *Morality and the Market in Victorian Britain* (Oxford University Press, 1998), p. 12.

6 Boyd Hilton, *The New Oxford History of England: A Mad, Bad, and Dangerous People? England 1783–1846* (Oxford University Press, 2006), p. 368.

7 Samuel Smiles, *Self Help: With Illustrations of Character, Conduct and Perseverance* (1859; Oxford University Press, 2002), p. 17.

CHAPTER 24

Music

Delia da Sousa Correa

'I think I should have no other mortal wants, if I could always have plenty of music. It seems to infuse strength into my limbs, and ideas into my brain' (*MF*, book 6, ch. 3). These words, spoken by Maggie Tulliver in *The Mill on the Floss*, also convey her creator's passionate appreciation of music. George Eliot's fiction is permeated with allusions to music and her correspondence is full of accounts of the inspiring and reviving effects of musical experience. In addition to the musical characters, scenes and figurative allusions found throughout her work, the soundscapes of her novels form a pervading undersong, as in the concerted sounds of scythes, bird-song and voices in *Adam Bede*, or the hypnotic thrumming waterwheel in *The Mill on the Floss*.

Music embodies the yearning for spiritual expansion and sympathetic communion that is central to George Eliot's work. A sense of music as a 'language of feeling', inherited from Romantic aesthetics and also from Feuerbach, is strongly evident throughout her writing.[1] A potent analogue for the writer's creativity, music also encompasses a communal ideal. Jubal, in her 1870 poem of that name, discovers music amidst 'the common store of struggling sound' (Poetry, 1: 49). Music provides a critical terminology for her assessments of other writers as well as a metaphorical treasure trove for her own art, which nevertheless insists on the heard as well as the figurative significance of the auditory.

Music was a preoccupation of George Eliot's life as of her work. When she and George Henry Lewes began their life together in Weimar in 1854, a friendship was forged with Liszt, whose playing she much admired and who introduced her to the music of Wagner. Her response to Wagner's music was always equivocal, exemplified by her mixed response on first hearing *Tannhäuser*: 'The overture and the first and second acts thrilled me, but the third I felt rather wearisome' (*J*, 26). Nevertheless, her 1855 essay 'Liszt, Wagner and Weimar' for *Fraser's Magazine* is one of the earliest appreciative accounts of Wagner's operas and operatic theories to have been published in the English press. Wagner's vision of musical development appealed as a progressive evolutionary theory and she was prepared to attribute her preference for Beethoven to the 'tadpole' stage of her own musical development (*Essays*, 102–3). She subsequently met Wagner in London, and her musical maestro Klesmer in *Daniel Deronda* embodies some of Wagner's theories (his character is generally thought also to incorporate elements of Liszt and the Russian Anton Rubinstein, another of the musicians whom she met in Weimar).

Musical experiences continued to form highlights in the many foreign travels of George Eliot and Lewes. At home in London, they frequently attended Philharmonic and Monday popular concerts where at first they sat in cheap shilling seats from which they could 'hear to perfection' (*L*, 3: 364). The music of Handel occupied a special place in George Eliot's life, as it did for many of her contemporaries: 'there are few things that I care for more in the way of music than his choruses performed by a grand orchestra', she wrote in 1859 (*L*, 3: 71); and anticipating a performance of *Judas Maccabaeus* in 1864 she asserted 'Handel's music always brings me a revival' (*L*, 4: 134). Handel from early on represented an ethical ideal that finds an echo in her 1867 poem 'O may I join the choir invisible' and throughout her work. 'When the tones of our voice have betrayed peevishness or harshness, we seem doubly haunted by the ghost of our sins', she had written in 1848, ' – we are doubly conscious that we have been untrue to our part in the great Handel chorus' (*L*, 1: 247). It is hardly surprising that she went on, in *Middlemarch*, to give her fellow countryman Caleb Garth a veneration for Handel that underpins his portrayal as a custodian of community values. For Garth, there is a 'sublime music' in the sounds of productive labour which finds its equivalent in the 'mighty structure of tones' of Handel's oratorios (*M*, chs. 24, 56). However, the degree to which George Eliot endorsed the commonly held view of Handel's music as the epitome of communal virtue was matched by her sense of its passionate expressiveness. It is with music from Handel's *Aecis and Galatea*, together with the 'wild passion and fancy' of Purcell's *Tempest* music, that Stephen Guest seduces Maggie in *The Mill on the Floss* (*MF*, book 6, ch. 3).

When she made sufficient money as a novelist to afford a grand piano, George Eliot took lessons in accompaniment, and musical evenings at 'The Priory' became a regular event. These were attended by literary figures, such as Robert Browning, and others including Herbert Spencer, who joined the singing. A visitor in later years was Edmund Gurney, future author of *The Power of Sound* (1880) and member of the Society for Psychical Research, who may have been in her mind when she created her musical hero Deronda. The make-up of these gatherings indicates in microcosm the contemporary social importance of music, and is also an indication of some of the many contexts for musical allusion in her work. Music was of serious interest to many of the evolutionary scientists of her acquaintance, including Spencer, Darwin and the psychologist James Sully. Darwin, mystified by music's function, was inclined to see it as a vestige of pre-human sexual selection, while Spencer was convinced that music had a progressive social purpose, specifically to influence the expressive power of speech, perfecting it as a mode of communication. Gurney's musical researches, like his interest in Spiritualism, were largely motivated by a desire to alleviate the suffering of the poor. Sully found analogies between music and narratives of personal identity. All these ideas animate George Eliot's references to music in her fiction.

The records of musical experiences and gatherings in her letters and journals are tantalising remnants of a rich world of music and conversation. Thanks to early recording technologies, her readers have the opportunity to hear one acoustical survival of her auditory life. 'We have been having much musical pleasure of late', she records in March 1878; 'a great baritone singer, Henschel, has taken up his abode in London and stirs one's soul by singing fine Handel and other songs' (*L*, 7: 18). The Leweses heard Henschel sing at large musical parties at which other musicians including Piatti, Agnes Zimmerman and Joachim also performed (see Figure 15). The precise auditory contexts of Victorian life and for George Eliot's writing seem irretrievably distant to us now, but, in this instance, we *can* reconstruct something of what she heard. In 1927, in his seventies, Henschel made a number of extraordinarily youthful recordings, accompanying himself at the piano. These offer an insight into the style of singing that George Eliot admired. In general, Victorian singers used more *portamento* (slides between notes) and less *vibrato* than later musicians. Henschel was extremely sparing with either technique and his style is the opposite of the self-indulgent, sentimentality that might be imagined as typically 'Victorian'. His performances of Lieder by Schubert, Loewe and others are quite spare and disciplined, with *tempi* considerably faster than modern performances and a minimum of embellishment. At the same time they are intimate, dramatic and moving, providing a rare opportunity for us to hear a physical echo of a voice that enraptured George Eliot in the 1870s.

Henschel also left us a musician's account of the writer, recording the attendance of George Eliot and Lewes at his concerts: 'they were both passionately fond of music' he notes, recalling her 'low musical voice and

Figure 15 George Eliot heard the baritone George Henschel (1850–1934) on a number of occasions, sometimes accompanying himself as in this portrait.

Sir Lawrence Alma-Tadema, *Portrait of the singer George Henschel playing Alma-Tadema's piano, Townshend House 1879* (oil on panel).

Private collection. Photo © Christie's Images. Reproduced by permission of The Bridgeman Art Library.

… very gentle, charming way of talking'.[2] She died too soon for us to have a recording of her voice, and thus we are left to imagine its attractive qualities as described by others. Voice was a more important aspect of historical and literary character for the Victorians than it is now and it is a crucial element in George Eliot's fiction. Not only are her novels populated by numerous singers, but the precise qualities of her characters' speaking voices are as significant as their other attributes. In *Adam Bede*, 'Dinah's mellow treble tones' have 'a variety of modulation like that of a fine instrument touched with the unconscious skill of musical instinct' (*AB*, ch. 2). In *Middlemarch* Dorothea's 'voice like music' brings to mind Handel's *Messiah* for Caleb Garth and her 'melodious fragments' of speech repeatedly remind Will Ladislaw of the Æolian harp (*M*, chs. 9, 56, 21). In *Daniel Deronda*, the rich tones of Deronda's speech, when compared with the '*adagio* of utter indifference' uttered by the villainous Grandcourt, are 'as the deep notes of a violoncello to the broken discourse of poultry' (*DD*, ch. 29).

This emphasis on voice, both singing and speaking, helps to generate sustained analogies with opera in George Eliot's fiction, from 'Mr Gilfil's Love Story' through the musical competition for Maggie's affections between Philip Wakem and Stephen Guest in *The Mill on the Floss* to *Daniel Deronda*. This last, with its constant allusions to the operatic repertoire and dramatisations of musical performances and encounters between characters, is the most persistently 'operatic' of her novels. In her work as a critic, the possession of a 'voice' becomes emblematic of joint affective power and moral authority, whether of Heine's poetry, or of Ruskin's aesthetic and social theories. This sense of the ethical pre-eminence of voice, evident in her early comment on 'the great Handel chorus', also imbues her fiction. 'Surely whoever speaks to me in the right voice, him or her I shall follow': Whitman's 'Vocalisation' provides a pivotal epigraph in her mysterious final novel, *Daniel Deronda*, where 'voice' shades into issues of 'vocation' – the Zionist vocation of the novel's Jewish characters and the vocational quests of others, especially women (*DD*, ch. 29). For women, singing is a possible vocation, and, in the direct sense of 'giving voice', a channel for emotions unutterable in speech. 'Poor wretch!' exclaims the singer Armgart of 'any murderess' in George Eliot's 1870 poem about an opera singer: 'The world was cruel, and she could not sing: | I carry my revenges in my throat' (Poetry, 1: 95). Armgart subsequently loses her voice on which her exceptional status depends; the figure of the singer suggests the power and vulnerability of the published female author.

In her portrayals of musical women, George Eliot engages with a particularly troubled aspect of contemporary debates over the education and roles of women. Music, on the one hand the most spiritual of the arts, was on the other a dangerous sensual influence. It enjoyed an equivocal status that mirrored that of women themselves and contemporary advice literature was often preoccupied with the need to set limits on women's musical expression. Through her musical women, she makes powerful claims for female artistry and emotional fulfilment, and, at the same time, dramatises the risks attendant on this. She also highlights the dangers for men in ideals of femininity and female education that encourage sirenic accomplishments. Lydgate, in *Middlemarch*, is seduced away from his devotion to medical science by Rosamond Vincy's singing of 'Meet me by moonlight', convinced that she is 'an accomplished creature … who would create order in the home and accounts with still magic, yet keep her fingers ready to touch the lute and transform life into romance at any moment' (*M*, chs. 16, 36).

George Eliot's professional singers, from Caterina Sarti in *Scenes of Clerical Life*, to Alcharisi in *Daniel Deronda*, have a supreme power of expression at their command – Armgart's 'channel to her soul' – but the price they pay is high (Poetry, 1: 95). The more convenient domestic scale of the singer Mirah's musicianship in *Daniel Deronda* was mocked by Henry James and remains a cause of discomfort to later readers ('it will never do for the public:– it is gold, but a thread of gold dust', she is told as a child, and Herr Klesmer later declares: 'I would not further your singing in any larger space than a private drawing-room' (*DD*, chs. 20, 39)). Nevertheless, this positive portrayal of a Jewish singer had radical implications in itself. Moreover, the 'private drawing room' of the day could include concerts for large audiences by major professionals (such as the concerts at which George Eliot herself heard Henschel sing). Klesmer's comment that 'here in London that is one of the best careers open' had its basis in the realities of contemporary musical life (*DD*, ch. 39).

In *The Mill on the Floss*, her portrayal of the heroine's response to music is informed by contemporary concerns about female sexuality, and particularly by her intense engagement with contemporary theories of psychology. In this novel, often read as exposing the human consequences of evolutionary theory, Maggie's involuntary response to music dramatises the workings of physiological psychology and biological inheritance, apparently exemplifying Spencer's accounts of nervous response as reflex actions, responses which, according to Darwin's account, extend back to the earliest emotional responses of our pre-human ancestors. Under the influence of Stephen Guest's singing, Maggie, who has 'little more power of concealing the impressions made upon her than if she had been constructed of musical strings', becomes a vibrating musical instrument, resonating sympathetic vibrations: 'When the strain passed into the minor, she half-started from her seat with the sudden thrill of that change … You might have seen the slightest perceptible quivering through her whole frame' (*MF*, book 6, ch. 7).

The principles of physical acoustics also underpin George Eliot's portrayals of emotional response. She took a keen interest in the acoustical phenomenon of sympathetic vibration, reading Helmholtz and later visiting him for a demonstration of the tuning forks by which he exemplified his theories. In *The Mill on the Floss*, the resonating strings of the Æolian harp become emblematic of the workings of physiology. *Daniel Deronda* further elaborates her joint commitment to Romantic aesthetics and contemporary science. Her musical maestro Julius Klesmer is as much a descendant of E. T. A. Hoffmann's Kapelmeister Kreisler as a figure modelled on the musicians of her acquaintance.[3] Johannes Kreisler in Hoffman's fiction is emblematic of the artist's dreams and sufferings, asserting the supremacy of art in the face of bourgeois obtuseness. Ridiculous from many aspects, he also possesses uncanny powers of magnetism and perception. In *Daniel Deronda*, vibrations from the playing of Klesmer (a near homonym of Kreisler) reveal to Gwendolen Harleth a terrifying apparition of her future. Like the magical figures of Hoffman's literature of terror, Klesmer has the burning and hypnotic gaze of a magician. An element of Hoffmanesque grotesque cohabits with his lofty statesman-artist status, underpinning his telepathic gifts of apprehension and mesmerising influence. Yet Klesmer's magnetic powers are but one aspect of the uncanny effects associated with music in a novel where expansions of sympathy challenge the usual limits of communication. Conversation between Deronda and Gwendolen is constantly about or through music. At a musical party where Gwendolen is under the jealous scrutiny of Grandcourt, the 'torrent-like confluences of bass and treble' are emblematic of their fervent empathy (*DD*, ch. 45). An acoustical image conveys the silent sympathy between Hans Meyrick and Mirah 'that yet seemed an agitated communication, like that of two chords whose quick vibrations lie outside our hearing' (*DD*, ch. 61).

In a novel where George Eliot contends that science and prophecy share an investment in 'second-sight', musically conveyed sympathies also challenge boundaries of time and causality (*DD*, chs. 28, 37, 38). The visionary Mordecai stands on Blackfriars bridge anticipating the appearance of Deronda, the embodiment of a long-remembered Zionist successor. Deronda is about to row out of the mist as landscape and thought blend together 'into a fine symphony to which we can hardly be said to listen' (*DD*, ch. 38). Deronda himself, singing the gondolier's refrain from Rossini's *Otello*, receives a premonition of Mirah. This is inspired by a synaesthetic mode of contemplation which, with the river-landscape an 'unfinished strain of music', unites thought and external materiality. In such passages, George Eliot's writing conveys its affinity with the impulse of Romantic poetry to commune with uncanny presences in nature.

'Musical' dramatisations of individual consciousness and music's association with sympathetic communication, empathy and transcendence are among the qualities of George Eliot's writing that reach towards the 'other side of silence' invoked in *Middlemarch* (ch. 20). At the same time, she employs musical allusion in *Daniel Deronda* to achieve her most trenchant scrutiny of national life, and most wide-ranging critique of gender. She took extreme care over the details of the repertoire to be sung by her characters; a connection with her readers' experience of music remains crucial (see *L*, 6: 184). Attentive reading of musical allusion in her work uncovers ways in which her knowledge of science engenders uncanny and unexpected literary effects. Yet music seems also to have represented an old language, 'remaining true' like sculpture 'in spite of Harvey & Bichat' ('Notes on Form in Art', *Essays*, 436). Music is implicated in George Eliot's experimental expansion of the limits of realist fiction, but the extraordinary extent and range of musical allusion in her work is an insistent reminder of the material conditions of imaginative life. Her adherence to the importance of heard experience means that her allusions to music are always more than metaphorical.

NOTES

1 Ludwig Feuerbach, *The Essence of Christianity*, trans. Marian Evans (1854; New York: Harper, 1975), pp. 3–4.
2 George Henschel, *Musings and Memories of a Musician* (London: Macmillan, 1918), p. 220. See also K. K. Collins (ed.), *George Eliot: Interviews and Recollections* (Basingstoke: Palgrave Macmillan, 2010), pp. 130–2 and 138–9, for other accounts of these occasions.
3 Kreisler figures in three novels by Hoffmann (1813, 1815, 1822) and elsewhere in his writings.

CHAPTER 25

Philosophy

Moira Gatens

A common approach to demonstrating the influence of philosophy on George Eliot's fiction is to show the ways in which her novels track the contours of this or that philosophy. For example, the appearance of 'the visible Madonna' in *Romola* might be taken to illustrate Auguste Comte's religion of humanity, or the stages of enlightenment of Dorothea in *Middlemarch* can be shown to match the three stages of knowledge outlined in Spinoza's *Ethics*.[1] This approach throws valuable light on her impressive philosophical repertoire, but the attempt to understand her novels as 'translations' of pre-existing philosophies runs the risk of obscuring her remarkable intellectual independence and the profoundly innovative character of her thought. Moreover, we know that she explicitly rejected pressure to make her novels conform to any given philosophical mould because this would be to lapse 'from the picture to the diagram' and thereby betray her commitment to write fiction that 'deals with life in its highest complexity' (*L*, 4: 300).

Marian Evans published her first work of fiction under the name George Eliot in 1858 at the age of thirty-eight. Prior to her career as a novelist, Evans worked as a translator and as the clandestine editor of the *Westminster Review*. She translated David Strauss's *The Life of Jesus, Critically Examined* in 1846. A translation of Ludwig Feuerbach's *The Essence of Christianity* followed in 1854 and she completed a translation of Benedict Spinoza's *Ethics* in 1856.[2] All three thinkers challenged the literal truth of the Bible and questioned the authority of theology. Their critiques of religion sought to reveal the latent meaning of Scripture and religion through a study of the projected desires, wishes and fears that religion masks in metaphor and allegory. These texts form part of a literature known as the 'Higher Criticism' and were influential in the development of the hermeneutic approach to the study of texts and cultures.

Jeremy Bentham and James Mill founded the *Westminster Review* in 1824 with the aim of disseminating the views of the Philosophical Radicals.

Editorship of this journal brought Evans into contact with many of the major thinkers of Victorian Britain including John Stuart Mill, Herbert Spencer, James and Harriet Martineau, Thomas Huxley and George Henry Lewes, who would become her partner-in-life. It is clear from her letters and journals that her early years in London were a period of intense intellectual excitement and growth. Much of her time was occupied reading, and debating ideas – in person and in print – with some of the most influential thinkers of her time. Virginia Woolf was exaggerating only mildly when she said of George Eliot: 'She knew everyone. She read everything.'[3] The milieux in which Evans moved certainly were eclectic but her principal interlocutors shared a great enthusiasm for the scientific method, based in observation and experiment.

Many leading British philosophers of the time shunned metaphysics and *a priori* knowledge in favour of empirically grounded approaches such as Utilitarianism (Bentham, J. S. Mill, Henry Sidgwick). The continental philosophers whom Evans especially praised are those who called for a sensual, embodied philosophy, such as Feuerbach, and those who applied scientific methods to the study of morality and society, such as Auguste Comte. I maintain that George Eliot's own preference for the 'experimental method' is what drives the ethical realism which arguably received its highest form in her fictional works. It is fair to say that some thinkers had a more dominant or active influence on her thought than did others. Spinoza and Feuerbach were dominant forces on the way that she thought about the imagination, religion and ethics. Lewes was a constant influence on the development of her thought, as she was on his. Much of the work they produced during their productive association may be viewed as the fruit of ongoing dialogue about their wide-ranging joint studies.

George Eliot's youthful rejection of religion judged that its dominant influence on 'individual and social happiness' was 'pernicious' but as she matured she came to respect religious tradition (*L*, I: 128). She understood these traditions as organic outgrowths that connect the past to present human life and values. The enduring presence of the past and the roles of imagination, memory and narrative in forming and sustaining the individual and community are essential features of her social and moral philosophy. She acknowledged necessity, or what she called the 'inexorable law' of the world of science, but she nevertheless insisted that our primary resource for understanding the self and others begins with the sympathetic imagination ('Progress', *Essays*, 31). Science cannot provide an exhaustive account of all aspects of life because life amounts to 'a great deal more than science' ('Natural History', *Essays*, 288). The integrated exercise of our imaginative, sympathetic and rational capacities is requisite to the attainment of moral knowledge. For George Eliot, the assertion that fellow feeling is the only 'universal bond' is as fundamental as Spinoza's assertion of the imitative and contagious nature of the affects (*L*, 1: 162).[4] She had faith in the sufficiency of that bond to found and nourish human community.

Although George Eliot endorsed Spinoza's critique of religion, she considered his model of the free man in the *Ethics* to be inscrutable to all but an elite few. She thought his explication of 'the nature and powers of the affects, and the power of the mind over them' through the deployment of the geometric method that 'considers human actions and appetites just as if it were a question of lines, planes, and bodies'[5] unlikely to engage non-philosophers. In a passage that could be interpreted as a response to Spinoza's geometric method, transposed to a modern idiom, she insisted that 'molecular physics is not the direct ground of human love and moral action any more than it is the direct means of composing a noble picture'. It is true, she admits, 'that every study has its bearing on every other' but still 'pain and relief, love and sorrow, have their peculiar history, which make an experience and knowledge over and above the swing of atoms' (*L*, 6: 99). Put differently, affective experience cannot be reduced to lines, planes and bodies. Her novels may be read as studies that chart the specificity of the interconnected histories of the pain and relief, love and sorrow, of her richly drawn characters. These studies, however, are presented in such a way that the general philosophical principles that determine human action and suffering are embodied in the particulars of each case because the specificity of the individual embodiment of pains and pleasures has ethical import. Although they suffer from similar affects, and endure similar legal and social disadvantages, the love and sorrow experienced by Rosamond Vincy is not ethically equivalent to the experiences of love and sorrow of Dorothea Brooke. The quality of their joys and sorrows – like their characters – is incomparable.

George Eliot's novels reveal deep agreement with Spinoza on many fundamental philosophical issues. She judged reward and punishment to be effects intrinsic to the deed. She conceived of the individual as an egotistic consciousness that imagines itself as the free centre of action rather than recognising itself as an insignificant 'speck' that is fully part of nature and connected to all else through complex webs of interconnected causes and effects (*M*, ch. 41). She was a determinist who nevertheless believed in freedom and the expansion of knowledge through human striving. Her novels richly confirm Spinoza's insight that different ways of being in the world and different ways of knowing the world are co-implicated. Each way of life gives rise to different habits of thought and diverse channels of association. Constantly conjoined perceptions create stable patterns of thought. Across time these habits become ever more deeply etched into our bodies and minds and new experiences tend to be interpreted within the frame of past experiences because we have a natural tendency to organise our experiences into the form of explanatory narratives. Spinoza's recommendations for the transformation of the passions necessarily involve social critique because context profoundly conditions the formation of our habits and dispositions and helps to determine which of our capacities can be realised or expressed. Freedom, by these lights, amounts to the ability to understand the causes and conditions that constitute our contexts of action. Although such understanding involves judgement, this is not reducible to a utilitarian calculation, or the application of a maxim, but rather involves reflection and deliberation. Virtue requires the cultivation of good habits – a task that George Eliot likened to the repeated exercise of a muscle in order to build strength (*TS*, ch. 13).

Feuerbach is not seen as an important figure in the history of philosophy but rather as a springboard for Karl Marx. For George Eliot, however, Feuerbach made a singular contribution to human self-understanding because he returned the vital powers of love and sympathy to their rightful possessor: humanity. It is only through the reclamation of these immanent powers that the human condition can be redeemed. It was for him that she reserved her strongest endorsement: 'With the ideas of Feuerbach I everywhere agree' (*L*, 2: 153). *The Essence of Christianity* offers an anthropological interpretation of religion as a primal and indirect form of self-knowledge. Religion involves the self-contemplation of human nature but only in a latent, indirect and imaginative form.[6] Feuerbach's aim was to demystify this confused self-knowledge. He explains religious experience as arising from our apprehension of our selves as particulars that belong to a natural kind (our 'species-being'). Only human beings invent religions because only human beings are aware of their species membership. Distinctively human thought and feeling – as distinct from mere 'animal sensation' – requires an other. In order to exist human consciousness requires both an 'I' and a 'thou'. Viewed as a whole, the human species possesses several admirable capacities – for example, benevolence, knowledge and love – that cannot be fully realised by any single individual. Rather than seeing these qualities as distributed throughout humanity, we project their perfect possession onto a single entity, God, who becomes the repository of our most cherished values. This hypostatised subject comes to be seen as the omnipotent Creator and the source of all benevolence. By exposing the imaginative projections at work in Christianity, Feuerbach sought to put an end to humanity's self-imposed alienation from its unique powers.

The real target of Feuerbach's critique is the metaphysical claims of theologians and not the entirely natural poetic expression of religious feelings. This critique opened the way for Feuerbach's reconstructive task, which is to show that although the subject of these admirable predicates is an illusion, the predicates are real. Our gratitude, love and adoration need to be directed away from illusory theological abstractions (the Holy Father, the Madonna, the Saints, Christ) and towards their proper objects: actual mothers and fathers who care for and protect us, embodied lovers and friends who compensate for and forgive our failings, and our fellow humans whose labour contributes to the viability of our distinctive human existence. It is these embodied relationships that spontaneously generate our sympathy, love, knowledge and morality. By exposing the illusory nature of our projections, Feuerbach hoped to put an end to the priestly hostility towards carnality and, by association, towards women. He argues that men and women complement each other, and when 'united they first present the species, the perfect man'.[7] In this earthly Eden it is the 'oxygen of sexual distinction', that engenders and sustains human life.[8] It is only together that man and woman constitute a whole human being, and only together can they realise humanity's full potential.

For both Spinoza and Feuerbach human beings are essentially embodied, passionate and imaginative and so require images and fictions through which to express their hopes and yearnings. This creative power of humanity is harmful only when metaphysical concepts (such as Being, God) are built upon these imaginings and then posited as the ultimate realities. George Eliot was strongly influenced by their accounts of the bivalent imagination. On the one hand, our imaginative projections can lead to destructive illusions and self-alienation; on the other hand, the imaginative identification that underlies the I–thou relation is the ground for human sympathy and morality. This is why, for both philosophers, an understanding of the relation between imagination and reason is a crucial task for philosophy. Within man, Feuerbach writes, there is 'an inward necessity which impels him to present moral and philosophical doctrines in the form of narratives and fables, and an equal necessity to represent that impulse as a revelation.'[9] George Eliot's novels can be seen as a continuation of the critical exploration of the relation between culturally inherited imaginative constructions and our capacity for critical reflection upon these constructions. Her novels seek to challenge the habituated ways in which her readers think about the I–thou relation, freedom, faith and redemption. Like the Bible, her fictions seduce through the pleasure of engaging the imagination in a vividly satisfying narrative. Unlike scripture, they do not claim the status of literal truth or divine revelation. Rather, she described her novels as 'a set of experiments in life'. These experiments are designed to provoke the reader to reflect on their religious, social and sexual imaginaries and to promote a critical awareness of the actual causes that determine the shape of human life. Her sceptical attitude towards the value of abstract philosophical theory motivated her preference for the genre of experimental realism. She expressed her increasing reticence 'to adopt any formula which does not get itself clothed for me in some human figure and individual experience' (*L*, 6: 216–17).

Lewes was a constant living influence on George Eliot's intellectual development. From 1854, when they eloped to Germany, until his death in 1878, they were inseparable. Whether they were attending opera, reading Aristotle, Goethe, Dante or Shakespeare, studying Darwin's *Origin of Species* or collecting anemones at the sea-side, George Eliot and Lewes enthusiastically supported each other's intellectual pursuits and they drew enormous emotional satisfaction from their union. It was Lewes who first encouraged her to try her hand at fiction and who protected her from the risks of public authorship. Although her interest in Spinoza pre-dated her relationship with Lewes, it was through him that she came to translate the *Ethics*.[10]

George Eliot and Lewes were among the first in Britain to theorise the novel as a serious art form that binds together aesthetic and ethical values. In one of his essays Lewes criticised the mistaken idea that 'art is independent of the truth of facts' because it is 'swayed by the autocratic power of Imagination'. He maintained, on the contrary, that the practices of science, art and philosophy all require imaginative thought.[11] In the same article, Lewes cryptically remarked that 'Philosophy and Art both render the invisible visible by imagination.'[12] While it may be tempting to understand this assertion as idealist, Lewes's comments elsewhere recommend caution in relation to what he meant by idealism. He insisted that 'realism is … the basis of all Art, and its antithesis is not Idealism, but *Falsism*'.[13] Such falsism is precisely the target of the last essay Evans wrote for the *Westminster Review* before launching her career as George Eliot. 'Silly Novels by Lady Novelists' may be read as an extended critique of falsism in literature. According to the criteria offered by Lewes and Evans, 'silly novels' are unworthy of the name of Art. Genuine artistic creation always bears the mark of veracity. Contrary to those who think of themselves as clever novelists, able 'to represent things as they never have been and never will be', George Eliot described the work of her own novels as obliging her 'to creep servilely after nature and fact'.[14] The humble and faithful study of nature, including human nature, does not preclude the imagination but nor should it neglect 'the pressure of that hard unaccommodating Actual, which has never consulted our taste and is entirely unselect' (*DD*, ch. 33).

George Eliot's understanding of her craft evolved over the course of her life. The faithful rendering of men and things as they had been 'mirrored' in her mind, to which she appealed in *Adam Bede* (1859), gave way to a more complicated view of the creative powers of the artist in *Impressions of Theophrastus Such* (1879). Theophrastus distinguishes between the 'arbitrary combinations' of fanciful imaginings, on the one hand, and the 'keen vision', the 'definite knowledge', the 'selective sensibility' and the 'strong, discerning perception' of the artist's imagination, on the other (*TS*, ch. 13). The difference between the two types of imagination reiterates the superiority of the selective imagination that creates new combinations from a store of patient and meticulous empirical observations.

George Eliot insisted on the specificity of art and its unique capacity to evoke wonder and reverence for nature and arouse sympathetic fellow feeling. Some have taken her rejection of crude materialism and naïve empiricism to be evidence of the lingering shadow of God. But these interpretations fail to note her frequent comments concerning the limits to what can be known, including the limits to self-knowledge. We are not capable of thoroughly knowing the nature of our selves and our actions, never mind all of their consequences. By her lights, human knowledge is still in its infancy. This epistemic modesty gave rise to George Eliot's distinctive empiricism and her preference for the experimental method. The intensive historical, cultural and psychological research that informs all her novels combines the painstaking task of establishing what are the facts with the artist's genius for the selection and recombination of facts, resonant with feeling, in order to create a work that shows the human condition in a clear light. These works give expression to those aspects of human life that are dimly felt but rarely distinctly seen. As Lewes put it, like philosophy, art also aims to make the invisible visible.

George Eliot perfected a new kind of art form that challenged religious and social imaginaries from within. Her re-staging of common cultural narratives, infused with unorthodox interventions, provided her readers with an opportunity to deliberate on conventional meanings and morals and to unmake their habitual chains of thought. Her narratives encourage readers to make new connections that open their minds to novel ways of being in the world. Her critical method is testament to the potential of art to improve and expand human knowledge. Her achievement went well beyond anything one finds in the philosophies with which she was familiar and signalled the advent of a new genre: the philosophical novel.

NOTES

1 See, for example, J. B. Bullen, 'George Eliot's *Romola* as a Positivist Allegory', *Review of English Studies*, n.s. 26 (1975), 425–35; and Miriam Henson, 'George Eliot's *Middlemarch* as a Translation of Spinoza's Ethics', *The George Eliot Review*, 40 (2009), 18–26.
2 Although the translation was complete in 1856 it was not published until 1981: Thomas Deegan (ed.), Baruch Spinoza, *Ethics, Salzburg Studies in English Literature: Romantic Reassessment 102* (Universität Salzburg, 1981).
3 Virginia Woolf, 'George Eliot' (1919), in Gordon S. Haight (ed.), *A Century of George Eliot Criticism* (Boston: Houghton Mifflin, 1965), p. 184.
4 Compare Spinoza, *Ethics*, Part III, Proposition 27: 'If we imagine a thing like us, toward which we have had no affect, to be affected with some affect, we are thereby affected with a like affect': Edwin Curley (ed. and trans.), *The Collected Works of Spinoza*, vol. I (Princeton University Press, 1985).
5 Spinoza, *Ethics*, Preface to Part III.
6 Ludwig Feuerbach, *The Essence of Christianity*, trans. Marian Evans (New York: Harper, 1975), p. 33.
7 Ibid., p. 156.
8 Ibid., p. 92.
9 Ibid., p. 208. Compare Spinoza on common fictions in the *Ethics*, Part I, Appendix.
10 Evans was translating Spinoza's *Tractatus Theologico-Politicus* as early as 1843. The translation was probably incomplete and is now lost. See Thomas Deegan, 'George Eliot, George Henry Lewes and Spinoza's Tractatus Theologico-Politicus', *George Eliot–George Henry Lewes Studies*, 22–3 (1993), 1–16.
11 'The Principles of Success in Literature' (1865), in Rosemary Ashton (ed.), *Versatile Victorian: Selected Critical Writings of George Henry Lewes* (London: Bristol Classical Press, 1992), pp. 226–7.
12 Ibid., p. 229.
13 'Realism in Art: Recent German Fiction', *Westminster Review*, n.s. 14 (1858), 493.
14 This phrase appeared in the discussion of the 'vocation of the novelist' in the first to ninth editions of *Adam Bede*, ch. 17, but was edited out in George Eliot's 1861 revision: see *AB*, 'Explanatory Notes'; also Carol A. Martin (ed.), *Adam Bede* (Clarendon edn, Oxford University Press, 2001), p. 164.

CHAPTER 26

Politics

Robert Dingley

H. H. Lancaster, writing in the *North British Review* in 1866, described George Eliot's title 'Felix Holt, *the Radical*' (his italics) as 'a good publisher's device, considering what political questions were mainly agitating the country when the book appeared' – a reference to the overwhelming pressure for an extension of the franchise which was to result in the passage of the 1867 Reform Act under Lord Derby's Conservative ministry. For Lancaster, however, it is precisely the topicality of George Eliot's novel that vitiates its usefulness, since her failure to produce an 'impartial representation' of the state of feeling in 1832 means that the book cannot provide an authentic source of instructive comparison with the present. Indeed, the book's eponym, Lancaster feels, 'the ideal Radical of 1832, is an entirely modern figure – an utter anachronism – a sort of cross between Mr Lowe and Lord Elcho'.[1] Since Lowe and Elcho were, in the mid 1860s, the leaders of the Liberal 'Adullamites', who implacably opposed any extension of the franchise whatever, Lancaster's implication is that Felix Holt's radical credentials would not only have been incongruous in 1832 but are still incongruous in 1866. After all, for most mid-Victorians, political radicalism was embodied in the portly figure of John Bright, and Bright – devout Quaker, tireless advocate of a vastly extended suffrage (for men), excoriator of the landed classes – represented almost everything Felix sets out to contest. 'We are little likely', announced a writer in *Blackwood's Magazine* in 1866, 'to adopt Radicalism of any shade; but if ever we see reason to change our political colours, we shall certainly follow Felix Holt rather than John Bright.'[2]

George Eliot's title, then, entails a provocative challenge to her audience, requiring it radically to reassess the meaning of 'radicalism'. True radicalism (from Latin *radix*, 'root') requires not mere acquiescence in fashionable slogans (which suffices Harold Transome) but a return to first principles – indeed, to a reconsideration of what those principles are. Felix's kind of radicalism, firmly rooted in independent judgement, can

Figure 16 John Tenniel, 'A leap in the dark', *Punch* (3 August 1867). Masquerading as a thoroughbred, Disraeli (who piloted the 1867 Bill through the Commons) gallops at a forbidding hedge labelled REFORM, while Britannia, terrified, shields her face. John Bright, Gladstone and Lord Derby have pulled up short.

thus be distinguished from what George Eliot, in 1848, called 'selfish radicalism' (*L*, 1: 254), the political advocacy of sectional or class interests which – and this was an accusation regularly levelled at Bright by opponents – could result only in social fragmentation.

That George Eliot could set out to present an alternative definition of the term 'radical' is, among much else, symptomatic of the flexibility of political language in the mid nineteenth century. Terms like 'radical', 'liberal' and 'conservative', before the imposition of stringent internal discipline on political parties (itself accelerated by the 1867 Act), exhibit a semantic indeterminacy which can encompass a baffling range of possible and seemingly incompatible attitudes. This problem is further complicated in the case of a writer like George Eliot, whose political thought is largely divorced from any close interest in contemporary practice. Thus, when in an 1868 letter to Clifford Allbutt, she describes 'the bent of my mind' as 'conservative rather than destructive' (*L*, 4: 472), she is very far from announcing her allegiance to the Tories ('the stupidest party', according to Mill[3]), though admittedly she was 'rather tickled' when Gladstone's Liberal ministry lost office in 1874 (*L*, 6: 22) and didn't 'mind' when Disraeli won the subsequent election (*L*, 6: 14). Her variety of conservatism, which she also described as 'meliorism' – her own coinage, she believed (*L*, 6: 333–4) – entails not merely an acceptance of change, but a conviction that change is in the long term synonymous with progress and that individuals can, indeed should, participate in furthering it. What chiefly distinguishes her conservative assumptions from those of a liberal like Mill (whose work she read closely) is the length of the term over which she believes that change should occur. Many of the dominant influences on her thought – Spencer, Comte, Darwin – predisposed her to view history as a process of continuous evolution, in which each successive stage incorporates and refines what has gone before. It is therefore essential for the proper unfolding of this process that disruptive attempts (like Savonarola's in Florence or Lydgate's in Middlemarch) to anticipate it by jettisoning the baggage of the past must fail: it is precisely from that baggage that the future will be unpacked. As George Eliot put it in her essay on Riehl's *Natural History of German Life*: 'The nature of European men has its roots intertwined with the past, and can only be developed by allowing those roots to remain undisturbed while the process of development is going on, until that perfect ripeness of the seed which carries with it a life independent of the root' (*Essays*, 288).

All of this raises as many difficulties as it resolves. It can easily seem, or become, indistinguishable from a romantic nostalgia of the sort professed by the narrator of 'Amos Barton', a 'tenderness for old abuses' and 'picturesque inefficiency' ('Amos', *SC*, ch. 1); it can result, as George Eliot concedes, in the kind of aporia which is 'in danger of paralysing' the young Daniel Deronda between his 'affections and imagination', which are 'intensely conservative', and a 'fervidly democratic … feeling for the multitude' (*DD*, ch. 32). More insidiously, the tendency to view political change in terms of a natural process of organic evolution – from the simple to the complex in Spencer's paradigm, or from primitive Theism to triumphant Positivism in Comte's – can too readily lend a specious authority to the judgement of contemporary issues. Mill noted of Comte that 'We fail to see any scientific connexion between his theoretical explanation of the past progress of society, and his proposals for future improvement',[4] and similar reservations can be advanced about George Eliot's metahistorical focus on such immediate questions as franchise reform. By what criteria, after all, do we decide that the evolutionary process has not yet equipped the working class to exercise the vote responsibly? Felix Holt argues, both in the novel and in his 'Address to Working Men', that workers (an imprecisely defined category) need to undergo a process of education at the hands of the cultured elite. It is only thus that they will learn to value the 'treasure of knowledge, science, poetry, refinement of thought, feeling, and manners, great memories and the interpretation of great records, which is carried on from the minds of one generation to the minds of another' ('Address', *Essays*, 425) and that they can then safely be entrusted with an electoral share in its maintenance. The difficulty with such a prescription (and even with more 'liberal' proposals like Mill's that would-be voters should pass basic tests in literacy and numeracy) is that its originator assumes the authority to decide and adjudicate the level of attainment that is consistent with the 'natural' process, to assess the correct pace at which history should unfold. And since that assessment entails an indefinite deferral of universal suffrage, it is hard not to see it as intellectual camouflage for the fear of mob rule.

George Eliot's position on the enfranchisement of women is similarly ambivalent. It would, of course, be consistent with her conviction that '[w]hat has grown up historically can only die out historically, by the gradual operation of necessary laws' ('Natural History', *Essays*, 287) to argue that the education which has been so far enjoyed by most women has unfitted them to exercise responsible political choice. The remedy for this, once again, is to reform education, and she was happy to contribute to projects like the establishment of Girton College in Cambridge. But her support for local initiatives co-exists with a willingness to relegate more general emancipation to the vague future, a willingness grounded in a broad endorsement of the 'separate spheres' ideology – her belief, as she told Emily Davies, in the need to conserve 'woman's peculiar constitution for a special moral influence' (*L*, 4: 468). In a letter to John Morley she clarified her conviction that 'growing moral force' could procure 'an approach to equivalence of good for woman and for man' – equivalence rather than identity, since the sexes are separated by 'distinctness of function' (*L*, 8: 402). A very similar argument is presented by Felix Holt when he proposes to working men that class distinctions 'have shaped themselves along with all the wonderful, slow-growing system of things' and that 'the only safe way by which society can be steadily improved' is by 'the turning of Class Interests into Class Functions' ('Address', *Essays*, 421). The trick, for women as for working men, is presumably to stop thinking of themselves as disadvantaged and start taking pride in their functional equivalence to, say, Viscount Palmerston. As Gilbert Murray shrewdly remarked: 'Most adherents of evolutionist or "meliorist" systems fall into the speculatively unsound position of justifying the present by the future.'[5]

George Eliot's radical conservatism, then, turns out to be less remote from its unsophisticated Tory namesake than the philosophical trimmings might suggest. But that is very far from the whole story. For, over the two decades of her novel-writing career, George Eliot explores with increasing insistence the conflicts and ambiguities in her own avowed political creed. The nature of this development becomes apparent in a comparison between *Adam Bede*, her first novel, and *Felix Holt*, her fifth. Both books are set retrospectively in periods of crisis – the years of the French Revolution and the Irish 'Rebellion' in the first, the time of uncertainty around the passing of the 1832 Reform Act in the second. Moreover, the conflict between a skilled artisan and a local squire for the love of a young woman – a conflict with the potential to represent class antagonisms – is central to both novels. In both, too, the removal, either voluntary or compelled, of disruptive elements permits the rural community to resume the even tenor of incremental change. It is, however, in these very areas of resemblance that the gulf separating the two texts becomes apparent. Most obviously, whereas upheavals in the wider world barely impinge on the pattern of life in Hayslope or on the consciousness of its inhabitants, in *Felix Holt*'s Treby Magna the pressure of external events is pervasive: election agents plan campaigns, disgruntled workers riot, prospects and principles are debated in pubs and drawing rooms.

More significant than these differing levels of overtly political investment, however, is what they suggest about a more general difference in the ways in which the rural settings are perceived. Hayslope's relative insulation means that it can, like the German communities described by Riehl, foster that 'gradual operation of necessary laws' ('Natural History', *Essays*, 287) whereby the slow evolution of the social system keeps pace with the slowly changing aspirations of the people who compose it. Adam's intelligence and industry, for example, enable him to achieve 'a broadening path of prosperous work'. but that is the extent of his 'ambitious longing' (*AB*, ch. 33) and it never occurs to him to question the rightness of Arthur Donnithorne's inherited status. What, indeed, regulates the rate of change in Hayslope and pre-empts any sudden fracture in its evolution is an almost reflex deference to traditional order, a deference which is ritually enacted on public occasions like the young Squire's birthday dinner and which asserts itself most dramatically when Adam, having knocked Arthur down for seducing Hetty, instantly reverts to respectful solicitude ('"Do you feel any pain, sir?" he said, tenderly, loosening Arthur's cravat' – ch. 28). George Eliot's novel antedates by nearly a decade the publication of her friend Walter Bagehot's classic study *The English Constitution* (1867), but it might almost have been written to exemplify one of his central theses: that the stability of the English political system is dependent on the fact that 'England is the type of deferential countries', that 'the mass of the people yield obedience to the select few'.[6] That is not, Bagehot explains, because the hereditary landowning class consists necessarily, or even very often, of conspicuously talented persons, but because 'it has the marks from which the mass of men always used to infer mind'.[7] It is, indeed, because the select few *symbolise* mind rather than being expected to exhibit it, that their position is secured.

From Bagehot's perspective, Adam Bede is the ideal citizen. He is properly 'susceptible to the influence of rank, and quite ready to give an extra amount of respect to every one who had more advantages than himself'; his 'respectful demeanour towards a "gentleman"' is a matter of 'impulse'. It is because of this 'large fund of reverence in his nature' that he will never develop 'theories about setting the world to rights' or become a 'proletaire with democratic ideas' (*AB*, ch. 16). Adam perfectly justifies Lord Palmerston's Whiggish confidence that mobility could somehow be reconciled with the status quo, that (as Palmerston optimistically declared) England was 'a nation, in which every class of society accepts with cheerfulness the lot which Providence has assigned to it', while 'at the same time, every individual of each class is constantly striving to raise himself in the social scale'.[8]

But the narrator's sardonically regretful reminder that since Adam 'was in his prime half a century ago, you must expect some of his characteristics to be obsolete' (*AB*, ch. 16) is confirmed by a glance at Felix Holt. Unlike Adam, Felix has little reverence for anything except his own opinions, but he too is content to remain an artisan and has no desire to rise above the station to which Providence (or heredity) has assigned him. In his case, however, failure to raise himself in the social scale is not only a matter of conscious decision rather than 'impulse' but of constant effort. He is, he tells Esther, 'a very ambitious fellow' and he likens his rejection of 'the scramble for money and position' to the 'harder discipline' of Catholic renunciation (*FH*, ch. 27). If Adam is a 'natural' artisan, Felix is an 'unnatural' one, willing himself to stay where he is in order to fulfil his chosen mission.

But Felix's obstinate refusal to evolve socially is not the only 'unnatural' choice in the novel. Like *Adam Bede*, *Felix Holt* ends with the squirearchy restored to its place after facing a crisis of identity, but whereas Arthur Donnithorne returns to his heritage at Hayslope after serving out his self-imposed sentence, the Transomes' continued occupancy of their mansion rests on a fiction. Harold is disqualified for his role both by his illegitimacy and because his right of possession is void under the complex terms of the entail. The novel ends with the real heir, Esther, leaving the district with Felix so that the Transomes can resume their 'hereditary' position. Once again, there is nothing natural about this development; instead, the entire community chooses to conspire in an act of oblivion so that life in Treby Magna can remain undisrupted.

Bagehot, as we have seen, argued that England is largely held together by symbolism and that its people 'defer to what we may call the *theatrical show* of society' because 'the higher world ... is a stage on which the actors walk their parts much better than the spectators can'.[9] In his introduction to the book's second edition (1872), Bagehot wonders whether this pageant and the attitudes it engenders will survive the 1867 Act's wholesale extension of the franchise, and there is a sense in which George Eliot raises the same question. Certainly, deference gets scarcer in the later novels (as Mr Brooke learns on the Middlemarch hustings), but there is also, as *Felix Holt* suggests, a troubled awareness that a community held together by its reverence for the traditional social hierarchy is held together by a mere fiction, that there is no substance sustaining the show of organic cohesion. While Bagehot, convinced of the supreme value of the Cabinet system, was able to believe that the real rulers are 'secreted in second-rate carriages' while the electorate gawps at 'Courts and aristocracies',[10] George Eliot, with neither great interest nor confidence in the day-to-day practice of government (her one professional parliamentarian, Ladislaw, is credited with no concrete achievements), becomes increasingly sceptical about the efficacy, even perhaps the continued possibility, of the politics of deference. Her scepticism culminates in Henleigh Grandcourt, whose immaculately turned-out existence is both exclusively concentrated and entirely dependent on getting himself deferred to. In Bagehot's terms, he would count as an exemplary role-player in the usefully diversionary spectacle of 'the higher world'. George Eliot concedes the point. Indeed, she goes further and notes that Grandcourt would have made a handy colonial governor (*DD*, ch. 48), but she also insists on his squalid pointlessness and speculates that if this is what a deferential polity has come to then it may be time to look elsewhere.

George Eliot's conservative meliorism was developed in a period – the long Whig Indian Summer, whose survival depended almost wholly on Lord Palmerston's, when piecemeal 'improvement' could be traded off against major constitutional change – in which her gradualist version of incremental progress within basically stable social conditions seemed to be underwritten by political consensus. With Palmerston's death in 1865, a dangerous volatility was – or appeared to be – injected into English life and George Eliot felt compelled to test in her fiction the strengths and limitations of her political convictions, as she had earlier tested the limits of her religious faith. It is the honesty of that exploration, the readiness to disclose patches and tears in the fabric of her own beliefs, that can still make her work seem – in a non-partisan but etymologically exact sense – radical.

NOTES

1 H. H. Lancaster, 'George Eliot's Novels', *North British Review*, 45 (September 1866), 110.
2 John Holmstrom and Laurence Lerner (eds.), *George Eliot and her Readers: A Selection of Contemporary Reviews* (London: Bodley Head, 1966), pp. 74–6.
3 John Stuart Mill, *Considerations on Representative Government* (London: Longman, 1882), p. 56n.
4 John Stuart Mill, *Auguste Comte and Positivism* (Ann Arbor, MI: University of Michigan Press, 1961), p. 118.
5 Gilbert Murray, *Stoic, Christian and Humanist* (London: Allen and Unwin, 1940), p. 62.
6 Walter Bagehot, *The English Constitution* (1867; London: Fontana/Collins, 1963), pp. 247–8.
7 Ibid., p. 121.
8 Asa Briggs, *The Age of Improvement* (London: Longmans, 1959), p. 404.
9 Bagehot, *The English Constitution*, p. 248.
10 Ibid., pp. 248–9.

CHAPTER 27

Race

Alicia Carroll

At first glance, Dorothea Brooke of George Eliot's *Middlemarch* (1871) and Fedalma of her epic poem *The Spanish Gypsy* (1868) seem to be daughters of different authors. And in fact most critics reading for the representation of race or ethnic identity in George Eliot read only *The Spanish Gypsy* or *Daniel Deronda* (1876), assuming that 'race' is not represented in her greatest work, *Middlemarch*, or her earliest novel, *Adam Bede* (1859). On the contrary, I propose that in Victorian culture diverse identities intertwine within a larger cultural discourse of heritage and 'race' or 'blood' that is always present. Even more problematically, in the Victorian period a symbolic economy of racial and ethnic difference becomes a body of knowledge in which the 'nature' of 'them' is most often investigated as a means of understanding the nature of 'us'. Therefore, even when an author such as George Eliot is writing of an 'other', implicitly this discourse always keeps questions of English identity central.

Victorians commonly used the interrogative mode to describe those groups whose identities were marginalised or threatening to mainstream culture. Hence, the position of Jewish people in Victorian culture was often described as 'The Jewish Question', just as the debate surrounding the social status and abilities of women was referred to as 'The Woman Question'. The claims of the Irish to self-rule were referred to by the British ruling class as 'The Irish Question'; similarly, the issue of the right to self-rule of people formerly enslaved in the British colonies was referred to as 'The Negro Question'. The term 'question' was generally used in a politically neutral way, though at times the very existence of a marginalised group was emphatically declared 'a problem', as in 'The Gypsy Problem'. Thomas Carlyle's 'Occasional Discourse on the Negro Question' (*Fraser's Magazine*, February 1849), however, was inflammatory. His position was characterised as vicious by liberal readers such as John Stuart Mill: in response, Carlyle provocatively retitled the piece 'Discourse on the Nigger Question' for republication as a pamphlet in 1853.

George Eliot famously espoused tolerance and intelligence in her representations of people of other races, ethnicities and religions. In her manifesto on representation and realism, 'The Natural History of German Life', she demonstrates her own belief in the importance of accurately 'experiencing' not just 'personal' identities but national characters in art as a remedy for egotism and narrow provincialism: 'Art is the nearest thing to life; it is a mode of amplifying experience and extending our contact with our fellow-men beyond the bounds of our personal lot. All the more sacred is the task of the artist when he undertakes to paint the life of the People' (*Essays*, 271).

This idea that a 'People' has a 'natural history' linked by 'blood' or 'race' to their national history was held by the foremost intellects of George Eliot's day. While it is accepted now that 'race' is a cultural construct which cannot be proven biologically, George Eliot deploys the term as her peers do, that is, as a biological reality. She engages a representational code that suggests character or personality is linked to place of origin and that 'blood' systematically assigns hereditary characteristics. For her gypsy queen Fedalma, then, race shapes her difference from within: 'in my blood | There streams the sense unspeakable of kind' (*SG*, 110). Race is a definitive factor of identity from which she cannot 'unmake' herself (112). This understanding of identity accounts for George Eliot's plots in which characters' latent feelings of difference are confirmed by the discovery of their origin of birth as an ethnic other, as gypsy or Jew in the cases of Fedalma or Daniel Deronda. As these plots suggest, the singular logic of 'the People' often leads to the expulsion, exclusion, or marginalisation of those who are *a* People, but not *the* one, those in possession of the privileged identity.

As William Baker explains, George Eliot's openness to Jewish religion and culture as well as her goal of complete accuracy in depicting such an important construct as a 'People' led to her scrupulous research into Jewish culture for *Daniel Deronda*. She read widely and took copious notes in 'Jewish mystical thought and German Jewish historians … [going] beyond the confines of her tradition and offer[ing] an alternative explanation of "the chequered area of human experience"'.[1] Her interest in Judaism was career-long, as evidenced from her study of Hebrew and her 'Oriental Memorandum' notebook in which she kept newspaper clippings on Jewish settlement in the state of Palestine.[2] She tasked herself to learn other cultures and to represent them. As we place George Eliot in context, it is possible to discern how she adopts the interrogative mode in constructing identities around questions that were central to her, not necessarily to the cultures represented.

Even as George Eliot challenges stereotypes of Jews in her representation of Judaism, she still, Reina Lewis argues, 'fantasizes the state of contemporary Judaism in relation to the concerns of the dominant English society'.[3] Michael Ragussis in *Figures of Conversion: The 'Jewish Question' and National Identity* (1995) has written extensively on how Jews in England represented a central figure of difference around which British national identity itself was formed. Indeed, if we place *Daniel Deronda* in the context of novels written by Jews themselves in the Victorian period, we see that these raise issues from within their community which are often not the same as those raised in George Eliot's work. While *Daniel Deronda* may stand out as the most canonical novel about a Jew in the Victorian period, Jewish writers, many of them women, wrote their own novels. They were well aware of the interrogative mode of inquiry; that they were perceived as a 'Question'. As one heroine in a novel by Emily Marion Harris states, 'the world judges us more with curiosity than respect'.[4] The interests of Jewish writers were diverse and included the position of women within the Jewish community and within Judaism historically, conflicts between the Anglo-Jewish and new immigrants from Eastern Europe, and of course the rights of Jews to full civil and religious liberties in England as well as the question most compelling to George Eliot, the construction of a Jewish homeland in Palestine. Discussions of race and ethnicity in George Eliot, then, should always be placed in a context that takes into account both her scholarly knowledge and her location in a culture that considers itself entitled to ask – if not define – questions of identity.

Indeed, this wider cultural discourse that treats 'others' as a question or problem is endemic to Victorian culture and was underscored through, for example, visual as well as print culture of the period. Victorian images of gypsies are especially revealing. Gypsy portraits were popular in British print culture before and after the publication of *The Spanish Gypsy*, and consistently place the subject in isolation, often in her 'environment' or 'costume', which is dutifully documented. In a typical portrait such as that in Figure 17, the girl (and it often is a girl), poses alone dressed in exotic attire. Her face is tilted in such a way as to be almost a defiant toss. This posture, though, has the effect of exposing her face for the viewer's education and each detail of her imagined ethnic difference is finely drawn: her wild, untamed hair, her hoop earrings, her strong features which seem both masculine and feminine, her dark inscrutable eyes which are so large as to seem almost equine, her full lips which mark her sensuousness. Such details were important to George Eliot, who noted similar ones as she researched her epic poem *The Spanish Gypsy*: 'Costume: silver rings in the

Figure 17 'The Gipsy Beauty', by W. H. Overend, an illustration from George Smith, *Gipsy Life: Being an Account of our Gipsies and their Children* (1880): characteristic of popular mid- to late-nineteenth-century images of gypsies.

ears. Kerchief on the head. Loose garment'.[5] The documentation of such garb makes no reference to Victorian fashion, propriety or modernity and inscribes the gypsy girl's identity as different from that of the middle- or upper-class viewer and artist, and yet disturbingly similar in her shared femininity and humanity. The absence of any reference to the gypsy's modernity intensifies her status as primordially female; the subject is immanent, caught in time, and the more traditional elements, of costume for instance, are captured, the more the painter proves himself or herself a master of his or her subject. While we see this kind of mastery of gypsy culture in Victorian visual culture, it is also evident at the linguistic level, when gypsy lorists refer in print to gypsies as 'ours'. Such research might respond to the gypsy 'question' by proclaiming comprehensive knowledge of 'a people' or 'tribe',[6] confirming the superior rational intellect of the British scholar or artist while marking the irrational, unhistorical mind of the gypsy. We see in such cases that two Victorian identities are developed that are fundamentally connected: as subjects gypsies are represented as primitives while the act of research and representation defines 'lorists' as sophisticates and masters.

As representations of gypsies, then, allowed European lorists to claim mastery and to ponder questions or anxieties clustering around other issues of the day such as 'The Woman Question', the gypsy's 'rebelliousness' came to be a popular trope for an increasing demand for civil status of the disenfranchised in the second half of the nineteenth century. George Eliot's interest in ethnicity, and the frequency with which representations of race and ethnicity occur in her writing, is a product of a wider interest in reform that is based in this post-Enlightenment discussion of the role of citizens in modern nations and their rights to representation and full participation in civic life. Concepts of ethnicity and heritage as well as religious freedom and difference feature significantly in such discussions and they lead to one of the central paradoxes that mark the limits of Victorian ideas of freedom and human rights within the modern nation state.

In the nineteenth century, the representation of the right of 'the People' to self-rule gained rhetorical impact from the idea that they share a common origin, religion, language and historical memory even if such unification is mainly mythical or imaginary. The distinctions which mark out an ethnic group or 'People', however, might elevate one identity's right to self-rule over another's. In the most extreme examples within the British empire, for example, 'a People' may often be a privileged group while 'a tribe' may be denigrated, primitivised and deprived of civil rights. At home and at its worst, this results in racist or anti-Semitic comments such as those by Thomas Arnold who wrote that 'England is the land of Englishmen, not of Jews' and 'the Jews have no claim whatever of political right'.[7] In this case, their right to full participation in civil society becomes dubious through their ethnic and religious identity that is subjugated to those of the dominant group.

Such privileging is clear even in a 'novel of the Midlands' of England like *Adam Bede*. The title character's identity is fundamentally linked to his ethnicity, which is signed by his venerable Saxon name and his distinctly 'Saxon' appearance that is mixed with marks of 'Celtic blood' (*AB*, ch. 1). As a proper specimen of British genealogy, Adam is marked as standard while no ethnic features are attributed to his brother who is clearly marked as Adam's inferior. It is Adam who is destined to become a first, an enfranchised 'master man' and a modern capitalist, while his brother will be his labourer. Likewise, purging the community of another British type and his progeny, the decadent squire Arthur Donnithorne and his bastard child, paves the way for a new British identity that is simultaneously sanitised of and sanctified by its past. A new 'us', carefully regulated in gendered, classed and ethnic qualities, emerges in the family formed at the end of the novel, signed by the duplication of Adam's features in the face of his son, the duplication of the mother's features in those of her daughter. This family is formed on the ashes of 'them'. The lesser Seth, who bears no distinctive ethnic features, is not to marry or reproduce. Passionate, dark-eyed, curly haired Hetty, also a sprig off a lesser side of the family tree, who works with her hands and recalls pagan goddesses such as Medusa or Hebe, is dead along with her baby. This remything of British identity is an illustration of the concept of *ethnie* 'defined as human populations with shared ancestry myths, histories and cultures, having an association with a specific territory and a sense of solidarity'.[8] Marking Adam's ethnic features helps to naturalise his privilege to become the ideal subject of a modern nation.

These new subjects, moreover, are properly secular. Although Dinah is often seen as cut off from her vocation of evangelical preaching on the grounds of her sex, her mysticism, Old Testament legalism and prophetic registry are also problematically neutralised as she is re-identified as Adam's wife at the end of the novel. Such qualities as mysticism and legalism are clearly troubling traces of difference in George Eliot's later work on Judaism as well. In addition to fears of ethnic 'contamination' from Jews, Victorians including George Eliot perceived Jewish 'character' as incompatible with the modern nation state because the Jewish religion was perceived as fundamentally medieval rather than modern, legalistic rather than reflective, and traditional rather than innovative in thought and practice. In her work on *Daniel Deronda* and cosmopolitanism, Amanda Anderson has explored the problem George Eliot faced in integrating a traditional identity such as Judaism into a modern nation state such as England. As Anderson argues, 'Being modern meant having a self-active or reflective relation to one's cultural heritage; Jewish culture, by contrast, was construed as a form of legalism (extrinsic law) that one followed unblinkingly'. George Eliot evades this problem, then, by modernising Daniel Deronda through his 'reflective and dialogical conception of nation-building'.[9] She underscores the link between origin and character through the intersecting stories of Daniel and Gwendolen; Gwendolen's landlessness is a source of her egotism and avarice, while Deronda's discovery of his 'birth-right' of a Jewish homeland is a deed to his morality and destiny. Constructing Deronda as a primarily secular Jew who succeeds the mystical Mordecai Cohen, George Eliot replaces Mordecai's mysticism with modern rationalism. Even so, the departure she constructs for Deronda effectively separates 'Jews' and 'Englishmen'.

Deronda's voluntary departure from England naturalises a kind of cultural sorting that is fundamental to Victorian identities and that foreshadows a continued source of conflict in modern nation states. Indeed, expulsion was to become one solution to the materially impracticable claims of 'ethnic minority' groups who as 'a People' too deserve full civil rights. Understanding this machinery goes a long way towards understanding why George Eliot's contemporary Abraham Lincoln believed both in granting Americans of African descent their 'freedom' and in 'returning' them to Africa although many enslaved people had lived their entire lives in the United States.[10] A similar impulse leads to the resettling of Fedalma's gypsy tribe in Africa in George Eliot's epic poem.

However, as her critical and insightful outsiders prove, although marginality in a culture may result in exclusion, it also provides a crucial critical perspective which may also amplify experience and extend 'our contact with our fellow-men beyond the bounds of our personal lot' ('Natural History', *Essays*, 271). The assumption clear in George Eliot's novels is that marginality provides a stimulus to insight, that a sense of exclusion fosters an analytical detachment, that a sense of geographical or metaphorical exile allows the critic a vantage point from which to accurately critique society. Will Ladislaw, the half-Polish liberal who is blasted as progeny of a 'thieving Jew pawnbroker' (*M*, ch. 77), walks this line of privilege *and* exclusion that allows George Eliot to critique her home culture.

We began by questioning the link between such disparate identities as Fedalma and Dorothea. Although each plot posits the question of its heroine's free will, each provides an answer based upon an encoded system of identity that George Eliot accepts as common sense. Her understanding of the limits and opportunities of identity determines the relationships of both Fedalma and Dorothea to the rights and burdens of inheritance. As Dorothea looks over her mother's jewels at the opening of the novel, she ponders which she will choose. Her rumination foreshadows the larger questions she actively considers throughout the novel, but it is fundamentally different from the destiny that Fedalma faces. Dorothea Brooke in *Middlemarch* is represented as a modern British woman whose privilege ultimately is to choose to help others; her gypsy sister is represented as a primitive whose duty is to lead her 'people'. Dorothea's mobility and all its attendant anxieties are piqued by contrast with the fixity of a character like Fedalma who is primitivised and essentialised. George Eliot is as fascinated by the possibilities of new identities for British people as she is entrenched in a system of difference that contrasts modern people with 'others' who are primitivised and encoded as such, as in the portrait of the gypsy girl.

That 'subject' deploys a view into the exotic in order to reflect upon the problem of female independence in modernity. Victorian identities do not live outside, but live within this complex code of representation.

NOTES

1 *George Eliot and Judaism* (Universität Salzburg, 1975), p. 180.

2 See Jane Irwin (ed.), *George Eliot's Daniel Deronda Notebooks* (Cambridge University Press, 1996), pp. 377–431.

3 Reina Lewis, *Gendering Orientalism: Race, Femininity, and Representation* (London: Routledge, 1996), p. 228.

4 Emily Marion Harris, *Estelle* (London: George Bell and Sons, 1878), p. 109. For a full discussion of this Jewish writer and others, see Nadia Valman, *The Jewess in Nineteenth-Century British Literary Culture* (Cambridge University Press, 2007).

5 Joseph Wiesenfarth (ed.), *George Eliot: A Writer's Notebook 1854–1879, and Uncollected Writings* (Charlottesville, VA: University of Virginia Press, 1981), p. 220.

6 See Lou Charnon-Deutsch's discussion of 'Our Gypsies', in *The Spanish Gypsy: The History of a European Obsession* (University Park, PA: Pennsylvania State University Press, 2004), pp. 179–239; also Deborah Epstein Nord's *Gypsies and the British Imagination, 1807–1930* (New York: Columbia University Press, 2006), and David Mayall's *Gypsy-Travellers in Nineteenth-Century Society* (Cambridge University Press, 1988).

7 Arthur Penrhyn Stanley, *The Life and Correspondence of Thomas Arnold, D.D., Late Head-Master of Rugby School, and Regius Professor of Modern History in the University of Oxford*, 4th edn, 2 vols. (London: B. Fellowes, 1845), vol. II, pp. 32–3.

8 Anthony Smith, *The Ethnic Origins of Nations* (Oxford: Basil Blackwell, 1986), p. 32.

9 Amanda Anderson, *The Powers of Distance: Cosmopolitanism and the Cultivation of Detachment* (Princeton University Press, 2001), pp. 126, 131.

10 Henry Louis Gates, Jr, 'Writing "Race" and the Difference it Makes', in *'Race', Writing and Difference* (University of Chicago Press, 1986), p. 3.

CHAPTER 28

Religion

Oliver Lovesey

George Eliot was regarded by many Victorians as a religious writer whose novels were 'second Bibles' (*L*, 6: 340). Though she did not subscribe to any Christian confession, she maintained that the religious impulse was one of the most valuable legacies of the Western cultural tradition. Moreover, she was a student of comparative religion with an omnivorous appetite for knowledge in all its forms for whom the misunderstanding of world religions was a damning species of intellectual myopia. She embraced Judaism, and she was particularly fascinated by the encounter of East and West, Islam and Judeo-Christianity, in Southern Europe and North Africa at moments of historical crisis. She expressed her religious inquiries in virtually all of the genres available to professional Victorian women writers: scholarly translation, periodical essay, poetry, verse drama and the novel. In particular, with the novel, the genre by which the Victorians knew they would be remembered, she embraced a genre that could allow a female writer to be part of 'a sort of natural priesthood' (*MF*, book 6, ch. 9) and mediate with a broad public on the historical, ethical and religious imaginary.

The wide tolerance and hybridity of George Eliot's later religious understanding might not have been anticipated by her own early religious experience. It is nearly impossible, moreover, to determine the exact nature of the heterodox secular humanism to which the mature George Eliot subscribed. In an oft-quoted conversation with F. W. H. Myers in 1873, she held forth on 'the three words which have been used so often as the inspiring trumpet-calls of men, – the words, *God*, *Immortality*, *Duty*, – [and she] pronounced, with terrible earnestness, how inconceivable was the *first*, how unbelievable the *second*, and yet how peremptory and absolute the *third*'.[1] These lofty pronouncements were recalled by Myers in 1881, eight years after the conversation, and the uncharacteristically absolute, even dogmatic, assurance of the phrasing has made some scholars question the accuracy of the statement, though Myers was acutely conscious that she was striving to make a memorable impression with 'words which should remain as an active influence for good'.[2] George Eliot acknowledged to Harriet Beecher Stowe in a letter of 1869 the importance of religion and her hope for its transformation which at least begins as a type of catechistic statement:

> I believe that religion too has to be modified – 'developed', according to the dominant phrase – and a religion more perfect than any yet prevalent, must express less care for personal consolation, and a more deeply-awing sense of responsibility to man, springing from sympathy with that which of all things is most certainly known to us, the difficulty of the human lot. (*L*, 5: 31)

While there is no single, definitive statement of George Eliot's religious position, she was fascinated by religion, and she was also enticed by grand narratives and totalising systems such as those of Auguste Comte, Ludwig Feuerbach, Herbert Spencer and Baruch Spinoza.

She came to her mid-career position of scepticism, reverence and curiosity after being raised in a rural Church of England congregation, followed by a period of intense religious piety and intolerance in adolescence. In this period, a Calvinistic Evangelical zeal led her to disdain novels, a disdain that in her later work signals moral short-sightedness in Tom Tulliver in *The Mill on the Floss* and Henleigh Grandcourt in *Daniel Deronda*. A youthful Mary Ann Evans wrote: 'The weapons of the Christian warfare were never sharpened at the forge of romance' (*L*, 1: 23). In the partially autobiographical *The Mill on the Floss*, Maggie Tulliver takes her passionate asceticism to such an extreme that she would burn all books save for three, including Thomas à Kempis's *The Imitation of Christ*. George Eliot gave a copy of *The Imitation*, obviously a work of profound significance for her, to her husband John Cross as a wedding gift. Her early questioning of faith after her period of Calvinistic enthusiasm, when her refusal to attend church inaugurated a 'holy war' with her father, first alienated her from her family, a hostility that would intensify when her beloved brother broke off communication after she went to live with G. H. Lewes. George Eliot's self-fashioning as one of the disinherited, partly due to her break with her family and faith, may have fostered her abiding sympathy with various others: the colonised, disabled, fallen, apostate, dissenter, Gypsy, Moslem and Jew.[3]

One of Mary Ann Evans's earliest projected writings, even before she wrote her first story at fourteen, was an outline of ecclesiastical history. A projected work, *The Idea of a Future Life*, was advertised in the *Leader* on 18 June 1853 as being by 'the Translator of Strauss's Life of Jesus' (*L*, 2: 90n) – the work of Marian Evans, published in 1846. In 1854 it was complemented by another translation from German, Ludwig Feuerbach's *The Essence of Christianity*. Strauss traces the synoptic nature of the Gospels, pointing to the manipulation of miracles to reinforce typological interpretation and to the Gospel writers' debts to Greek philosophy. Feuerbach advances a demythologised Christianity in which the religious impulse is interpreted as an expression of the best in humanity, suggesting that such aspirations should be worshipped and the numinous cut away, but that Christian worship should be continued even by disbelieving priests. Evans also translated the *Ethics* of the radical Jewish moral philosopher Spinoza, having earlier translated his Latin critique of biblical miracles, the *Tractatus Theologico-Politicus*. *Ethics* – unpublished in her lifetime – attempted to ground morality in a non-religious or at least non-theological context.

Just as there was a variety of types of Victorian belief, there was also a variety of types of Victorian doubt and causes for that doubt. While primarily the province of Victorian intellectuals, apostasy had a broad appeal, shown when the census of 1851 recorded significant drops in church attendance. Victorian apostasy was fuelled by historical criticism of the Bible, but also by disenchantment with the Church establishment due to a perception of its corruption, opposition to social reform, and hostility to Dissenting congregations. The continuing stark inequality in volume of work and remuneration between clerical livings, instances of nepotism and even bribery in hiring and promotion, and inadequacy of preparation for sacred office, despite ongoing attempts to reform the ancient institution, reinforced perceptions of its reactionary, moribund nature and calls for disestablishment. In light of this view of the established Church, the vibrancy of Dissenting chapels springing up to minister to swelling populations in industrial areas and to challenge conventional religious practice in rural ones – inspired in some cases by the pentecostal fire of charismatic preachers – presented for many a positive development, though it was sometimes disparaged by the establishment as being somehow illegitimate, radical, enthusiastic, vulgar and unEnglish. These perceptions led to a questioning of the spiritual status quo.

In addition, advances in science reinforced dissatisfaction with revealed religion. Geology demonstrated that the earth's origin pre-dated Bishop Ussher's 4004 BCE, and Charles Darwin explained the process of evolution through natural selection. George Eliot recognised the importance of *On the Origin of Species*, but sagely noted that it did not address the far more interesting 'mystery' behind evolution (*L*, 3: 227).

George Eliot's apostasy was partly a wide-ranging textual, hermeneutic experience, though a willingness to live in the presence of uncomfortable truths without recourse to opium – intellectual or otherwise – is admired everywhere in her fiction. In *Romola*, the fifteenth-century Dominican friar Girolamo Savonarola becomes the spiritual teacher of the titular character, who comes to a sceptical but mature understanding by reading his prison writings.[4] The most sympathetically portrayed clergymen in her early novels – Tryan in 'Janet's Repentance', Irwine in *Adam Bede*, Kenn in *The Mill* and Farebrother in *Middlemarch* – all experience a crisis of faith. Her least-sympathetic clerics, *The Mill*'s Stelling and Gascoigne in *Daniel Deronda*, have been attracted to the Church solely by the professional, gentlemanly status it affords. Perhaps her most intensely religious figure is Daniel Deronda, an embodiment of Zionist zeal, at whose hands 'the Orient has plans made for it'.[5] Deronda finds in faith an answer to a lifelong anxiety about identity, though finally the assurance of this faith lies in Hebrew texts he cannot read which will enable a Cabbalistic transmutation of souls that he has anticipated earlier in the novel. He had humorously referred to the myth about the Buddha offering himself to a starving tigress as the embodiment of this notion. Buddhism had a powerful appeal for Victorian intellectuals like George Eliot because of its well-formulated ethics and the clear alternative it offered to seemingly moribund conventional religious forms.[6] Her marginalia in her copy of Charles Taylor's *Sayings of the Jewish Fathers* note the similarity between the notion of the centrality of the Thorah, Worship and 'the bestowal of Kindnesses' in Judaism, and, as she writes, 'Bouddha Dharma'.[7]

The essays and reviews that George Eliot published before she began writing novels establish a poetics of fiction for her mature novels and go some distance towards explaining her early narratives' direct engagement with religious matters. 'Silly Novels by Lady Novelists,' an omnibus book review offering a classification of the genus and species of dead forms, can be read as her literary manifesto. In addition to advancing the moral responsibility of novels and novelists, she gestures to an unexamined subject: '[t]he real drama of Evangelicalism' (*Essays*, 318). She argues, furthermore, in 'The Natural History of German Life' that novelists should be natural historians or anthropologists of the Christian church that is part of the moral fabric of provincial English life. Her first published fiction, 'The Sad Fortunes of the Reverend Amos Barton', was collected in *Scenes of Clerical Life* and suggests a plan for an anatomy of clerical figures. The longest and most nuanced of the *Scenes*, 'Janet's Repentance',

JAN. 8, 1881 THE GRAPHIC 29

1. CHILVERS COTON CHURCH AND VICARAGE. ("Shepperton Church as it was in the old days, with its outer coat of rough stucco, its red-tiled roof, its heterogeneous windows patched with desultory bits of painted glass, and its little flight of steps, with their wooden rail running up the outer wall, and leading to the schoolchildren's gallery."—*Amos Barton, Chap. I.*)—2. "MILLY'S GRAVE," CHILVERS COTON CHURCHYARD.—3. MARKET PLACE, NUNEATON. ("Milby . . . was a dingy-looking town, with a strong smell of tanning up one street, and a great shaking of handlooms up another, and even in that focus of Aristocracy, Friar's Gate, the houses would not have seemed very imposing."—*Janet's Repentance, Chap. II.*)—4. NUNEATON CHURCH AND VICARAGE ("Milby"). ("Old Mr. Crewe, the curate, in a brown Brutus wig, delivered inaudible sermons on a Sunday, and on a weekday imparted the education of a gentleman to three pupils in the Upper Grammar School."—*Janet's Repentance, Chap. II.*)—5. RIBBON WEAVER, Single Hand-Loom. ("Every other cottage had a loom at its window, where you might see a pale, sickly-looking man or woman pressing a narrow chest against a board, and doing a sort of treadmill work with legs and arms."—*Amos Barton, Chap. II.*)

REMINISCENCES OF "GEORGE ELIOT"

Figure 18 Soon after the publication of *Scenes of Clerical Life*, 'Shepperton Church' was identified with that at Chilvers Coton, and the town of Milby with Nuneaton. 'Reminiscences of "George Eliot"' (*Graphic*, 8 January 1881) depicts several of the places depicted in *Scenes*, including a ribbon weaver at a handloom (mentioned in 'Amos Barton': Silas Marner is not George Eliot's only weaver).

focuses on the relationship of mutual confession that springs up between Janet Dempster, driven to drink by her abusive husband, and the youthful Reverend Tryan, a reforming Evangelical, whose sympathy is less the product of his earlier spiritual doubts than guilt over his seduction of a woman who falls into degradation and dies. As in *Romola* and *Daniel Deronda*, what might occasion a clerical romance between a chastened woman and her spiritual advisor provides a liberating education in disappointment. George Eliot's publisher wanted her to accommodate popular taste by presenting a really good clergyman, and her notes for a novel after *Daniel Deronda* suggest the inclusion of such a figure,[8] but when writing 'Janet's Repentance,' she would not depart from what she regarded as the moral dictates of realism. Her famous statement about realism in chapter 17 of *Adam Bede* appears as part of an apology following the portrait of the fallible Reverend Irwine.

George Eliot's early fiction often represents the nineteenth-century clergyman – the 'parson' or first person of the parish, the local representative of a powerful state apparatus – as the embodiment of fine Old England. The rural parson in this period was becoming increasingly a figure of nostalgia or controversy, appearing out of step with history in a climate of competitive professionalisation, bitter ecclesiastical party politics, and widespread reform. The novels' critical perspective is muted by their being set a generation or two in the past and by their focus on clerical romance and amateur pursuits. The flawed, pluralist parson Irwine forsakes marriage to care for an elderly mother, but he fails to confront the young squire and prevent Hetty Sorrel's seduction. By contrast, Dinah Morris voices the passionate piety of eighteenth-century female lay preachers. Based on George Eliot's own Aunt Samuel, Dinah embodies Methodism's pentecostal zeal until she is prohibited from preaching (banned by the Methodist Conference in 1803), her calling subsumed in marriage. This is perhaps the first radical foreclosing of a noble woman's ambition in George Eliot's works, but not the first instance in which clerical romance challenges vocation. 'Mr Gilfil's Love-Story' and *Felix Holt*'s story of the Dissenting minister Rufus Lyon show the religious figure profoundly shaken by an infatuation with an 'exotic' foreign woman. Disappointed romance marks the Reverend Farebrother in *Middlemarch*, though it does not disrupt his passion for natural science. The more calculating Reverend Casaubon in that novel, also preoccupied with extra-clerical scholarly, orientalist pursuits, misinterprets the devotion of Dorothea who hopes to assist his quest for 'the Key to all Mythologies' and extend the range of his clerical responsibilities (*M*, ch. 7).

The Victorian novel was both pulpit and podium for professional female writers. Denied positions in the Church above the status of churchwarden, or in parliament, or in the legal or medical professions and the civil service – despite the fact that a woman was the head of the Church of England and the country's monarch – Victorian women writers had access to the periodical press and the circulating library. The novel was recognised as a distinctly pious but also polemical forum for women, and novelists like Margaret Oliphant in her *Chronicles of Carlingford* (1861–76), for example, soon took up George Eliot's idea of a series of clerical novels. While George Eliot was certainly not a preacher, the narrators in her novels perform a mediating role between character and reader, fostering altruistic identification leading to sympathy, a demythologising gesture that mimics the thematic pattern leading from egotism to sympathy via confession.[9] Richard Simpson in 1863 recognised these signs of demythologised religious transformation in the early novels, but attacked what he regarded as their intellectual dishonesty.[10] For George Eliot, the novel had begun to supplant poetry as the genre of religious exploration, and her later work continued to examine the natural history of religion and traces of pre-Christian mythological systems in the broadest terms. As a student of the mythographer Max Müller, George Eliot gave pre-Christian myth and ritual significant attention. An extensive exposition of fetishism, rural mythology, fatalism and superstition appears in her transitional novel *Silas Marner*, which explores the diverse channels adopted by characters to express a longing for meaning.

George Eliot would become one of the best-known Victorian scholars and popularisers of Judaism. She advocated for a Jewish homeland, though her work promotes an idealised, essentialist notion of racial and national identity. In her essay 'The Modern Hep! Hep! Hep!', Theophrastus Such, the son of a clergyman, emphasises the affinity between the English and the Jews. Jewish 'ideas have determined the religion of half the world' and Jewish 'literature has furnished all our devotional language' (*TS*, ch. 18). George Eliot situates her appeal for understanding within an attack on religious imperialism, and a type of eugenic fantasy about racial 'fusion' and immigration. She acknowledges that in relations with the 'Hindoos' of India, the Chinese, the Irish, and the indigenous peoples of North America, the English 'are a colonising people', though her position is not an undifferentiated endorsement of religious or national diversity, for she excludes the Ottoman Empire. The essay confronts English anti-Semitism, while allowing that Jewish exclusiveness, itself a response of the powerless to oppression, can foster vices. While accepting that racial 'fusion' is probably inevitable in 'the growing federation of the world', she dreads the threat to the English language of unmitigated linguistic hybridity.

Daniel Deronda embodies prophetic religious yearning within Deronda, a world-historical figure, a modern Daniel, who wishes to explore the return to the promised land that for him is an unpopulated, blank space on the map. In 'Notes on "The Spanish Gypsy"', George Eliot articulated a somewhat more direct, poetic treatment of the religious encounter of East and West, and the return to an African homeland, at another moment of historical crisis (Cross, 3: 41–9). As in 'O May I Join the Choir Invisible', her hymn for the English branch of the Comtean Religion of Humanity, in which the departed gain immortality in the memory of the living making an 'undying music in the world' (Poetry, 2: 85), music in *Daniel Deronda* and her epic verse drama, *The Spanish Gypsy*, embodies or transmits religious inheritance and racial memory. Her idealised, romantic vision of the religious conflict in Spain's Golden Age is of a piece with the Zionism of her last novel.

The Spanish Gypsy is set in fifteenth-century Spain around the time of the expulsion of the Jews in 1492. The foundling Fedalma was raised by the noble mother of Don Silva who fights in the holy war against the Moors. He seeks to wed Fedalma, but she hears music in the square that moves her to dance, and the music and movement conjure a 'race memory', like Deronda's reaction to hearing chanting in the Frankfurt tabernacle. Her enslaved father Zarca acquaints her with her Gypsy identity and demands she assume her destiny. She becomes Queen of the Gypsies and leads her people, the Zíncali, on a doomed quest for their African homeland. George Eliot's conception was based on the notion of 'holy war' taken from a Zoroastrian legend,[11] within which the Gypsies are used as pawns in a confrontation between Christianity, Islam and Judaism, though there are a number of possible sources.[12]

The Gypsies' faith is presented as a living creed, residing in fidelity to the ties of kinship (for instance at *SG*, 229), while their faith also rests in a shared status as the 'most forsaken', most abject people (204). Zarca's faith is transmitted to Fedalma (as Mordecai's faith is transmitted to Deronda), to be carried henceforth by one who regards herself as the priestess of the temple of this faith and its 'funeral urn' (261). Instead of the wandering Jew, Fedalma will become the bearer of the 'Gypsy's wandering tomb' (265), though her people will eventually 'propagate forgetfulness' (256). The Moors have facilitated the Gypsies' plan to escape exile in Africa, but 'Moslem subtlety' casts a calculating and wary eye upon the enterprise (254). The Moors speculate on whether there will be sufficient space for the Gypsies within, not Africa, but a Jewish, Christian, Moslem or Gypsy hell (254).

Islam in George Eliot's work is less sympathetically and far less extensively treated than Judaism, and generally associated with calculation or fantastical self-sacrifice or ecstasy. At the beginning of *Middlemarch*, for example, possessed by a 'national idea', Saint Theresa of Avila in early sixteenth-century Spain, after reading the lives and deaths of saints, embarks on a children's crusade with her brother Rodrigo, to 'seek martyrdom in the country of the Moors' (*M*, 'Prelude'). For her, Moslem lands are places for Christians to die. In *Daniel Deronda*, the possibility of the extravagance of even a 'Moslem paradise' is held out as an inadequate consolation for the intense psychological torture to which Gwendolen is subjected by Grandcourt and her own guilt (*DD*, ch. 54).

Religion in George Eliot's work is a matter of anthropological investigation, intellectual scepticism and emotional reverence, as well as a web of intersections between nationalism, politics and race, at moments of 'global' crisis. Impelled by her perception of kinship with the ostracised, disinherited and misunderstood, George Eliot's portrayal of religious 'others' in her later work, like her translation of theological works, periodical essays, early studies of the natural history of religion in provincial England and studies of religious confrontation at moments of historical and cultural crisis, was an attempt to advance understanding and promote tolerance of hybridity.

NOTES

1 *Century Magazine*, 23 (November 1881), 62–3. George Eliot described herself as a 'meliorist', as her husband John Cross notes (Cross, 3: 301).
2 Ibid., 62.
3 Bernard Semmel, *George Eliot and the Politics of National Inheritance* (New York: Oxford University Press, 1994), p. 17.
4 Oliver Lovesey, *The Clerical Character in George Eliot's Fiction* (Victoria, BC: ELS Editions, 1991), pp. 73–6.
5 Edward Said, *Orientalism* (New York: Vintage, 1979), p. 169.
6 J. Jeffrey Franklin, *The Lotus and the Lion: Buddhism and the British Empire* (Ithaca, NY: Cornell University Press, 2008), pp. 21, 42.
7 Marginalia in George Eliot's copy of Charles Taylor's *Sayings of the Jewish Fathers* (Cambridge University Press, 1877), p. 26.
8 William Baker, 'A New George Eliot Manuscript', in Anne Smith (ed.), *George Eliot: Centenary Essays and an Unpublished Fragment* (London: Vision, 1980), p. 18, n. 3.
9 J. Hillis Miller, *The Ethics of Reading* (New York: Columbia University Press, 1987), pp. 61–80.

10 [Richard Simpson], 'George Eliot's Novels', *Home and Foreign Review* (October 1863), 522–49. K. K. Collins identifies the contemporary alarm at George Eliot's controversial life and her work's treatment of the sacred, in his *Identifying the Remains: George Eliot's Death in the London Religious Press* (Victoria, BC: ELS Editions, 2006), pp. 1–6.

11 Joseph Wiesenfarth, *George Eliot's Mythmaking* (Heidelberg: Carl Winter Universitätsverlag, 1977), p. 212.

12 See Semmel, *George Eliot and the Politics National Inheritance*, pp. 105–7; Avrom Fleishman, *George Eliot's Intellectual Life* (Cambridge University Press, 2010), p. 137; William Baker, 'Preface', *SG*, pp. xvi–xxi.

CHAPTER 29

Romanticism

Joanne Wilkes

The narrator of *Middlemarch*, referring to the late 1820s, characterises it as a period when 'Romanticism ... had not yet penetrated the times with its leaven and entered into everybody's food' (*M*, ch. 19). The implication is that by the time of writing, the early 1870s, this absorption had taken place. The comment further suggests why, in studying George Eliot's fiction, written from the 1850s to the 1870s, it is not a straightforward venture to identify what she owes to Romanticism. The artistic and intellectual trends associated with Romanticism have become part of her 'food' as well.

Among the many intellectual influences on George Eliot, European Romanticism of the late eighteenth and early nineteenth centuries was prominent. She was especially familiar with its Germanic and French dimensions as well as with developments in Great Britain. Moreover, she was alive to the wide variety of creative endeavours that the movement encompassed: pictorial art and sculpture; fiction (with Gothic and historical fiction being notable Romantic genres), drama and poetry; music, including opera. While Romanticism inflected her intellectual interests, such as historiography, philosophy and politics, this chapter will concentrate on creative literature.

While nursing her dying father in 1849, Marian Evans writes to Sara Sophia Hennell that 'Rousseau's genius has sent that electric thrill through my intellectual and moral frame which has awakened me to new perceptions, which has made man and nature a fresh world of thought and feeling to me' (*L*, I: 277). Although he died in 1788, the publications of Swiss-French writer Jean-Jacques Rousseau had an immense impact on European culture and politics, and served as precursors to Romanticism.

The future George Eliot, responding particularly to the *Confessions*, makes the point that Rousseau has not induced her to adopt all his beliefs – in this respect, she says, he is like other writers who have influenced her 'profoundly'. Such a caveat reminds us that the novelist's engagement with writers and thinkers of any kind would never involve a straightforward acceptance of their ideas. Rather, 'the rushing mighty wind of his inspiration has so quickened my faculties' that her own ideas have taken more definite shape, and she has been able to 'make new combinations' from the fusing of 'old thoughts and prejudices' (*L*, I: 277).

The way the future novelist describes Rousseau's impact on her is redolent of the characteristics which his works emphasised, and which were central traits of Romantic texts: powerful sensation ('electric thrill'), 'new perceptions' which relate to both 'man and nature', the linking of 'thought and feeling', the creative endeavour resulting in 'new combinations'. Romantic writing usually valorised powerful feeling: Romanticism is often seen as in part a reaction against a perceived overvaluing of intellect and ratiocination during the eighteenth-century Enlightenment. The interactions between thought and feeling, including the potentially transformative power of feeling over thought, were also vital concerns. 'New perceptions', meanwhile, were believed possible because, in tandem with the valorising of feeling itself, came a privileging of subjectivity. The human mind, rather than a passive blank slate on which impressions from the outside world were made, was seen more as an individualised power: perceptions varied between people, and each percipient brought some feeling of their own to the process, such that perception had a creative dimension to it. Those possessing the most intense – and thus the most creative – powers of perception, were artistic geniuses. The Romantics' focus on subjectivity also fostered a fascination with the human psyche, and with the individual's inner life. Rousseau wrote autobiographical works which catalysed this interest (his *Confessions*, 1781–7, and *Rêveries d'un promeneur solitaire*, 1782), as well as a very influential novel (*Julie, ou la Nouvelle Héloïse*, 1761). Psychological analysis of characters' inner lives became a prominent feature of nineteenth-century fiction, and George Eliot's novels arguably represent the culmination of this trend.

In Britain, the writers traditionally most identified with the Romantic movement are the poets Blake, Wordsworth, Coleridge, Byron, Percy Shelley and Keats. The significance of poets such as Felicia Hemans and Letitia Elizabeth Landon is now recognised, along with the poet and novelist Sir Walter Scott and the novelist Mary Wollstonecraft Shelley. George Eliot's writings show that she was familiar with all these authors, but the ones who figure most strongly are Wordsworth, Scott and Byron. They are also the three who made most impact on nineteenth-century literature in general, and not only in Britain.

Scott's recuperation of old ballads (*Minstrelsy of the Scottish Border*, 1802–3) and his series of poems beginning with *The Lay of the Last Minstrel* (1805) and *Marmion* (1808) focused on Scottish legends from earlier centuries contributed to people's fascination with the distant (and especially the medieval) past, and with cultures that seemed remote and exotic to metropolitan readers. Some of Scott's novels fostered similar interests and, for George Eliot, they demonstrated how sympathy might be aroused for lower-class people of a kind outside readers' personal experience. In 'The Natural History of German Life' (1856), written just before she began to publish fiction which self-consciously discusses writers' efforts to render lower-class life, she declares that 'a picture of human life such as a great artist can give, surprises even the trivial and the selfish into that attention to what is apart from themselves, which may be called the raw material of moral sentiment'. She adduces as an example 'Luckie Mucklebackit's cottage', the dwelling of an old Scottish peasant woman of the late eighteenth century described in Scott's novel *The Antiquary* (1816) (*Essays*, 270).

Another example of the same effect is Wordsworth's poem 'Poor Susan'. Published in the second edition (1800) of his first important collection of poems, *Lyrical Ballads*, the poem expresses the experience of a woman trapped in a poor area of London, who hears every morning the song of a thrush: this music recalls to her the beautiful region in which she grew up: 'A mountain ascending, a vision of trees', a river, '[g]reen pastures', and finally 'a single small cottage, a nest like a dove's, | The one only dwelling on earth that she loves'.[1]

If Rousseau's writings could offer George Eliot 'new perceptions' of 'man and nature', so too did Wordsworth's. Both lived in beautiful rural areas, and celebrated the influence of the natural world on the human mind and spirit, contrasting its effects with what they saw as the corrupting impact of life in cities. This was a major theme of Wordsworth's poetry, in which the natural world is a source of solace, of emotional healing and of moral regeneration. It is also – more than for Rousseau – the locale of humble people whose lives are worth the attention of middle- and upper-class urban readers. Wordsworth's Preface to the *Lyrical Ballads* (1800, 1802) highlighted the interaction between people of 'low and rustic life' and their surroundings, arguing that 'in that condition the essential passions of the heart find a better soil in which they can attain their maturity', and that these passions are 'incorporated with the beautiful and permanent forms of nature'.[2]

Although George Eliot's novels do not suggest that rural people are necessarily morally superior to urban dwellers because of their greater exposure to nature, her earlier works in particular urge readers to expand their minds and sensibilities to understand the feelings and experiences of characters assumed to have very different backgrounds from their own. *Adam Bede*, as well as addressing its readers in this way (notably in chapter 17), offers a largely attractive picture of farming life and its rhythms and processes, and also of the rural craftsman in Adam himself. Meanwhile in *Silas Marner*, Silas, after being ostracised by an urban religious sect, is eventually integrated into a rural village which, for all its shortcomings, is a cohesive community with longstanding traditions: when Silas revisits the town, his old quarter and its inhabitants have been swallowed up in urban development.

George Eliot told John Blackwood that Wordsworth might have liked *Silas Marner* (*L*, 3: 382), and she provided the novel with an epigraph from his poem 'Michael' (also from the 1800 edition of *Lyrical Ballads*):

> A child, more than all other gifts
> That earth can offer to declining man,
> Brings hope with it, and forward-looking thoughts (ll. 149–51)

The quotation obviously foreshadows the role that Eppie is to play in Silas's life: making him think of the future, and leading to his integration into the Raveloe community. A related dimension of Romantic thought taken up by Wordsworth was the celebration of the child's special intuitive powers. Rather than being afflicted by original sin, the child embodied innocence; it also possessed capacities of perception and responsiveness, especially to the natural world. An adult might lose some of these, but could still access them through a child.

The role played by memory in Silas's integration into Raveloe is also crucial, and again can be connected with Wordsworth. Eppie's pull on Silas's emotions comes partly from how she reminds him of his dead younger sister. Even before Eppie appears in his life, Silas's openness to affection is demonstrated by his attachment to his old water-pot, which he has kept despite its being broken. In 'Michael', the shepherd Michael's son Luke (unlike Eppie) is irretrievably corrupted by city life and has to leave England, but Michael remains emotionally drawn to the unfinished sheepfold that he and Luke had worked on together.

The power of memories, and especially memories relating to the natural world, is a central motif of Wordsworth's poetry. For him such memories could effect emotional healing, and in *The Mill on the Floss*, George Eliot takes up this theme in dealing with Tom and Maggie Tulliver, for instance when the narrator declares that, although '[l]ife did change' for the pair, 'the thoughts and loves of these first years would always make part of their lives', and suggests that such experience is a general human one. The love we feel for natural phenomena like trees and flowers in our childhood continues through our lives, and can 'thrill ... deep and delicate fibres' within us (*MF*, book 1, ch. 5).

Memory is clearly important to this novel, as Maggie's sense of identity is closely bound up with her memories and the loyalties she associates with them. But whereas in Wordsworth's poetry memories are often integrated into the speaker's experience and help him move forward (his 'Lines Written a Few Miles Above Tintern Abbey', 1798, is an exemplary instance), Maggie is constantly torn between the ties linked to her memories and newer possibilities – there is no straightforward resolution. It is also worth noting that the rural communities portrayed in *Adam Bede* and *Silas Marner* belong to the late eighteenth and early nineteenth centuries – around the period of Wordsworth's *Lyrical Ballads* – and these novels do raise the issue of how far the positive elements of such communities have been, or can be, retained in George Eliot's present.

The connection between 'thought and feeling' (to recall the letter about Rousseau) was another focus of Wordsworth's Preface to the *Lyrical Ballads*. It famously declared that 'all good Poetry is the spontaneous overflow of powerful feelings', but went on to stress that poetry of value could only be produced by 'a man who, being possessed of more than usual organic sensibility, had also thought long and deeply'.[3] *Middlemarch* in particular was to give attention to the interplay of thought and feeling. The medical researcher Tertius Lydgate is described as possessing 'intellectual ardour' (*M*, ch. 15) – and when he fails, it is less an intellectual defeat than a depletion of emotional energy arising from his unwise marriage. When the novel's other protagonist, Dorothea, starts to register how her husband Edward Casaubon has 'an equivalent centre of self', the narrator describes this needed awareness as a transmutation of thought into emotion, something Dorothea has to 'conceive with that distinctness which is no longer reflection but feeling – an idea wrought back to the directness of sense' (*M*, ch. 21).

The development of feeling described here is a moral process, an emergence from that state of 'moral stupidity' where we take 'the world as an udder to feed our supreme selves' (*M*, ch. 21). But another strand of Romanticism, that which George Eliot associated with the immensely popular poet Lord Byron, was one that she saw as privileging subjective feeling in an egoistic way, rather than stimulating empathy. Wordsworth and Byron are both evoked in telling ways in *Felix Holt, the Radical*, which is set in the early 1830s. Mrs Transome, we are told, had in her youth 'laughed at the Lyrical Ballads', and this and her other once-fashionable literary opinions are sardonically placed in the novel as, thirty years on, both out of date and offering her no emotional sustenance. Her unthinking Toryism seeks to suppress 'the obtrusiveness of the vulgar' (such as those populating *Lyrical Ballads*), while her memories are painful rather than healing (*FH*, ch. 1). Meanwhile, Esther Lyon is given the chance to become the next Mrs Transome, and the traits in her which make this fate temporarily tempting are linked with her fascination with the heroes of Lord Byron.

In the second decade of the nineteenth century, Byron published a series of poems focused on a glamorous male figure. The heroes of *Childe Harold's Pilgrimage* (1812–1818), *The Giaour* (1813), *The Bride of Abydos* (1813), *The Corsair* (1814), *Lara* (1814), *The Siege of Corinth* (1816) and *Manfred* (1817) were powerful personalities with generally similar traits: an air of mystery, usually connected with secret wrongdoing, a charismatic influence on others, a disillusioned and misanthropic attitude, ceaseless restlessness, a capacity for powerful passion and a devotion to a single love. These traits were often identified with Byron himself. But, like contempt for Wordsworth, enthusiasm for Byron is in *Felix Holt* an undesirable sentiment, and Felix's influence dissipates it in Esther. A working man, Felix derides Byron's heroes as pretentious, self-absorbed and artificial. He calls Byron a 'misanthropic debauchee ... whose notion of a hero was that he should disorder his stomach and despise mankind', so that his heroes 'are the most paltry puppets that were ever pulled by the strings of lust and pride', and 'gentlemen of unspeakable woes, who employ a hairdresser, and look seriously at themselves in the glass' (*FH*, ch. 5). The novel sets up Felix as a kind of antitype to the Byronic hero – a man of humble background who learns to suppress his own pride, and, rather than expressing contempt for others, commits himself to a life of engaging with quotidian realities and small-scale efforts at social betterment. That Esther in effect abandons Byron for Felix is a sign of her moral growth.

A more complex treatment of the Byronic figure emerges in *Middlemarch*'s Will Ladislaw (who is even called a 'sort of Byronic hero' by the catty but sharp Mrs Cadwallader (*M*, ch. 38)). Ladislaw is an outsider – he is partly foreign and doubly disinherited – but his outsider status has exposed him to European culture, and thus to a world beyond Middlemarch's narrow-minded provincialism. He is artistic, and also interested in politics, but for much of the novel he lacks direction. It is through his love for Dorothea that his energies find a definite political channel.

The Romantic movement itself was associated with political change. Rousseau's political ideas influenced the French Revolution; Wordsworth and Coleridge were caught in the ferment of French revolutionary ideas, although both became conservative in middle age. Shelley was a political radical, while Byron was involved in struggles to free Italian states from Austrian rule, and died trying to liberate Greece from Ottoman control. George Eliot's novels implicitly respond to such ambitions. In *Felix Holt, the Radical*, the radicalism is to do with reforming individuals morally rather than with initiating widespread political change, while in *Middlemarch*, although Ladislaw (unlike Lydgate) remains 'ardent', the political 'hopefulness' of his generation has been 'much checked' by the 1870s (*M*, ch. 87).

For all her reservations about Byronic egoism, George Eliot's novels constantly focus on characters with aspirations for more than their society offers them, thwarted by a combination of their own traits and the limitations of their social environments. One influence here was that of the great German Romantic dramatist Friedrich Schiller (1759–1803). Possessing more of a moral vision (in George Eliot's terms) than Byron, Schiller demonstrated the dilemmas arising from his characters' high ideals in conflict with social and historical reality, while at the same time recognising the dangers inherent in the idealising mind.[4] But whereas Schiller's idealists usually die, revealing the impossibility of realising their ideals in the social realm, George Eliot's idealists, with the exception of Maggie Tulliver, reach some accommodation with their societies – as happens with Romola, Felix, Dorothea, Lydgate and Ladislaw – though often with a sense of opportunities missed.

Although set in the 1860s, a generation or more after the Romantic movement, George Eliot's last novel shows fascinating developments in her treatment of Romantic motifs. *Daniel Deronda* presents for the first time in her career a fully fledged genius of Romantic tendencies: Julius Klesmer, a figure who has been related to various European performers and composers, including Franz Liszt (whom she had met). Like Will Ladislaw, he is an outsider, but more so than Ladislaw, he has a successful career. Meanwhile, idealistic aspirations are incarnated in Mordecai and Daniel Deronda – both also Jews and thus outsiders – and the novel's open ending gestures towards the potential achievement of their proto-Zionist goals. The implications are different, however, when George Eliot locates male Byronic self-will and charisma in significant female characters, in

Gwendolen Harleth and Daniel's artist mother the Alcharisi. Neither woman attains a lasting outlet for her aspirations, and there is no clear endorsement of them in the text. Thus, considering George Eliot's treatment of female ambition through the lens of Romanticism – just as from other perspectives – reveals the novelist's ambivalence about it.

NOTES

1 William Wordsworth and Samuel Taylor Coleridge, *Lyrical Ballads*, ed. Michael Mason (London and New York: Longman, 1992), pp. 266–7.
2 Ibid., 60.
3 Ibid., 62.
4 Deborah Guth, *George Eliot and Schiller: Intertextuality and Cross-Cultural Discourse* (Aldershot and Burlington, VT: Ashgate, 2003) provides extensive discussion of George Eliot's fiction in relation to Schiller's plays.

CHAPTER 30

Rural life

Carol A. Martin

The year 1856 saw the emergence of Mary Ann Evans as a writer on rural life. In September she began what would become her first published work of fiction, two months after she had articulated her theory of the importance of accurate representation of rural life in the July number of the *Westminster Review.* This theory was to inform her fiction throughout her career:

> Art is the nearest thing to life; it is a mode of amplifying experience and extending our contact with our fellow-men beyond the bounds of our personal lot. All the more sacred is the task of the artist when he undertakes to paint the life of the People. Falsification here is far more pernicious than in the more artificial aspects of life. It is not so very serious that we should have false ideas about evanescent fashions … but it *is* serious that our sympathy with the perennial joys and struggles, the toil, the tragedy, and the humour in the life of our more heavily-laden fellow-men, should be perverted, and turned towards a false object instead of the true one. ('Natural History', *Essays*, 271)

A keen observer of rural life from her childhood as the daughter of the steward of a landed estate in Warwickshire, Mary Ann Evans grew up during a period when the rural landscape was being dramatically altered. At the 1851 census, though agriculture remained the largest single source of employment, it had lost its pre-eminence. Change was most evident in the Midlands and the North, where new industrial towns like the cotton manufacturing centre, Birmingham, had grown up close to George Eliot's home town of Coventry. Although rural life is at the centre of both *Scenes of Clerical Life* and *Adam Bede*, the author was keenly aware of how the urban–rural dynamic had changed over the first half of the century. More and more people were moving to London or to other urban centres like Birmingham, which had 71,000 residents in 1801 and 233,000 fifty years later, and Manchester, which grew from 75,000 to 303,000.[1] In her novels, George Eliot had frequent occasion to point out the proximity of industrial squalor and agricultural plenty, as in the coach journey in the 'Introduction' to *Felix Holt* where the contrasts among fields and towns, and mines and other scars of industry, are indicated.

Coventry, the urban centre closest to George Eliot's childhood home at Griff, was described by William Cobbett in 1820:

> Coventry … is a City containing about twenty thousand souls, and the business of which is, principally, Watch-making and Ribbon-weaving. It is in the County of Warwick, and is within a few miles of the centre of England. The land all around it, for many many miles is very rich indeed … and yet, good God! What a miserable race of human beings! What a ragged, squalid, woe-worn assemblage of creatures![2]

But when Mary Ann Evans moved with her father from Griff, the home of her youth, into Coventry in March 1841, it had become 'a pleasant town of some 30,000 inhabitants, of whom about 5,000 were employed as ribbon weavers'.[3] From the Evans house Bird Grove in Foleshill, it was about a mile to that of the ribbon manufacturer Charles Bray, his wife Cara and her sister Sara Hennell, who became her close friends. Years later, in *Middlemarch*, George Eliot pictured the gradual erosion of the boundary between rural and urban in her description of the house of the Caleb Garth family as 'a little way outside the town – a homely place with an orchard in front of it … now surrounded with the private gardens of the townsmen' (*M*, ch. 24).

In her retrospective essay 'How I came to write fiction', George Eliot records having written 'an introductory chapter describing a Staffordshire village and the life of the neighbouring farm houses' (*J*, 289), and although no fragment of this chapter is extant, her description fits well the first story in *Scenes*, 'The Sad Fortunes of the Reverend Amos Barton'. From this modest beginning of ten chapters and a brief conclusion, George Eliot went on to be hailed as a notable recorder of English rural life.

Only traces of England's demographic changes appear in *Scenes*, as the author draws on the rural life she knew from her Warwickshire childhood. 'The Sad Fortunes of the Reverend Amos Barton' opens in the parish church of Chilvers Coton where Mary Ann Evans was baptised and which she attended over the years (see Figure 18). The description of Cheverel Manor, the remodelled Gothic mansion in the second tale, 'Mr Gilfil's Love Story', is closely based on the Newdigate family seat, Arbury Hall, where the young Mary Ann visited in the housekeeper's room while her father went on his rounds taking care of estate business. In the third of the *Scenes*, 'Janet's Repentance', the narrator's description of Mr Jerome's lush garden of fruit and flowers grown for aesthetic pleasure and domestic use offers only temporary relief from the political, personal and religious tensions in the town of Milby ('Janet', ch. 8). This story includes vividly depicted scenes of alcoholism and abuse. Frequently noted in news accounts in the London papers of the 1850s and exposed twenty years later in Frances Power Cobbe's *Contemporary Review* essay 'Wife-Torture in England', the brutality of husbands towards their wives was a social problem not limited to the metropolis. Responding to John Blackwood's objections to the details of alcoholism and domestic brutality in Milby, George Eliot argued for the reality of her representation, pointing out that 'the real town was more vicious than my Milby' (*L*, 2: 347).

The work that established George Eliot's reputation as a recorder of rural life was her first full-length novel, *Adam Bede*, which opens during the Napoleonic Wars, when agriculture in England flourished. The specific date in the opening paragraph, 'the eighteenth of June, in the year of our Lord 1799', marks the distance in time of the setting of the novel from the time of its publication – sixty years, or the conventional two generations. The carpenters' workshop, where door panels are carved by hand, is a reminder for readers in 1859 of how thoroughly labour had been mechanised over the past six decades (*AB*, ch. 1). The conversation following Mr Irwine's afternoon church service (country parsons often held Sunday services in multiple locations) would have reminded readers of England's agricultural prosperity during the Napoleonic Wars. At this point in the story, though, Hayslope residents' connection with the war is manifested for instance in the confidence expressed by the gardener Mr Craig that the English will beat the French because he has had 'upo' good authority as it's a big Frenchman as reaches five foot high, an' they live upo' spoon-meat mostly' (*AB*, ch. 18). The Poysers' income depends on dairy products and grain, but another important part of the national economy was iron and steel production to meet the growing need for munitions. And Dinah Morris's work in the mills in aptly named Stonyshire shows the impact of industry and the fragmentation of traditional communities.

Scenes like the Poysers' leisurely walk to church with Mrs Poyser's meditations on the milk-producing merits of different cows and the Poyser sons' discovery of the speckled turkey's nest reminded urban readers of the pleasures of a farm family's limited leisure time. Jane Welsh Carlyle spoke for many when she wrote to George Eliot: 'It was as good as *going into the country for one's health*, the reading of that Book was! … I could fancy in reading it, to be seeing and hearing once again a crystal-clear, musical, Scotch stream, such as I long to lie down beside and – *cry* at (!) for gladness and sadness; after long stifling sojourn in the South; where there [is] no *water* but what is stagnant or muddy!'[4] Reviewer Anne Mozley celebrated the accuracy of the author's representation: 'We do not know whether our literature anywhere possesses such a closely true picture of purely rural life as *Adam Bede* presents. Every class that makes up a village community has its representative; and not only is the dialect of the locality accurately given but the distinct inflection of each order.'[5] For an author who wrote and rewrote the dialect of the 'rustics' in *Adam Bede*, this comment must have been particularly gratifying given the concerns of both Lewes and Blackwood about its intelligibility to the reader.

Less nostalgic and more realistic are the representations of landowners like old Squire Donnithorne who tries to persuade his tenants the Poysers to accept a disadvantageous move from the Hall Farm. The Squire's veiled threat not to renew the Poysers' lease elicits Mr Poyser's meditation on the farm family's vulnerability: 'I should be loath to leave th' old place. We should leave our roots behind us, I doubt, and niver thrive again' – a reminder that landlords held the upper hand (ch. 32). His grandson Arthur enjoys the privileges of his position as heir to the estate, but demonstrates a lack of awareness of his responsibilities. His congenial façade in pretending to admire Mrs Poyser's dairy conceals his desire to see the dairymaid Hetty Sorrel and arrange their first meeting in the wood – a meeting with dreadful consequences for both.

As urban spaces became more crowded, city dwellers were likely to have fewer opportunities than those in the country to be closely informed (accurately or not) about their neighbours' lives, past and present. In *Scenes of Clerical Life*, country gossip circulates rumours about Amos Barton's naive but innocent friendship with the Countess Czerlaski: 'There's fine stories i' the village about her', and even the earnest but unsophisticated Amos is tainted ('Amos', ch. 7). In *The Mill on the Floss* the narrator satirises Aunt Glegg's sanctimonious capacity for keeping track of what her neighbours are up to: 'Mrs Glegg had both a front and a back parlour in her excellent house at St Ogg's, so that she had two points of view from which she could observe the weakness of her fellow-beings, and reinforce her thankfulness for her own exceptional strength of mind' (*MF*, book 1, ch. 12). She is outwitted by the talents of Bob Jakin, whose ventures as an itinerant packman lead to further entrepreneurial initiatives indicative on a small scale of England's growing trade in manufactured goods. Tom Tulliver too becomes part of the new capitalist economy, paying back his father's creditors by his activities in trade and earning a place in his uncle Dean's business.

"'*You may run away from my words, Sir,' continued Mrs. Poyser.*"—PAGE 302.

Figure 19 Illustration by William Small, engraved by James D. Cooper, for *Adam Bede*, chapter 32, 'Mrs Poyser "has her say out"', in Blackwood's Illustrated Edition (1867).

Of George Eliot's first four works of fiction, *Silas Marner* (1861) goes farthest back in time, to 'the days when the spinning-wheels hummed busily in the farmhouses – and even great ladies, clothed in silk and thread-lace, had their toy spinning-wheels of polished oak' (ch. 1). Its Wordsworthian view of nature is established at the start through its epigraph from 'Michael, A Pastoral Poem': 'A child, more than all other gifts | That earth can offer to declining man, | Brings hope with it, and forward-looking thoughts.' Perhaps reminding readers of the fate of Michael's son Luke when he goes off to the city, the urban setting serves especially to contrast the treachery of Silas's *soi-disant* friend from Lantern Yard in the city with the humanity and generosity of spirit of such rustic characters as Dolly Winthrop and even the men at the Rainbow. Although the story is set back in time, the rural setting of the village of Raveloe is not far distant from that known to George Eliot's contemporaries: 'it lay in the rich central plain of what we are pleased to call Merry England, and held farms which, speaking from a spiritual point of view, paid highly desirable tithes. But it was nestled in a snug well-wooded hollow, quite an hour's journey from any turnpike' (*SM*, ch. 1). While this account of the setting may lack her usual precision in drawing rural scenes, its strength lies in the evocation of a rural past well beyond the memory of most readers in 1861. E. S. Dallas in his review in *The Times* praised its realism and truthfulness, calling it 'a plain statement of the everyday life of the people'.[6]

After her Italian novel *Romola* (1863), George Eliot returned to the English landscape in *Felix Holt*, *Middlemarch* and *Daniel Deronda*, but with a focus on urban spaces and political and social issues that sets these novels apart from her earlier works. As cities grew and city dwellers waxed nostalgic for clear air, clean water and the greenery of rural England, the purchase of a country estate became increasingly attractive to those who had made a sufficient fortune in London, Manchester, Birmingham, Leeds and other centres of industry and commerce, for reasons of status as well as environmental concerns. Such estates were, however, not readily available given the concentration of land in relatively few hands. One of those landowners is *Middlemarch*'s Mr Brooke, whose mismanagement of his land and irresponsible treatment of its tenants at once undercuts his credibility as a candidate in the parliamentary election of 1832, and epitomises the need for reform.

In line with the nineteenth-century philanthropic movement for improving the conditions of workers, both rural and urban, Brooke's niece Dorothea draws plans for new cottages and goes so far as to pick out models, urging Brooke with a Carlylean argument: 'I think we have no right to come forward and urge wider changes for good, until we have tried to alter the evils which lie under our own hands.' Brooke's resistance is finally overcome in a confrontation with his drunken tenant Dagley, who argues that 'there's to be a Rinform, and them landlords as never done the right thing by their tenants 'ull be treated i' that way as they'll hev to scuttle off' (*M*, ch. 39). Despite his shocked surprise at Dagley's speech, Brooke's eventual agreement to hire Caleb Garth to manage the property sets the scene for Fred Vincy's finding an out-of-doors career more suitable than the clerical one his father envisioned for him. *Felix Holt, the Radical* also centres on property issues and the extension of the franchise, but the rural setting is less consequential than in *Middlemarch*.

George Eliot's last novel, *Daniel Deronda*, is set mainly in London and Europe. For the most part its rural scenes are set on large estates, with gradations of rank and issues of social mobility sharply delineated. Yet even in this, her least rural novel, she emphasises the importance of rootedness:

> A human life, I think, should be well rooted in some spot of a native land, where it may get the love of tender kinship for the face of the earth, for the labours men go forth to, for the sounds and accents that haunt it, for whatever will give that early home a familiar unmistakable difference amidst the future widening of knowledge: a spot where the definiteness of early memories may be inwrought with affection, and kindly acquaintance with all neighbours, even to the dogs and donkeys, may spread not by sentimental effort and reflection, but as a sweet habit of the blood ... But this blessed persistence in which affection can take root had been wanting in Gwendolen's life. (ch. 3)

The values are those that inform her early novels, but *Daniel Deronda* explores rootedness in a more complex way appropriate to its nearly contemporary setting and its international reach, from its opening in a gambling casino on the continent to Daniel Deronda's embracing his roots in Europe's Jewish community and seeking a new life in Palestine.

NOTES

1 Anthony Wohl, *Endangered Lives: Public Health in Victorian Britain* (Abingdon: Routledge, 1984), p. 4.
2 Frederick Smith, *Coventry: Six Hundred Years of Municipal Life* (London: Corporation of the City of Coventry in association with the *Coventry Evening Telegraph*, 1945), pp. 201–2, quoting Cobbett's *Political Register*, 25 March 1820.

3 Rosemary Ashton, *George Eliot: A Life* (London: Hamish Hamilton, 1996), p. 34.
4 David Carroll (ed.), *George Eliot: The Critical Heritage* (London: Routledge and Kegan Paul, 1971), p. 72.
5 Ibid., p. 97.
6 Ibid., p. 179.

CHAPTER 31

The science of the mind

Pauline Nestor

In October 1855 George Eliot reported to her friend Sara Hennell that she was reading William Carpenter's *Principles of Human and Comparative Physiology* and 'trying to fix some knowledge about plexuses and ganglia in my soft brain' (*L*, 2: 220). Her modesty was playfully disingenuous. As the same letter makes clear, George Eliot was in fact deeply immersed in and expertly conversant with contemporary developments in the burgeoning field of the science of the mind. In addition to Carpenter's text, which had by then run to a fourth edition and been expanded to include a substantial section on physiological psychology, she also writes of reading Franz Gall and Karl Spurzheim, the founders of phrenology, and she comments knowledgeably on her friend Herbert Spencer's seminal *History of Psychology* (1855). Her study in these matters was thorough and systematic, reading aloud and note-taking in collaboration with her partner, George Henry Lewes, himself a significant commentator on, and contributor to, debates in physiology and psychology. Indeed, so well versed was George Eliot in the field that after Lewes's death in 1878 she was able to revise for publication the last two volumes (*The Study of Psychology* and *Mind as a Function of the Organism*) of his five-volume *Problems of Life and Mind*.

Writing of 'The New Psychology' in 1879, William Courtenay claimed that nothing was 'more remarkable than the change which has come over the study of psychology in England within the last fifty years'.[1] The two major developments in that progress were the shift to materialist analyses of the brain with 'the indispensable union of the physiological with the psychological', and the application to the mind of 'the revolutionary principle of development, and the inclusion of it within the larger philosophy of evolution', pioneered by Herbert Spencer.[2] More generally, the Positivist spirit of mid-Victorian England gave rise to a range of investigations of subjectivity shaped by the aspirations of scientific methodology to measure, to hypothesise and to verify. At the heart of each was a determination to examine and know the self as a subject of science. Where once theology or philosophy might have been expected to provide insight into the human mind, now, according to Lewes, only the 'Method of Science' could yield true knowledge, and that one method 'must be followed in all investigations, whether the investigations relate to Physics, to Psychology, to Ethics, or to Politics'.[3]

This preoccupation with the science of the mind was not simply restricted to the elite intellectual classes in which George Eliot moved. It was also a matter of lively and extensive interest in the popular imagination due to the widespread interest in physiognomy and phrenology, to the fascination with various manifestations of spiritualism, and to the influence of the novel, the pre-eminent art form of mid-Victorian England and the genre which most profoundly offered readers new dimensions of psychological analysis and complexity.

In 1789 the first English translation of Johann Lavater's work, *Essays in Physiognomy*, appeared and, according to John Graham, 'was reprinted, abridged, summarized, pirated, parodied, imitated, and reviewed so often that it is difficult to imagine how a literate person of the time could have failed to have some general knowledge of the man and his theories'.[4] Lavater held out the prospect of systematically deducing moral qualities through the meticulous measurement and analysis of facial characteristics. The popularity of this 'new science' permeated the cultural and intellectual life of the first half of the nineteenth century in a variety of ways, its merits being debated over many decades in the periodical press.

Despite physiognomy's pretensions to measurement and analysis, it ultimately failed to satisfy its promise of scientific rigour and exactitude. Nevertheless, if physiognomy ultimately proved to be a false taxonomic dawn in the march towards a science of the mind, the related discipline of phrenology, while still purporting to read character from the surface of the body – in this case, the shape of the skull – promised more in terms of scientific rigour. Gall's phrenological system outlined a division of the brain into twenty-seven separate portions, each assigned a corresponding faculty: Johann Spurzheim, 'the improver' of the system, subsequently added a further eight. Together, they proposed a comprehensive taxonomy of character which offered, according to George Eliot's long-time friend Charles Bray, the 'clearest analysis of the mental constitution that has perhaps yet been given'.[5]

Phrenology enjoyed enormous popularity in the first half of the nineteenth century, due in no small measure to the influence and reach of George Combe's *The Constitution of Man*, which popularised Gall's theory, promising a systematic and scientific account of Moral and Political

Philosophy. First published in 1828, Combe's book had sold 100,000 copies by 1860, ensuring 'the seepage of phrenology into every chink and cranny of public opinion', according to the *Spectator* in 1841, and leading Lewes to suggest in 1846 that phrenology was 'the only psychological [doctrine] which counts a considerable mass of adherents'.[6] While Lewes adjudged Gall's theories overall as 'defective' and 'inaccurate', he nevertheless contended that phrenology had given 'an immense impulse to research' through its 'truly scientific' study of the mind, its recognition of 'the constant relation between structure and function', and its attention to 'inherited structures and inherited aptitudes'.[7]

George Eliot was not untouched by the phrenological craze, thanks in part to her close friendship with Charles Bray, an enthusiastic proponent of this new 'science'. Indeed, it was in Bray's company that she travelled to London in 1844 to have a phrenological cast of her head taken. However, while she was *au fait* with phrenological language, her use of it was invariably playful or sardonic, and she was intellectually ill-disposed to accept a theory which offered to read depth from surface: 'It is possible that such a supposed relation has a real anatomical basis', she wrote to Dante Gabriel Rossetti; 'But in many particulars facial expression is like the expression of hand-writing: the relations are too subtle and intricate to be detected, and only shallowness is confident' (*L*, 5: 79).

She was similarly sceptical about spirit communication, confessing only a 'feeble interest' to Harriet Beecher Stowe in 1872, and leaving a séance held at the home of Erasmus Darwin in 1874 'in disgust' (*L*, 5: 280; 6: 6n). In this she stood against the tide of the mid-Victorian fascination with altered states of consciousness – mesmeric trance, hallucination, somnambulism, telepathy and the like – which led to a remarkable conjunction of popular and scientific interests in psychology and psychophysiology, and provoked extensive debate about the nature of consciousness and volition. So, for example, in 1848 Catherine Crowe's anthology of ghost stories, *The Night-side of Nature*, offered both best-selling entertainment and a commentary, drawing on 'German authorities', which called for rigorous scientific examination of psychic phenomena; while in 1882 the Society for Psychical Research collated the testimony of 25,000 members of the public for their vast Census of Hallucinations in order to prove the truth of telepathy and bury the scientific incredulity that greeted psychic research 'under a heap of facts'.[8]

Psychic research's claim to scientific method extended in the case of some researchers to the use of scientific apparatus. As the increasing specialisation and elitism of science in the second half of the nineteenth century came to depend in part on the sophistication of its equipment, psychic researchers drew upon an arsenal of scientific paraphernalia. William Crookes, for example, devised an elaborate self-registering spring-balance and concluded that he had discovered a new 'Psychic Force', and photography was similarly enlisted to establish 'as a scientific fact the objective existence of invisible human forces'.[9] As well as their claim to the methods of science, psychical researchers also appropriated the language and theory of contemporary science. William James, for one, saw the attempts to understand the relationship between mind, body and spirit, including the Society for Psychical Research's investigations of trance personalities, telepathy and spirit possession, as all part of the emerging 'science of the soul', which he characterised as 'like Physics before Galileo's time'.[10] Similarly, electricity and other emerging technologies of Victorian England, particularly the telephone and the telegraph, were offered as compelling analogies for the understanding of telepathy. For all concerned, a recognition of the new and coercive cultural authority of science compelled them to submit the deepest questions of human identity to scientific analysis.

The mid-Victorian novel was the third force in popularising the science of the mind, contributing substantially to the psychological literacy of the period. Accordingly, works of the period often stressed a correlation between reading and self-awareness. Thus in *The Mill on the Floss* the dark-haired and rebellious heroine Maggie Tulliver shows her first inkling of the high cost extracted for female deviance through her interpretation of the story of the witch in Daniel Defoe's *History of the Devil.* Subsequently, she sees a version of herself in the tragic heroine of Germaine de Staël's influential best-seller *Corinne* and is moved to protest against the injustice of social constructions of beauty, goodness and conformity: 'I'm determined to read no more books where the blond-haired women carry away all the happiness … If you could give me some story, now, where the dark woman triumphs, it would restore the balance' (*MF*, book 5, ch. 4).

Much more than a knowledgeable observer, George Eliot was in fact a significant contributor to contemporary scientific debate, exemplifying in her work both the porous boundaries between amateur and professional scientific realms in the period and the particular aptitude of the novel genre for psychological investigation. In 'The Development of Psychology', for example, James Collier suggested that the literature of the day was 'drenched with metaphors' from psychology and its physical science precursors, and similarly the first edition of the journal *Mind* described psychology as 'a *critique*, a method, a certain thoughtful attitude in science, morals and literature'.[11] Beyond simply providing subject matter, science shaped George Eliot's way of seeing the world, and whether through organicist metaphors of a web of life or allusions to scientific optics, it furnished her with a whole vocabulary for analogy and analysis.

More particularly, her fiction grappled with the same fundamental problems as the emerging science of psychology. Appropriately, she saw her novels as 'a set of experiments', representing an extended, particularised and dramatic investigation of 'what our thought and emotion may be capable of' (*L*, 6: 216). At the heart of her fiction – and pivotal to mid-century debates on the mind – was the question of will. All of the pioneering psycho-physiologists – Bain, Carpenter, Huxley, Spencer, Lewes – challenged the existence of free will and, under the guise variously of 'ideo-motor' or 'secondarily automatic' action, 'automatism' and 'unconscious cerebration', proposed permutations on a theory of reflex as the foundation of action. With volition, the cornerstone of ethical responsibility, thus called into question, these theorists were left searching for an escape from the straitjacket of rigid determinism. This took the form of naturalising the will as a 'developed reflex', a process achieved through restraint, education and directed attention: 'it is over *the formation of habits* that the will can exert its greatest power, by fixing attention on one set of motives to the exclusion of other motives'.[12] George Eliot was similarly drawn in her early fiction to this idea of ethical vigilance, as, for example, with Adam Bede's aspiration to cultivate an emotional self-consciousness which might lead him 'to dread the violence of his own feeling' and to keep always in mind 'the irrevocableness of … wrong-doing' (*AB*, ch. 48).

Nevertheless, George Eliot's later work provided its own critique of such prospects for complete self-regulation. As Lewes argued, one important consequence of the recognition of 'unconscious sensual and volitional processes' was that the developing science of psychology could not limit itself 'to the facts of Consciousness; for this would exclude the greater part of our mental life'.[13] George Eliot took on this challenge in her fictional explorations of the vulnerability that arises from the unconscious – the existence of 'a possible self, a self not to be absolutely predicted about' (*DD*, ch. 13). *The Mill on the Floss*, for example, is charged with a sense of the forces which undermine the sovereignty of the will. It is a work haunted by violence and madness – real, incipient or feared – in which forms of vacancy, amnesia and unconsciousness repeatedly thwart intention, and the pervasive metaphors of the twin tides of the river and music conjure the disruptive forces of destruction and desire.

This recognition that the limits of consciousness circumscribe the capacity for self-regulation meant that, for George Eliot, ethical evolution was not quite as assured as Herbert Spencer contended in his 1857 paean to the perfectibility of man, 'Progress: Its Law and Cause'. At its simplest, as Lewes argued, 'unconscious processes cannot … fall within the range of introspection', or, as George Eliot noted in *Adam Bede*, motivation was sometimes the result of the 'backstairs influence' of an 'unrecognised agent secretly busy' in the mind (ch. 16).[14] Nevertheless, if complete self-regulation was not a likely achievement in her fiction, it was a worthy aspiration. Habits of self-reflexivity and the exercise of moral imagination, nourished importantly by art, held out the greatest promise of meeting the ultimate ethical challenge of living vigilantly conscious of the fact that that other 'has an equivalent centre of self' (*M*, ch. 21).

The second central preoccupation that George Eliot shared with the mental scientists of the period was with psychology's 'new frontier', the so-called 'social factor'. James Collier insisted that 'the inclusion of the environing world in the definition of the science of the mind' was the 'first notable advance' in psychology's progress.[15] George Eliot, likewise, insisted that the 'Social Factor in Psychology' was 'the supremely interesting element in the thinking of our time' (*L*, 7: 161). She took the term from the title of the fourth chapter of Lewes's *Study of Psychology* in which he argued that psychology must be based on a recognition that the Mind is 'an expression of organic and social conditions' and it must study man 'as a social animal … a social unit: he lives in society, is mentally developed by it and for it'.[16] Accordingly, her novels repeatedly demonstrate that 'there is no creature whose inward being is so strong that it is not greatly determined by what lies outside it' (*M*, 'Finale') – and characters like Tertius Lydgate and Gwendolen Harleth, who harbour fantasies of self-determination, confidently expecting to shape their own fate, are inevitably destined for a hard lesson.

Not surprisingly, then, when Joseph Jacobs defended experimental psychology six years after George Eliot's death, he referred to fiction as having the 'closest connection with psychology' and providing an 'unworked field for psychologists':

> For the last fifty years we have had a large number of persons whose life has been passed in examining and exhibiting the processes of other men's minds. From their experience the science of human nature ought to be able to learn something. I need only refer to the stores of acute observation contained in the works of George Eliot and George Meredith.[17]

NOTES

1 William Courtenay, 'The New Psychology', *Fortnightly Review*, n.s. 26 (1879), 318.

2 George Henry Lewes, *Problems of Life and Mind* (London: Trubner, 1879), vol. IV, p. 14; James Collier, 'The Development of Psychology', *Westminster Review*, n.s. 45 (1874), 396.

3 George Henry Lewes, *A Biographical History of Philosophy from its Origins in Greece down to the Present Day* (1846; New York: Appleton, 1857), p. 779.

4 John Graham, 'Lavater's *Physiognomy* in England', *Journal of the History of Ideas*, 22 (1961), 562.

5 Charles Bray, *The Education of the Feelings* (London: Taylor and Walton, 1838), p. 16.

6 Harriet Martineau, 'George Combe', *Biographical Sketches 1852–1875* (London: Macmillan, 1888), p. 270; Lewes, *Biographical History of Philosophy*, p. 748.

7 Lewes, *Problems*, vol. IV, p. 77.

8 Henry Sidgwick, *First Presidential Address to the Society for Psychical Research*, quoted in Arthur Conan Doyle, *The History of Spiritualism* (London: Cassell, 1926), vol. II, p. 58.

9 Wallace, 'A Defence of Modern Spiritualism', *Fortnightly Review* (1 January 1874), 792, 796.

10 Quoted in Deborah Blum, *Ghost Hunters: William James and the Search for Scientific Proof of Life After Death* (London: Century, 2007), p. 168.

11 Collier, 'The Development of Psychology', 391; *Mind*, 1 (January 1876), 451.

12 W. B. Carpenter, *The Doctrine of Human Automatism* (London: The Sunday Lecture Society, 1875), p. 31.

13 Lewes, *Problems*, vol. IV, p. 19.

14 Ibid., p. 94.

15 Collier, 'The Development of Psychology', 403.

16 Lewes, *Problems*, vol. IV, pp. 6, 38.

17 Joseph Jacobs, 'The Need for a Society for Experimental Psychology', *Mind*, 11 (1886), 51.

CHAPTER 32

Secularism

Michael Rectenwald

Secularism is an orientation to life that places paramount importance on the matters of 'this world', and considers observation and reason the best means by which the things of this world can be known and improved.[1] It has its roots in a response to religious belief, but is not necessarily a form of religion in itself. In some forms, secularism has been preoccupied only with the elimination of religious belief; in others, it is concerned with substituting a secular creed in its place. This latter form of secularism was embraced by such 'advanced' middle-class writers of the Victorian period as Thomas Carlyle, John Stuart Mill, Matthew Arnold and George Eliot.[2] The encounter with secularism of such thinkers was often accompanied by a 'crisis of faith', a crisis that had social, intellectual and moral implications for the newly converted non-believer. George Eliot at once represents the reach of secularist philosophy into middle-class circles, and provides its best expression in Victorian fiction.

In 1841, at the age of 22, Mary Ann Evans, then an evangelical Christian, had a life-changing encounter with secular thought. To this point she had followed her father's staunch adherence to the customs of the Church of England, at times practising very strict religious observances. Mary Ann was led into religious doubt when introduced to heterodox texts by new Coventry friends, Charles Bray, his wife Cara and her sister Sara Hennell. The source of their religious scepticism was the new biblical or 'Higher Criticism'. Originating in Germany and imported into Britain, this historical and naturalistic approach to the Bible held that the Scriptures, like other ancient texts, involved myths, legends and allegory. The 'events' in the Bible and the existence of the texts themselves could be accounted for on purely naturalistic terms and without recourse to divine authorship. In fact, scholars maintained, given the Bible's historical inaccuracies, theological inconsistencies and dubious morality, divine authorship was especially improbable.

Probably the first work of biblical criticism that Evans encountered was *An Inquiry into the Origins of Christianity* (1838), by Charles Christian Hennell, brother of Cara and Sara. She soon engaged in the propagation of biblical criticism in English, when she took over from Charles's wife, the former Rufa Brabant, the massive task of translating from the German David Strauss's *The Life of Jesus* (published in 1846). Strauss's controversial study represented an important contribution to the new form of historicism because of its demonstration that supposedly miraculous events, especially in the New Testament, were in fact mythical. She later translated Ludwig Feuerbach's *The Essence of Christianity* (1854), another significant work in this vein, which in a complex argument proposes that God is the outward projection of individual human natures.

George Eliot's reading also included the new secular social studies, which influenced her outlook and work. The French philosopher and historian Auguste Comte argued in *Positive Philosophy* (1830–46) that, like natural phenomena, social phenomena could be studied in terms of natural law. Comte held that society and all branches of knowledge pass through three stages: the theological, the metaphysical and the scientific or positive. According to this Positivist schema, religious belief was part of the infantile stage of humanity that was paralleled in the lives of individuals. Belief in the supernatural was thus equated with childhood fantasy. At the time of his writing, Comte argued that the social world was still being treated in theological and metaphysical terms and that his own work marked the beginning of the scientific approach. Comte suggested that an understanding and submission to natural law in the social realm was no less necessary than in the natural realm.

In 1851, Marian Evans reviewed for the *Westminster Review* R. W. Mackay's *The Progress of the Intellect* (1850), a work of Comtean orientation. By this time a sympathiser with Comte's Positivism, her characterisation of this tendency in thought was exemplary: she wrote 'The master key to this revelation, is the recognition of the presence of ... that invariability of sequence which is acknowledged to be the basis of physical science, but which is still perversely ignored in our social organization, our ethics and our religion' (*Essays*, 31). The language of the Mackay review is echoed in a *Middlemarch* passage describing the 'long pathways of necessary sequence' of Lydgate's studies (*M*, ch. 16). Ironically, Tertius Lydgate, the ambitious medical reformer in *Middlemarch*, does not apply the same scientific approach to his personal life that he does to his research. He fails to recognise that the relationships he is establishing in Middlemarch – with Nicholas Bulstrode, the self-serving religious hypocrite, and Rosamond

Vincy, Lydgate's self-centred and demanding wife – will have necessary, mostly negative, consequences.

Like the poet Alfred Tennyson, George Eliot read with keen interest the major scientific works that supported the secular worldview under formation at the time, including Charles Lyell's three-volume treatise, *The Principles of Geology* (1830–3). This masterwork, which laid the foundation of modern geology, ridiculed the biblical explanations for geological findings, including the Mosaic flood. According to Lyell, those studying the earth's surface had allowed for 'dramatic and even supernatural causes' – massive floods, earthquakes, a 'plastic force' in nature – and explained the otherwise inexplicable by reference to 'the origin of things'.[3] Lyell suggested that no such catastrophes could be allowed if geology was to become scientific. Instead, the history of the earth demonstrated an uninterrupted uniformity – natural forces affecting the earth's surface uniformly across time. Although he maintained that humanity had been created by a special theistic fiat, Lyell explained all other geological and biological phenomena with reference to uniform natural causes.

In *The Mill on the Floss*, George Eliot deals with uniformity in nature and the social order, and the enormity of geological causes as they compare to the minuscule scale of human drama. While the flood in the novel may seem to have some of the supernatural power of the Mosaic flood, the narrator makes clear that it is one of many that have taken place in the past and of more that will take place in the future. The Floss is described in the novel as 'the great river [that] flows forever onward, and links the small pulse of the old English town with the beatings of the world's mighty heart' (*MF*, book 4, ch. 1). The river has no regard for human affairs and is an instantiation of the unalterable uniformity of causes that operate on the surface of the earth and on its several inhabitants, including human beings.

George Eliot also read the major evolutionary treatises of the period, which had a great impact on her views and those of many of her contemporaries. Evolutionary works prompted religious doubt and were used to support a secular worldview. One of the most influential was the anonymously published *Vestiges of the Natural History of Creation* (1844) which introduced evolutionary ideas into the drawing rooms of the middle class. While its author, the Scottish journalist Robert Chambers, maintained a providential source for the beginning of the universe (the 'Divine Author'), all subsequent developments, including the introduction of human beings, were the results of evolution, not God's creative intervention.

Of course, George Eliot also read Charles Darwin's works, which form the basis of modern evolutionary biology: *On the Origin of Species* (1859) and *The Descent of Man* (1871). In the *Origin*, Darwin explained the introduction of all species, including, by implication, human beings, in terms of the law of natural selection acting on randomly appearing variations. In *The Descent of Man*, he fully naturalised human beings, treating them as animals descended from a pre-human ancestor. He also treated human sexual behaviour, invoking 'sexual selection' to explain the relationship between the sexes in terms of evolutionary adaptation.

George Eliot's treatment of evolutionary theory is best illustrated in *Middlemarch*, where she explores several aspects of evolutionary thinking, including Darwin's and Herbert Spencer's theories of sexual selection as applied to human beings. She also portrays a model of an organic social economy operating according to the same causal forces which act in the natural economy, as depicted in the *Origin*. In the provincial town of Middlemarch, every element has its impact on other elements, and the whole is tied together in a 'web' of relations that is too complex for even the narrator to grasp fully. This organic web mirrors the incredibly complex set of relationships that obtains in nature.

George Levine has recently argued that the prevalence of secularism among the Victorian middle class may have been overstated by twentieth-century readers and critics, based on the attention paid to the writings of a small, yet influential, group including Carlyle, Mill and George Eliot. Yet religious defection among the working classes was no 'mirage'.[4] From the early 1800s, waning church attendance among working-class men and women in industrial towns was already a cause for concern. By the 1851 religious census, working-class attendance was lower than that of other groups. Working-class radical secularists saw the Church and state as a piece in an oppressive 'Old Corruption'. The Anglican Church buttressed the dominant classes ideologically and, at the same time, the state Church and its clergy were supported materially by taxes. Together, for artisanal and working-class radicals, the unholy alliance represented a bar against progressive change. Until the 1840s, working-class 'infidels' – a term of derogation suggesting that irreligion represented a moral and social deficiency – faced imprisonment and fines for their expression of anti-clericism and unbelief.[5]

George Eliot represented working-class infidelity in her most explicitly political novel, *Felix Holt, the Radical*, where the trade-unionist speaker expresses his hostile attitude towards established religion:

> It's part of their monopoly. They'll supply us with our religion like everything else, and get a profit on it. They'll give us plenty of heaven. We may have land *there*. That's the sort of religion that they like – a religion that

> gives us working men heaven, and nothing else ... We'll give them back some of their heaven, and take it out in something for us and our children in this world. (*FH*, ch. 30)

As an unbeliever, Felix Holt accepts the anti-supernaturalist aspect of the speaker's diatribe, but nevertheless rejects his proposed solution for working-class ills – voting reform. According to Felix, 'something else [must come] before all that'. As he makes clear in an 'Address to Working Men, By Felix Holt' (first published in *Blackwood's Magazine* in January 1868 and later appended to the novel), this 'something' is the moral improvement of the working class through education. The 'Address' was solicited by John Blackwood as an intervention in the second Reform Bill debate in 1867 – to counter Benjamin Disraeli's speech delivered to working men in October 1867 and to convince working men that they needed to improve morally before any improvement in society might be effected by their exercise of the vote. *Felix Holt* and the 'Address' thus exemplify the political differences between George Eliot's secularism and that of working-class radicals, especially before 1850. For her, a secularist faith in an all-subsuming natural law did not signify the kind of political upheaval that it did for working-class infidels. On the contrary, for Comtean secularists like George Eliot, natural law was seen as the regulatory mechanism for social and political conservatism.

Working- and middle-class secularism shared a philosophical lineage and drew support from each other's efforts. This is apparent in the Bray circle of which Eliot was a part. Charles Bray was a supporter of freethought, election reform, and many other progressive working-class concerns, including the Utopian socialist philosophy of Robert Owen. In May 1842, he attended the opening of Owen's Millennium Hall in Queenswood, Hampshire. Bray read and recommended the standard works on which the working-class radicals relied in their periodical campaigns against theism, including Baron d'Holbach's *System of Nature* and C. F. Volney's *Ruins of Empire* (Haight (1968), 37–8; 45–6).

On the other side, working-class secularism, then known as 'freethought' or 'infidelity', was well under way before it found expression among middle-class thinkers.[6] As early as 1842, well before Mary Ann Evans's translation, working-class radicals had reviewed Strauss's work in the *Oracle of Reason*, according to its editor 'the only exclusively atheistical print that has appeared in any age or country'.[7] Working-class infidels endured prison sentences for blasphemy and sedition and fought for the removal of legal sanctions against the expression of anti-clerical and anti-theistic views. By the 1850s, they had already won a wider toleration for freethought.

Until the 1850s, the middle-class sceptics had, for the most part, eschewed working-class infidels for fear that such associations would threaten their 'respectability'. Then George Jacob Holyoake steered working-class freethought away from vitriolic cleric-baiting and Bible-roasting when he founded Secularism proper in 1851. At this point, the views of working- and middle-class secularists came to resemble each other more closely. Holyoake's strain of Secularism was a 'positive' form of unbelief. Like Comte, Holyoake sought not strictly to destroy religious belief, but to supersede it with a scientific morality and epistemology. His moderation and the emphasis he placed on 'positive' Secularism won him middle-class support.

In 1850, the two secularist lines finally crossed. Holyoake's periodicals had earned him a reputation among middle-class reformers as a stalwart and capable publisher. The *Reasoner*, founded in 1846, defined and promoted his brand of Secularism and ran reviews and notices of liberal theological and heterodox middle-class writers, including his own review of George Henry Lewes's *Robespierre* (1849). The *Leader*, the periodical founded by Lewes and Thornton Hunt in 1850, positioned itself at the forefront of liberal opinion. Holyoake's notoriety as a leading radical with sober judgement had earned him entrance into middle-class radical society, where he met and discussed politics and philosophy with the legatees of philosophical radicalism, including Francis Place, Robert Owen, Francis Newman, Thornton Hunt, Louis Blanc and others. Some of these writers even contributed articles to the *Reasoner*. At the *Leader*, where George Lewes was responsible for the reviews of literature and the arts and Marian Evans assisted him with editing and writing, Holyoake was brought on as the business manager. He also contributed articles on the co-operative movement under the pseudonym 'Ion'. He had become good friends with Lewes, and later befriended Marian Evans.[8]

Although little evidence of the connection is extant in George Eliot's writing, Holyoake paid tribute to her and Lewes, stating that until he was received by such company, he had been 'an outcast name, both in law and literature'. His inclusion in the *Leader* was 'the first recognition of the kind I have received'.[9] This recognition was seen by many of Holyoake's older working-class acquaintances as the gentrification of working-class infidelity and its merging with the gradualist, middle-class scientific meliorism avowed explicitly by George Eliot: 'I will not answer to the name of optimist, but if you like to invent Meliorist, I will not say that you call me out of my name.'[10]

Thus, middle-class secularism benefited legally and ideologically from the working-class freethought movement, which parted ways with radical

Figure 20 George Eliot's grave in Highgate Cemetery, with Jacob Holyoake's nearby (at the left of the image).

By permission of Mustapha Ousellam.

working-class politics as the latter tended towards the negative secularism of Charles Bradlaugh on the one hand, and Marxian socialism on the other. Holyoake's brand of Secularism was likewise legitimated by middle-class unbelievers.

In a fitting ending to the story, the mingling of these groups found its ultimate expression at Holyoake's funeral in Highgate Cemetery. Years before, Holyoake had purchased a plot at the head of the graves of George Eliot and Lewes, where his ashes were buried in January 1906 during a service attended by thousands of Owenite co-operators and old friends (see Figure 20).[11]

Secularism was an important context for George Eliot's life and works. She was essentially a secularist; her own personal values were demonstrably secular, and she produced works of fiction in which characters, plots and outcomes were explained and evaluated in secular, naturalistic terms. While many of her characters, like Bulstrode, have religious beliefs, such believers are often caught in contradictions and hypocrisy, and the failure of individuals is explained in terms of natural, dense and complicated causality. The view that Charles Bray and others ascribed to her, although of uncertain provenance, rings true to her character and work:

> She held as a solemn conviction … that in proportion as the thoughts of men and women are removed from the earth … are diverted from their own mutual relations and responsibilities, of which they alone know anything, to an invisible world, which alone can be apprehended by belief, they are led to neglect their duty to each other, to squander their strength in vain speculations … which diminish their capacity for strenuous and worthy action, during a span of life, brief indeed, but whose consequences will extend to remote posterity.[12]

This is a quintessential expression of the secular outlook.

NOTES

1 George Holyoake, *The Reasoner* (London: Holyoake and Co., 1852), vol. XII, p. 1.

2 See Edward Royle, 'Freethought: The Religion of Irreligion', in Denis G. Paz (ed.), *Nineteenth Century English Religious Traditions: Retrospect and Prospect* (Westport, CT: Greenwood Press, 1995), p. 181.

3 James A. Secord (ed.), Charles Lyell, *Principles of Geology* (1830–3; London: Penguin Books, 1997), p. 9.

4 See George Levine, *Realism, Ethics and Secularism: Essays on Victorian Literature and Science* (Cambridge University Press, 2008), pp. 210–44.

5 See George Jacob Holyoake, *The History of the last trial by jury for atheism in England: a fragment of autobiography* (London: Watson, 1851).

6 Royle, 'Freethought', pp. 172–3.

7 *The Oracle of Reason, or, Philosophy Vindicated* (London: Field, Southwell & Co., 1841–3), vol. I (1842), pp. 239, ii.

8 See Joseph McCabe and Charles William Frederick Goss, *Life and Letters of George Jacob Holyoake* (London: Watt & Co., 1908), vols. I and II.

9 George Jacob Holyoake, *Bygones Worth Remembering* (London: T. F. Unwin, 1905), p. 64.

10 Quoted in Edith Simcox, 'George Eliot', *The Nineteenth Century*, 9 (May 1881), 787.

11 Lee Grugel, *George Jacob Holyoake: A Study in the Evolution of a Victorian Radical* (Philadelphia, PA: Porcupine Press, 1976), p. 155.

12 Charles Bray, *Phases of Opinion and Experience During a Long Life: An Autobiography* (London: Longmans, Green, 1884), p. 73.

CHAPTER 33

Theatre

Lynn Voskuil

In Victorian England, the institution of theatre took multiple forms, and George Eliot – her reputation as one of the world's greatest novelists notwithstanding – was fascinated by many of them. Throughout her adult life, she attended various theatrical performances in London and elsewhere, melodramas and pantomimes as well as Shakespeare and classical dramas. Her partner George Henry Lewes participated in the theatre world as an actor, playwright and critic, while George Eliot revealed her own theatrical investments in a number of characters and works, including her dramatic poem 'Armgart' (1871) and her poetic drama *The Spanish Gypsy* (1868), as well as fictional characters like Rosamond Vincy, Gwendolen Harleth, Mirah Cohen and of course Daniel Deronda's mother Leonora Alcharisi, an imposing figure who was modelled on the real-life Jewish actress Rachel Felix. George Eliot has often been portrayed as unyieldingly antitheatrical, a novelist whose commitments to fully realised interiority and psychological realism precluded any affinities for the outward displays of theatre, especially the melodramatic theatre so pervasive in the nineteenth century. As her novels themselves suggest, however, her engagement with theatre was at once complex and critical, betraying a paradoxical and sometimes contradictory fascination with the spectacles that animated her culture.

The Victorian stage is best known for its melodrama, a theatrical genre whose features made their way into novels and poetry as well as plays of the period, including George Eliot's. As a stage genre, European melodrama emerged in the late eighteenth century, with the first English play actually called a 'melodrama' – Thomas Holcroft's Gothic *A Tale of Mystery* – produced in 1802. Melodrama's generic features include suspenseful plotting, frequently with an explicit sense of poetic justice; the effusive expression of strong emotion, usually by means of what would today seem to be an obvious, even exaggerated style of acting (a style honed, it should be noted, in large theatres with dim lighting before cinematic close-ups were technologically possible); and a reliance on stock characters that audiences would immediately recognise. Also central to melodrama was the use of music to set moods, signal entrances and exits, and establish leitmotifs for central characters.

These characteristics of melodrama differentiate it starkly from the finely honed psychologies of George Eliot's characters and the innovative structures of her plots, especially in her two greatest novels, *Middlemarch* and *Daniel Deronda*. Yet it is in these novels that theatrical characters and motifs figure most prominently, signalling her complex relation to the Victorian stage. In *Middlemarch*, Lydgate's first love is Laure, a melodramatic actress who murders her real husband on stage, and is followed in Lydgate's affections by Rosamond Vincy, a woman who 'acted her own character,' according to the narrator (*M*, ch. 12). And in *Daniel Deronda*, all three central female characters are theatrical in varying ways. In their criticism, both George Eliot and Lewes had critiqued the modes of characterisation typical of melodrama. When Lewes, for example, complained of characters that 'have the air of Keepsake beauties',[1] he was objecting to the practice of modelling characters on predictable, sentimental examples from decorative Victorian gift books – the kinds of characters, in other words, that appeared frequently in stage melodrama and even in novels. In *Daniel Deronda*, Mirah Cohen nonetheless makes her first appearance as a pathetic, destitute figure on the banks of the Thames, ready to plunge to her death – the sort of figure that many readers would have recognised from the melodramatic stage.

Although George Eliot and Lewes were prone to criticise 'Keepsake beauties', then, they were also clearly influenced by their melodramatised cultural context. Lewes, in fact, participated fully in the professional theatre world. He acted in a number of temporary companies assembled by Charles Dickens for benefit performances; wrote and performed in *The Noble Heart*, a drama in Elizabethan blank verse that was produced in Liverpool, Manchester and London; and translated and adapted a number of French plays for the English stage. George Eliot attended *The Chain of Events*, one of Lewes's French adaptations, with Herbert Spencer in 1852, a play that was itself melodramatic. 'As a series of tableaux I never saw anything equal to it', she wrote to Cara Bray after seeing it. 'But to my mind it is execrable moral taste to have a storm and shipwreck with all its horrors on the stage. I could only scream and cover my eyes' (*L*, 2: 18). Lewes was also a sophisticated drama critic and theorist, authoring widely read columns in both the *Leader*, a radical newspaper published from 1850 to 1854 – for which he adopted the persona of 'Vivian', a witty man-about-town – and later in the *Pall Mall Gazette*. In addition, he published occasional pieces on theatre and drama in a number of leading intellectual journals, including *Blackwood's Edinburgh Magazine*, *Fraser's Magazine* and the *Westminster Review*, and strongly influenced later Victorian critics like William Archer and George Bernard Shaw, who learned much from Lewes's wit and urbanity in the *Leader* columns. Lewes's theatrical experience gave him a healthy respect for Victorian audiences – even audiences who preferred melodrama – and he emphasised the importance of 'playing to a Public' that included all classes rather than catering only to the aristocracy.[2]

If Lewes admired many Victorian playgoers, a night at the theatre in Victorian England would nonetheless try the patience of most theatregoers now. Accepted conduct today – the dimming of overhead lights, the expectation of quiet attention to the stage, and the polite applause at appropriate moments – became habitual and expected only at the very end of the Victorian period (and then only in certain theatre spaces). Before that, audiences were much more boisterous, expressing their pleasure or displeasure with the entertainment very noisily and vociferously. 'Has the reader ever seen a piece, on its first production, condemned? or, to use theatrical phraseology, "damned," – in any of the larger establishments?' wrote James Grant in *The Great Metropolis*, his account of urban life in London in the 1830s.

> No one who has not witnessed such a scene can form any idea of it. The audience, on such occasions, are in a perfect hubbub ... The great majority of the audience seem to make the matter a personal one. They feel as if some insult had been offered to them individually by the luckless wight of an author, and the scarcely less unfortunate proprietor of the theatre. They will in such cases rise from their seats, and express their indignation, not only in loud hisses, groans, &c., but by the most violent gestures.[3]

As Grant's account suggests, theatre seating was stratified by class, with working-class playgoers occupying the galleries and benches in the 'pit' (an area close to the stage with inexpensive backless benches) and wealthier patrons seated in boxes or stalls. In playgoers' freedom to voice opinions loudly in the theatre, some recent scholars have found a certain limited amount of agency and power for the working classes.[4] But however socially energised London's poorer citizens may have been by their visits to the theatre, the relations among classes in the theatre cannot be reduced to simple opposition. Indeed, as numerous Victorian accounts make clear, Victorian audiences of all classes shared a love for spectacle. '[Theatres] may be said to be the principal source of amusement to all classes of the inhabitants [of London],' wrote Grant. 'The highest and the

SCENE FROM "THE WICKED WORLD," AT THE HAYMARKET THEATRE.

Figure 21 An illustration by D. H. Friston of a scene from W. S. Gilbert's play *The Wicked World* (1873) at the Haymarket Theatre, London.
Illustrated London News, 8 February 1873, courtesy of John Weedy.

lowest, the most intellectual and most illiterate, evince an equal partiality to them. The people of London are a theatre-going people, in the largest and broadest acceptation of the phrase.'[5]

During a typical evening at the theatre, playgoers not only expressed their opinion of the entertainment but also talked among themselves and consumed various kinds of food and drink which they could buy from circulating vendors. This kind of conduct was encouraged by a four-to-five-hour-long evening featuring a number of interludes and acts in addition to a central feature. People could enter for reduced prices later in the evening, and often socialised at least as much as they watched the stage; in a typical evening, a playgoer could meet friends, eat dinner, chat with neighbours, and even secure a prostitute (if so inclined) for an after party as well as watch the stage. It is exactly these kinds of theatres in which Mirah Cohen is made to perform in *Daniel Deronda* and these kinds of spectators whom she dreads. With her aversion to spectacle and self-display, Mirah experiences as a professional actress only 'the glare and the faces, and my having to go on and act and sing what I hated, and then see people who came to stare at me behind the scenes' (*DD*, ch. 20). While theatre managers like Marie and Squire Bancroft began actively to discourage rowdy conduct among playgoers in their Prince of Wales theatre in the 1860s (in part by reducing the number of inexpensive seats and thus also the patronage of working-class playgoers), it persisted until late in the century, when music halls began to attract the rowdiest audiences and theatres became the preserve of wealthier patrons.

The professional stage, while very popular, was but one arena in which Victorians satisfied their intense taste for theatre. All sorts of ephemeral travelling entertainments – from impromptu performances in penny gaffs (temporary stages that charged a penny for admission) to 'booth theatres' at fairs and Punch and Judy shows – could be found in the streets of the major urban centres, attracting many working-class patrons. The respectable classes (or people who aspired to those classes) participated in the widely popular 'private theatrical' performances that were staged, often lavishly, and performed in domestic drawing rooms. In *Daniel Deronda*, Gwendolen Harleth expends much of her time and energy in the opening chapters producing a scene from *The Winter's Tale* in the drawing room at Offendene. These scenes are typical in that they give Gwendolen an acceptably modest space in which to express herself theatrically. With its reputation as a marketplace for prostitutes (at least in the first half of the nineteenth century), the professional theatre was shunned by some respectable Victorian women who cared about their moral reputations, a prohibition that extended to playgoing as well as acting professionally. Stage actresses were tainted with at least the hint of promiscuity throughout much of the century, a stigma that often held regardless of the actress's actual lifestyle. In private drawing rooms, though, upper-class women like Gwendolen could perform with (relative) impunity.

Gwendolen's choice of *The Winter's Tale* for her performance points to another important characteristic of nineteenth-century theatre, both public and private: its uses of Shakespeare. Like many playgoers today, the Victorians venerated Shakespeare – but they adapted, excerpted, bowdlerised and melodramatised his work as well. In other words, they couldn't get enough Shakespeare, and they adjusted his plays to meet a variety of aesthetic and cultural ends, as Gwendolen's performance attests. After 1843, when certain theatrical regulations changed, many of the minor theatres quickly developed excellent Shakespearean repertoires. In north-east London, for example, Samuel Phelps successfully transformed the Sadler's Wells Theatre into what amounted to a Shakespeare repertory company for his working-class clientele, producing no fewer than thirty-one Shakespeare plays in his eighteen years as the theatre's manager.[6] From Edmund Kean at the beginning of the nineteenth century to Henry Irving at its end, a number of actors made their reputations playing Shakespearean heroes and villains. While acting remained a socially risky profession for women throughout the century (like most public professions, it should be noted), a number of actresses also played Shakespeare to great acclaim, including Helen Faucit and Ellen Terry. Faucit, in fact, was a friend of the Leweses, and George Eliot once pondered writing a theatrical piece for her. Even Sarah Bernhardt, the scandalous French actress, whom George Eliot also saw on stage, performed several Shakespearean parts in London, including (in crossdress) the role of Hamlet – a novelty that intrigued a late-Victorian public whose restrictive gender ideologies were beginning to moderate in the 1880s and 1890s.

As Bernhardt's experiment suggests, nineteenth-century theatre and theatricality had important ramifications for Victorian gender ideals, especially for women. In Victorian England, feminine modesty, chastity and decorum were culturally and ideologically valued, even more so than they had been in previous centuries, an emphasis that pitted gender ideals squarely against the spectacle and display of the stage. Respectable women, it was believed, were not theatrical. In this cultural context, it is significant that Gwendolen selects an actress for her role model, for it signals her desire to be on display – to challenge, that is, the cultural premium placed on feminine modesty and decorum – and betrays her fundamental ignorance of the professional stage, a lack of understanding that Klesmer exposes. If her choice has disastrous results for Gwendolen, it also illuminates the paradoxical position in which Victorian women were placed: cautioned to be modest and retiring, they were also required to attract eligible suitors in order to marry well (the only acceptable 'profession' open to respectable women for much of the nineteenth century), a process that required a certain amount of self-display and theatricalised awareness. Like Rosamond Vincy in *Middlemarch*, Gwendolen hones her theatrical skills in the domestic drawing room and never on the professional stage, performing 'her own character' for the same reasons Rosamond does: in order to make a good match. The Victorians' taste for theatre, however ambivalently felt, thus put women like Rosamond and Gwendolen in an almost impossible position, a position that required them to be theatrical and self-effacing at the same time. This paradox is registered in the pages of both *Middlemarch* and *Daniel Deronda*. It could be argued that

Rosamond and Gwendolen each respond to cultural pressures on women to perform their romantic and domestic roles effectively – and then are punished for doing so.

The real-life actress Rachel reappears in *Daniel Deronda* as the inspiration for the character of Leonora Alcharisi, Deronda's long-lost Jewish mother who also happens to be a highly acclaimed professional actress. Both George Eliot and Lewes had seen Rachel perform, though George Eliot distanced herself from the awe Charlotte Brontë had professed when she saw Rachel on stage and then in her novel *Villette* modelled the character 'Vashti' on the actress. 'I have not yet seen the "Vashti" of Currer Bell in Rachel', George Eliot wrote laconically to friends after an 1853 performance (*L*, 2: 104). Lewes, however, was deeply impressed with Rachel's performances, describing her in the *Leader* as an exemplar of what he called 'natural acting'.[7] This concept of acting – one that was widespread in the nineteenth century – influenced George Eliot's own idea of 'sincere acting', the term used to describe Alcharisi's very sense of being in *Daniel Deronda* (ch. 51). If Alcharisi is fatally ill when Deronda finally meets her, she is nonetheless a deeply impressive figure whose carefully framed scenes in the novel cannot be summarily dismissed as 'antitheatrical.' Her flawed, ambiguous figure further captures the paradoxes of George Eliot's perspectives on gender and theatre, in part because Alcharisi renounced motherhood in order to pursue a professional career, not unlike George Eliot herself.

Alcharisi registers yet one more crucial feature of the nineteenth-century theatre world: the debate over 'drama' versus 'theatre' and the pursuit of a 'literary drama'. In London as well as Paris, Rachel had played classical roles like Phèdre and Andromaque to appreciative audiences, and her appearance in *Daniel Deronda* signals the novel's affiliation with what Victorians called 'literary drama'. For much of the century, copyright law and contractual arrangements made it far more lucrative to write novels than plays, with the result that many Victorian stage dramas were adaptations of novels or French plays (of the sort that Lewes translated) rather than original scripts. Nonetheless, advocacy for a 'literary drama' that could reconnect Britain with its Shakespearean heritage gathered steam as the century waned, with late-century playwrights such as the non-native Henrik Ibsen and the native George Bernard Shaw positioned within this movement. Before cultural conditions were ripe for these changes on the professional stage, figures like Alcharisi registered the widespread hope, at least among the intelligentsia, for the rebirth of such a 'literary drama' in England. Eliot's experiments with verse drama in 'Armgart' and

The Spanish Gypsy – texts that have not been widely analysed by critics – may also be seen as related to this movement.

George Eliot's affiliation with literary drama notwithstanding, her fascination with theatre in general, including melodrama, is captured in her novels, especially the later ones. Her fascination is due in no small part to the central role played by Lewes in her personal and professional life. The same people who devoured her novels and lionised her public persona – itself significantly theatricalised, as Nina Auerbach has argued – also eagerly patronised the London and provincial theatres.[8] Both Lewes and George Eliot wrote for a living, a position that incorporated them into a community that included at once the Victorian intelligentsia and the mass audiences Lewes valued so highly. In this context, George Eliot's longstanding popularity registers not only her aesthetic greatness but also the sophistication of the Victorian reading and playgoing public.

NOTES

1 [George Henry Lewes], 'Realism in Art: Recent German Fiction', *Westminster Review*, n.s., 14 (1858), 493.

2 George Henry Lewes, *Life and Works of Goethe: With Sketches of His Age and Contemporaries, from Published and Unpublished Sources*, 2 vols. (London: Smith, Elder, 1875), vol. II, p. 241.

3 James Grant, *The Great Metropolis*, 2nd edn, 2 vols. (London and New York: Saunders and Otley, 1837), vol. I, pp. 91–2.

4 See Marc Baer, *Theatre and Disorder in Late Georgian England* (Oxford University Press, 1992), pp. 18–36; and Elaine Hadley, *Melodramatic Tactics: Theatricalized Dissent in the English Marketplace, 1800–1885* (Stanford University Press, 1995), pp. 34–76.

5 Grant, *The Great Metropolis*, vol. I, pp. 23–4.

6 Michael Booth, *Theatre in the Victorian Age* (Cambridge University Press, 1991), p. 46.

7 The term appears frequently in Lewes's theatre criticism. See Lynn Voskuil, *Acting Naturally: Victorian Theatricality and Authenticity* (Charlottesville, VA: University of Virginia Press, 2004), pp. 40–55.

8 Nina Auerbach, *Romantic Imprisonment: Women and Other Glorified Outcasts* (New York: Columbia University Press, 1986), pp. 254–6.

CHAPTER 34

Transport

Ruth Livesey

Writing of her return to London from a journey to the North of England in 1852, Marian Evans described the still relatively new experience of long-distance rail travel in terms of an exotic romance. 'To get into a first-class carriage, fall asleep, and awake to find oneself where one would be', she wrote to her friends, the Brays, 'is almost as good as having Prince Hussein's carpet' (*L*, 2: 65). To many living through the great transport revolution of the mid-nineteenth century, the speed of the railway and its rapid transformation of place and distance could only be compared to the magical or uncanny: Dickens's journalism, for example, is thick with analogies between rail travel and a dreamscape drawn from fairy tales. If the non-fiction writer and editor Marian Evans was drawn to this fantastical side of transport, however, as the novelist George Eliot she took a different perspective. Transport in George Eliot's fiction is almost always a means to the real: it establishes the historical setting of her works; confirms the social and economic position of characters; and helps to map local and international communication.

The landscape of George Eliot's youth can itself be mapped by the milestones of transport development in Britain. She grew up at Griff by the side of a turnpike road carrying passengers, goods and post from Coventry and further south to Nuneaton, and into Leicestershire and beyond. The flows of horse-drawn traffic on the Coventry to Hinckley turnpike and the interest of her father, Robert Evans, in such matters write in small the great national significance of improved road engineering in rapid communication in the early nineteenth century: a boom in road investment peaked in the 1820s. The countryside surrounding Griff House was cross-cut by a network of canals and sophisticated locks, testament to the late eighteenth-century technological vision of Sir Francis Newdigate and his development of the Arbury estate that was Robert Evans's primary employer. Although many of the outlying canal branches had fallen into disuse by the 1830s and 1840s, the main arteries remained essential in the development of the collieries that reshaped this part of north Warwickshire. While the first public railway, from Stockton to Darlington, had opened in 1825, the development of a national network took at least another twenty years, with development focused on connecting major industrial cities. It is worth noting that, as a result, though Coventry was part of a national rail transport system by 1838 (and surveys had been undertaken for it in 1829, accurately reflected in chapter 56 of *Middlemarch*), a line to Nuneaton with a stop near Griff did not open until 1850. The modes of transport in George Eliot's work invoke this range of forms on the doorstep of the nineteenth-century traveller: the pedestrian wanderings of packmen and outcasts; the dreamy river journey of Maggie Tulliver; the cosmopolitan rapid rail transit of *Daniel Deronda*. But whatever the means of mobility, the narratives underscore how the technological developments in transport in the nineteenth century inscribe a self-conscious modernity in George Eliot's railway-travelling implied reader: a stark contrast, more often than not, with fictional characters drawn from the earlier part of the century.

By the late 1860s the dominance of the railway over national communications in Britain was complete. Although the industrial revolution had been underpinned by the development of a network of canals, and fast stage and mail coaches transformed the circulation of print culture from the late eighteenth century, the railway, then and now, came to symbolise the decisive modernity of the Victorian age. While the final, rural, stages of many long journeys (whether of persons or mail bags) continued to be completed by coach into the early 1870s, by the time George Eliot came to write her novels a world dominated by road transport and the regular passage of stage and mail coaches was a thing of the past – though within living memory. This revolution in transport created an odd conjunction in the sense of speed and modernity: adults experiencing the dizzy pace of mass rail transport from the 1840s were only a single generation away from those to whom the new fast mail coaches of the early nineteenth century had seemed a dangerous disruption of the steady plod of packhorses and drifting of the canal boat. Scholarship by Wolfgang Schivelbusch and Nicholas Daly, among others, has helped draw attention to how the new sensations of the railway make their way into the concerns of fiction during the period from 1830 to 1860, but less notice has been taken of the fact that the steam train was part of a rapid succession of ever-accelerating forms of transport over the foregoing century.

The coming of the railway, from this perspective, is not so much of a dramatic rupture through which passengers move from old, slow ways, to modernity; but part of a much longer pattern of history in which each generation experiences change and (relative) modernisation, and sees the landscape of youth move towards obsolescence. George Eliot's works demonstrate an exceptional awareness of this historicity. This is most notable, perhaps, in *Middlemarch* (1872) where the survey of what looks to be a specific moment in the transformation of 'Old provincial society' in the early 1830s is radically reframed by the narrator concluding: 'In fact, much the same sort of movement and mixture went on in old England as we find in older Herodotus' (*M*, ch. 11). But a close look at George Eliot's use of transport reveals a deflection of simple linear narratives of history as 'progress' here too, not least through the voices of rural labour. In *Middlemarch*, for example, Old Timothy Cooper protests against Caleb Garth's insistence that 'the railway's a good thing' and emphasises the uneven nature of nineteenth-century progress – the fiction that it takes all forwards together:

> Aw! good for the big folks to make money out on … I'n seen lots o' things turn up sin' I war a young un – the war an' the pe-ace and the canells, an' the oald King George, an' the Regen', an' the new King George, an' the new un as has got a new ne-ame – an' it's been all aloike to the poor mon. What's the canells been t' him? They'n brought him neyther me-at nor ba-acon, nor wage to lay by … Times ha' got wusser for him sin' I war a young un. An' so it'll be wi' the railroads. They'll on'y leave the poor mon furder behind. (ch. 56)

Transport might be the way that George Eliot's fictions signal their precise realist historical setting – as with the disquiet over the coming of the railway line in *Middlemarch* – but it is also one of the means by which these carefully evoked historical moments are placed in a much broader pattern of constant change and repetition. Timothy's response to the railway is framed as 'an undeniable truth' which he has come to know 'through a hard process of feeling': something that cannot be refuted by arguments for abstract 'social benefits'. If the railway belongs to a cosmopolitan world of technology and rational linear progress in George Eliot's works, then her rustic, labouring pedestrians serve to symbolise an enduring, cyclical – and seemingly more natural – world of 'the manifold wakings of men to labour and endurance' (*M*, ch. 80).

The most explicit use of transport to mark the historical nature of George Eliot's fiction displays a similar unsettling of a linear model of history as 'progress'. At the opening of *Felix Holt, the Radical* (1866) the narrator asks the reader to compare high-speed journeys to long-distance travel on the outside of a stagecoach as it was 'Five and thirty years ago',

Figure 22 The opening paragraph of *Felix Holt* evokes the glory of 'the old coach-roads' and 'the rolling swinging swiftness' of coaches like the Birmingham Tally Ho, depicted here by James Pollard (1792–1867).

Image after James Pollard, 'The Birmingham Tally Ho Coaches', sourced from Encore Editions.

concluding that 'the slow old-fashioned way of getting from one end of our country to the other is the better thing to have in the memory'. Shooting past landscape, 'like a bullet through a tube', can 'never lend much to picture and narrative; it is as barren as an exclamatory O!' (*FH*, 'Introduction'). This connection between modes of transport and states of feeling, between geographical journeys and the unfolding of narrative, does much to establish the complex attitude to reform and modernisation in *Felix Holt*. Old-fashioned coach travel enables passengers to understand stories and localities in context thanks to the informed perspective of the narrator/coachman whereas modern rail travel, as Schivelbusch suggests, obliterates such in-between places in haste to get from A to B.[1] Modern communication (in all senses of that word) is direct, but impoverished.

The transition from stagecoach to rail forms an unspoken parallel with the major concern of the novel: political reform and demands for the vote for all working men. Such Radicalism forms the backdrop to the action of *Felix Holt*, which opens soon after the passage of the relatively limited Reform Act of 1832. The 'Introduction' addresses an implied reader not only used to rail travel, but also conscious of the imminent passage of the second Reform Act of 1867 which introduced something closer to democracy in Britain, extending the franchise to the majority of working men. The analogy between the revolution in transport and the question of political reform implies that democratisation may also do much to denude the nation of its rich texture, variety and interconnections in favour of a functional allocation of rights. But it also undercuts the sense that reform and modernisation are epoch-making or new. Elderly 'gentlemen in pony-chaises' regard the 'rolling swinging swiftness' of the stagecoach nervously as a novelty, remembering the slower era of the packhorse; the coachman, on the other hand, is embittered by the near prospect of the expansion of railways and full of information about the negotiation of local landowners with canal companies over the previous decades (*FH*, 'Introduction). In a similar fashion, the author's suggestion that the 'departed evils' of the past she evokes included 'pocket boroughs [and] a Birmingham unrepresented in parliament' would be rich with irony to contemporary readers ('Introduction'). The campaign for parliamentary reform in the 1860s publicised the continued existence of a number of corrupt 'pocket boroughs' each with only a handful entitled to vote and willing to bring in whomever the local patron nominated, while Birmingham still only had a tiny proportion of enfranchised voters compared to its size. Change is constant and its effects are uneven and often unexpected: the coach to modernity can only seat a certain number of relatively privileged passengers and it leaves the shepherd standing in the field behind, struggling even to lift his glance 'accustomed to rest on things very near the earth' to this symbol of a 'mysterious distant system of things called "Gover'ment"' ('Introduction').

Modes of transport were sharply defined in terms of social class in the nineteenth century, and George Eliot's fiction carefully observes how walking on foot, riding on horseback, travelling in a smart yellow gig, a carrier's cart or the stagecoach indicates a specific economic position. In *Adam Bede* (1859), for instance, the novel opens with an unnamed traveller on horseback stopping to look down (albeit with admiration) on Adam striding from his workshop and the pedestrians wandering to the preaching in Hayslope. The symbolic significance of this overview from horseback emerges fully only in chapter 45 where the rider is named as Colonel Townley, a magistrate. Such a dual perspective – the privileged view from horseback; the labouring view from foot – continues throughout the narrative. It is this demarcation of class by mode of transport that makes Adam's encounters with Arthur Donnithorne on foot in the woods all the more striking in terms of an exploration of 'natural' as opposed to 'social' hierarchies of moral and physical strength: they are, unusually, on a level in these confrontations over Hetty. Hetty's own fall is matched by her means of progress down to Windsor and back: she takes the stagecoach to Stoniton, and rides in carriers' carts through the Midlands, before spending all she has on one last stagecoach to Windsor and then reverting to pedestrian wanderings off the road returning northwards. The contrast between these broken stages and Arthur Donnithorne's purposeful return to Hayslope by mail coach and persistent galloping to ensure Hetty's reprieve from the death penalty indicates the great void of experience between the landed gentry and the respectable labouring classes. Arthur – moving at a gallop – has an utterly different apprehension of place and speed from Adam who, for all his exceptionally brisk pace, cannot catch up with the swift communication of Hetty's crime that reaches Mr Irwine by mail coach.

George Eliot's evocation of rural locality is often tied to the transport links that connect village life to the wider world. It is crucial to the construction of the self-contained, historic world of Raveloe in *Silas Marner* (1861), for instance, that it lies 'quite an hour's journey on horseback from any turnpike, where it was never reached by the vibrations of the coach-horn, or of public opinion' (*SM*, ch. 1). In a similar vein, the lively critical spirit of the inhabitants of Shepperton is contrasted with the resigned grumbling in the neighbouring parish of Knebley in 'Mr Gilfil's Love Story' (1857): the former has 'turnpike roads and a public opinion, whereas, in … Knebley, men's minds and wagons alike moved in the deepest of ruts' ('Gilfil', ch. 1). Both comments reflect the rapid increase in the circulation of information – of newspapers and journals – with the improvements of roads and the new mail coaches in the last decades of the eighteenth century. To be near the turnpike road, along which travelled the mail coaches, meant a substantial advantage in speed of communication of important national and international events. National transport by road is, in this estimate, crucial to the making of public opinion in the first half of the nineteenth century; but such improved communication and collective information is not a straightforward good in George Eliot's works and we should be alert to the irony of just what informed 'public opinion' might be in Shepperton. Certainly, in *The Mill on the Floss* (1860), Maggie Tulliver's disgrace is maintained by misinformed public opinion after she is spotted in Mudport with Stephen Guest: news travels home faster than her own 'automatic' random travels by stagecoach after she leaves him (*MF*, book 6, ch. 14).

The complexities of a world in which people and information travel at speed unsettling local attachment are at the heart of *Daniel Deronda* (1876). This – the most contemporaneous of Eliot's novels – is the only one in which characters travel by rail. A good part of the dark humour of Grandcourt's visit to his mistress Lydia Glasher to demand the return of the family diamonds results from the railway timetable. While Grandcourt is often depicted mastering his means of transport – whether a horse, a yacht, or his entourage – in this case he is stuck at Gadsmere after 'scorching words' have passed as 'there was no suitable train earlier than the one he had arranged to go by' (*DD*, ch. 30). By contrast, Gwendolen Harleth travels from Leubronn back home to Offendene in a mere three days, her 'whirling journey' an echo of the random spinning of the roulette wheel she quits on losing her fortune (ch. 2). Such speed of travel in this novel seems to have as its necessary corollary a loss of place and belonging. The Offendene that Gwendolen returns to is not a childhood home; she is not 'well rooted in some spot of a native land' but an untethered searcher like so many others in this narrative (ch. 3).

Despite – and, perhaps, because of – its setting in a modern railway world in which information can travel from point to point at speed, the narrative structure of *Daniel Deronda* is famously indirect. Gwendolen sets out on her three-day rail journey from Leubronn, for example, at the end of chapter 2 but only arrives home nineteen chapters later after a retrospective diversion through her earlier life and that of Daniel. The novel features more letters and more journeys than any other of George Eliot's works – and the news of Grandcourt's death travels by telegram – but lacking roots and connections, these communications are often barren ones between strangers that prevent and delay richer exchange. Think, for example, of Deronda's anonymous note to Gwendolen sent with the necklace he redeems from the pawnshop for her (ch. 2); of the brief and peremptory notes Deronda receives from his 'unknown mother' (ch. 50); or of Deronda's cold rejection of an inquiry about his parentage when visiting the synagogue in Frankfort which could have revealed the key to his identity (ch. 32). Technological advances in transport and communication seem to go hand in hand with increasing estrangement between those who should have the closest of dialogues: potential lovers; mothers and children; family friends. In this world of high-speed but barren communications George Eliot returns to the alternative mode of travel by water which she had used so fruitfully to suggest 'automatic' unconscious attraction in *The Mill on the Floss*.[2] It is rowing down the Thames that Daniel first encounters Mirah and where Mordecai sees him as the fulfilment of his vision; Gwendolen's desire to see Grandcourt dead is realised out at sea off Genoa. These portentous encounters happen outside the technological world of modern transport but provide routes to a sense of home – a rooted new beginning in life – for both characters.

NOTES

1 Wolfgang Schivelbusch, *The Railway Journey: Trains and Travel in the Nineteenth Century*, trans. Anselm Hollo (Oxford: Blackwell, 1980), p. 13.

2 For more on how this watery journey reflects Eliot's interest in nineteenth-century psychology see Carolyn Burdett, 'Sexual Selection, Automata, and Ethics in George Eliot's *The Mill on the Floss* and Olive Schreiner's *Undine* and *From Man to Man*', *Journal of Victorian Culture*, 14 (2009), 26–52.

CHAPTER 35

Travel and tourism

Judith Johnston

George Eliot was eleven when the first railway from Manchester to Liverpool opened in 1830, and her novels capture the wonder and anxiety as the railway network rapidly criss-crossed the English countryside heralding the modern age of travel. In the famous opening to *Felix Holt, the Radical* (1866) a ghostly coach lumbers across the pages, in a scene that is nostalgic but also recognises the new age of speed. And *Middlemarch* (1871–2), set in that important period of change and reform, 1829 to 1832, records local rural anxiety as a team of surveyors prepares plans for laying future trackwork. Caleb Garth's reassurance that the railway is 'a good thing' (*M*, ch. 56) was certainly true for women in enabling safe, affordable travel. Early in 1852 George Eliot was returning to London from a visit to the Brays in Coventry. She writes to Cara Bray:

> I had a comfortable journey – all alone, except from <Rugby> Weedon to Blisworth. When I saw a coated animal getting into my carriage, I thought of all horrible stories of madmen in railways, but his white neck-cloth and thin mincing voice soon convinced me that he was one of those exceedingly tame brutes, the clergy. (*L*, 2:3)

Her mockery of the more sensational encounters of traveller's tales reveals a woman now very used to travelling alone.

As the years went by, George Eliot was to travel extensively. Though steam power was critical in making travel quicker and less arduous, whether by land or sea, at mid century travel especially to the continent was no longer the prerogative of the wealthy. After the Napoleonic Wars, the British middle class began to travel in numbers, and Thomas Cook developed a whole new market for tourist group excursions from 1845 on. George Eliot's many journeys within Britain and abroad were made independent of such services. She did not venture to exotic destinations like America or Egypt, preferring places in France, Germany and Italy.

George Eliot's first journey abroad was made in June 1849, shortly after the death of her father, travelling with her friends the Brays across France and Italy to Geneva. She stayed on alone in Switzerland for some months. John Cross's account of her stay in Switzerland may well have been informed by the journal pages he apparently removed (*J*, xvii). He describes the area surrounding the *pension* Campagne Plongeon in highly conventional terms, then the tone becomes more personal as the focus shifts to solitude:

> In the first few months following a great loss it is good to be alone for a time – alone especially amidst beautiful scenes – and alone in the sense of being removed from habitual associations, and yet constantly in the society of new acquaintances, who are sufficiently interesting, but not too intimate. (Cross, 1: 208–9)

In October she left Plongeon where she found the company eventually uncongenial, 'people so little worth talking to' (*L*, 1: 315). Instead, she lodged with M. and Mme D'Albert-Durade, who became valued friends with whom she shared her passion for music and art.

In 1854 George Eliot undertook the defining journey of her life when she ran away to Germany with George Henry Lewes. While not her first trip to Europe, this was the watershed journey for her, both personally and professionally. The decision to embrace a new life which she knew would place her beyond the pale in polite Victorian society required courage, and sets this major journey apart from her previous respectable journeys. A revealing passage in her journal has her arriving early at St Katharine's Docks, London, and waiting anxiously for Lewes to appear (*J*, 14). Similarly, her troubled heroines, Maggie Tulliver and Romola, at the most significant turning points in their lives, also take to boats in the hope of escaping the gendered ideology which thwarts and trammels their ambitions and desires. Maggie yearns that she might 'glide along with the swift, silent stream, and not struggle any more' (*MF*, book 6, ch. 13). And Romola, drifting away in the night, 'was alone now: she had freed herself from all claims, she had freed herself even from that burthen of choice' (*R*, ch. 61).

Even while eloping, George Eliot as traveller remains the consummate journalist, recording her thoughts and feelings as she gazes on the passing scene or engages with the exigencies of travel. As their ship passes up the River Scheldt on the first night of her new life with Lewes, she describes the dawn in terms highlighting the romance of this journey:

> The crescent moon, the stars, the first faint blush of the dawn reflected in the glassy river, the dark mass of clouds on the horizon, which sent forth

> flashes of lightning, and the graceful forms of the boats and sailing vessels painted in jet black on the reddish gold of the sky and water, made up an unforgettable picture. (*J*, 14)

The ongoing journey to Weimar was recorded in careful detail in her diary, and later in 'Recollections of Weimar 1854' and 'Recollections of Berlin 1854–55'.

While we can access some of the reactions of George Eliot as traveller from her letters, journals and diaries, her 'Recollections' and her published articles, others appear in new dress in the novels. The interlude describing journeying down the Rhone on a summer's day in *The Mill on the Floss* is a good example (book 4, ch. 1). The article 'Three Months in Weimar', published in 1855 in *Fraser's Magazine*, offers a sample of public writing, based on 'Recollections of Weimar 1854', that is revelatory of the personal relationship on which she had embarked. Superficially it seems to be an account of two male companions travelling together, a blurring of gender lines that the anonymous journalism of the period allowed:

> after a ten hours' journey from Frankfort, I awoke at the Weimar station. No tipsiness can be more dead to all appeals than that which comes from fitful draughts of sleep on a railway journey by night. To the disgust of your wakeful companions, you are totally insensible to the existence of your umbrella, and to the fact that your carpet bag is stowed under your seat, or that you have borrowed books and tucked them behind the cushion. (*Essays*, 83)

George Eliot's travel journals contain numerous instances contradicting the statement of a legendary 'elderly man' at the start of *Felix Holt*, that travel by train 'can never lend much to picture and narrative' (*FH*, 'Introduction'). The description of the journey to Munich in 1858, as it moves in and out of various scenes, records with great clarity the pleasure of the traveller as each new picture lends itself to her gaze:

> I enjoyed looking at the landscape as we went along the railway. It ran through a well-cultivated plain, studded with villages and small towns – some of the villages charming to see. I remember one particularly where the little church stood perched on a steep rocky eminence that rose quite suddenly from among the little cluster of houses on the level. Sometimes we passed through long fir and pine woods, then we came out on tracts of tilled ground, where the hop-poles were standing in tent-like stacks, then on wide-stretching plains, all smooth green and brown. (*J*, 309)

Rail was not the only mode of transport. In 1860, to cross Mount Cenis into Italy they travelled by sledge when embarkation's 'human bustle and confusion made a poetic contrast with the sublime stillness of the starlit heavens' (*J*, 336). Arriving at Suza, 'breakfast and the railway came as a desirable variety after our long mountain journey and long fast' (*J*, 337).

During their years together George Eliot and Lewes travelled the length and breadth of Great Britain, sometimes for research. The journey to Lincolnshire in September 1859, for instance, was to check out facts needed for *The Mill on the Floss*. Lewes noted in his diary that the journey was undertaken 'on artistic grounds, Polly wanting to lay the scene of her new novel on the Trent' (*L*, 9: 345). Other travels were for recreation and for the sake of health; several expeditions to Malvern in the early 1860s were to allow Lewes to take the water cure.

The only domestic travels which occasioned 'Recollections' essays were scientific expeditions to Ilfracombe and Tenby in 1856, and the Scilly Isles and Jersey in 1857, designed specifically for Lewes to develop his newly awakened interest in marine biology. On these trips they placed some reliance on the advice of Philip Gosse, who was largely responsible for the contemporary popularity of sea-side studies among the middle classes, and used his works as guide books. George Eliot made reference in 'Recollections of Ilfracombe, 1856' to *A Naturalist's Rambles on the Devonshire Coast* (1853) as a guide to lodgings, commenting that the 'reasons for his recommendation were not very patent to us when we saw the shabby ill-furnished parlour and bedroom' (*J*, 263); and elsewhere noted that Caldy Island is a place 'where Gosse tells us there are treasures to be found' (*L*, 2: 256). Gosse had recently published *Tenby: a Sea-Side Holiday* (1856), and John Murray's *Handbook for Travellers in South Wales* (1860) would record that Gosse made Tenby famous (*J*, 260). In following Gosse, Lewes was tapping into a saleable commodity in a period when he and George Eliot were beset with money worries. Their scientific tourism was, however, principally a means of acquiring a range of new knowledges. A visit to Hele's shop provided 'a considerable stretch to my knowledge of animal forms', George Eliot noted, and the 'tide-pools made me quite in love with sea-weeds' (*J*, 266, 267).

In the 'Recollections of Ilfracombe' George Eliot is at her liveliest, fascinated by the collecting of specimens at low tide which she twice terms a 'glorious hunt' (*J*, 60, 61):

> when one sees a house stuck on the side of a great hill, and still more a number of houses looking like a few barnacles clustered on the side of a great rock, we begin to think of the strong family likeness between ourselves and all other building, burrowing house-appropriating and shell secreting animals. The difference between a man with his house and a mollusc with its

shell lies in the number of steps or phenomena interposed between the fact of individual existence and the completion of the building. (*J*, 265)

This wonderful comparison of human habitations to those of molluscs was incorporated by Lewes into the first of a series of articles titled 'Sea-side Studies' published in *Blackwood's*.[1] In a letter to Sara Hennell, George Eliot reported that Lewes 'has written a very nice paper (in my opinion) describing our "Sea-side Studies"', suggesting her sense of participation in a joint project (*L*, 2: 259; *J*, 261). Fossicking on the sea-coast permitted a range of healthy activities, including long walks which are described in vivid detail. Ilfracombe is 'a ravishingly beautiful place' and the scenery and zoology 'have been terribly unpropitious to my work' (*L*, 2: 254). Yet famously, it was while they were at Tenby that she began seriously to consider the writing of fiction, and she was well embarked on *Scenes of Clerical Life* before setting off in March 1857 on their next trip in the interests of science, to the Scilly Isles and Jersey. They were away for five months. By now they were both *Blackwood's* authors, Lewes's 'New Sea-Side Studies I', based on this expedition, being published side by side with Part 4 of 'Mr. Gilfil's Love Story' (written at Scilly) in June 1857, while Part 3 of 'Janet's Repentance' immediately preceded 'New Sea-Side Studies IV' in the September issue.

George Eliot and Lewes would travel to the continent many times. As with their sea-side studies, their travels were often directed by research interests: 'This has been a red-letter day', she wrote enthusiastically in Munich on 27 April 1858. They had talked with scientists, Professors Wagner and Martius, visited the *atelier* of the artist Kaulbach, been introduced to the poet Johann Heyse, and met Liebig, Professor of Chemistry, summed up by George Eliot as 'charming – with well cut features, a low quiet voice, and gentle manners. It was touching to see his hands, the nails black from the roots, the skin all grimed' (*J*, 314). Such encounters and conversations find their place in one form or another in the later novels. Reading for this journey included unlikely travel reference works such as Anna Mary Howitt's *An Art Student in Munich* (1853). Seeing the snow-covered Alps was a watershed moment, George Eliot declaring them to be a '[s]ight more to me than all the art in Munich, though I love the Art nevertheless. The great wide-stretching earth and the all-embracing sky … are what I most care to look at after all' (*J*, 311).

As their financial position improved, so their itineraries concentrated more on cultural tourism, and beginning in 1860 with the journey to Italy, they depended more on guide books. Murray's *A Handbook for Travellers in*

Southern Italy was the presiding genius. The 1864 journey was undertaken in company with the artist Frederic Burton, who had never been to Italy before. His presence, doubtless as an authority on art generally, explains in part the almost tedious catalogue of artworks and paintings which dominates George Eliot's short 'Italy 1864' journal in considerable contrast to the fullness of 'Recollections of Italy 1860'. It is in this latter essay that she records her traveller's philosophy, that the main object of travel must be 'the enlargement of one's general life', together with her awareness of the anxiety which accompanies the 'delight of seeing world-famous objects', that the moment will not be sufficiently enjoyed because 'the faculties are not wrought up into energetic action' (*J*, 336). However, the 1864 journal records the purchase of souvenirs and, in keeping with the modernity of the age, photographs. Those by Carlo Ponti, along with a Ponti Alethoscope, were especially sought out on their last day in Venice in 1864 (*J*, 371, 376).

The impact of the European journeys emerges most forcefully when George Eliot brilliantly incorporates her varying travel experiences into her fiction writing (see Figure 23). That contest between art and landscape noted in Munich is revived in *Middlemarch* when the reader discovers the newly married Dorothea 'sobbing bitterly' in Rome:

> She had been led through the best galleries, had been taken to the chief points of view, had been shown the grandest ruins and the most glorious churches, and she had ended oftenest choosing to drive out to the Campagna where she could feel alone with the earth and sky, away from the oppressive masquerade of ages. (*M*, ch. 20)

Middlemarch contains numerous references to and reworkings of Italian history and art, often appearing as sly and subtle similes and metaphors, in particular with regard to the characterisation of Dorothea, her puritan instincts bewildered by 'smirking Renaissance-Correggiosities' (*M*, ch. 9). Possibly the most famous outcome of the Italian tourism is *Romola* (1862–3), set in early Renaissance Florence, which is notoriously weighed down with historical detail, much of it gleaned during a second trip to Italy in 1861 for research purposes. Once more in Genoa, George Eliot is delighted with Lewes's reaction to the city as 'his first vision of anything corresponding to his preconception of Italy', adding, 'Genoa la Superba is not a name of the past, merely' (*J*, 338). The detailed travel description of the 'Recollections' is finely nuanced, however, when Daniel Deronda arrives in that city: the reader is provided with a Genoa intensified by sound, heat and light, 'till all strong colour melted in the stream of moonlight which

Figure 23 Like many travellers, George Eliot initially found Rome overpowering and gained relief by driving into the countryside – an experience shared with Dorothea Casaubon in chapter 20 of *Middlemarch*. Corot's painting of the Campagna *c.* 1830–1 depicts the area as Dorothea might have seen it.

Jean Baptiste Camille Corot (French, 1796–1875), *La Cervara, the Roman Campagna* (*c.* 1830–1831). Oil on fabric, 97.6 × 135.8 cm. The Cleveland Museum of Art. Leonard C. Hanna, Jr. Fund 1963.91.

made the streets a new spectacle with shadows, both still and moving, on cathedral steps and against the façades of massive palaces' (*DD*, ch. 50). In the intense atmosphere of Genoa, key revelations are made and issues resolved. *Daniel Deronda* is a novel in which peripatetic characters undertake both actual journeys, and what John Rignall deems journeys 'of the imagination… beyond the bounds of physical travel'.[2]

The journey through Normandy and Brittany in 1865 offers the reader occasionally more personal, and therefore more interesting, accounts of where the Leweses went and what they saw. This journal is interlarded with long verbatim quotations from Murray's *Handbook for Travellers in France* (see, for instance, *J*, 382). The journey to Spain at the start of 1867 is only recorded in a few letters, the relevant journal having been sold in 1923 and then broken up to be bound into Houghton Mifflin's 1924 limited edition of *The Works of George Eliot* (*J*, xviii, n. 5). No pages from this dismembered journal have ever surfaced. In letters, however, Lewes and George Eliot describe revelling in the warm sunny climate and adjure their friends to '[b]elieve none of the fictions … about the horrors of Spanish hotels and cookery, or the hardships of Spanish travel' (*L*, 4: 344).

George Eliot's last journey abroad was almost as significant as that elopement in 1854. In May 1880 she married John Cross, and after the ceremony and the signing of wills, the pair set off for Dover, crossing the Channel 'delightfully in a private cabin on deck' (*J*, 203). There is little record of their travels apart from brief notes in her diary of the French towns they passed through and the sightseeing undertaken on the road to Venice. Her letters are more forthcoming and from them, along with cryptic notes in the diary, we learn that Ruskin is the guiding light of their time in Venice: 'We edify ourselves with what Ruskin has written about Venice in an agreeable pamphlet shape, using his knowledge gratefully and shutting our ears to his wrathful innuendoes against the whole modern world' (*L*, 7: 294–5). Wealthy, and legally married, her circumstances were now very different from when she went off with Lewes so many years before. On this honeymoon journey she revisited many of the places she had journeyed to with Lewes, remarking that while Cross 'has entered with great interest into the art of all the wondrous towns from Milan to Venice … to me the journey has been a precious revival of memories fifteen or sixteen years old' (*L*, 7: 299). For Cross himself, the effect of travel on his wife was a revelation: 'from the day she set her foot on Continental soil, till the day she returned to Witley, she was never ill – never even unwell … I had never seen her so strong in health … the atmosphere seemed to have a magical effect' (Cross, 3: 417–18). It was not so for him. In Venice on 16 June he threw himself into the Grand Canal, either a suicide attempt or an act of delirium. Cross notes only that he became 'thoroughly ill' (Cross, 3: 408). His wife's version of the incident is that he suffered a 'sharp but brief attack at Venice', but notes of herself: 'I have been amazingly well through all the exertions of our travels' (*L*, 7: 307–8). This honeymoon tour was George Eliot's final journey. She died just six months later.

NOTES

1 *Blackwood's Edinburgh Magazine* (August 1856), 195.
2 John Rignall, 'George Eliot and the Idea of Travel', *The Yearbook of English Studies*, 36.2 (2006), 151.

CHAPTER 36

Visual arts

Leonée Ormond

In July 1858 George Eliot paid her first visit to the Picture Gallery in Dresden, a defining event in her enthusiasm for the fine arts. One painting in particular, Raphael's *Sistine Madonna*, was momentous. Often described as the 'Dresden Madonna', it had been painted for the Order of St Sixtus in Piacenza and was obtained for the Gallery in 1754. The *Sistine Madonna* shows the Virgin, framed by curtains, standing on the clouds with the Holy Child in her arms. Kneeling beside her are St Sixtus and St Barbara. The two child angels below, their arms on a parapet, are well known in many forms, even on occasion appearing as part of Christmas decorations in London's Oxford Street (see Figure 24).

At the time when George Eliot saw the *Sistine Madonna* it was hanging in a section of the Picture Gallery arranged in the form of a chapel. She would have known the image from prints, but she was overwhelmed in the presence of the actual painting:

> I sat down on the sofa opposite the picture for an instant, but a sort of awe, as if I were suddenly in the living presence of some glorious being, made my heart swell too much for me to remain comfortably, and we hurried out of the room. On subsequent mornings we always came in the last minutes of our stay to look at this sublimest picture. (*J*, 325)

George Eliot's experience of the *Sistine Madonna* lies behind the narrator's comment in *Adam Bede*, then being written, concerning Seth Bede's thoughts of Dinah Morris. During the dance at Donnithorne Chase Seth looks with distaste at the Hayslope girls: 'just as one feels the beauty and the greatness of a pictured Madonna the more, when it has been for a moment screened from us by a vulgar head in a bonnet' (*AB*, ch. 26). In a later novel, *The Mill on the Floss*, Philip Wakem tells Maggie Tulliver that the 'greatest of painters only once painted a mysteriously divine child; he couldn't have told how he did it, and we can't tell why we feel it to be divine' (*MF*, book 5, ch. 1).

Figure 24 George Eliot shared the opinion common in her day that Raphael was the greatest of all painters. The Sistine Madonna ('this sublimest picture' – *J*, 325) especially moved her during her stay in Dresden in 1858, when she and Lewes frequently visited the Old Masters Gallery.

Among other works in the Gallery which attracted the lasting admiration of George Eliot and George Henry Lewes was Titian's *Tribute Money*, a print of which later hung on their wall at 'The Priory'. Here Christ, holding a coin marked with Caesar's head, tells the Pharisee who plans to entrap him: 'Render therefore unto Caesar the things which are Caesar's.' George Eliot refers to the painting by name in *Daniel Deronda* where the narrator, describing the faces of Daniel and Mordecai Cohen, wishes that she 'could perpetuate those two faces, as Titian's "Tribute Money" has perpetuated two types presenting another sort of contrast' (*DD*, ch. 40).

Two other Dresden favourites of the novelist were the *Madonna* by Hans Holbein (now known to be a copy of his *Darmstadt Madonna*) and a 'wonderful portrait' by the same artist. In this latter case, although the attribution to Holbein has been upheld, the identification of the sitter has changed dramatically. George Eliot was convinced that the man who looks challengingly out of the canvas as he handles an elaborate dagger was a goldsmith. Now he is known to have been an aristocrat, Charles de Solier, the French ambassador in London. In her journal the novelist tells us that she 'especially enjoyed looking at' this image of 'nothing more lofty than a plain weighty man of business, a goldsmith; but the eminently fine painting brings out all the weighty calm good sense that lies in a first rate character of that order' (*J*, 325). This vehemence suggests, that, had she known the true identity of the sitter, her enthusiasm might have been tempered by his high social class.

On George Eliot's earlier visit to Germany, in 1854–5, she had seen a number of collections of old masters including that in Berlin. On this second tour she was able to make many visits to the galleries of Munich and Dresden. It is generally agreed that a painting by the seventeenth-century Dutch artist Gerrit Dou, *The Spinner's Prayer*, seen by her in the Alte Pinakothek in Munich in 1858, was one inspiration for the well-known passage in chapter 17 of *Adam Bede.* Here, Eliot praises artists of the seventeenth-century Dutch school for their realism, for turning their attention to the life of working people like 'an old woman bending over her flower-pot, or eating her solitary dinner, while the noonday light, softened perhaps by a screen of leaves, falls on her mob-cap, and just touches the rim of her spinning-wheel, and her stone jug, and all those cheap common things which are the precious necessaries of life to her' (*AB*, ch. 40).

Such a defence of the ordinary is not out of place in a novel set in a rural world with carpenters and farm labourers among the characters. In Dresden, as in Munich and Berlin, George Eliot admired works by other Dutch and Flemish genre painters, 'Teniers, Ryckaert, Gerard Dow, Terburg, Mieris and the rest' (*J*, 326).

In her praise of realism in art, George Eliot was following in the footsteps of John Ruskin, the third and fourth volumes of whose *Modern Painters* she had recently reviewed in the *Westminster Review* (February and April 1856). Not surprisingly, she often writes with pleasure of the work of a later Dutch master, Rembrandt. In Dresden she praised his portraits, but was less keen on his subject works, which included a drinking scene with the artist as the prodigal son, and a picture of Samson and Delilah at the dinner table. She was frankly disgusted by Rembrandt's *Ganymede* showing Zeus as an eagle carrying off the crying and urinating child. Enthusiasm for portraits can be anticipated in a novelist known for her powerful sense of character. Her liking for images which render the human face with striking insight and accuracy is a recurring feature of George Eliot's accounts of visits to art galleries and collections.

The overview which emerges from George Eliot's account of her experience of old master paintings during her travels in Germany is a complex one. Chapter 17 of *Adam Bede* can be interpreted as her credo and it is easy to pigeonhole her as an advocate for realism and for secular art. 'It is for this rare, precious quality of truthfulness that I delight in many Dutch paintings, which lofty-minded people despise', she writes; 'I find a source of delicious sympathy in these faithful pictures of a monotonous homely existence' (*AB*, ch. 17). Her appeal to her readers to rate the Dutch school as highly as 'cloud-borne angels', 'prophets, sibyls, and heroic warriors' should be read carefully, however (ch. 17). It is apparent from her accounts of galleries that George Eliot was far less single-minded than this would suggest. The woman who was overwhelmed by the *Sistine Madonna* did not denigrate idealised images of the Madonna however passionately she might defend paintings of old women at their spinning wheels. She asked that both should be appreciated for their own qualities.

> Paint us an angel, if you can, with a floating violet robe, and a face paled by the celestial light; paint us yet oftener a Madonna, turning her mild face upward and opening her arms to the divine glory; but do not impose on us any aesthetic rules which shall banish from the region of Art those old women scraping carrots with their work-worn hands. (*AB*, ch. 17)

One can anticipate that George Eliot would admire the paintings of beggar boys by the seventeenth-century Spanish painter Murillo. She expressed her approval in her review of Wilhelm Riehl's *Natural History of German Life* of 1856 and her journal records delight at seeing examples of his 'low life' paintings in the Dulwich Art Gallery in 1859. In Dresden, however, her praise was bestowed upon an overtly Catholic and deeply religious work by the artist, *Saint Rodriguez.* Here, the martyred saint, holding a palm branch, is crowned by a cherub. George Eliot's description reminds us that, for all her retreat from Christianity, she still responded emotionally to the representation of inspired religious experience: 'The attitude and expression are sublime, and strikingly distinguished from all other pictures of saints I have ever seen. He stands erect in his scarlet and white robes, with face upturned – the arms held simply downward, but the hands held open in a receptive attitude. The silly cupid-like angel holding the martyr's crown in the corner spoils all' (*J*, 325–6). Again, we have to qualify our judgement, and not assume that George Eliot always thought of 'cupid-like' angels as 'silly'. When writing of a famous group of paintings by Correggio in the Dresden collection, she noted that 'the little cherub riding astride a cloud' in the *Madonna with Saint Sebastian* remained with her 'vividly' (*J*, 325). One cherub is commended for its liveliness, the other condemned as faintly ridiculous.

In admiring Raphael, Rubens and Murillo, George Eliot was squarely mid Victorian. Her intense dislike for the 'superlatively odious' religious paintings of the seventeenth-century Bolognese artist Guido Reni, relates her to a growing reaction against a school formerly regarded as the touchstone of high art, and much praised by Sir Joshua Reynolds among others (*J*, 326). Her attraction to Titian and Rembrandt was rather more forward-looking. At this time Dante Gabriel Rossetti was beginning to pose his half-length female models in the manner of Titian. A quarter of a century before, Alfred Tennyson had been entranced by Titian's *Allegory of Vanity* in the Louvre, and attempted to recreate the effect of the picture in a poem published in 1842, 'The Gardener's Daughter'. On the whole, George Eliot preferred the Venetian painter's religious works and his portraits to his pagan subjects. However, she liked the *Sleeping Venus* in Dresden, then attributed to Titian, now given jointly to Titian and Giorgione, believing this famous nude to be as much an example of 'purity and sacred loveliness' as the religious works which surrounded it (*J*, 325). Another full-length Titian nude which Lewes and George Eliot praised was the *Danae* in the Kunsthistorisches Museum in Vienna. However, she found his much praised *Ecce Homo* in the same gallery 'splendid in composition and colour, but the Christ is abject, the Pontius Pilate vulgar: amazing that they could have been painted by the same man who conceived and executed the Christo del Moneta [*The Tribute Money*]!' (*J*, 323). Here, as in her approach to portrait painting, George Eliot's judgement is based upon her belief that faces and demeanour should be appropriate to the story. As so often, even in her approach to works like the *Sistine Madonna*, it is the human truth that she is looking for. She found the paintings in Vienna by Titian's contemporary, Veronese, 'splendid and uninteresting' (*J*, 323). With typical independence of mind, however, she was 'converted' to Veronese when she saw his *Marriage Feast at Cana* in the Louvre in 1859 (*J*, 78).

Much of this discussion has concerned works by Italian old masters. George Eliot visited Italy for the first time in 1860 and it was there that, encouraged by Lewes, she conceived the idea of a novel about the Italian renaissance, eventually published as *Romola*. Once the idea had taken hold, the novelist found herself studying art works, like the frescoes of Domenico Ghirlandaio with their precise representation of fifteenth-century Florentine life, and relevant texts, particularly *The Lives of the Painters* by Giorgio Vasari, as part of the background work for her novel. Several Florentine painters appear as characters in *Romola*, particularly Piero di Cosimo. George Eliot gives him a largely fictional oeuvre, inventing works to reflect the relationships of her characters. Like a novelist, Piero creates through his understanding of human nature. So, he paints a triptych showing Romola and Tito as Ariadne and Bacchus, an indirect reference to Tito's 'rescue' of Romola from her life with her father. Occasionally George Eliot refers to a 'real' painting or statue in the novel: for example, she tells us that Bernardo Dovizi, Cardinal Bibbiena, 'now looks at us out of Raphael's portrait' in the Pitti Palace (*R*, ch. 20).

George Eliot does not use the device of ekphrasis, the detailed description of an actual work of art, in the manner of Henry James. She comes closest to it when writing of Fra Angelico's *Crucifixion* in the chapter house of the Convent of San Marco, where one of her leading characters, Savonarola, was among the fathers. Women were not permitted to visit Savonarola's cell on the upper floor of the Convent, so Lewes had to supply her with descriptions of the Fra Angelico frescoes on the corridor walls there. Both novelist and heroine were subject to the same restriction. They could, however, see the *Crucifixion*. Romola, entering the chapter house, is 'just conscious that in the background there was a crucified form rising high and pale on the frescoed wall, and pale faces of sorrow looking out from it below' (ch. 15).

Romola largely reflects the taste of its time; the artists mentioned or presented as characters were usually those who appeared in the guide books. Today we think of Botticelli as the outstanding artist of Savonarola's generation. However, in the 1860s few English people knew of him, and his name is notably absent from the novel. *Romola* was written at a time when discerning critics and collectors had begun to praise what were then known as 'goldbacks' or 'primitives', Italian paintings and frescoes from the thirteenth and fourteenth centuries.

In building up a picture of the Florentine art world for *Romola*, George Eliot did not neglect sculpture. The 'old Florentine' Spirit of the novel's 'Proem' 'paid many florins … for disinterred busts of the ancient immortals' and, in her account of the city, she refers to two statues by Donatello, *Plenty* and *Judith*. She demonstrates her knowledge of Ascanio Condivi's life of Michaelangelo when she mentions Condivi's reference to a missing statue of a Faun. Generally, however, she was ambivalent about Michaelangelo and hostile to the work of his baroque successors.

George Eliot preferred classical statues. Once settled in London she became familiar with the British Museum, and Lewes and she were frequently to be found studying ancient sculpture on their continental journeys. These works were an occasional source of telling references in the novels. Hetty Sorrel in *Adam Bede*, for example, has the 'passionate passionless lips' of the *Rondanini Medusa* in Munich (ch. 37). The most striking parallel of all comes in *Middlemarch* where Dorothea Brooke is seen beside the *Ariadne* in the Vatican Gallery (ch. 19). The narrator notes that the statue had been thought to be of Cleopatra, but Ariadne, abandoned by Jason, is a perfect parallel for Dorothea, abandoned on her honeymoon by a husband more concerned with his researches in the library.

Among contemporary or near contemporary sculptors, the young George Eliot admired the work of Bertel Thorwaldsen, the Danish neo-classical artist, and owned a small cast of his *Resurrected Jesus* that helped sustain her when she was 'Strauss-sick' during the translation of the *Life of Jesus* (*L*, I: 205). Ludwig Schwanthaler's 'colossal Bavaria' in Munich impressed her mightily in 1858 (*J*, 311).

Like other writers of her time, George Eliot took an intelligent interest in contemporary artists. On her visits to Germany she showed surprisingly little enthusiasm for the work of the Nazarenes, the group of German painters initially drawn together in the early nineteenth century, who looked back to early Italian art as an inspiration. She was more impressed by one of the founding Nazarenes, Friedrich Overbeck, when she met him in Rome in 1860, and Naumann, in *Middlemarch*, is clearly an artist of that school.

George Eliot had a closer knowledge of the comparable English group, the Pre-Raphaelite Brotherhood, founded in 1848. As a regular visitor to the Royal Academy, she commented on their work in her journal and letters. In the 1850s she singled out the paintings of William Holman Hunt and John Millais. She much admired Millais's *The Huguenot*, a picture of a Catholic woman vainly endeavouring to protect her Protestant lover from the massacre of St Bartholomew's Eve. Hunt's *The Hireling Shepherd* struck her as a fine piece of landscape painting marred by 'a pair of peasants in the foreground who were not much more real than the idyllic swains and damsels' ('Natural History', *Essays*, 268). The context for this criticism was her review of Riehl's *Natural History of German Life*, in which she attacks those artists who present country people as though they were figures from opera or ballet. In fact, George Eliot missed the point of Hunt's painting, which criticises clergy so preoccupied with points of religious debate (represented by the death's head moth in the shepherd's hand) that they neglect their pastoral duties.

Eventually, George Eliot came to know all three leading Pre-Raphaelite artists. Dante Gabriel Rossetti discussed his drawings with her and sent her photographs of his work. Her closest relationship, however, was with one of the next generation of Pre-Raphaelites, Edward Burne-Jones. When he showed a group of paintings at the Dudley Gallery in 1873, she was particularly impressed by two of them, *Love Among the Ruins* and *The Hesperides*. Five years later she wrote to the artist:

> I want in gratitude to tell you that your work makes life larger and more beautiful to us – I mean that historical life of all the world in which our little personal share of her seems a mere standing room from which we can look all round, and chiefly backward … the sadness is so inwrought with pure elevating sensibility to all that is sweet and beautiful in the story of man and in the face of the earth, that it can no more be found fault with than the sadness of midday when Pan is touchy like the rest of us. (*L*, 5: 391)

If one side of George Eliot felt that Burne-Jones's work was not sufficiently involved with everyday life, the other side, which responded to inspiration and to emotional truth, deeply admired his paintings.

For many Victorian writers, work with an illustrator was their closest contact with the art world. Some, like Alfred Tennyson, disliked what they felt to be a misrepresentation of their writing. When she heard that Frederic Leighton, who had made his name as a painter of Italian renaissance subjects, was to illustrate *Romola*, George Eliot was naturally delighted. However, for a time she experienced disappointment that Leighton's drawings did not exactly match her own vision of her characters, as expressed through the text. Finally, however, after talking it over with Lewes, she concluded that the 'exigencies' of his 'art must forbid perfect correspondence between the text and the illustration' and that 'illustrations can only form a sort of overture to the text' (*L*, 4: 41, 55). Appropriately enough, the novelist asked the artist, who was visiting Florence, to check the accuracy of her account of fifteenth-century dress from the frescoes of Ghirlandaio. Art and literature were, as so often in George Eliot's writing, completely intertwined.

Further reading

GENERAL

Levine, George (ed.), *The Cambridge Companion to George Eliot* (Cambridge University Press, 2001).

Rignall, John (ed.), *Oxford Reader's Companion to George Eliot* (Oxford University Press, 2000).

GEORGE ELIOT'S LIFE; THE BIOGRAPHICAL TRADITION

Ashton, Rosemary, *G. H. Lewes: A Life* (Oxford University Press, 1991).

George Eliot: A Life (London: Hamish Hamilton, 1996).

142 Strand: A Radical Address in Victorian London (London: Chatto and Windus, 2006).

Bodenheimer, Rosemarie, *The Real Life of Mary Ann Evans: George Eliot Her Letters and Fiction* (Ithaca, NY: Cornell University Press, 1994).

Collins, K. K., *Identifying the Remains: George Eliot's Death in the London Religious Press* (Victoria, BC: ELS Editions, 2006).

Collins, K. K. (ed.), *George Eliot: Interviews and Recollections* (Basingstoke: Palgrave Macmillan, 2010).

Fleishman, Avrom, *George Eliot's Intellectual Life* (Cambridge University Press, 2010).

Fulmer, Constance M. and Margaret E. Barfield (eds.), *A Monument to the Memory of George Eliot: Edith J. Simcox's 'Autobiography of a Shirtmaker'* (New York and London: Garland, 1998).

Haight, Gordon S., *George Eliot and John Chapman: With Chapman's Diaries* (New Haven, CT: Yale University Press; Oxford University Press, 1940).

George Eliot: A Biography (Oxford: Clarendon, 1968).

Hardy, Barbara, *George Eliot: A Critic's Biography* (London: Continuum, 2006).

Henry, Nancy, *The Life of George Eliot* (Oxford: Wiley-Blackwell, 2012).

Hughes, Kathryn, *George Eliot: The Last Victorian* (London: Fourth Estate, 1998).

Maddox, Brenda, *George Eliot: Novelist, Lover, Wife* (London: Harper, 2009).

PUBLISHERS AND PUBLICATION; EDITIONS OF GEORGE ELIOT'S WORK

Baker, William and John C. Ross, *George Eliot: A Bibliographical History* (New Castle, DE and London: Oak Knoll Press and The British Library, 2002).
Huxley, Leonard, *The House of Smith Elder* (London: Smith, Elder, 1923).
Oliphant, Margaret, *Annals of a Publishing House: William Blackwood and His Sons, their Magazine and Friends*, 2 vols. (Edinburgh and London: William Blackwood and Sons, 1897).
Porter, Mrs Gerald, *Annals of a Publishing House: John Blackwood* (Edinburgh and London: William Blackwood and Sons, 1898).
Sutherland, J. A., *Victorian Novelists and Publishers* (London: Athlone Press, 1976).

GENRE

Hadjiafxendi, Kyriaki, 'The Cultural Place of George Eliot's Poetry', Special Issue of *George Eliot–George Henry Lewes Studies*, 60–1 (2011).
Orel, Harold, *The Victorian Short Story: Development and Triumph of a Literary Genre* (Cambridge University Press, 1986).
Prins, Yopie, 'Victorian Meters', in Joseph Bristow (ed.), *The Cambridge Companion to Victorian Poetry* (Cambridge University Press, 2000), 89–113.
Sanders, Andrew, *The Victorian Historical Novel, 1840–1880* (London: Macmillan, 1978).

AFTERLIFE

Dolin, Tim, *George Eliot* (Oxford World's Classics, Oxford University Press, 2005).
Easley, Alexis, *Literary Celebrity, Gender, and Victorian Authorship, 1850–1914* (Newark, DE: University of Delaware Press, 2011).
Giddings, Robert and Erica Sheen (eds.), *The Classic Novel From Page to Screen* (Manchester University Press, 2000).
Kucich, John and Diane Sadoff, *Victorian Afterlife: Postmodern Culture Rewrites the Nineteenth Century* (Minneapolis: University of Minnesota Press, 2000).

CRITICAL FORTUNES

Atkinson, Juliette (ed.), *Bloom's Classic Critical Views: George Eliot* (New York: Infobase, 2009).
Blake, Kathleen, 'George Eliot: The Critical Heritage', in George Levine (ed.), *The Cambridge Companion to George Eliot* (Cambridge University Press, 2001), 202–25.
Carroll, David (ed.), *George Eliot: The Critical Heritage* (London: Routledge and Kegan Paul, 1971).

Haight, Gordon S. (ed.), *A Century of George Eliot Criticism* (London: Methuen, 1965).
Holmstrom, John and Lawrence Lerner (eds.), *George Eliot and her Readers: A Selection of Contemporary Reviews* (New York: Barnes and Noble, 1966).
Hutchinson, Stuart (ed.), *George Eliot: Critical Assessments*, 4 vols. (Mountfield: Helm, 1996).
Marshall, Gail (ed.), *Eliot, Dickens and Tennyson by their Contemporaries, Volume 1: George Eliot* (London: Pickering and Chatto, 2003).
Perkin, J. Russell, *A Reception-History of George Eliot's Fiction* (Ann Arbor, MI: UMI Research Press, 1990).
Wilkes, Joanne, *Women Reviewing Women in Nineteenth-Century Britain: The Critical Reception of Jane Austen, Charlotte Brontë and George Eliot* (Farnham: Ashgate, 2010).

CLASS

Adams, James Eli, 'The Boundaries of Social Intercourse: Class in the Victorian Novel', in Francis O'Gorman (ed.), *A Concise Companion to the Victorian Novel* (Oxford: Blackwell, 2005), 44–70.
Cottom, Daniel, *Social Figures: George Eliot, Social History, and Literary Representation* (Minneapolis: University of Minnesota Press, 1987).
David, Deirdre, *Intellectual Women and Victorian Patriarchy* (Ithaca, NY: Cornell University Press, 1987).
Eagleton, Terry, *Criticism and Ideology: A Study in Marxist Literary Theory* (London: Verso, 1978).
Gallagher, Catherine, *The Industrial Reformation of English Fiction: Social Discourse and Narrative Form, 1832–1867* (University of Chicago Press, 1985).
Homans, Margaret, 'Dinah's Blush and Maggie's Arm: Class, Gender, and Sexuality in Eliot's Early Novels', *Victorian Studies*, 36 (1993), 155–79.
Langland, Elizabeth, *Nobody's Angels: Middle-Class Women and Domestic Ideology in Victorian Culture* (Ithaca, NY: Cornell University Press, 1995).
Lesjak, Caroline, *Working Fictions: A Genealogy of the Victorian Novel* (Durham, NC: Duke University Press, 2006).
Williams, Raymond, *Culture and Society, 1780–1950* (London: Chatto and Windus, 1958).

DRESS

Cunnington, C. Willett, *English Women's Clothing in the Nineteenth-century* (London: Faber and Faber, 1938).
Harvey, J., *Men in Black* (London: Reaktion, 1995).
Hollander, Anne, *Seeing Through Clothes* (Berkeley, CA: University of California Press, 1993).
Hughes, Clair, *Dressed in Fiction* (Oxford and New York: Berg, 2005).

EDUCATION

Beer, Gillian, *George Eliot*, Key Women Writers (Bloomington, IN: Indiana University Press, 1986).

Burstyn, Joan N., *Victorian Education and the Ideal of Womanhood* (London: Croom Helm, 1980).

Ellis, Alec, *Educating Our Masters: Influences on the Growth of Literacy in Victorian Working Class Children* (Aldershot: Gower, 1985).

Gargano, Elizabeth, *Reading Victorian Schoolrooms: Childhood and Education in Nineteenth-Century Fiction* (New York and London: Routledge, 2008).

Green, Laura, '"At Once Narrow and Promiscuous": Emily Davies, George Eliot, and *Middlemarch*', *Nineteenth Century Studies*, 9 (1995), 1–30.

Educating Women: Cultural Conflict and Victorian Literature (Athens: Ohio University Press, 2001).

Hilton, Mary, and Pam Hirsch, *Practical Visionaries: Women, Education, and Social Progress, 1790–1930* (Harlow: Longman, 2000).

Lacey, Candida Ann (ed.), *Barbara Leigh Smith Bodichon and the Langham Place Group* (New York: Routledge and Kegan Paul, 1986).

McClure, Laura, 'On Knowing Greek: George Eliot and the Classical Tradition', *Classical and Modern Literature: A Quarterly*, 13:2 (Winter 1993), 139–56.

Paxton, Nancy L., *George Eliot and Herbert Spencer: Feminism, Evolutionism, and the Reconstruction of Gender* (Princeton University Press, 1991).

Robertson, Linda K., 'From Reality to Fiction: Benefits and Hazards of Continental Education', in John Rignall (ed.), *George Eliot and Europe* (Aldershot: Scolar Press, 1997), 156–65.

The Power of Knowledge: George Eliot and Education (New York: Peter Lang, 1997).

ETIQUETTE

Adonis, Andrew and Stephen Pollard, *A Class Act: The Myth of Britain's Classless Society* (London: Hamish Hamilton, 1997).

Czikszentmihalyi, Mihaly and Eugene Rochberg-Halton, *The Meaning of Things: Domestic Symbols and the Self* (New York: Columbia University Press, 1981).

Davidoff, Leonore, *The Best Circles: Society, Etiquette and the Season* (London: Croom Helm, 1973).

Ehrenreich, Barbara and Deirdre English, *For Her Own Good: 150 Years of the Experts' Advice to Women* (London: Pluto, 1979).

Mintz, Steven, *A Prison of Expectations: The Family in Victorian Culture* (New York University Press, 1983).

Mitchell, Sally, *Daily Life in Victorian England* (Westport, CT: Greenwood, 1996).

FAMILIES AND KINSHIP

Beer, Gillian, *Darwin's Plots: Evolutionary Narrative in Darwin, George Eliot and Nineteenth-Century Fiction*, 2nd edn (1983; Cambridge University Press, 2000).

Behlmer, George K., *Friends of the Family: The English Home and Its Guardians, 1850–1940* (Stanford University Press, 1998).
Chase, Karen and Michael Levenson, *The Spectacle of Intimacy: A Public Life for the Victorian Family* (Princeton University Press, 2000).
Cohen, Paula Marantz, *The Daughter's Dilemma: Family Process and the Nineteenth-Century Domestic Novel* (Ann Arbor, MI: University of Michigan Press, 1991).
Corbett, Mary Jean, *Family Likeness: Sex, Marriage and Incest from Jane Austen to Virginia Woolf* (Ithaca, NY: Cornell University Press, 2008).
Davis, Philip, *The Victorians* (Oxford English Literary History, vol. 8, 1830–80, Oxford University Press, 2002).
Langland, Elizabeth, *Nobody's Angels: Middle-Class Women and Domestic Ideology in Victorian Culture* (Ithaca, NY: Cornell University Press, 1995).
Mount, Ferdinand, *The Subversive Family: An Alternative History of Love and Marriage* (London: Cape, 1982).
Nelson, Claudia, *Family Ties in Victorian England* (Westport, CT: Praeger, 2007).
Sanders, Valerie, *The Brother–Sister Culture in Nineteenth-Century Literature* (Basingstoke: Palgrave, 2002).
Wohl, Anthony S., *The Victorian Family* (London: Croom Helm, 1978).

GENDER AND THE WOMAN QUESTION

Ablow, Rachel, *The Marriage of Minds: Reading Sympathy in the Victorian Marriage Plot* (Stanford University Press, 2007).
Caine, Barbara, *Victorian Feminists* (Oxford University Press, 1992).
Chase, Karen, 'George Eliot and the Woman Question', in John Rignall (ed.), *Oxford Reader's Companion to George Eliot* (Oxford University Press, 1998, 467–71.
Hadjiafxendi, Kyriaki, '"George Eliot," the Literary Market-Place, and Sympathy', in Kyriaki Hadjiafxendi and Polina Mackay (eds.), *Authorship in Context: From the Theoretical to the Material* (Basingstoke: Palgrave, 2007), 33–55.
Easley, Alexis, *First-Person Anonymous: Women Writers and Victorian Print Media, 1830–70* (Farnham: Ashgate, 2004).
Langland, Elizabeth. *Nobody's Angels: Middle-Class Women and Domestic Ideology in Victorian Culture* (Ithaca, NY: Cornell University Press, 1995).
Levine, Caroline and Mark Turner, 'Introduction: Gender, Genre and George Eliot', *Women's Writing*, 3.22 (1996), 95–6.
Paxton, Nancy L., *George Eliot and Herbert Spencer: Feminism, Evolutionism, and the Reconstruction of Gender* (Princeton University Press, 1991).

HISTORIOGRAPHY

Buckley, Jerome Hamilton, *The Triumph of Time: A Study of the Victorian Concepts of Time, History, Progress, and Decadence* (Cambridge, MA: Harvard University Press and Oxford University Press, 1967).

Burrow, J. W., *A Liberal Descent: Victorian Historians and the English Past* (Cambridge University Press, 1981).
Crosby, Christina, *The Ends of History: Victorians and the Woman Question* (New York and London: Routledge, 1991).
Dodd, Valerie A., *George Eliot: An Intellectual Life* (Basingstoke: Macmillan, 1990).
Fleishman, Avrom, *George Eliot's Intellectual Life* (Cambridge University Press, 2010).
Kenyon, John, *The History Men: The Historical Profession in England since the Renaissance*, 2nd edn (London: Weidenfeld and Nicolson, 1993).
McCaw, Neil, *George Eliot and Victorian Historiography: Imagining the National Past* (Basingstoke, Macmillan and New York: St Martin's Press, 2000).
Vargish, Thomas, *The Providential Aesthetic in Victorian Fiction* (Charlottesville, VA: University Press of Virginia, 1985).

INDUSTRY AND TECHNOLOGY

Beer, Gillian, 'What's Not in *Middlemarch*', in Karen Chase (ed.), *Middlemarch in the Twenty-First Century* (Oxford University Press, 2006).
Deane, Phyllis, *The First Industrial Revolution*, 2nd edn (Cambridge University Press, 1979).
Flint, Kate, 'The Materiality of *Middlemarch*', in Karen Chase (ed.), *Middlemarch in the Twenty-First Century* (Oxford University Press, 2006).
Givner, Jessie, 'Industrial History, Preindustrial Literature: George Eliot's Middlemarch', *English Literary History*, 69.1 (2002), 223–43.
Ketabgian, Tamara, *The Lives of Machines: The Industrial Imaginary in Victorian Literature and Culture* (Ann Arbor, MI: University of Michigan Press, 2011).
Knoepflmacher, U. C. and Logan D. Browning (eds.), *Victorian Hybridities* (Baltimore, MD: Johns Hopkins University Press, 2010).
More, Charles, *Understanding the Industrial Revolution* (London: Routledge, 2000).
Novak, Daniel A., *Realism, Photography, and Nineteenth-Century Fiction* (Cambridge University Press, 2008).
Otis, Laura, *Networking: Communicating with Bodies and Machines in the Nineteenth Century* (Ann Arbor, MI: University of Michigan Press, 2001).
Sussman, Herbert L., *Victorians and the Machine: The Literary Response to Technology* (Cambridge, MA: Harvard University Press, 1968).
Van Dulken, Stephen, *Inventing the Nineteenth Century* (London: British Library, 2001, and New York University Press, 2007).

INTERIORS

Appadurai, Arjun (ed.), *The Social Life of Things: Commodities in Cultural Perspective* (Cambridge University Press, 1986).

Ayres, James, *Domestic Interiors: The British Tradition, 1500–1850* (London and New Haven, CT: Yale University Press, 2003).

Banham, Joanna, Sally Macdonald and Julia Porter, *Victorian Interior Design* (London: Cassell, 1991).

Barrett, H. and J. Phillips, *Suburban Style: The British Home 1840–1960* (London: Macdonald, 1987).

Bourdieu, Pierre, *Distinction: A Social Critique of the Judgement of Taste*, trans. R. Nice (Cambridge, MA: Harvard University Press, 1986).

Bryden, Inga and Janet Floyd (eds.), *Domestic Space: Reading the Nineteenth-century Interior* (Manchester University Press, 1999).

Cohen, Deborah, *Household Gods: The British and their Possessions* (London and New Haven, CT: Yale University Press, 2006).

Gloag, John, *Victorian Comfort: A Social History of Design from 1830–1900* (London: Adam and Charles Black, 1961).

Grier, K., *Culture and Comfort: Parlor-Making and Middle-class Identity* (Washington, DC: Smithsonian, 1988).

Heidegger, Martin, 'Building, Dwelling, Thinking', in N. Leach (ed.), *Rethinking Architecture: A Reader in Cultural Theory* (London: Routledge, 1997).

Logan, Thad, *The Victorian Parlour* (Cambridge University Press, 2001).

LANDSCAPE

Grimble, Simon, *Landscape, Writing and 'The Condition of England': 1878–1917, Ruskin to Modernism* (Lewiston, Queenston, and Lampeter: Edwin Mellen Press, 2004).

Helsinger, Elizabeth K., *Rural Scenes and National Representation: Britain, 1815–1850* (Princeton University Press, 1997).

Price, Martin, 'The Picturesque Moment', in F. W. Hilles and Harold Bloom (eds.), *From Sensibility to Romanticism: Essays Presented to Frederick A. Pottle* (Oxford University Press, 1965), 259–92.

Rignall, John, 'History and the "Speech of the Landscape" in Eliot's Depiction of Midland Life', *George Eliot–George Henry Lewes Studies*, 24–5 (1993), 147–62.

Salvesen, Christopher, *The Landscape of Memory: A Study of Wordsworth's Poetry* (London: Edward Arnold, 1965).

Witemeyer, Hugh, *George Eliot and the Visual Arts* (New Haven, CT and London: Yale University Press, 1979).

LANGUAGE

Beer, Gillian, *Darwin's Plots: Evolutionary Narrative in Darwin, George Eliot and Nineteenth-Century Fiction*, 2nd edn (1983; Cambridge University Press, 2000).

Ermarth, Elizabeth Deeds, 'George Eliot and the World as Language', in Stephen Regan (ed.), *The Nineteenth-Century Novel: A Critical Reader* (New York: Barnes and Noble, 1971), 320–9.

Raines, Melissa, 'George Eliot's Grammar of Being', *Essays in Criticism*, 58 (2008), 43–63.

George Eliot's Grammar of Being (London: Anthem, 2011).

Shuttleworth, Sally, *George Eliot and Nineteenth-Century Science: The Make-Believe of a Beginning* (Cambridge University Press, 1984).

LAW

Cornish, W. R. and G. de N. Clark, *Law and Society in England 1750–1950* (London: Sweet and Maxwell, 1989).

Dolin, Kieran, *Fiction and the Law: Legal Discourse in Victorian and Modernist Literature* (Cambridge University Press, 1999).

A Critical Introduction to Law and Literature (Cambridge University Press, 2007).

Finn, Margot, 'Victorian Law, Literature and History: Three Ships Passing in the Night', *Journal of Victorian Culture*, 7 (2002), 134–42.

Frank, Cathrine O., *Law, Literature and the Transmission of Culture in England, 1837–1925* (Farnham: Ashgate, 2010).

Petch, Simon, 'Legal', *A Companion to Victorian Literature and Culture*, ed. Herbert Tucker (Oxford: Blackwell, 1999), 155–69.

Pettitt, Clare, 'Legal Subjects, Legal Objects: The Law and Victorian Fiction', in Francis O'Gorman (ed.), *A Concise Companion to the Victorian Novel* (Oxford: Blackwell, 2005), 71–90.

Patent Inventions: Intellectual Property and the Victorian Novel (Oxford University Press, 2004).

Rodensky, Lisa, *The Crime in Mind: Criminal Responsibility and the Victorian Novel* (Oxford University Press, 2003).

Schramm, Jan-Melissa, *Testimony and Advocacy in Victorian Law, Literature and Theology* (Cambridge University Press, 2000).

Welsh, Alexander, *George Eliot and Blackmail* (Cambridge, MA: Harvard University Press, 1985).

Strong Representations: Narrative and Circumstantial Evidence in England (Baltimore, MD: Johns Hopkins University Press, 1992).

METROPOLITANISM

Alter, Robert, *Imagined Cities: Urban Experience and the Language of the Novel* (New Haven, CT and London: Yale University Press, 2005).

Bradbury, Malcolm, 'The Cities of Modernism', in Malcolm Bradbury and J. McFarlane (eds.), *Modernism 1890–1930* (Harmondsworth: Penguin, 1976), 96–104.

Rignall, John, *Realist Fiction and the Strolling Spectator* (London: Routledge, 1992).

George Eliot: European Novelist (Farnham: Ashgate, 2011).

Williams, Raymond, *The Country and the City* (London: Chatto and Windus, 1973).

The English Novel from Dickens to Lawrence (London: Chatto and Windus, 1970).

MONEY

Delaney, Paul, *Literature, Money and the Market: From Trollope to Amis* (Basingstoke: Palgrave, 2002).
Feltes, N. N., *Modes of Production of Victorian Novels* (University of Chicago Press, 1986).
Gallagher, Catherine, *The Body Economic: Life, Death, and Sensation in Political Economy and the Victorian Novel* (Princeton University Press, 2006).
Henry, Nancy, *George Eliot and the British Empire* (Cambridge University Press, 2002).
Henry, Nancy and Cannon Schmitt (eds.), *Victorian Investments: New Perspectives on Finance and Culture* (Bloomington, IN: Indiana University Press, 2009).
Herbert, Christopher, 'Filthy Lucre: Victorian Ideas of Money', *Victorian Studies*, 44 (2002), 185–213.
Kynaston, David, *The City of London: Volume 1, A World of its Own, 1815–1890* (London: Chatto and Windus, 1994).
Lalor, J., *Money and Morals, A Book for the Times* (London: John Chapman, 1842).
O'Gorman, Francis (ed.), *Victorian Literature and Finance* (Oxford University Press, 2007).
Poovey, Mary, *Genres of the Credit Economy: Mediating Value in Eighteenth and Nineteenth-Century Britain* (University of Chicago Press, 2008).
Wagner, Tamara S., *Financial Speculation in Victorian Fiction: Plotting Money and the Novel Genre, 1815–1901* (Columbus, OH: Ohio State University Press, 2010).
Weiss, Barbara, *The Hell of the English: Bankruptcy and the Victorian Novel* (Lewisburg, PA: Bucknell University Press, 1986).

MUSIC

Beer, Gillian, '*The Mill on the Floss*: "more instruments playing together"', in Penny Gay, Judith Johnston and Catherine Waters (eds.), *Victorian Turns, NeoVictorian Returns: Essays on Fiction and Culture* (Newcastle upon Tyne: Cambridge Scholars Publishing, 2008), 78–90.
Gray, Beryl, *George Eliot and Music* (Basingstoke: Macmillan, 1989).
Picker, J. M., *Victorian Soundscapes* (Oxford University Press, 2003).
da Sousa Correa, Delia, *George Eliot, Music and Victorian Culture* (Basingstoke: Palgrave, 2003).
'George Eliot and the "Expressiveness of Opera"', *Forum for Modern Language Studies*, 48(2) (2012), pp. 164–77.
Weliver, Phyllis, *Woman Musicians in Victorian Fiction, 1860–1900: Representations of Music, Science and Gender in the Leisured Home* (Aldershot: Ashgate, 2000).

PHILOSOPHY

Anger, Suzy, 'George Eliot and Philosophy', in George Levine (ed.), *The Cambridge Companion to George Eliot* (Cambridge University Press, 2001), 76–97.
Ashton, Rosemary, *The German Idea: Four English Writers and the Reception of German Thought, 1800–1860* (Cambridge University Press, 1980).
Atkins, Dorothy, *George Eliot and Spinoza*, Salzburg Studies in English Literature, Romantic Assessment, No. 78 (Universität Salzburg, 1978).
Beer, Gillian, *Darwin's Plots: Evolutionary Narrative in Darwin, George Eliot and Nineteenth-Century Fiction* (Cambridge University Press, 1983).
Fleishman, Avrom, *George Eliot's Intellectual Life* (Cambridge University Press, 2010).
Gardner, Catherine, *Women Philosophers: Genre and the Boundaries of Philosophy* (Boulder, CO: Westview, 2004).
Knoepflmacher, U. C., 'George Eliot, Feuerbach and the Question of Criticism', *Victorian Studies*, 7 (1964), 306–9.
Levine, George, *Realism, Ethics and Secularism: Essays on Victorian Literature and Science* (Cambridge University Press, 2008).
Paris, Bernard J., *Experiments in Life: George Eliot's Quest for Values* (Detroit, MI: Wayne State University Press, 1965).
Shuttleworth, Sally, *George Eliot and Nineteenth-century Science: The Make-Believe of a Beginning* (Cambridge University Press, 1984).
Wright, T. R., *The Religion of Humanity: The Impact of Comtean Positivism in Victorian Britain* (Cambridge University Press, 1986).

POLITICS

Brantlinger, Patrick, *The Spirit of Reform: British Literature and Politics, 1832–1867* (Cambridge, MA: Harvard University Press, 1977).
Briggs, Asa, *Victorian People: A Reassessment of Persons and Themes, 1851–67* (University of Chicago Press, 1955).
Gallagher, Catherine, *The Industrial Reformation of English Fiction: Social Discourse and Narrative Form, 1832–1867* (University of Chicago Press, 1985).
Henry, Nancy, 'George Eliot and Politics', in George Levine (ed.), *The Cambridge Companion to George Eliot* (Cambridge University Press, 2001), 138–58.
Myers, William, *The Teaching of George Eliot* (Leicester University Press, 1984).
'George Eliot: Politics and Personality', in John Lucas (ed.), *Literature and Politics in the Nineteenth Century* (London: Methuen, 1971), 105–29.
Watson, George, *The English Ideology: Studies in the Language of Victorian Politics*, (London: Allen Lane, 1973).
Williams, Raymond, *Culture and Society, 1780–1950* (London: Chatto and Windus, 1958).

RACE

Anderson, Amanda, *The Powers of Distance: Cosmopolitanism and the Cultivation of Detachment* (Princeton University Press, 2001).

Carroll, Alicia, *Dark Smiles: Race and Desire in George Eliot* (Athens, OH: Ohio University Press, 2003).

Charnon-Deutsch, Lou, *The Spanish Gypsy: The History of a European Obsession* (University Park, PA: Penn State University Press, 2004).

Gates, H. L. (ed.), *'Race,' Writing, and Difference* (University of Chicago Press, 1986).

Henry, Nancy, *George Eliot and Empire* (Cambridge University Press, 2002).

Irwin, Jane (ed.), *George Eliot's Daniel Deronda Notebooks* (Cambridge University Press, 1996).

Lewis, Reina, *Gendering Orientalism: Race, Femininity, and Representation* (London: Routledge, 1996).

Meyer, Susan, *Imperialism at Home: Race and Victorian Women's Fiction* (Ithaca, NY: Cornell University Press, 1996).

Nord, Deborah E., *Gypsies and the British Imagination, 1807–1930* (New York: Columbia University Press, 2006).

Ragussis, Michael, *Figures of Conversion: The 'Jewish Question' and National Identity* (Durham, NC, Duke University Press, 1995).

Said, Edward, *Orientalism* (Harmondsworth: Penguin, 1978).

Valman, Nadia, *The Jewess in Nineteenth-Century British Literary Culture* (Cambridge University Press, 2007).

RELIGION

Baker, William, *George Eliot and Judaism* (Universität Salzburg: Institut für Englische Sprache und Literaturen, 1975).

Carroll, David, *George Eliot and the Conflict of Interpretations* (Cambridge University Press, 1992).

Cheyette, Bryan, *Constructions of 'The Jew' in English Literature and Society: Racial Representations, 1875–1945* (Cambridge University Press, 1993).

Cunningham, Valentine, *Everywhere Spoken Against: Dissent in the Victorian Novel* (Oxford: Clarendon Press, 1975).

Himmelfarb, Gertrude, *The Jewish Odyssey of George Eliot* (New York: Encounter Books, 2009).

Hodgson, Peter C., *Theology in the Fiction of George Eliot: The Mystery Beneath the Real* (London: SCM Press, 2001).

Jay, Elisabeth, *The Religion of the Heart: Anglican Evangelicalism and the Nineteenth-Century Novel* (Oxford: Clarendon Press, 1979).

Knight, Mark and Emma Mason, *Nineteenth-Century Religion and Literature: An Introduction* (Oxford University Press, 2006).

Lovesey, Oliver, *The Clerical Character in George Eliot's Fiction* (Victoria, BC: ELS Editions, 1990).

Nurbhai, Saleel and K. M. Newton, *George Eliot, Judaism and the Novels: Jewish Myth and Mysticism* (Basingstoke: Palgrave Macmillan, 2002).

Qualls, Barry, 'George Eliot and religion', in George Levine (ed.), *The Cambridge Companion to George Eliot* (Cambridge University Press, 2001), 119–37.

Ragussis, Michael, *Figures of Conversion: 'The Jewish Question' and English National Identity* (Durham, NC: Duke University Press, 1995).

Semmel, Bernard, *George Eliot and the Politics of National Inheritance* (Oxford University Press, 1994).

Shaffer, Elinor S., *'Kubla Khan' and The Fall of Jerusalem: The Mythological School in Biblical Criticism and Secular Literature, 1770–1880* (Cambridge University Press, 1975).

Wiesenfarth, Joseph, *George Eliot's Mythmaking* (Heidelberg: Carl Winter Universitätsverlag, 1977).

ROMANTICISM

Dolin, Tim, *George Eliot* (Oxford World's Classics, Oxford University Press, 2005).

Dramin, Edward, '"A New Unfolding of Life": Romanticism in the Late Novels of George Eliot', *Victorian Literature and Culture*, 26: 2 (1998), 273–302.

Easson, Angus, 'Statesman, Dwarf and Weaver: Wordsworth and Nineteenth-Century Narrative', in Jeremy Hawthorn (ed.), *The Nineteenth-Century British Novel* (London: Edward Arnold, 1986), 17–30.

Guth, Deborah, *George Eliot and Schiller: Intertextuality and Cross-Cultural Discourse* (Aldershot and Burlington, VT: Ashgate, 2003).

Mann, Karen B., 'George Eliot and Wordsworth: The Power of Sound and the Power of Mind', *Studies in English Literature*, 20 (1980), 675–94.

Newton, K. M., *George Eliot: Romantic Humanist. A Study of the Philosophical Structure of Her Novels* (Basingstoke: Macmillan, 1981).

Rignall, John (ed.), *George Eliot and Europe* (Aldershot: Scolar, 1997).

RURAL LIFE

Gill, Stephen, *Wordsworth and the Victorians* (Oxford University Press, 1998).

Carroll, David, *George Eliot and the Conflict of Interpretations* (Cambridge University Press, 1992).

Graver, Suzanne, *George Eliot and Community: A Study in Social Theory and Fictional Form* (Berkeley, CA: University of California Press, 1984).

Handley, Graham, *George Eliot's Midlands: Passion in Exile* (London: Allison and Busby, 1991).

Mingay, G. E. (ed.), *The Victorian Countryside*, 2 vols. (London: Routledge and Kegan Paul, 1981).

Wiesenfarth, Joseph, *George Eliot's Mythmaking* (Heidelberg: Carl Winter Universitätsverlag, 1977).

THE SCIENCE OF THE MIND

Bourne-Taylor, Jenny and Sally Shuttleworth (eds.), *Embodied Selves: An Anthology of Psychological Texts 1830–1890* (Oxford University Press, 2003).

Cooter, Roger, *The Cultural Meaning of Popular Science: Phrenology and the Organisation of Consent in Nineteenth-century Britain* (Cambridge University Press, 1984).

Davis, Michael, *George Eliot and Nineteenth-Century Psychology: Exploring the Unmapped Country* (Aldershot: Ashgate, 2006).

Hamilton, Peter and Roger Hargreaves (eds.), *The Beautiful and the Damned: The Creation of Identity in Nineteenth-century Photography* (Aldershot: Lund Humphries, 2001).

Luckhurst, Roger, *The Invention of Telepathy 1870–1901* (Oxford University Press, 2002).

Rhys Morus, Iwan (ed.), *Bodies/Machines* (Oxford: Berg, 2002).

Richards, Graham, *Mental Machinery: The Origins and Consequences of Psychological Ideas 1600–1800* (London: Athlone, 1992).

Rylance, Rick, *Victorian Psychology and British Culture 1850–1880* (Oxford University Press, 2000).

SECULARISM

Budd, Susan, *Varieties of Unbelief: Atheists and Agnostics in English Society, 1850–1960* (London: Heinemann Educational, 1977).

Butler, Lance St John, *Victorian Doubt: Literary and Cultural Discourses* (New York: Harvester/Wheatsheaf, 1990).

Chadwick, Owen, *The Secularization of the European Mind in the Nineteenth Century* (Cambridge University Press, 1990).

Holyoake, G. J., *The Principles of Secularism Illustrated* (London: Book Store, 282, Strand; Austin and Co., 17, Johnson's Court, Fleet Street, 1871).

The Trial of Theism, by George Jacob Holyoake… (London: Holyoake, 1858).

Levine, George L., *Realism, Ethics and Secularism: Essays on Victorian Literature and Science* (Cambridge University Press, 2008).

The Joy of Secularism: 11 Essays for How We Live Now (Princeton University Press, 2011).

Paxton, Nancy L., *George Eliot and Herbert Spencer: Feminism, Evolutionism, and the Reconstruction of Gender* (Princeton University Press, 1991).

Royle, Edward, *Victorian Infidels: the Origins of the British Secularist Movement, 1791–1866* (Totowa, NJ: University of Manchester and Rowman and Littlefield, 1974).

Taylor, Charles, *A Secular Age* (Cambridge, MA: Belknap Press, 2007).

Warner, Michael, Jonathan VanAntwerpen, and Craig J. Calhoun, *Varieties of Secularism in a Secular Age* (Cambridge, MA: Harvard University Press, 2010).

THEATRE

Bodenheimer, Rosemarie, 'Ambition and Its Audiences: George Eliot's Performing Figures', *Victorian Studies*, 34 (1990), 7–33.

Franklin, J. Jeffrey, *Serious Play: The Cultural Form of the Nineteenth-Century Realist Novel* (Philadelphia, PA: University of Pennsylvania Press, 1999).

Litvak, Joseph, *Caught in the Act: Theatricality in the Nineteenth-Century English Novel* (Berkeley, CA: University of California Press, 1992).

Marshall, David, *The Figure of Theater: Shaftesbury, Defoe, Adam Smith, and George Eliot* (New York: Columbia University Press, 1986).

Marshall, Gail, *Actresses on the Victorian Stage: Feminine Performance and the Galatea Myth* (Cambridge University Press, 1998).

Miller, Renata Kobetts, 'The Exceptional Woman and Her Audience: Armgart, Performance, and Authorship', *George Eliot Review*, 35 (2004), 38–45.

Voskuil, Lynn, *Acting Naturally: Victorian Theatricality and Authenticity* (Charlottesville, VA: University of Virginia Press, 2004).

TRANSPORT

Daly, Nicholas, *Literature, Technology and Modernity, 1860–2000* (Cambridge University Press, 2004).

Dames, Nicholas, *Amnesiac Selves: Nostalgia, Forgetting and British Fiction, 1810–1870* (Oxford University Press, 2001).

Headrick, Daniel, *When Information Came of Age: Technologies of Knowledge in the Age of Reason and Revolution, 1700–1850* (Oxford University Press, 2000).

McDonagh, Josephine, 'Space, Mobility, and the Novel: "the spirit of place is a great reality"', in Matthew Beaumont (ed.), *Adventures in Realism* (Oxford: Blackwell, 2007), 50–67.

Menke, Richard, *Telegraphic Realism: Victorian Fiction and Other Information Systems* (Stanford University Press, 2008).

Pawson, Eric, *Transport and Economy: The Turnpike Roads of Eighteenth Century Britain* (London: Academic Press, 1977).

Plotz, Jon, *Portable Property: Victorian Culture on the Move* (Princeton University Press, 2008).

Schivelbusch, Wolfgang, *The Railway Journey: Trains and Travel in the Nineteenth Century*, trans. Anselm Hollo (Oxford, Blackwell, 1980).

Shuttleworth, Sally, *George Eliot and Nineteenth-Century Science: The Make-Believe of a Beginning* (Cambridge University Press, 1987).

Williams, Raymond, *The Country and the City* (London: Chatto and Windus, 1973).

TRAVEL AND TOURISM

Buzard, James, *The Beaten Track: European Tourism, Literature and the Ways to Culture, 1800–1918* (Oxford: Clarendon Press, 1993).

Harris, Margaret, 'The Travels of George Eliot', *Studies in Travel Writing*, 12:3 (2008), 291–9.

Henry, Nancy, *George Eliot and the British Empire* (Cambridge University Press, 2002).

Martin, Carol A., 'The Reader as Traveller, the Traveller as Reader in George Eliot', *George Eliot Review*, 29 (1998), 18–23.

McCormack, Kathleen, *George Eliot's English Travels: Composite Characters and Coded Communications* (New York: Routledge, 2005).

Rignall, John, 'George Eliot and the Idea of Travel', *Yearbook of English Studies*, 36:2 (2006), 139–52.

Rignall, John (ed.), *George Eliot and Europe* (Aldershot: Scolar, 1997).

Thompson, Andrew, *George Eliot and Italy: Literary, Cultural and Political Influences from Dante to the Risorgimento* (Basingstoke: Macmillan, 1998).

VISUAL ARTS

Ormond, Leonée, 'Angels and Archangels: *Romola* and the Paintings of Florence', in Caroline Levine and Mark W. Turner (eds.), *From Author to Text* (Aldershot: Ashgate, 1998), 181–190.

'Mines of Misinformation: George Eliot and Old Master Paintings: Berlin, Munich, Vienna and Dresden, 1854–5 and 1858', *George Eliot Review*, 33 (2002), 33–50.

'George Eliot and the Victorian Art World', *George Eliot Review*, 36 (2005), 25–38.

Witemeyer, Hugh, *George Eliot and the Visual Arts* (New Haven, CT and London: Yale University Press, 1979).

Index

Academy, 70
Adam Bede, 8, 15, 17, 18, 25, 36, 37, 41, 42, 52, 56, 57, 65, 66, 67, 86, 98, 100, 105, 109, 116, 117, 118, 131, 146, 150, 154, 160, 161, 174, 178, 183, 184, 201, 206, 210, 220, 226, 230, 234, 241, 243, 251, 258, 259, 268, 291, 303, 305, 306, 309
'Address to Working Men, by Felix Holt', 17, 40, 101, 113, 225, 275
advice books, 122, 125, 126, 164, 211
Africa, 10, 236, 245
All the Year Round, 36
Allardyce, Alexander, 42
Allingham, Helen, 168
American Civil War, 54
Angelico, Fra, 308
Anglicanism, 241
apostasy, 240
Arbury Estate, 157, 287
Arbury Hall, 3, 4, 54, 257
Archer, William, 281
Aristotle, 219
  Poetics, 38
'Armgart', 34, 210, 279, 285
Armstrong, Isobel, 141
Armstrong, Nancy, 85
Arnold, Matthew, 86, 156, 271
Asher & Co., 30
Ashton, Rosemary, 35, 48, 89
Athenaeum, 49, 68
Austen, Jane, 67, 68, 78, 85, 89
  Mansfield Park, 86
Austen, Zelda, 83
Australasian, 30, 31

Bagehot, Walter, 227, 228
Bain, Alexander, 268
Baker, William, 231
Balzac, Honoré de, 74, 191, 193, 195
  Lost Illusions, 193
Beaty, Jerome, 45, 81
Beauvoir, Simone de, 60
Beer, Gillian, 49, 84, 87, 119
Beethoven, Ludwig van, 194, 207
Beevers, Geoffrey, 57
Bentham, Jeremy, 184, 185, 214
Bernhardt, Sarah, 284
Bildungsroman, 157
Blackstone, William, 184, 187
Blackwood, John, 6, 9, 12, 23, 24, 25, 26, 27, 30, 41, 42, 174, 202, 243, 251, 258, 275
Blackwood, William, 21, 53
Blackwood, William ('the Major'), 21, 27
Blackwood, William and Sons, 9, 23, 24, 38, 43, 48, 53, 197
Blackwood's Edinburgh Magazine, 12, 17, 24, 25, 36, 40, 42, 222, 275, 281, 299
Blake, Kathleen, 84
Blake, William, 249
Blanc, Louis, 276
Blind, Mathilde, 45, 68
Bodenheimer, Rosemarie, 49, 89
Bodichon, Barbara, 15, 41, 119, 137, 140, 186, 194
Bonnell, Henry Houston, 74
Boston Public Broadcasting System, 59
Botticelli, Sandro, 308
Bourl'honne, Pierre, 47
Bowen, Charles Synge Christopher, 185, 188
Bowker, Richard Rogers, 70
Bradbury and Evans, 28
Bradlaugh, Charles, 277
Bray, Cara, 5, 6, 42, 45, 257, 271, 280, 295
Bray, Charles, 5, 13, 42, 45, 46, 187, 199, 202, 257, 265, 266, 271, 275, 277
Briggs, Asa, 79
Bright, John, 137, 222
British Broadcasting Corporation, 58
British Museum, 309
Brontë, Charlotte, 55, 67, 83, 147
  Jane Eyre, 52, 86, 116, 130, 141, 161, 187
  Villette, 193, 285
Brontë, Charlotte, Emily and Anne, 52, 89

Brontë, Emily, 55
'Brother and Sister', 10, 141
'Brother Jacob', 19, 20, 37, 38, 200
Browne, Matthew, 69
Brownell, William Crary, 74
Browning, Oscar, 193
Browning, Robert, 69, 207
Buddhism, 241
Burke, Edmund, 147
Burne-Jones, Edward, 9, 310
Burne-Jones, Georgiana, 9
Burton, Frederic, 47, 300
Byron, George Gordon, Lord, 249, 252, 253, 254
Byronic hero, 253

Caldwell, Janis Maclaren, 88
Call, Wathen Mark Wilks, 42
Cambridge, 118, 125, 149, 189, 225
Carey, Peter, 59
Carlyle, Jane Welsh, 66, 258
Carlyle, Thomas, 145, 151, 156, 198, 204, 230, 262, 271, 274
Carpenter, William, 264, 268
Carroll, Alicia, 87
Carroll, David, 88
Cecil, David, 78
Chalmers, Thomas, 201
Chambers, Robert, 273
Chapman, John, 5, 6, 13, 14, 34, 43, 47, 48, 190
Chapman and Hall, 21
Chilvers Coton, 46, 257
Christianity, 238
circulating libraries, 17, 20, 21, 23, 24, 25, 30, 66, 244
class, 85, 86, 115, 125, 155, 164, 176, 178, 225, 226, 227, 234, 250, 271, 274, 276, 281, 290, 291, 295
Cleveland, Rose Elizabeth, 39
Clifford, Lucy, 46
Cobbe, Frances Power, 258
Cobbett, William, 257
Coleridge, Samuel Taylor, 147, 249, 254
Collier, James, 267, 269
Collins, Kenneth K., 46
Collins, William Wilkie, 166
Colvin, Sidney, 69
Combe, George, 14, 265
Companies Act 1862, 187
Comte, Auguste, 88, 146, 214, 215, 224, 239, 245, 272, 276
Condivi, Ascanio, 309
Conrad, Joseph, 78
Contemporary Review, 258
Cornhill Magazine, 18, 19, 20, 23, 24, 28, 37, 45, 68, 197
Correggio, Antonio, 307
Cosimo, Piero di, 308
Cottom, Daniel, 85
Courtenay, William, 264
Cousin, Victor, 15
Coventry, 4, 42, 52, 53, 54, 55, 190, 256, 257, 271, 287, 288, 295
  Coventry Herald and Observer, 13, 34
'The Creed of Christendom', 14
Cross, John Walter, 3, 10, 189, 203, 239, 302
  George Eliot's Life, 4, 7, 20, 32, 42, 43, 47, 48, 53, 71, 79, 89, 157, 189, 296, 302
Crowe, Catherine, 266
Currer Bell. *See* Brontë, Charlotte

D'Albert Durade, François, 47, 296
Dallas, Eneas Sweetland, 66, 67, 143, 261
Daniel Deronda, 4, 10, 12, 21, 31, 39, 53, 56, 58, 70, 78, 84, 86, 87, 96, 102, 108, 109, 116, 118, 134, 146, 154, 163, 164, 166, 169, 176, 181, 187, 188, 189, 195, 196, 203, 207, 210, 211, 212, 213, 230, 232, 235, 241, 245, 246, 254, 262, 280, 282, 283, 284, 285, 293, 301, 305
Dante Alighieri, 38, 219
Darwin, Charles, 9, 56, 87, 129, 208, 212, 219, 224, 240, 274
Darwin, Erasmus, 266
David, Deidre, 85
Davies, Emily, 119, 137, 225
Davis, Michael, 88
Defoe, Daniel, 267
dialect, 69, 178, 259
Dickens, Charles, 33, 36, 38, 41, 52, 53, 55, 56, 59, 66, 68, 78, 116, 139, 147, 155, 160, 166, 167, 187, 192, 195, 196, 203, 204, 280, 287, 314, 320
  Great Expectations, 193
  Hard Times, 155
  Nicholas Nickleby, 116
  Oliver Twist, 37
  Our Mutual Friend, 28, 166
  The Pickwick Papers, 52
Dictionary of National Biography, 45
Disraeli, Benjamin, 28, 224, 275
Dodds, Valerie, 49
Dolin, Tim, 59
Donatello, 309
Dow, Gerard, 305, 306
Dresden, 303, 305, 306, 307
dress, 233
  mourning, 108, 126, 127, 128
  wedding, 107
  women's fashion, 166
Du Maurier, George, 47

Eagleton, Terry, 85
Eastlake, Charles, 161
Edgeworth, Maria, 115, 117
Edinburgh Review, 70
Edmundson, Helen, 57
Education Act 1870, 95, 115
education, women's, 119, 140, 141, 211, 225
Edwards, Lee, 83
Eliot, George
adaptations of her works, 54, 55, 56, 58, 89
appearance and personal attributes, 4, 13, 46, 47, 75, 210
centenary of birth, 54, 57, 60, 75
centenary of death, 11, 55
collected editions, 53
Cabinet Edition, 26, 28, 31, 32, 38
'Cheap Edition', 19, 27, 28
Clarendon Edition, 32
'Illustrated Edition', 31
'New' or 'Stereotyped' Edition, 32, 46
Standard Edition, 32
criticism of morality, 70
as editor and reviewer, 5, 6, 14, 15, 34, 35, 36, 41, 95, 147, 148, 149, 168, 169, 170, 190, 191, 201, 214, 219, 224, 241, 250, 256, 272, 276, 287, 306
education, 4, 117
finances, 14, 187, 188, 202, 203
humour, 66, 68
language proficiency, 4, 117, 176, 177, 178
literary criticism, 35, 65, 117, 144, 169, 214, 241
literary earnings, 14, 17, 19, 20, 25, 27, 28, 29, 30, 31, 53, 197, 201
memorials to, 11, 55, 56
as moral sage, 67, 68, 71, 75
music, love of, 4, 8, 206, 207
names and pseudonyms, 3, 6, 7, 8, 12, 14, 17, 23, 36, 40, 41, 54, 65, 66, 138, 139, 177, 190
novels as autobiography, 45, 66, 76, 78, 79, 130
as poet, 38, 39, 69, 206, 210
political conservatism, 97, 224, 226
reading, 48, 117, 195, 212, 231, 272, 299
relationship with George Henry Lewes, 3, 6, 8, 8, 41, 42, 43, 65, 71, 179, 187
relationship with John Walter Cross, 10, 302
religious belief, 4, 5, 43, 70, 71, 146, 215, 238, 239, 241, 271, 307
residence, places of
142 Strand, 5, 13, 190
Blandford Square, London, 8
Cheyne Walk, 11
Foleshill, 4
Griff House, 3, 55, 287
'The Heights', 10, 190
'The Priory', 9, 47, 75, 124, 162, 165, 207, 305
Richmond, 13
Wandsworth, 193
serial publication, 10, 19, 23, 28, 30, 68
half-volume parts, 21, 30, 31
settings of her novels, 8, 9, 37, 101, 129, 146, 252, 254, 257, 258, 261, 262, 287, 289, 298
translations of her works, 26, 27, 30, 31
as translator, 5, 13, 14, 34, 41, 117, 135, 146, 177, 190, 201, 214, 240, 272
travels abroad, 6, 10, 19, 191, 193, 296, 299, 305
travels in Britain, 298
Works, *see individual titles*
Eliot, Thomas Stearns, 40, 78
The Waste Land, 195
Elton, Oliver, 77
Engels, Friedrich, 195
English Woman's Journal, 15, 139
Ermarth, Elizabeth Deeds, 178
Essays and Leaves from a Notebook, 32, 53
The Essence of Christianity. See Eliot, George: as translator; Feuerbach, Ludwig
ethnic identity, 102, 230, 231, 234, 245
Evans, Christiana (later Clarke, GE's sister), 4, 8
Evans, Christiana (née Pearson, GE's mother), 3, 4
Evans, Fanny (later Houghton, GE's half-sister), 191
Evans, Isaac (GE's brother), 4, 5, 8, 42, 45
Evans, Robert (GE's father), 3, 4, 5, 53, 201, 287
evolution, 87, 129, 131, 240, 273, 274
Examiner, 71

Faraday, Michael, 56
Faucit, Helen, 284
Felix Holt, the Radical, 9, 20, 29, 39, 68, 78, 86, 89, 101, 116, 118, 132, 143, 146, 154, 155, 156, 158, 171, 172, 182, 184, 188, 222, 226, 227, 252, 253, 254, 257, 262, 274, 289, 295, 297
Felix, Rachel, 279, 285
feminist criticism, 77, 83, 84
Feuerbach, Ludwig, 147, 206, 215, 217, 218, 239
GE's translation of *Der Wesen des Christenthums*, 5, 13, 14, 34, 41, 67, 135, 146, 190, 191, 214
Finkelstein, David, 53
Flaubert, Gustave, 78, 195
L'Education sentimentale, 195
Fleishman, Avrom, 48
Flint, Kate, 107, 138
Foleshill, 257
Ford, Ford Madox, 75, 173

Fortnightly Review, 17, 35
Foster, Myles Birket, 172
Foster, Shirley, 84
four-volume novel, 20, 30, 31
Francillon, Robert Edward, 70
Fraser's Magazine, 15, 206, 281, 297
Fremantle, Anne, 47
Frith, William Powell, 168
Froude, James Anthony, 6, 34

Gall, Franz, 264, 265
Gallagher, Catherine, 86
Gaskell, Elizabeth Cleghorn, 55
  Life of Charlotte Brontë, 42
  Mary Barton, 37, 98, 155
  North and South, 155
  Round the Sofa, 36
Geneva, 120, 296
George Eliot Fellowship, 55
George Eliot Review, 55, 89
George Eliot–George Henry Lewes Studies, 55, 89
'German Wit: Heinrich Heine', 15
Ghirlandaio, Domenico, 308, 311
Gilbert, Sandra and Susan Gubar, 83
Giorgione, Giorgio, 307
Girton College, 119, 140, 225
Gladstone, William Ewart, 43, 224
Goethe, Johann Wolfgang von, 219
  G. H. Lewes's *The Life and Works of Goethe*, 6, 15, 42
Gosse, Edmund, 75, 76
Gosse, Philip, 298
Grant, James, 281
Graphic, 46
Great Exhibition 1851, 153, 160, 163, 190
Greg, William Rathbone, 14
Gurney, Edmund, 207
gypsies, 232, 245

Haight, Gordon Sherman, 14, 32, 43, 47, 79, 89
Handel, Georg Friedrich, 207, 208, 210
Hardy, Barbara, 49, 80, 104
Hardy, Thomas, 52, 85, 171
Harper and Brothers, 25, 26, 27, 28
Harper's New Monthly Magazine, 31
Harper's Weekly, 30
Harris, Margaret, 49
Harrison, Frederic, 183, 188
Harvey, William John, 81
Hegel, Georg Wilhelm Friedrich, 147
Heine, Heinrich, 15, 210
Helmholtz, Hermann von, 212
Hemans, Felicia, 249
Henley, William Ernest, 72
Hennell, Charles Christian, 5, 272
Hennell, Sara, 5, 6, 42, 45, 137, 248, 257, 264, 271, 299
Henry, Nancy, 87
Henschel, George, 208
Heyse, Johann, 299
'Higher Criticism', 5, 146, 214, 271
Highgate Cemetery, 11, 277
Hodgson, Peter, 88
Hoffmann, Ernst Theodor Amadeus, 212
Holbein, Hans, 305
Holcroft, Thomas, 279
Holloway, John, 79
Holyoake, George Jacob, 276
Homans, Margaret, 85
Horowitz, Evan, 86
Household Words, 36
'How I came to write fiction', 257
Howe, Irving, 86
Howitt, Anna Mary, 299
Hughes, Kathryn, 49, 89
Hunt, Thornton, 6, 14, 276
Hunt, William Holman, 310
Hutton, Richard Holt, 67, 68
Huxley, Thomas Henry, 137, 194, 215, 268

imperialism, 87, 244
Impressions of Theophrastus Such, 10, 23, 31, 34, 40, 43, 70, 71, 154, 159, 170, 171, 190, 203, 220, 244
'In a London Drawing Room', 194
industrial novel, 155
Industrial Revolution, 154, 155, 156, 157, 288
'The Influence of Rationalism', 17
Islam, 238, 245, 246
'Italy 1864', 300

Jacobs, Joseph, 102, 269
James, George Payne Rainsford, 37
James, Henry, 9, 46, 56, 68, 69, 70, 71, 78, 111, 211, 308
James, William, 267
'Janet's Repentance', 7, 12, 13, 17, 25, 116, 134, 146, 158, 184, 187, 189, 241, 257, 299
Jefferies, Richard, 173
Jews/Judaism, 70, 78, 86, 87, 210, 230, 231, 232, 234, 235, 238, 241, 244, 245
Joachim, Joseph, 208
Johnston, Judith, 49
Jones, Owen, 163
Joyce, James, 40

Karl, Frederick, 49
Kaulbach, Wilhelm von, 299
Keats, John, 249
Kempis, Thomas à, 239

King, Henry, 58
Kingsley, Charles, 15
Kipling, Rudyard, 171
Kitchel, Anna T., 47
Knoepflmacher, Uhlrich C., 81

Landon, Letitia Elizabeth (L.E.L.), 39, 249
Langford, Joseph, 12, 13, 18, 21, 30
Langland, Elizabeth, 84
Laurence, Samuel, 47
Lavater, Johann, 265
Lawrence, David Herbert, 78, 160
Le Fanu, Sheridan, 36
Leader, 14, 15, 35, 199, 239, 276, 280, 285
'Leaves from a Notebook', 37
Leavis, Frank Raymond, 78, 79
'The Legend of Jubal', 39, 206
The Legend of Jubal and Other Poems, 30
Leighton, Frederic, 20, 28, 310
Lesjak, Carolyn, 86
Levine, Caroline, 84
Levine, George, 274
Lewes, Agnes, 6, 187
Lewes, Charles, 8, 53, 188
Lewes, Elinor Southwood (later Ouvry), 47
Lewes, George Henry, 6, 12, 13, 14, 17, 21, 32, 35, 41, 42, 48, 53, 88, 139, 215, 219, 239, 276, 279, 280, 296, 302
  Problems of Life and Mind, 31, 264, 269
  scientific work, 179, 219, 264, 266, 268, 298, 299
  'Sea-side Studies', 299
Lewes, Gertrude, 53
Lewes, Thornton, 10
Lewis, Maria, 4, 117
Liebig, Baron Justus von, 299
'Life and Opinions of Milton', 186
'The Lifted Veil', 8, 18, 37, 88, 173
Liggins, Joseph, 7, 9, 42
Liszt, Franz, 206, 207, 254
'Liszt, Wagner and Weimar', 15, 206
literary tourism, 54
London, 190, 196
London Quarterly Review, 67
Longman, William, 28
Louise, Princess (daughter of Queen Victoria), 9, 47, 137
Lyell, Charles, 273
Lytton, Edward Bulwer, 18, 20, 21, 24, 37

Macaulay, Thomas Babington, 148, 149, 150
Mackay, Robert William, 14, 34, 147, 272
Macmillan's Magazine, 18, 24
Maine, Henry, 185
Malleson, Elizabeth, 138
Mallock, William Hurrell, 70
Marcet, Jane, 201
'Margaret Fuller and Mary Wollstonecraft', 119
marriage, 84, 122
  wedding etiquette, 123
Married Women's Property Acts, 138, 186
Martin, Carol P., 17, 25
Martineau, Harriet, 14, 201, 215
Martineau, James, 215
Martius, Karl Friedrich Philipp von, 299
Marx, Karl, 217
Marxist criticism, 85, 96
Mayall, John Edward, 47
McDonagh, Josephine, 99
meals, 125, 126
medicine, 88
meliorism, 224, 276
melodrama, 66, 99, 279, 281, 286
Menke, Richard, 88
Meredith, George, 75, 76, 269
Meyer, Susan, 87
Michaelangelo Buonarroti, 309
Middlemarch, 10, 20, 21, 30, 37, 39, 45, 55, 56, 58, 59, 69, 71, 75, 76, 77, 83, 84, 87, 88, 96, 99, 104, 107, 113, 116, 117, 118, 119, 127, 128, 134, 141, 142, 146, 151, 153, 154, 155, 156, 158, 161, 163, 164, 165, 169, 170, 174, 180, 184, 185, 186, 187, 188, 193, 197, 207, 210, 211, 214, 230, 241, 246, 248, 252, 253, 254, 257, 261, 262, 274, 280, 284, 288, 289, 295, 300, 309
  one-volume edition 1874, 30, 172
Midlands, 3, 8, 9, 154, 156, 168, 170, 173, 234, 256, 292
Mieris, Franz Van the elder, 306
Mill, James, 214
Mill, John Stuart, 6, 39, 141, 145, 146, 154, 202, 215, 224, 230, 271, 274
The Mill on the Floss, 8, 18, 19, 27, 36, 42, 43, 57, 58, 60, 67, 83, 87, 96, 100, 105, 113, 116, 118, 128, 129, 133, 135, 141, 146, 154, 157, 158, 165, 168, 169, 173, 180, 185, 189, 192, 200, 202, 206, 210, 211, 212, 239, 241, 251, 259, 267, 268, 273, 292, 293, 296, 297, 298, 303
Millais, John, 310
Miller, J. Hillis, 81
Millett, Kate, 83, 138
Milton, John, 38
Mind, 267
modernism, 40
modernity, 154, 157, 192, 193, 233, 235, 237, 288, 300
Moers, Ellen, 104, 138
Morley, John, 68, 141

Mozley, Anne, 259
'Mr. Gilfil's Love Story', 7, 12, 146, 210, 257, 292, 299
Mudie's Circulating Library, 17, 18, 19, 23, 25, 28, 30
Müller, Max, 244
Munich, 297, 299, 300, 305, 309
Murillo, Bartolomé, 306, 307
Murray, John: travel handbooks, 298, 300, 301
Murray, John Condon, 88
Myers, Frederick William Henry, 46, 238

Napoleonic Wars, 199, 258, 295
'The Natural History of German Life', 15, 35, 97, 99, 148, 150, 169, 176, 177, 178, 185, 191, 192, 204, 215, 224, 225, 226, 231, 236, 241, 250, 256, 306, 310
Nazarene painters, 309
'The Nemesis of Faith', 34
neo-Victorian fiction, 59
'New Woman', 141
New York, 196, 203
Newdigate Estate, 3
Newdigate family, 287
Newman, Francis, 276
North British Review, 222
Norton, Caroline, 186
'Notes on Form in Art', 39, 213
'Notes on "The Spanish Gypsy"', 245
Nuneaton, 3, 4, 7, 9, 42, 46, 53, 54, 55, 57, 287

'O may I join the choir invisible', 207, 245
Oliphant, Margaret, 24, 28, 138, 139
  Chronicles of Carlingford, 36, 244
opera, 206, 207, 210, 213, 219
Oracle of Reason, 275
Overbeck, Friedrich, 309
Owen, Richard, 194
Owen, Robert, 275, 276
Oxford, 118, 149
Oxford University Press, 32

Pall Mall Gazette, 17, 40, 280
Palmerston, Viscount (Henry John Temple), 226, 227, 229
Paris, 193
Paris, Bernard J., 81
Parkes, Bessie Rayner (later Belloc), 14, 15, 47, 137, 139
Paterson, Arthur, 47
Pattison, Mark, 118
Paul, Charles Kegan, 42, 46
Penguin, 32, 59
Pestalozzi, Johann, 115
Phelps, Elizabeth, 138
philology, 177
photography, 88, 267, 300
phrenology, 264, 265, 266
physiognomy, 69, 169, 265
physiological psychology, 69, 179, 211, 264
Piatti, Alfredo Carlo, 208
Picciotto, James, 70
picturesque, 46, 68, 169, 170
Pinney, Thomas, 79
Place, Francis, 276
'Poetry and Prose from the Notebook of an Eccentric', 34
political change, 86, 101, 254, 261, 290, 291, 295
Political Economy, 197, 198, 201, 202, 204
Ponti, Carlo, 300
Poovey, Mary, 200
position of women, 116, 119, 125, 137, 151, 186, 210, 225, 244, 284
Positivism, 146, 224, 264, 272
postcolonial criticism, 86
Pre-Raphaelite Movement, 160, 309, 310
'The Progress of the Intellect', 14, 34, 147, 149, 150, 215, 272
Proust, Marcel, 169
psychological theory, 88, 180, 211, 267
publishing industry, 18, 23, 24, 32, 33
Punch, 124
Purcell, Henry, 207

radicalism, 222, 254, 276, 290
railway, 145, 154, 287, 288, 289, 293
Ranke, Leopold von, 149
Raphael (Raffaello Sanzio), 307, 308
  Sistine Madonna, 303, 306
realism, 15, 35, 37, 65, 66, 67, 95, 100, 104, 142, 143, 160, 169, 177, 179, 183, 188, 213, 215, 219, 231, 243, 261, 279, 305, 306
Reasoner, 276
'Recollections of Berlin 1854–55', 297
'Recollections of Ilfracombe', 298
'Recollections of Italy 1860', 300
'Recollections of Weimar 1854', 15, 297
Reform Act 1832, 84, 101, 145, 155, 184, 226, 290
Reform Act 1867, 95, 101, 102, 222, 228, 275, 291
religion, 271
  Anglicanism, 240, 271, 274
  Dissent, 240
  Evangelical Christianity, 88, 183
  Evangelicalism, 201, 241, 271
religion of humanity, 214, 245. *See also* Comte, Auguste
Rembrandt van Rijn, 306
Reni, Guido, 307
Reynolds, Joshua, 307

Ricardo, David, 202
Riehl, Wilhelm Heinrich, 15. *See also* 'The Natural History of German Life'
Rome, 108, 300, 309
Romilly, Samuel, 184
Romola, 8, 19, 20, 23, 28, 37, 58, 68, 71, 104, 106, 109, 120, 133, 134, 146, 149, 151, 154, 161, 197, 214, 241, 296, 300, 308, 309, 310
Rosenberg, Tracey S., 84
Rossetti, Dante Gabriel, 266, 307, 310
Rossini, Gioacchino Antonio, 213
Rousseau, Jean-Jacques, 115, 248, 249, 250, 254
Rubens, Peter Paul, 307
Ruskin, John, 35, 95, 102, 160, 168, 169, 170, 173, 174, 204, 210, 302, 306
Ryckaert, David, 306
'The Sad Fortunes of the Reverend Amos Barton', 6, 12, 97, 104, 146, 241, 257

Said, Edward, 86
Saintsbury, George, 70, 71, 72
Saturday Review, 15, 65, 67, 68, 71
Scenes of Clerical Life, 13, 17, 23, 25, 36, 41, 42, 65, 69, 104, 117, 154, 158, 178, 201, 259, 299
Schiller, Friedrich, 254
Schwanthaler, Ludwig, 309
science fiction, 37
scientific thought, 69, 87, 88, 176, 180, 212, 215, 264, 267
Scott, Walter, 27, 37, 68, 71, 74, 150, 165, 171, 249, 250
Semmel, Bernard, 87
Senior, Jane (née Hughes), 113, 138
Shakespeare, William, 38, 55, 68, 70, 219, 279, 281, 283, 284
Shaw, George Bernard, 281, 285
Shelley, Mary Wollstonecraft, 249
Shelley, Percy Bysshe, 249, 254
short fiction, 36, 37, 38
Showalter, Elaine, 60, 83, 84
Shuttleworth, Sally, 88, 180
Sibree, John, 120
Sibree, Mary (later Cash), 43
Silas Marner, 8, 19, 27, 37, 38, 56, 67, 68, 101, 133, 134, 146, 150, 154, 157, 178, 184, 199, 200, 244, 251, 261, 292
'Silly Novels by Lady Novelists', 6, 15, 36, 104, 201, 219, 241
Simcox, Edith, 49, 69, 71
Simpson, Richard, 244
Smiles, Samuel, 202
Smith, Barbara Leigh. *See* Bodichon, Barbara
Smith, Elder, 9, 19, 23, 29
Smith, George, 9, 17, 19, 20, 23, 28, 29, 197
Smith, Thomas Southwood, 160
Smith, W. H., 24, 30
social calls, 124
Society for Psychical Research, 207, 266, 267
The Spanish Gypsy, 10, 29, 32, 34, 69, 230, 232, 245, 279, 286
Spectator, 67, 266
Spencer, Herbert, 6, 14, 43, 115, 207, 211, 215, 224, 239, 264, 268, 274, 280
Spinoza, Baruch, 177, 215, 216, 218, 239
  Ethics, 214, 240
    GE's translation, 219
  Tractatus Theologico-Politicus, 240
spiritualism, 265, 266
Spurzheim, Karl, 264, 265
St James's Magazine, 69
St Theresa of Avila, 143, 246
Staël, Germaine de, 267
stagecoaches, 158, 171, 288, 289, 292, 295
steam power, 153, 157, 288, 295
Stein, Gertrude, 40
Stephen, Leslie, 45, 71, 74, 75, 76
'Story-Telling', 40
Stowe, Harriet Beecher, 37, 239, 266
Strachey, Lytton, 75
Strauss, David Friedrich, 147, 275
  GE's translation of *Das Leben Jesu*, 5, 13, 34, 41, 146, 199, 214, 240, 272, 309
Sully, James, 208
Sutherland, John, 18, 21, 23, 24

Tauchnitz, 25, 26, 27, 28, 29, 30, 31
telegraph, 119, 153, 154, 267, 293
telephone, 153, 154, 158, 267
Teniers, David, 306
Tennyson, Alfred, 69, 273, 307, 310
Terburg, Gérard, 306
Terry, Ellen, 284
Thackeray, William Makepeace, 56, 176, 195
  The Adventures of Philip, 19
  Lovel the Widower, 19
Thomas, Edward, 173
Thompson, Edward Palmer, 96
Thorwaldsen, Bertel, 309
'Three Months in Weimar', 15, 191, 297
three-volume novel, 17, 18, 21, 23, 24, 33
Ticknor and Fields, 30
Tillotson, Geoffrey, 79
The Times, 66, 67, 261
Times Literary Supplement, 76
Titian (Titziana Vecellio), 307
  Tribute Money, 305
Tolstoy, Leo, 79
Toynbee, Arnold, 156

Trench, Richard Chenevix, 177
Trollope, Anthony, 176, 188, 203
  Barsetshire series, 36
  An Editor's Tales, 36
  Framley Parsonage, 19
  The Last Chronicle of Barset, 165
  The Prime Minister, 21
Trübner, Nicholas, 25
Turner, Joseph Mallord William, 168
Turner, Mark, 84
Tush, Susan Rowland, 89
Tyndall, John, 194

Unitarianism, 5
University of London, 55, 119, 140
urbanisation, 95, 99, 145, 168, 256
Utilitarianism, 183, 197, 198

van den Broek. Antonie Gerard, 32
Van Ghent, Dorothy, 80
Vasari, Giorgio, 308
Venice, 10, 300, 302
Veronese, Paolo, 308
Victoria, Queen, 66
visiting cards, 124

Wagner, Andreas, 299
Wagner, Richard, 206
Warren, Samuel, 24
Warwickshire, 3, 9, 45, 53, 55, 256, 257, 288
Weed, Elizabeth, 83
Weimar, 191, 206, 297
Westminster Review, 6, 13, 14, 15, 34, 35, 42, 170, 183, 190, 214, 219, 256, 272, 281, 306
  'Belles Lettres' section, 14, 15, 35
Westward Ho!, 15, 149
Wharton, Edith, 75
White, William Hale, 43
Williams, Raymond, 85, 192
Witemeyer, Hugh, 169
Wollstonecraft, Mary, 119
'Woman in France: Madame de Sablé', 15
'The Woman Question', 230, 234
Woolf, Virginia, 40, 59, 60, 76, 77, 215
Wordsworth, William, 38, 67, 168, 169, 187, 197, 249, 250, 251, 252, 254, 261
World's Classics, 32
'Worldliness and Other-Worldliness: the Poet Young', 15, 169, 191

Zimmerman, Agnes, 208